RURAL RIDES *OF THE*
BRISTOL CHURCHGOER

Joseph Leech at approximately seventy-five.

RURAL RIDES *OF THE* BRISTOL CHURCHGOER

Joseph Leech

Edited with an introduction

by Alan Sutton

NONSUCH

High Street, Bristol with Christ Church in the background.

First published in weekly instalments
in the *Bristol Times* between
2 September 1843 and 26 July 1845.
First published in this format 1982
This edition 2004

Nonsuch Publishing Limited
The Mill, Brimscombe Port,
Stroud, Gloucestershire, GL5 2QG
www.nonsuch-publishing.com

British Library Cataloguing in Publication Data.
A catalogue record for this book is available from the British Library.

ISBN 1-84588-001-3

Typesetting and origination by Nonsuch Publishing Limited
Printed in Great Britain by Oaklands Book Services Limited

Contents

Sources of illustration

ILLUSTRATIONS: Frontispiece; Joseph Leech at approximately seventy-five, MISS M. FAYLE: p. 4, High Street, Bristol, DELINEATIONS OF GLOUCESTERSHIRE (DG): p. 8; Joseph Leech outside his office, REECE WINSTONE: p. 26; Churchgoer, an enlargement of the block from 1843, BRISTOL TIMES AND BATH ADVOCATE (BTBA): p. 27; Churchgoer, enlargement of frontispiece of 1845, THE CHURCHGOER: BEING A SERIES OF VISITS TO THE VARIOUS CHURCHES OF BRISTOL: p. 30; Mary-le-Port, BRISTOL PAST AND PRESENT (BPP): p. 33; Commercial Rooms, DESCRIPTIVE HISTORY OF BRISTOL (DHB): p. 34; Clifton Church, BPP: p. 48; St. Nicholas, BPP: p. 56; St. John the Baptist, BPP: p. 65; St. Phillip and Jacob, BPP: p. 71; Churchgoer at home, CHURCHGOER ETC. BRISTOL: p. 72 St. Augustine's the Less, BPP: p. 80; St. Werburgh's, BPP: p. 87; St. Stephen's, BPP: p. 89; The Quay, DG: p. 98; St. Michael's, BPP: p. 102; The Bristol Riots, 1831, BPP: p. 103; Temple or Holy Cross, BPP: p. 112; Chirst Church, BPP: p. 129; St. John's Bedminster, BPP: p. 196; Churchgoer, an enlargement of the block from 1844, BTBA: p. 145; Churchgoer at the Dorcas, THE CHURCH-GOER. RURAL RIDES; OR CALLS AT COUNTRY CHURCHES: p. 160; Box Tunnel, 1846, SCIENCE MUSEUM, LONDON: pp. 163-4; Keynsham Church, THE CHURCH-BUILDER: p. 183; Henbury Church, BPP: p. 205, Thornbury Church, DG: p. 216, Westbury-on-Trym, parvise over southport, THE CHURCHBUILDER: p. 231; Slimbridge Church, NOTES, HISTORICAL AND ARCHITECTURAL ETC., SLIMBRIDGE: p. 236; Chew Stoke acient parsonage, DELINEATIONS OF THE NORTH WESTERN DIVISION OF THE COUNTY OF SOMERSET (DNWS): p. 248; Lympsham Church and rectory, DNWS: p. 259; Long Aston Church. HISTORY AND ANTIQUITIES OF THE COUNTY OF SOMERSET: p. 267; Bitton Church, THE HISTORY OF THE PARISH OF BITTON p. 272; Almondsbury Church, A COLLECTION OF GLOUCESTERSHIRE ANTIQUITIES: p. 276; John Locke's house, DNWS: p. 282; Weston-Super-Mare, DNWS:

Preface

The writings of Joseph Leech were first brought to my attention in 1979 by Dr. Robert Dunning, and throughout the editorial processes he has kindly helped in solving reference problems and offered assistance. I am also indebted to Miss Elizabeth Ralph, Dr. Nigel Scotland and Mr. David Evans for the helpful suggestions they made at proof stage; Miss Ralph also introduced me to Miss M. Fayle, Joseph Leech's grand-daughter, who helpfully supplied me with invaluable biographical information, and the photograph of Joseph that appears as the frontispiece.

All the articles published here were first published in weekly instalments in the Bristol Times from 1843 to 1845, and subsequently most of them were reissued in the three Churchgoer volumes listed in the bibliography. In this volume, the only articles which appeared in the newspaper only are Portishead and Long Ashton. The dates above each entry relate to the date of the Saturday of publication in the *Bristol Times*, and this will explain why articles relating to Christmas anachronistically appear dated mid January. The articles, as published in the Churchgoer volumes, were jumbled, but here they have been published in chronological sequence. This volume contains articles published between September 1843 and August 1845, a second volume now in preparation entitled The Bristol Churchgoer and his Visit to Bath contains articles published between September 1845 and March 1847.

In editing, all the social references have been retained, but some of the architectural notes and details of the sermons have been removed, as have his latin and classical quotations. Generally I have tried to retain his flow whilst removing his verbosity.

Finally I would like to thank my wife, Melinda, for her assistance and patience whilst visiting the churches of south Gloucestershire and north Somerset armed with our typescript, Pevsner and Ordnance Survey map.

Alan Sutton
Frampton-on-Severn
Gloucestershire
March 1982

Joseph Leech outside the office of the *Bristol Times & Mirror, c.* 1870.

Introduction

Just shut your eyes for a moment, and fancy yourself in the church, a hundred years ago, listening to this very same discourse from Kings, amongst the congregation who then occupied these seats, and retrospect will possibly prompt the same reflection, that in another century some such simple memorial of us will suggest to a race sitting in the pews where we now sit.

Joseph Leech was in a reflective mood when he wrote these words after his visit to Stone Church in October 1845, prompted by his picking up a prayer book and reading 'Eleanor Bennett, Feb. 10, 1741'. The coincidence here is of interest, for Eleanor Bennett was probably of the same family as James Bennett, author of *The History of Tewkesbury* (1830), a contemporary of Leech and a local historian, who was born and spent his childhood in the Falfield and Stone area.

The simple memorial that takes us back 100 years is the collection of writings left by Leech relating to his peregrinations around the city churches of Bristol, and the country churches of south Gloucestershire and north Somerset. These were published in the *Bristol Times* on the Saturdays following the Sunday trips, and most of them were later published in three volumes entitled *The Churchgoer* and *Rural Rides*. (*See the bibliography for precise details.*)

Joseph Leech was born on 19 March 1815 in Ennis, County Clare, the son of John Leech, the proprietor of a substantial hardware business. The family came from County stock in Galway, according to a family legend handed down verbally over two hundred years. Apparently, Joseph's father John, when very young, was sent out of the room with his brother on the arrival of a fine lady who drove up in a carriage and pair. The fine lady was shown in to John's mother, and after spending a few minutes with her left, leaving John's mother in tears. The legend is that John's father had married beneath him, and was cut off by the family, the fine lady being sent by the family to take one or both boys back to Galway. Whatever the truth of this, John remained and developed a good business, married, and had at least two children, a girl and Joseph.

After leaving Ennis College, Joseph went to live with his sister and brother-in-law at Maryborough, Queen's County (now Port Laoise, Laoise) and worked on the staff of his brother-in-laws' newspaper. In 1838, at the age of twenty-three, he took a holiday of several weeks in London, and when he ran short of money he went to Bristol to await a ship to Ireland. Having to wait several days for the arrival of his ship home, he lodged at the White Lion in Broad Street and amused himself by looking around the city, taking especial interest in his own trade — the newspapers of the city, *Felix Farley's Journal*, the *Bristol Mirror* and the *Bristol Mercury*. Glancing through these he concluded there was scope for a fresh approach to journalism in Bristol, and on returning to Ennis asked his father for financial assistance. His father gave him £500 on the understanding that he would get nothing more later, this in effect being his inheritance.

Back in Bristol, Leech lodged in Redcliff Street, where he set up his type and began to produce a newspaper called the *Bristol Times*, and it was there that he was wakened one night by the noise of someone creeping around his room. Thinking he was back in Ennis he called out 'Is that you Paddy?' An English voice said 'Douse the glim' and a flicker of light went out across the room. Leech jumped out of bed and threw himself on the first man he came to; two men rushed out of the room, and taking a wrong turn ended up in a downstairs store room where Schweppes & Co. stored empty bottles. There the fight continued — one of the men knocking a colleague out in the dark, mistaking him for Leech. The arrival of two policemen rescued Leech from the unequal struggle, but not before he had fallen on some bottles that had been smashed in the fight, cutting his thigh badly. The three would-be thieves had recently been released from prison and were subsequently transported. Leech had to sit through the trial because of his injuries, but from this episode he earned the soubriquet 'the mad Irishman'.

The first edition of his new venture, the *Bristol Times*, appeared on Saturday 2 March 1839. The paper was Conservative and aimed at the gentry and middle classes. Opportunities for newspaper proprietors had increased in 1836 when Stamp Duty was reduced from 4*d* to 1*d*, but even so the total cost of the paper at 5*d* was beyond the means of most, and readership would have been small, the circulation probably not exceeding 6,000. Leech's office was soon too cramped and he moved to 33 Broad Street, next door to one of his opponents, the *Bristol Mercury*. In 1849 he moved again, this time to 18 Small Street. Four years later the tax on advertisements, previously 18*d* each, was dropped. This incentive to the newspaper industry prompted him to expand, and he bought the goodwill of *Felix Farley's Journal*, established in 1714, and assimilated that into the *Bristol Times* (rechristened *Bristol Times and Journal*). The last major expansion was in January 1865 when Leech heard that his major opponent, T.D. Taylor, was considering selling the *Bristol Mirror*. Leech suggested that they merge and change the paper to a daily instead of a weekly. Taylor agreed, and the *Bristol Times and Mirror* was born. Newspaper circulation had now increased dramatically. The population of Bristol quadrupled between 1839 and 1889, and in 1855 the last penny Stamp Duty had been abolished, or at least made optional in as much as the payment of one penny ensured free postal delivery. Now with both Stamp Duty and Advertisement Tax gone, newspapers came within the means of a much larger section of the literate population. Leech also had newspaper involvements in Bath. He was joint proprietor of the *Bath Chronicle* for sixteen years with Charles Thring Bleeck, who became his brother-in-law in 1852 following Leech's marriage to Adelaide (Ada) Elizabeth Bleeck, daughter of Dr. Alfred Bleeck who had a wealthy practice at Redcliff Parade. They were married in St. Mary Redcliff, and started their married life at Kingsdown Parade. Shortly after the death of their first child they moved to Albert Villas in Canynge Square. They finally moved to Burwalls, Leigh Woods, in 1872.

In his earlier days at the newspaper, personalities were freely attacked and this comes across quite clearly in the *Churchgoer* articles. Leech invited libel several times, and there are many 'letters to the editor', a good many of which seem to have Leech's style, and which he could well have written himself to encourage the controversy and debate. He was adept in following the prevailing fashion, dealing his blows freely when he considered he could hit with advantage, and his wit, humour and playful satire were soon looked forward to each Saturday. The style he developed was individualistic and cavalier. At public dinners he would usually attend himself, commit the principal speeches to memory and later dictate them to his wife, who would write them down. Even with the best of memories this must have been an impossible task, and is shown as such throughout the pages of Churchgoer. His fondness for literary quotations is evident on many pages, and yet in every case he misquotes, thus showing they are from memory. He evidently cared little for accuracy — the main gist was sufficient, and this seems to go for his spelling, proof-reading, standardization of punctuation and presentation.

Leech's wife, Ada, once asked him why he had his books printed in such small type and on such bad paper. His reply was to the effect that he would not spend good money on books that no-one would read. This must have reflected an element of modesty, for the books went through several editions each and were extremely popular, notwithstanding his verbosity and adjectival indulgence. His style today might be considered heavy, and his prose considerably overdone, but it fitted in well with the early Victorian genre of writing. His general popularity is reflected in the invitations received to speak at public dinners. He delighted in good stories on which to hang a tale that would quickly set the table in a roar — a fact that many members of the *Grateful Society* of which he was the respected 'father' remembered long after. The fun and merriment he brought into play on its November gatherings were brought to an annual crescendo when he had to propose a toast to 'The Churchwardens of All Saints', an office always reserved for him. Another similar society was the St. Stephen's Ringers, (*see* page 85) of which Leech was not eligible for membership, neither living on or working in the required parish. He was often at their banquets where he was called upon to speak, and in one speech he pleaded for admission on the grounds that he drew water that he needed for his business from St. Stephen's conduit. He was eventually admitted, and paid his quarterages for a few years in the 1850s.

Leech was a staunch Conservative and disapproved of Free Trade, and at least twice his strong feelings over particular issues nearly landed him dead or bankrupt. In December 1845 a paragraph appeared in the *Bristol Times*, stating that a situation in the Custom House had been conferred upon an Irishman, and that this was the second or third instance in which — probably through the remissness of those who were expected to look after such matters — the patronage of the Government offices had been snatched by other localities. At a meeting of the True Blue Club, Charles Blisset characterized this statement as "a wilful and deliberate falsehood." Leech requested an explanation, but Blisset only replied that the committee were of the same opinion as himself. Henry Shute, the 'friend' of Leech, thereupon requested Blisset to appoint a 'friend' with a view to a duel; but Blisset declined the challenge, firstly because he said he could substantiate the charge, and secondly because every other of his committee who adopted his opinion would be liable to a similar attack, "so that Mr. Leech, in addition to his title as a public slanderer, may have to add to that of a murderer also." Leech then published his defence as follows: In November 1844, the chief promoters of the True Blue Club published a poll book of the municipal election for Clifton Ward, with the avowed object of depriving Liberal tradesmen of Conservative patronage. This it appeared Mr. Leech had condemned, whereupon, 'the fiat went forth, that the paper that would not defend exclusive dealing was unworthy of confidence, and must be crushed.' This obviously shows Leech in a good light. Although he tied his colours firmly to the Tory mast, he would not stand for any false dealings. An example of his genuineness and of his considerable accrued wealth was his assistance to the Union of London and Smith's Bank, for when Finzels, the sugar merchants, went bankrupt, there was a run on the bank which was stopped by Leech transferring all his money there.

The issue that nearly bankrupted him was the great libel case of 1875 between Handel Cossham (plaintiff) and Leech & Taylor and the *Bristol Times* (defendants). The case, heard on 3-6 November 1875, was of great complexity and the subject of a book published by the defendants the following year. Briefly, the case was one of alleged libel by Leech against Handel Cossham and his handling of the affairs of the bankrupt company Shackleton, Ford & Co., railway carriage manufacturers, of which Cossham had been a director. Leech and Taylor won the case.

At one point Leech was offered a knighthood as a reward for carrying out some nefarious deed (the subject of which is unknown), but he considered it underhand and would have nothing to do with it. In reprisal, Reuters and other news agencies refused to send him telegrams, so he had to rely on telegrams sent to the Commercial Rooms. His good character earned him several offices which included a directorship of the Bristol Waterworks Company and, later. Deputy Chairman of the Clifton Suspension Bridge Company. It was as holder of this office that he once received news that a man was going to throw himself off the Bridge clothed in an inflatable rubber suit for a wager. Two men had bet that he would not be injured on landing. Leech hurried to the Bridge and had the gates closed. The cab drew up and the jumper was pea-green, but the backers were mad with rage at not being allowed onto the bridge, and turned back after a furious row.

Leech married Adelaide Elizabeth Bleeck in 1852, and they had six children: Alfred, Nora, Ada, Mary, Mabel and Joseph. Joseph Leech died on 13 August 1893 and was buried in Long Ashton churchyard, alongside his eldest son, Alfred, who had died in 1878, and his daughter Nora who had died in 1891. Adelaide followed him in 1897. In his will he left £107,000, a considerable sum by nineteenth-century standards. His other publications included *Three Weeks in Wet Sheets*, and *Brief Romances from Bristol History*.

THE CHURCHGOER

The following letter from the *Bristol Times*, full of Leech's style and obviously written by him is worthy of entry here. It embodies the sense of fun Leech obtained from this, his best brainchild to date. The Churchgoer series had been preceded by *Local Leaves by a Street Lounger* (1842), and from the style it would have been obvious to the readers that the writers were the same.

To the Churchgoer

VENERABLE SIR, — I am sorry you are not as indefatigable in your rustic pilgrimages as you were in your city rounds. When confining your observations to Bristol, you hardly allowed a week to pass without giving the public a paper on some church or another; now you suffer a fortnight to elapse between your contributions, and sometimes rather more.

My object, venerable sir, in addressing you now is, to endeavour to incite you to increased activity, that we country parsons may have the pleasure or pain of seeing ourselves a little sooner in letter-press, than we can possibly expect to do, if you take such very long rests between your trips. We want to have our suspense ended — our fate decided; not to be left for twelve months to come in nervous doubt as to whether each Sunday morning may bring the Church-Goer to our venerable old country church or not.

Though I say we, I do not address you for my own sake; for I am only a curate, and I perceive we poor seventy pounders are sufficiently insignificant to escape your notice — *aquilla non petit muscas*. You seldom condescend to criticise or victimize anything below a vicar, and I, therefore, do not presume to expect that I shall either gain or lose by your visit; but I really feel for my worthy old rector, who has not had an easy moment, I verily believe, since he first heard of your intention to take "rural rides," and read that you had purchased a horse. His feelings are a mixture of nervous hope and fear; he is afraid of your coming, and yet he hardly wishes you to stay away; I really pity the "restless ecstacy" in which he is. He invariably takes a peep of late into the church from the vestry door before advancing to the reading-desk, to see if there be any suspicious-looking stranger amongst the congregation; and if there should happen to be one who resembles you, either in age or appearance, he is quite in a tremble for that day and the following six, and waits with the greatest anxiety until the next Saturday to see if he is in the paper; or rather he has not the patience to wait, for he will sometimes go to meet the postman, and get the *Times* from him on the road. Returning to the parsonage a few Saturday mornings since, I met him on the bridge, and the first question he asked was, if I saw the postman. At other times, when he does happen to be at breakfast on the arrival of the paper, you should see how the fried potatoes and bacon (my rector is very fond of this dish for breakfast,) are neglected, or rather not remembered at all, for the moment; while with tremulous haste he breaks the wrapper, and turns to the fourth page to see if ours be the "church for the day," and then you should witness the relief, not unmingled, I sometimes think, with disappointment, which he experiences on finding he is not there: he breathes freely, lays down the paper, and attacks the fried potatoes and bacon. For the last two months, (and this confirms me in my impression, that he is not indisposed to be distinguished,) he has preached invariably in the morning, though he often previously conceded me that privilege, as well as the afternoon also; and his sermons have been freshened up, with an evidently increased ambition. Last Sunday being a wet one, he, I suppose, made sure you would not come, so he left at home the sermon that he had been getting up during the week with the greatest care, in anticipation, or perhaps apprehension, of you, and took with him an old one which he had not preached for twelve months. It turned out, however, that just as he was about to enter the reading-desk, he perceived close by the north side of the chancel arch a little old-fashioned man (but who, I could plainly see, was not of your diameter by a dozen inches), with spectacles. This apparition quite altered his arrangement: he pocketed the old sermon, and beckoning one of his daughters to him from the rectory pew, sent her home for the new one, which he preached with great spirit, and I hope to the edification of the flock, though the stranger in spectacles turned out, as we ascertained next day, to be a travelling vendor of Blacking. I therefore beg you will come at once, and let us know the best or the worst without delay, for the rector's excitement will not pass away until the visit is over. Besides, it is attended with inconvenience not only to himself but to the household: for instance — he has always brewed for the family and the other day he made a mistake in the hops, whereby the beer was so bitter that nobody could drink it; rather an annoyance you will confess, considering that I reside at the Rectory. Then he runs the risk of making a mistake in the Psalms, by constantly looking towards the door as each person enters, expecting it may be you. Even the family participate in his nervousness, for the other day, after your visit to Keynsham, his three daughters (the parish gossips are kind enough to appropriate the eldest to your humble servant) entered the church with needles and threads innumerable to see if there was the slightest rent in the pulpit fringe, the Churchwarden's pew, or window curtains; and I have actually had a clean washed surplice every second Sunday of late on the strength of it, while the clerk has been enjoined, under penalty of dismissal, to come in a white neckcloth.

Be, therefore, so good as to pay your visit at once, and thereby relieve the anxious suspense of my rector, and

Your humble servant,

THE CURATE OF ....

To poet and parson I have but one answer to return, I shall be with you all, and eat your dinners, and hear your sermon in good time. I hope, however, there is no clergyman who does not do his best on all occasions. To take pains with his sermon, merely because the "Church-Goer" is expected, is a poor compliment to his flock, to say nothing of more serious considerations.

Joseph Leech was above medium height with an abundance of wavy hair! He was Protestant, Irish, and at the time of his first church-visiting article, twenty-eight years old. His alter-ego, 'Churchgoer' was the opposite. He was of medium height, 'portly', balding, old-fashioned in dress and fifty-five years old. This alternant character was a source of great amusement to Leech and a convenient mouth-piece for his favourite hobby-horses. In reading his articles carefully one can deduce a caring Christian with a social conscience. However, he was not a man out of his times, and the mid-nineteenth century attitude of— 'the rich man in his castle, the poor man at his gate' as evinced in *All things Bright and Beautiful* shows through in several places. The poor are *expected* to show humility, the rich are only criticised for the lack of any *semblance* of humility when listening to the Word.

The rich must worship it is true, as well as the poor, and agreeable spectacle as it is to see the poor attend in truth and sincerity, the rich joining in the services of the church in humbleness and reverence are a still more gratifying sight. . . . The congregation of Clifton, too, generally carry the easy lounge of the drawing-room into the church: they make themselves as comfortable as they can during the reading of the Confession, Litany, and other prayers, in contempt, if of nothing else, of the 18th canon, which says, 'All manner of persons then present shall reverently kneel . . . *(Clifton)*

But of course we must make some allowance for Leech — he could go so far, but he did not want to lose his patronage and bite the hand that fed.

The social attitudes generally, however, are of great interest. The vast difference between the rich and poor is not easy to exemplify, and the moral obligations of the wealthy were only seen as being to their maker (with reservations) and not to their fellow poorer humans.

Then for singing, the ladies for the most part, at least as far as I could see, seemed too genteel to do that for themselves, thinking it quite enough to pay an organist, and give a number of charity boys an annual coat (with buttons) of grey with trousers to match, to that business for them. *(Henbury)*

And as for the humility of the poor:

(The) congregation are the simplest and humblest as well as the most attentive . . . They look as if they have come to worship, not to show themselves. *(St. John the Baptist)*

The attitude that the poor have a definite and subservient position in society was an obvious and unspoken fact that was taken for granted:—

"It's a piece with everything else they have done," said the old lady; "the positions in the church have been all regulated by the amount paid, and now the tickets are disposed of on the same principle. It is all very well to keep out common people, but to refuse a gentlewoman! . . . I'm told the first ten or twelve pews have given over one hundred pounds each to the church, and a friend of mine, who gave thirty, is halfway down the nave."

"Well Ma'am," said I, "all cannot have the first pews, and it is only fair the highest sums should have the highest seats."

"Oh certainly, certainly," replied the old lady, who didn't think of disputing any point —

"quite delightful I'm sure — so popular; and the poor people I'm told, too, are to be allowed to pay half-a-crown each for their sittings in the aisle — did you hear that?"
   (The Consecration of Christ Church Clifton)

Cheltenham, Bath and Clifton were at this time fashionable spas where the elegant lived, but rarely worked; where life revolved around social refinement, and money was something that one had, but did not speak of. Leech constantly refers to these places, openly and allegorically — especially when some absentee parson is practising his social refinements there instead of looking after his parish — left to a curate or 'guinea coast' stand-in.

Many incumbents, if not at a fashionable spa, were enjoying two livings, and this pluralism was one of Leech's favourite themes for attack; and the recipients of repeated salvoes were absentee incumbents. Pluralists did not fit into his idyll of the English village. To him a curate was not enough, and although not denigrated in any way, they are made out to be victims of the system — seventy-pounders — impoverished and living in cold lodgings or vicarages which they could not afford to keep up — eating cold bacon and potatoes while the absentee incumbent derives the benefit, throwing crumbs out to the curate. Often there was not even a curate, and the parish might be served by a subsidy — a stand-in for the fee of a guinea:

The Bath subsidy (poor old gentleman) was, God knows, weak enough, for he had hardly physical strength to go through the prayers; he began the wrong psalms, and was corrected by the clerk, and upon the whole it struck me that he ought rather to be in bed than in the reading desk. 'He will never be able to get through the sermon thought I after the second singing . . .' *(Kelston* (not in this volume)

The rector of Kelston was also Dean of York. He obviously received the *Bristol Times* or was posted one by a colleague or relation, for in the following weeks vitrolic correspondence poured out from York and was answered in the *Bristol Times* in the columns of 'letters to the editor'.

Another parish where the problem of pluralism cropped up was Slimbridge:—

I asked who the parson was. They said a Mr. Goldspur or Goldsburgh, I think: but that he had another living (Oh! these 'other livings!') in Somersetshire, where he resided: there were, however, two curates, which they seemed to think a very good substitute for one rector. *(Slimbridge)*

Another problem that Leech was fond of pointing out was the large parish run with insufficient, or in some cases no curates:—

The whole service was performed and sermon preached by the clergyman whom I saw enter, I should therefore conclude the vicar keeps no curate. *(Keynsham)*

This was not true, the Rev. W.G. Hawtayne was curate at this time, but Leech did not concern himself with accuracy too often. If it suited his theme he could easily and unfairly denigrate an incumbent. He considered Keynsham church to be in bad state of repair, and dirty. He expands on what he would do if he were the clergyman, and regarding the cleanliness:—

If there were none else to keep the church clean, I should make my own servants do it.

So it would seem that when it came down to social attitudes Leech falls into his own trap. He does not elaborate on who would clean the church if he had no servants!

Newspaper readership comprised the affluent portion of the community and this is reflected in Leech's comments to his dear readers, especially in relation to Weston and Uphill:

. . . the Channel seemed as broad and bright as if it were not three parts mud; and Brean Hill and many a bold headland, ran out like great bullies into the sea, as if to meet and repel it. But everyone must know the ground as well as I do. I cannot fancy there is one who takes up this paper, who has not at some time or another been for a month or so in summer to inhale the fine sand and sea breezes in this locality, and ride donkeys to every eminence in the neighbour-hood, for the benefit — of those who hire them out. *(Lympsham)*

Some of the comments on the poor show how carefully Leech separates them into two distinct categories: the hard-working, upright and clean artisan; and the unwashed operative, loitering outside the beerhouses.

On entering, I had hardly cast my eyes round with that enquiring glance which says I wonder where I shall get a seat, when a young woman, seemingly a mechanic's wife, very civilly opened a pew in which she was — a tacit, but very intelligible invitation which I thankfully accepted, albeit the seat was far from the summit; for it is hard if the humblest spot in the houses where God deigns to dwell be not good enough for the best of us erring mortals . . . seeing the young woman had no Prayer Book, I offered her a share of mine; but suddenly reddening up, she de-clined my courtesy: there was no mistaking the cause of her confusion — she could not read, and I felt I had been the innocent instrument of creating pain . . .

The congregation of St. Philip and Jacob is mainly composed of substantial tradesmen and numbers of the poor of the parish, who deported themselves with the utmost decency and much seeming attention. *(St. Philip and Jacob)*

Here the unwashed operative, with the beard of a week's growth, and luxuriating in the un-shaved and untended laziness of an idle morning, loitered about with his face turned far often-er in the direction of a public house than the parish church, and looking still more repulsive in the filthy contrast he presented to the thrifty and tidily dressed artisan . . .
(Holy Trinity, St. Philip's Out)

To the steam-boat passenger coming up the river. Pill, with its sickly yellow hovels and beer-shops rising out of and surrounded by slime and mud, and its group of tarry sailors and tattered women leaning overw dirty half-doors and crumbling walls, is unpicturesque and unpleasant enough; but until you traverse its narrow broken streets, which, but for courtesy, might better be called kennels, and see the traces, not so much of poverty as of filth, vice, and intemperance which abound, you have no idea of the commonwealth of dirt and degradation which a community of sailors can raise around them.

(*St. Georges, Somerset or Easton in Gordano*)

The slightly patronizing attitude in his descriptions of the hard working artisan, and the analogy he draws between the unwashed operative and dogs extends to one of cynical hostility when he refers to the Chartist riots of 1831. Leech was a Tory, and certainly did not believe in a universal franchise.

. . . A dense volume of smoke, then a spiral burst of flame from the dun mass, followed by a loud cheer, as the red flakes showered thick as snow-fall on the crowd beneath! Frolicsome darlings! thought I, bless your merry hearts, but you do enjoy yourselves; seeing what a little thing gives you pleasure — what an amiable and innocent way you have of disporting yourselves; what despot should ever think of curtailing the homely pastimes of the poor — for a holy day's amusement only hand them over a moderate sized square, a row or two of dwellings, half a dozen warehouses, and they are as happy as the day is long — they'll make fun for themselves. Another volume of smoke, and the flame now leaps up from a new quarter, and the people have extended their sport in another direction. *Vive la bagatelle!* who says you are not fit for freedom, — who asserts that those merry fellows, whose cheerful voices are now ringing in my ears up from the streets of that piled and close built city beneath, might not be discreetly entrusted with an enlarged franchise? None but some silly old Tory, who distrusts the wisdom, prudence, judgment, and moderation of 'the many', thinks it as well they should not have an opportunity of serving Church and State . . . (*St. Michaels*)

When deciding upon his Churchgoer character Leech did not set down many parameters, but week by week a new piece of information was given out, enabling his readers to build a fair mental picture of Churchgoer's rotund and amiable form. It would be interesting to know if Leech had anyone in particular in mind when he devised the character.

My years are about fifty-five, my stature five feet seven, my dress a snuff coloured coat, waistcoat black, and trousers Oxford grey; a bamboo cane and a pair of spectacles complete my appearance, and I generally get the highest seat I can in the synagogue, not through pride of heart, but because I am hard of hearing. If you should identify a person amongst your congregation at any time during the next three months answering this description, do not feel alarmed, and make no allusion to irreverent spies or church-going gossips, for I am an advocate for propriety in all places, and would escape observation in most.

He does, however, sometimes slip up:—

... he pulled out a tin snuff box from his pocket and offered me a pinch. I don't take snuff, but to gratify him I put my finger in the box ...
   (*St. Augustine's the Less*)

For fifty years I have eschewed it myself (marriage), and nothing short of a pinch of snuff sustains me when an elongated list of banns is being published.
   (*St. James's Church*)

The character building goes on throughout the series, Leech throwing another crumb out here and there, although 'Churchgoer' appears to remain fifty-five for the next four years. He is said to have an annuity of £150, his spectacles are green, he is hard of hearing, and he is fond of growing geraniums. Sometimes a complete piece of fabrication is put in to make the scenario more credible:

I was at the time lodging in Queen's Square, and had furnished apartments for my own accommodation, so when I saw my 'household goods all shrivelled around me, to prevent further mistake, and lest the pretty play-fellows (the Bristol rioters, 1831) should in their most humorous fancy carry out the amiable pastime against my own person, I betook myself to the summit of St. Michael's ... (*St. Michael's*)

What fun he must have had! How many people knew? Many readers of the *Bristol Times* must have associated the style of the articles with the editorial columns and concluded that they came from the same pen, as also the preceding articles, *Local Leaves by a Street Lounger*, and a common (contrived) correspondent to the paper:— *An Unfortunate Father of a Family*. Apart from those who knew Leech personally, and either guessed, or were in on the secret, there must have been many who were taken in, or even if they did guess that it was the editor himself, would not have known that the editor looked any different from Churchgoer. Of those who supposedly came up to him in the articles to say 'I believe I have the pleasure of addressing the Churchgoer', how many would have come up to Leech during his genuine city peregrinations and as acquaintances, with a knowing wink, have said the same? Each of the articles probably comprises part fact, part fun, and part allegory — a common constituent part of the 'lectures' that Leech used the column for, as a lesson to the affluent on being a little more humble, or the pluralist parsons for being a little more considerate.

Leech's opinions were, it appears, more liberal than many in an age when feelings were running high. Within the Church of England itself, the Evangelicals had for nearly a century formed a distinctive movement, led by such figures as William Wilberforce, Hannah More, Francis Close, Henry Venn and Charles Simeon. They and their followers stood for the revival of Christian life by preaching guilt, forgiveness and conversion, a life having as necessary consequences a political morality in which personal accountability was paramount, and a concern, notably in the foreign mission field, for the social as well as the spiritual value of the Christian message.

By the time Leech was writing the Evangelical Movement was facing a challenge from those who deplored a liberalizing tendency in theology. The challenge came from a group of Oxford scholars, led by John Henry Newman, John Keble and Edward Pusey, whose *Tracts for the Times*, published between 1833 and 1841, were at first highly controversial attempts at the restoration of a more rigorous religious life, with an emphasis on authority and a return to some of the liturgical practices of the medieval church. Leech's comments on Pusey at Clifton Church, (see p.34) were, perhaps, more restrained than might have been expected, and his own personal, and somewhat advanced, preference for Gothic architecture gave him more sympathy for the Tractarians than his background might suggest. There was, in truth, very much of the outside observer about Leech in such matters, for in a piece about Uphill and Weston Super Mare, published in his *Supplemental Papers* he described the arrangements at Evangelical Weston where:

the most ingenious processionist could do nothing in the chancel, seeing there is not room to place another camp stool there.

Tractarian Uphill was a place for—

visitors with soft hats and straight collars, who like long coats and short sermons, having the prayers chanted, and the east the cardinal point for the creed.

Whatever its internal divisions, the Church of England was the spiritual home of Joseph Leech, and he was clearly uncomfortable with Dissent. His scathing remarks were relatively few, for was not Bristol an important focus of Nonconformity, Wesley's second home and the centre of ministerial training; and were not some of the country's leading Nonconformist families involved in Bristol manufacturing trade? But he cannot resist a swipe or two at what he saw as the extremism of Dissent:

On entering Winterbourne I noticed a good many going into a bare-looking Dissenting chapel, with 1829 in immense figures in front; so, as the inscription was in that part of the building where the denomination of the sect assembling there is usually placed, I concluded this was number 1829 of the two thousand varieties of dissent. *(Winterbourne)*

The chapel in Winterbourne with immense letters is actually dated 1816. This is probably another example of a fact committed to memory, and then recalled incorrectly.

He had to admit, however, that there was something to be said for the Nonconformists. Much of their support had resulted from the perpetuation of the class system within the Church which had alienated the poor. The singing, too, was far better in Chapel, and Leech comments on the 'Momentary elevations' which it caused, one of the undoubted reasons for the popularity of dissenting worship. Perhaps his best piece on Nonconformity was the 'Empty Cans' passage at the beginning of his journey to Blagdon:

As I rode through Bedminster on the morning of my visit to Blagdon, a kind of Cobourg or market-cart, in which were a number of young men with black coats and white neckcloths, passed me; and soon pulled up, and deposited one of its semi-clerical-looking company in front of something like a conventicle. The conveyance then proceeded on its way; and as I was curious enough to wish to know what this meant, I pushed John to 'a prettier pace,' and was enabled to keep up with it, until another black coat and white neckcloth popped out near Bishport; the Cobourg still continuing its course, and, doubtless, dispensing more young ministers, like a shower of manna, by the way. This, I afterwards learned, was a conveyance belonging to the Baptist College in Stoke's Croft, from which it starts every Sunday morning for the country, with a cargo of young students, who are dropped in the manner referred to along a given line, and amongst congregations who are waiting their advent. The Cobourg having conveyed the 'last man' to the remotest chapel, waits until he has preached; and then, retracing its road, picks up the others in its progress, after they have got rid of their pent-up orations also. This is, doubtless, a good plan for young men to try their nascent theology and rhetoric on rural audiences; but, without wishing to say anything disrespectful of the College or the students, (who are also named on such occasions 'supplies') the return career of the Cobourg resembled, in my imagination, calling for empty cans, inasmuch as each young man had by that time discharged himself of his discourse. *(Blagdon)*

During his visit to St. Philip and Jacob Leech says he is sure it is the constant hymning that fills half the dissenting houses:

for the poor wish to feel themselves as it were worshipping; the evil of it is that in too many instances amongst seceders it is carried to a dangerous excess, and leads to a morbid excitement more to be deplored than even the coldness of those of quality who seem to think (I say it with reverence) they can praise God by deputy, and that they do enough towards harmony and devotion when they pay twenty shillings a year to an organist, two tenors, a treble, and a bass. *(St. Philip and Jacob)*

During his visit to Mary-le-Port he was able to hear the singing in the adjoining chapel, and in a magniloquent and conceited manner declare to his readers (who doubtless would have been happy to agree with him), that the lower orders were unable to discern the difference between the 'short lived ecstacy' of hymn singing, and devotion:

One of the greatest inconveniences of Maryport is its close contiguity to Bridge Street Independant Chapel, with regard to which it stands in a parallel situation little more than, if so much as, twelve yards apart. From where I sat in the church I could see the people rising up and sitting down, and going through all their evolutions close by, and while the first and second lessons were being read, we had the advantage of their melody 'next door,' with a distinctness which convinced me that they in their turn must have the full use of our organ. I confess this 'confusion of tongues,' was far from having a double effect of any very desirable kind upon our devotion; especially as the major part of most dissenting worship consists in singing, which has a rather distracting effect when put in competition with sober reading. It is not strange, when you consider this, that for the lower orders nonconformity should have such attractions: this constant singing, in which all bear a part, has an exciting influence on rugged and undisciplined natures; they mistake the momentary elevation which it imparts to their feelings for devotion; so frequent is this hymning, that the short-lived ecstacy which it creates has hardly time to subside when they hymn again. *(Mary-le-Port)*

It is said in the family that Leech even had a down on the Irish Church Mission because 'it turned good Catholics into bad Protestants!' Indeed Leech has nothing good to say of Ireland at all, despite the fact that it comprised his whole family background, education and life-style until he was twenty-three — a mere six years earlier. He came of affluent stock — and was therefore obviously Protestant with a natural antipathy to 'popery'. Perhaps his attitude was part of the character building, and did not reflect his true feelings, although the episode with the True Blue Club where he complained of the situation at the Custom House going to an Irishman adds to the riddle. He could not, however, completely get rid of his background; he carried a strong Irish brogue to the grave.

One of Leech's favourite targets was the parish clerk — a breed he would do without if he had the choice. At St. John's, Bedminster he thought it would be quite as well if the clerk would speak a little more through his mouth . . . and at *Henbury*:—

the incumbent repeated the Creed in so low a tone that it was quite impossible from where I was to hear him . . . though the clerk, I confess, had voice enough for himself, priest, and people

and finally at *St. Mary Redcliff*:—

I don't know whether or not parish clerks may be out of my province: if it were not taking a liberty, however, I would meekly beg that the rev. the vicar might devote a spare hour to teaching the clerk to deport himself with more reverend humility in his business: he lolled upon the left hand with an air of the utmost complacency, and casting a side-long glance towards the ceiling said, 'We beseech thee to hear us, good Lord,' as if it did not greatly concern him whether his prayers were complied with or not.

Leech was very proud of his architectural knowledge, and used every opportunity to show it. He was partial to the gothic style, thinking, like Pugin, that the classical style was more suited to secular buildings and gothic to ecclesiastical buildings. His interest extended to the use of the terms 'Early English, Decorated and Perpendicular', rather novel at that time, having come from Thomas Rickman's *An Attempt to Discriminate the Styles of Architecture in England from the Conquest to the Reformation*, (1817), and which must have influenced Leech considerably. This was, of course,' the great era of new church building in the Victorian gothic style, and many of the churches Leech visited had been recently opened, or he commented on others that were in construction, as at Filton when on his trip to Almondsbury. He was not, however, in full sympathy with the Camden Society, which he felt took things to excess, paying more attention to the style and balance of domestic architecture in a rectory rather than utility. How saddening he would think it today to see how many of these new churches had such short lives.

One of the most amazing recurring themes throughout the series is the 'vendetta' which for no apparent reason Leech brings to the Churchgoer columns. The most cruel of these are comments made about David Williams, rector of Bleadon in Somerset and a geologist of some repute. He was elected a Fellow of the Geological Society in 1828 and was quite eminent amongst his fellow contemporary geologists, although now, many of his opinions have been questioned or proved incorrect. John Rutter in his *Delineations of the North Western Division of the County of Somerset* (1829); gratefully acknowledged Williams for his assistance, and in the section on Uphill there are lists of Williams' excavations of the Uphill caverns. David Williams also carried out repairs to his church, the cross in the churchyard being repaired at his own expense after being struck by lightning in 1827. Wherever a reference can be got in Leech makes use of it — what was the basis of this animosity?

Immediately under you is Bleadon, and thence, some mile or mile and a half distance, may be seen amongst a clump of trees, the handsome embattled, but leaning tower of Lympsham Church. If I had time when passing Bleadon, I think I should have looked in to my friend Parson Williams, and told him how freely people talk about his parish, and how frequently they refer to it in familiar comparisons: the very sparrows which perch upon the old cross seem to twitter their remarks; and rooks that crowd cawing about the pinnacles of the church are nowhere else so significantly loquacious. A set of open mouthed, talkative, scandalous fellows are these same rooks; and I sometimes think, as they wing their way from parish to parish, and alight in garrulous coteries on the summit of one tower after another, they amuse themselves in canvassing the merits of the ministers of the various churches at which they call. *(Lympsham)*

Leech tended to use several sources before diving headlong into publication, and these were not always reliable. When making enquiries amongst parishioners he was quite capable of questioning someone with an unwarranted grudge, and publishing the result without further check. In some instances he berated an incumbent for not keeping a curate, when the Clergy List for that year, the prior year, and subsequent year, show that a curate was in residence. As can be shown over and over, Leech gathered facts quickly and committing things to memory was often unfair:

The Rev. David Williams was in the reading desk when I entered .... he seemed to be suffering from flatulency, for at every other verse he was obliged to pause, afterwards wiping his mouth with an old brown handkerchief, and occasionally varying the act by using the sleeve of his surplice (which was far from clean) for the purpose. There was no singing or musical service whatever, the Rev. Gentleman objecting to it, as I have heard, on the grounds that it affects his head, but he has never complained of it affecting his heart. On some occasions, however, the Uphill singers have come over, and been permitted to "perform;" but not very long since, being rather too energetic in their exertions, they were publicly, perhaps justly, rebuked by the Rector for their overpowering vocalism — "If you can't sing better," said he, "don't sing at all — shut up that noise!" (Bleadon)

On balance Joseph Leech comes through at the end of this book as a caring Christian. Many of the social abuses he mentions have been recognised and eradicated although the unwashed operative, luxuriating in laziness and looking towards the public house is still with us, and is a perennial problem. One day he knew that Bristol and Clifton would meet — the green fields between being eradicated, but what would he think if he saw it today? The grand families gone, the large houses now bedsits or trendy flats. The docks as he knew them gone, and half the city churches destroyed on one day in November 1940. Leech saw many of the major changes in the city before his death in 1893. The railway mania he saw come and go, in fact he wrote on it, for according to John Latimer the following piece appeared in the *Bristol Times* some years after the fever by a contributor who could be easily identified!

"Fairy legends had no wonders for us like that time. You saw a man today in the streets of Bristol whom you would not trust with the loan of a five pound note; tomorrow he splashed you with the wheels of a new Long-acre carriage. He was as suddenly transformed from a twenty pound house to a mansion in the country, and though small beer refreshed him during the greater part of his life, he now became critical in the taste of Bordeaux. A railway, in fact, was not a means of transport but a thing to bet and gamble about. . . Once in the height of the sorrowful farce, I had occasion to call on a couple of 'bold brokers' in a certain street not a mile from the centre of Bristol. The flavour of the Havannahs and new scrip filled the place; the clerks were having chops and tomato sauce, and a silver-necked bottle proved they enjoyed at least a reversion of the Saint Peray from the principals' apartment, into which I was summoned. Softly I trod on a Turkey carpet; a tray well furnished stood on a sideboard; and piles of prospectuses flanked the fine ponderous bronze inkstand of the man of projects who sat in a richly cushioned chair. Voices issued from the neighbouring room where the second principal saw others on business, and the click of plates and occasional flying of corks proved how actively the business of allotments was progressing. But they came like shadows, and so departed."

They came like shadows, and so departed. In a similar reflective theme Leech 'saw in' the New Year of 1845 with ringers in a belfry:

Millions will pass from amongst us during the twelve months we have now ushered in with such a clamorous peal, and yet of these doomed millions not one person seriously believes that he will die. His relative or his neighbour may die, but he is not to die: there is nothing in which we willingly give precedence to other people but in death. 'After you, Sir,' is the comfortable feeling, is not the complaisant expression in all these matters. In my own mind I was at that moment verifying the truth of my own thoughts, for while I was thus reflecting *for others*, I never once fancied that I ought to think for myself. "And you, smooth old gentleman in the snuff-coloured coat," some monitory spirit seemed to whisper in my ear — "have you ever dreamt there is the slightest — we'll say the *slightest* possibility of your being one of the unconscious millions for whose coffin the oak planks are now seasoning?" "Certainly not," thought I, "no, no; I am going to live, of course, and write Church-Goers for years to come".

Returning now to the beginning of this introduction, and Leech's reflections on Stone church, we can correct his misquote that appears in a slightly later piece of writing and say 'It will be all the same a hundred years hence'.

The City Churches

12 September 1843
The Cathedral

Having breakfasted on Sunday, the— day of—, I looked out for a moment from my window at the well-dressed groups that passed to and fro 'like a freed vernal stream,' before I could determine as to my particular destination for that day. My mind halted between Clifton Church and the Cathedral, but as there is always difficulty in getting a seat in the former, I decided in favour of the latter. I reached the Green some ten minutes before the bell began to ring, and experienced the soothing effect of a quiet walk between the old trees, which in the midst of a densely populated city and a great thoroughfare, still preserve their advanced age and contiguity to a venerable Cathedral, an air of seclusion rendered even more graceful by refreshing contrast with the scene around. This is said to have been a favourite walk with the poet Coleridge, where he 'chewed the cud' of fancy and opium for hours together; and I can easily imagine that at an earlier date it was equally the resort of the black friars of St. Augustine: be that as it may, however, I found many others like myself making use of the agreeable shade which the old trees shed around, to shelter them from the morning sun, until the bell in the tower and the crazy portals of the south door opening almost simultaneously, at once announced, and enabled us to avail ourselves of the permission to enter.

Having passed through the groups of loungers who pay more attention to the epitaphs than their prayer books, I found myself with others in the choir, looking at locked pews, and wondering if ever, like the gates of Jerusalem, they would open of their own accord. A little white-headed, ruddy faced man, in drab smalls and long gaiters to match, and a black serge cloak, the skirts of which floated out behind the rapidity of his movements, flitted restlessly about, and eyed each person that entered, opening a pew for some, but seemingly profoundly ignorant that others were equally in want of accommodation. Nor was his selection made on the principle of 'first come, first served,' for I noticed that he seated several who arrived subsequently to your humble servant, though he must have seen me, for I stalked up and down the aisle, and gave him many significant looks and nods, intended to convey an equal amount of meaning, all tending to imply that I should feel much obliged for the temporary use of twelve square inches of horizontal timber; but whether owing to a want of expression on my part, or an abundant obtuseness on his, the hint

was not taken, until enlightened by some sleight of palmistry which I saw
pass between him and a person who was preferred before me, I inserted my
forefinger and thumb with a certain caballistic sign into my waistcoat pocket,
and presently a pew door stood invitingly open, as though I had said, 'Sesame.'
Wondering at my previous ignorance I entered and composed myself as well
as I could, to take the full benefit of twelve pennyworth of prayers. Others I
afterwards saw select their seats in economical humility in the aisle; so that
it is only fair if people are permitted to make them a marketable commodity.
What the cost is I can't say, but I intend when next I pay the Cathedral a visit,
to charter the Bishop's throne if it be not too expensive.

A Cathedral congregation is ever a motley one; the only invariable and legitimate attendance being, if I may so speak, those little antiquated young
urchins, who look as if, like Rip Van Winkle, they had risen from a sleep of
a hundred years in the dress of that period who seem to have 'flourished in
perpetual youth' for nearly a century, and who are destined, I devoutly hope,
long to remain living monuments in red stockings to the well directed and
enduring benevolence of Bristol's best of benefactors. The other portions of
the congregation are composed of persons who have quarrelled with their own
parish authorities about pews, or their own parish ministers about opinions
— persons who are fond of music, or fancy they can sing chaunts; and persons
who have gone there so long that they forget the cause of their first visit, and
never missed a Sunday for thirty years.

The Rev. Canon Harvey's[1] manner is equable, mild, and impressive; and he
wins one's interest, and attracts one's attention more by the matter of his sermon, than the mere harmony of his words, though his language is pure, and his
style clear and pleasing. He evidently does not effect eloquence, and that 'grand
nonsense' which Johnson pronounced 'insupportable,' has not the slightest allurement for him, though his sermons are obviously written with care, and
delivered with a sincere yet subdued feeling; he uses little action, and his voice,
though not very variable, is impressive. The Rev. Canon Harvey, who is about
sixty years old, was, I heard, tutor to Prince George of Cambridge, is Canon of
Bristol Cathedral, and Rector of Bradford, in Wilts. He is considered to hold
what are called by people who make distinctions, high church opinions, and is
much esteemed as a preacher by those who frequent the Cathedral.

16 September 1843

Mary-le-Port

Soon after ten o'clock I found myself in the Commercial Rooms[1] on a certain Sunday not long since, waiting until one of the many churches round about should be opened for morning service. There were perhaps a dozen persons like myself lounging at the tables, curious to gain a glimpse of the evening papers before proceeding to prayers. The swell of bell-ringing, so general in this quarter, so all-pervading, too, as to appear monotonous, seemed to fill the rooms, and no other sound was heard, save when now and again the rustle of a *Sun*, *Globe*, or *Standard* in the hands of some heavy politician, or the tapping at the weather-glass by some wet-wishing corn-jobber, met the ear. A dull and drowsy atmosphere prevailed through the apartment; a blue-bottle or two that on ordinary days would be scared by the voice of business flitted buzzing about, and the porter of the rooms, poor fellow, in order to console his conscience for a breach of the Sabbath, was reading his Bible at the bar.

Not caring to stay longer than necessary in so fusty an atmosphere, I turned to the list of churches in the Directory, and one of the first that met my eye was 'Maryport, Sundays, 11 forenoon, 6 evening,' &c., &c.

Maryport, Maryport, thought I, and, strange to say, I never, to my knowledge had been in Maryport; in all my rambles I never even saw the church, though I knew there was such an one packed up and thrust away somewhere to the rear of High Street, but so ingeniously surrounded with human dwellings that unless one went specially in search of it, he was not likely to find it. I soon found it, however, perhaps as much attracted by the popular reputation of its new minister, who had succeeded from the Scottish Church to Episcopacy, and been lately presented with this incumbency, as anything else. I am always curious to see when a man gains a new name, how he wears it and deserves it, for I not unfrequently find that those whom the public speak most about are not most to my mind; whether the want of taste or judgement lie most with me or the public, it is, of course, for others to decide.

Following some respectable families to the west entrance, I was soon and civilly installed in a pew. To my surprise, Maryport — for I expected from its backward and retired situation to find it little larger than a capacious saltbox — was a good sized, exceedingly well attended, and handsome Church.[2] Its very situation adds, in my opinion, to its interest; it is essentially an old city church, time-worn and venerable outside, and forming with its little grass-grown churchyard, upon whose

ancient gravestones the lattices of the contiguous dwellings have for centuries looked out, a small, sombre, sleepy square, where the busy echoes of the surrounding streets may be heard, though protected itself in its retirement from much intrusion or thoroughfare. It is just the church—being as it is in the heart of the city —where one can fancy for hundreds and hundreds of years successive generations baptized, and married, and buried in its vaults and about its buttresses.

But though these days are gone by, Maryport is still well attended, has still its attentive and respectable congregation. Amongst the latter I noticed several persons from other and even remote parishes of Bristol — moveable church-goers, as I may call them, who, like myself, are afflicted with a love of novelty, and are in the habit of 'going to and fro' amongst the many places of worship within the city.

Maryport, which is composed of a nave, north aisle, and good sized chancel, is commodious, and capable of containing a fair number. It has, what is rather common amongst the old churches of Bristol, and distracts your modern architectural amateurs so much, a Grecian altar-screen; but for my part, though I think it is better for the *future* to avoid such solecisms, I am quite sure God will not keep away from where two or three are gathered together in His name merely because a Corinthian column and architrave raise their proportions in the east end of a Gothic church. I am an advocate for order and arrangement in all place; but I think it possible to carry punctillio to a fastidious excess.

One of the greatest inconveniences of Maryport is its close contiguity to Bridge Street Independant Chapel, with regard to which it stands in a parallel situation little more than, if so much as, twelve yards apart. From where I sat in the church I could see the people rising up and sitting down, and going through all their evolutions close by, and while the first and second lessons were being read, we had the advantage of their melody 'next door,' with a distinctness which convinced me that they in their turn must have the full use of our organ. I confess this 'confusion of tongues,' was far from having a double effect of any very desirable kind upon our devotion; especially as the major part of most dissenting worship consists in singing, which has a rather distracting effect when put in competition with sober reading. It is not strange, when you consider this, that for the lower orders non-conformity should have such attractions: this constant singing, in which all bear a part, has an exciting influence on rugged and undisciplined natures; they mistake the momentary elevation which it imparts to their feelings for devotion; so frequent is this hymning, that the short-lived ecstacy which it creates has hardly time to subside when they hymn again.

The Rev. Mr. Marshall[3] is an extempore preacher. There are two kinds of extempore preachers. First, those who write their sermons, get them well off, and afterwards deliver them: when a man has time to do this —as affording him more scope for elocution — I think it the most effective, as it is a finished composition carefully and painfully prepared to the best of the preacher's ability, so as to apply to all conditions and characters of men, and yet capable of being delivered with a freedom and force of action upon which one cannot venture, when he has to read the matter throughout with little aid from practised repetition: but few men who have parochial duties to attend to, and who have two services each Sunday, can find time for this. The other class of extempore preachers are those who consider but do not write their sermons; who, making themselves acquainted with the subject, trust to their capacity and fluency for giving expression to the ideas and impressions they have previously formed, and the appeal and exhortation with which they can apply them. That many men have been able to do this with eminent success, I am quite well aware, but they have been and must be also men of eminent talents; there is always, however, a danger of looseness, vagueness, and iteration about this pulpit improvisatizing. When the incumbent of Maryport on the present instance commenced his sermon, which he did in a quiet, tempered, and impressive manner, showing in a clear and most happy style of application, that the case of the lawyer ignorant of the law it was his business to expound, was no singular one, many of us being ignorant of that eternal code in which we are so vitally concerned, and by which we are to be judged, and which it is our first business to become acquainted with. For the first ten minutes there was a perspicuity, a compression and finished correctness both in thought and diction, which led me to believe that he must belong to the first class of extempore preachers, and that he was then delivering without book, a sermon which he had carefully written; but as he proceeded the not unfrequent repetition of the same phrases, and the frequent use of words, which I think he would have expunged from a written sermon, induced me to change my mind, and give him credit for being an excellent extempore preacher of the second class, while I honestly confess that I all but disapprove of that class altogether, because I think there are few men who cannot on most occasions produce something better with preparation than they can without it. A man if he would deliver an honest and sound sermon under these circumstances, must feel a strain on him throughout; or if on the other hand he will be eloquent at the expense of his matter and commonsense, he must resort to empty declamation or sounding expletives, more characteristic of the conventicle than the church. The latter was far from being the case on this occasion: there was no rant or abortive attempts at fine preaching: on the contrary his manner was temperate but impressive; his language pure, scholarlike, and correct; and his matter orthodox and good: but the consequence of extempore preaching was also evident, some things were said more than once, and other things might have been as well and more forcible said in fewer words. On the whole, notwithstanding these little imperfections, I was much pleased; there was an earnest and an honest wish to do good — and I am sure he must do good. He had, too, a happy manner of introducing the happiest scripture quotations, and in the happiest moments; and his explanation of our duty to our neighbour — a duty, perhaps, may be often least understood by those who fancy they know most, not only of that but their duty to their God — was intrepid and direct, that of a conscientious man, who scorned to spare the hollowness of the selfrighteous and superficial. Mr. Marshall's expression is grave and unpretending; he uses considerable but not ungracious action, though he sways his body rather too much, and partially closes his eyes at times during his delivery; we are told, however, of Bourdaloue that his eyes were closed throughout the entire sermon. The rev. gentleman, whose age is about 50, was until, I believe, the last two years, a Minister of the Church of Scotland, which, however, he left through conscientious scruples: he was subsequently ordained to the Church of England, when the incumbency of Maryport becoming vacant, it was, with a small directed liberality, conferred on him by the patron, Mr. Isaac Cooke.

1. The Commercial Rooms, Corn Street, built 1811.
2. Destroyed by enemy action, 24 November 1940, the tower alone remains.
3. James Marshall, 1796-1855. Presbyterian minister who joined the Church of England. Mary-le-Port 1842-7, Christchurch, Clifton 1847-55.

The Commercial Rooms

Clifton Church

As I stood by the porch of Clifton church, a lofty perked-up looking dowager approached, followed by one of those non-descripts, made of buttons and braid, called 'a page.' Like all of his class it was impossible to tell his age; a long dark fur on his upper lip, and a certain hardness of feature told one he had arrived at that mysterious epoch where man and boy meet; while the childishness attempted to be imparted to his figure in other respects, showed that an effort had been made by his aspiring mistress to convert him into something between a Cupid and a Ganymede. He was so packed and squeezed into his jacket and trousers, and all the protuberances of his body were so pressed in and imprisoned, you felt in contemplating him a most uncomfortable misgiving lest, like most things too cruelly imposed upon, they would one day or another revolt, and laughing to scorn all the ingenuity of tailoring and the power of stitches, burst forth in native fullness and form to the world. This poor boy had certainly parted not only with his liberty, but with his second prerogative, for he was like nothing in nature but — *a page*: save for the rows of buttons and the hat, which he held up with his ears, the creature would have looked like a crocodile, and even that would have been preferable, for better be like a crocodile than nothing. He carried a small gilt edged prayer book, about the size of a set of ivory tablets, for his mistress, and to bear this and himself upright seemed his principal business. She had romantically, too, re-baptized him 'Alphonse.' Alphonse walked up to the pew, and placing the prayer book there, turning on his heel, took up his position in the gallery by the full-blown footman.

One, two, three, four feathered dowagers, a fifth, a sixth, and the line threatens to stretch out to the crack of doom— each occupying for the most part a whole pew to herself, while several anxiously looking for a place crowded round the door. Young and old, all finely clad, nodding plumes and flowing dresses, swept on, and still the expectants stood by the porch seeming more uncomfortable and more painfully embarrassed as others were accommodated, and the well trained sextoness flitted by from time to time, affecting of course to understand nothing of the significant though almost imploring glances meant to make interest as it were for the humblest portion of the humblest pew in the church. The impotent man in scripture waiting for someone to place him in the pool, was hardly more helpless than these people waiting for places, for though they could walk themselves, they saw many 'step in before them' to vacant seats, of which they dare not avail themselves: any of the five porches of Bethseda were at least open to those who could first approach them, but unless you can find someone to allow the sexton to 'put you in,' your strength of limb or priority of attendance is of little use in Clifton, or, in fact, in any of our fashionable churches. And should it be more difficult to reach the river of life now under the Christian dispensation, than of old the healing waters of the Hebrew pool, the virtues even of which were limited to far too few? The bold and broad invitation of the inspired writer was not given in this niggard way; it was not directed to the 'first,' or second, or the third that 'stepped in:' 'ho everyone that thirsteth, come ye to the waters; and he that hath no money, come ye buy and eat; you come buy wine and milk without money and without price,' How different this announcement to what we occasionally read in the advertising columns of the local papers — 'Two or three pews to be let in Clifton Church, without money or without price? Just try and see — and in good situations, too, where your feathers will wave, and your fan flutter, and your sapphire-mounted smelling bottle send forth its incense, amongst the foremost of fashion: where you may see and be seen, and note the look and mark the dress of your neighbours — this means a good situation, where a commanding view and a good prospect of the surrounding congregation may be had. You that thirst, come not near the sacred soft-cushioned preserve — vested property, freehold interest, or anything or any term you please for the privilege which one man pays for, under the invidious pew system of shutting another out of the house of God. Were I a Sampson Agonistes I'd pull, not the pillars of the temple down, but the pews up; for while several in the present instance were standing by the entrance or in the aisle, crushed or thrust aside by each person that entered, nearly half a dozen pews in my own neighbourhood had but one or two persons, in each; and as if their isolation was not already sufficiently provoking, they kept the doors open, moving them to and fro upon their hinges to create a gentle breeze.

Clifton church, though a parish church, and a church capable of accommodating a large number, is not to any extent the church of the parishioners; the rich and the non-resident occupy the reserved seats, and those few that are still nominally free are filled by servants, as impatient as their masters of the poor man's contiguity to their lace and livery. It is not the church of the poor man; he has no business there in that atmosphere of eau de Cologne and bouquet de la Reine, where the glitter of gilt-edged prayer books and the rustle of brocades present sounds and sights extraordinary to humble comprehensions. The rich must worship, it is true, as well as the poor, and agreeable spectacle as it is to see the poor attend in truth and sincerity, the rich joining in the services of the church in humbleness and reverence are a still more gratifying sight; but the poor ought not to be kept out of their own parish church — from the pews by the rich, and from the free seats by their powdered footmen.

The congregation of Clifton, too, generally carry the easy lounge of the draw-ing-room into the church: they make themselves as comfortable as they can during the reading of the Confession, Litany, and other prayers, in contempt, if of nothing else, of the 18th canon, which says, 'All manner of persons (no ex-ception, you see, for magnificos) then present shall reverently kneel upon their knees when the general Confession, Litany, and other prayers are read, and shall stand up at the saying of the Belief, according to the rules in that behalf prescribed in the Book of Common Prayer.' That there are many exceptions, I willingly and with pleasure admit, to this irreverent negligence.

Four clergymen were engaged in the performance of the service — the rec-tor, two curates, and the celebrated Dr. Pusey,[1] who read the communion ser-vice. When I saw the latter I was most amazingly disappointed. Oh, how often has my poor old aunt trembled with fear and rage as she read the *Record* until the spectacles were almost agitated from her nose, and all at the mention of this man's name. Smithfield she thought was again to blaze with Reformers and the Pope to preach at St. Paul's, and all was to be the doing of Dr. Pusey — he sacrificed a lamb, she assured me, every Friday, and I in return assured her his butcher's bill must be enormous. And this poor, sickly man, with a voice plaintive, and a face melancholy with the pale cast of thought and illness, a figure tall and stooped and a step slow, telling of infirmity not from age, (for his hair is still dark) but from ill health — this was the ogre of my aunt's imagination and of mine, at the mention of whose name my little nephews and nieces were set asleep, and crouched locked in each other's arms, with their heads beneath the bedcovering. After the victories of Blenheim, Malpaquet, and Oudenard, the word 'Malbrook!' from its mother would have frightened into quiet the most refractory infant in France: amongst the little impracticables of our domestic circle the name of 'Pusey!' was equally talismanic — a shadow of dread which none but the curate of our parish had the power of exorcising. And there was that 'Doctor,' no ogre, no monster, a poor, plain, pensive man, who seemed all unconscious of the hubbub he was raising around him. Oh, how my aunt, good old soul, had she been there, would have stared to see that he had neither hoofs nor horns — that his eyes were not like basilisks', and that the murderous mark of Cain was not written on his forehead, and that he did not walk in with that scarlet lady of bad repute under his arm, and that he did not feast upon heccatombs of slaughtered innocents. He read with a slow, plaintive, almost sad voice, and his utterance, from physical weakness, was subdued: he appeared to me the last man — looking, as he did, like some recluse just come from his cloister — to set the world by the ears, or lead in any great movement, innovation, or restoration, as you will have it. Luther was a man of stern muscular power, and immense firmness and obstinacy by nature; Melanchthon,[2] too, was a hero; but Dr. Pusey's greatness would seem forced upon him like Malvolio's, by circumstances — if he has been lifted into note, it would seem none of his doing or seeking. He seems to have the capacity neither physical nor moral for battling in the vanguard of a great movement; there is none of that vigour, or strength, or activity of character required for one taking the part and position he does in the English Church of the 19th century. He is a scholar of deep erudition, and a theologian of large and extensive acquirements, especially amongst the earlier fathers of the Christian church; but he is far from forward, neither eloquent, nor energetic, and even his writings, while they attest rather than display profound study, vast reading, and painful elaboration, want that lucidness, force, and originality which are the characteristics so often of decision, and with the multitude most attractive. Report speaks of him as an amiable, charitable, and pious man in private life: on doctrines I am not learned enough to speak.

The sermon was preached by one of the curates.[3] It was smoothly written, and not particularly calculated to make his 'highly respectable congregation' uncomfortable.

1. Edward Bouvierie Pusey, 1800-82. Leader of the Oxford Movement from 1841. Later this year (1843) he was suspended from the office of university preacher (Christ Church, Oxford) on a charge of heresy.
2. Philipp Melanchthon, German Protestant reformer, 1497-1560.
3. The curates are not listed in *The Clergy List*. The incumbent was James Taylor (1795).

14 October 1843

Redcliff Church

"Allow me, Madam," said I, offering my arm to an old lady who happened at the moment to be descending from a fly close by the gate leading from Redcliff Hill. She thanked me and availed herself of the proffered assistance, and as she seemed bound for Church I begged she would double the obligation by continuing to lean on me until we reached the porch. The weather was stormy, and the wind as we crossed the churchyard caught up the sear and yellow leaves of autumn, and flung them with a sort of boisterous sport in the old lady's face, and mine, as if in mockery of our newly-formed acquaintance. The soft red earth, too — the fat rich loam, fed with many a meal of mortality, was thrown up in several directions around, as if Death, mole-like, had been working beneath us, and showed his subterraneous progress in each fresh grave. I noticed the circumstance to my venerable companion. "The old gravedigger," said I, "Madam, seems to have made preparations hereabouts for the reception of more than one guest, who may arrive in the course of the day, and lie in those newly decked beds, which like a good host he has got ready for them". Whether I was too poetical to be intelligible, or too plain to be pleasant, I cannot say, but the old lady merely answered 'yes', and changed the subject by enquiring what Sunday it was. "The seventh Sunday after Trinity, Madam," said I, and by this time we had entered the church.

Having lent the old lady the use of my arm, I thought the least she might do was to offer me the use of her pew, but she did not: so I nodded to the sexton, and the sexton nodding in return showed me into one, where there were two young ladies, more than an equivalent you will probably say for one old one. I made a slight apologetic bow to the fair interns, and sat me down in *vis-à-vis* to both on a bare seat, for not content with one cushion, and probably expecting no other visitor, they had made themselves a little more comfortable by laying their foundations upon two. I gave rather a significant glance to our relative conditions, but they did not seem to understand me. I thought for a moment of sitting between them, but the space was so small, and my years being fifty-five, I questioned if the freedom would be taken in good part, so I remained as I was. 'I wonder who are my fair companions,' thought I, and I dare say they asked a like question of themselves — 'Who is that queer old quiz in the snuff-coloured coat?' — for the casual contiguity of a stage-coach or a church pew usually beget such speculations.

People are tired of hearing Redcliff Church praised — its grand proportions, and exquisite details; and not unnaturally so; for it is the never-ending theme of all our local antiquarians and little letter writers: but tire of silently, deeply, and devoutly admiring it you never can: all the affected prattle of the art cannot convey the feeling with which for the first time long drawn aisle, graceful column, solemn arch, and groined ceiling burst upon the view, and fill the mind with all the influence of grandeur, symmetry, unity, and beauty combined. Nor does it at all diminish the effect to consider that the history, origin, and date of the building are lost in the dim distance and defective records of the past — that the splendid structure has outlived its own annals. Whether it owes its erection to Canynges or Hardinge, De Brytonne or another, let us be content to take it as a sublime monument of the liberality and pure taste of a by-gone age: as the individual author, founder, or finisher has ere this I hope received his reward.

Redcliff Church, for a building so old, does not abound in monuments; the most remarkable I noticed was a heap of quartern loaves, which partially blocked up one of the windows of the north aisle. Whoever the ancient worthy may have been by whose munificence this Sunday supply is distributed, his descendants seem determined to make his works so shine before men that they shall not forget them: nor have I any serious objection, only that is gives that part of the church the appearance of a baker's shop. There is a sprinkling of weeping willows, smoking torches, and tea urns, the usual illustrations of surviving affection and departed worth: these, with the monument of some ferocious defunct, who has surmounted his tablet with a brace of ten-pounders, a tattered banner, and a battered helmet, form the principal mural curiosities of the place. There is, of course, the usual board of bygone mayors, which with a laudable pride is preserved in every parish church, and in the present instance contains a list of names from William Canynges to Kerle Haberfield — the gold leaf which records the first is a little dimmed, but it grows brighter by degrees through his successors, until it shines forth in dazzling splendour in the last — not least — of those recounted.[1]

The congregation seem respectable and civil, though I should have been able to say more for the latter quality, had the young ladies before alluded to lent me a cushion. I was never well-looking, and there is a sobriety about my snuff-coloured coat which is not eminently attractive: to these circumstances I suppose I must attribute the fact of neither offering me during the first singing a share of their hymn-books: in the second, however, some gentleman in the next pew noticing my destitute situation, and seeing from my musical face that if supplied with the means I might probably prove of good service to the choir, kindly handed me one of those tiny tomes, thus rebuking the incivility of my fair neighbours, and I now take this opportunity to thank him for his attention.

The service was performed and the sermon preached by a gentleman to me a stranger. His text was the 14th Chap 11 v. of the Gospel of St. Luke, 'For whosoever exalteth himself shall be abased; and he that humbleth himself shall be exalted,' His view of the subject was just, and his mode of treating it lucid: his illustrations apt, and his language, though not showy or ornamental, was smooth and flowing; but he rather read than delivered his sermon, and his tone and manner were both monotonous. The mechanical aid of elocution should not be overlooked so much as it is, and no man should think his matter so good that it may not receive some assistance from action and intonation.

There are few places where humility might not be appropriately preached, and Bristol need not of course be excepted from the number. Go where you will and you find a great man or men in his or their own opinion: draw the smallest circle you can of society, and you see amongst them envyings, self-exaltations, &c. — the least village has its great man, the smallest hamlet its degrees of comparison: a large city like this cannot, therefore, be. without its gradations, and its sets, and its ranks, and its so called good, bad and indifferent society. Nor is it alone to the highest that these lessons of humility should be taught, for there are few people from the man of moderate competence, who do not attempt to look down upon or up to other people: few think the acquaintance of their equals worth having, and feel far more proud of a nod of condescension from a person who is in his turn a toadyer to someone else, than the cordial handshake of an honest neighbour; there is a restless and unnatural striving to get out of our sphere, and when we have got out of it, we find that those amongst whom we have got are striving in turn to get out of theirs, only to find the same uneasy aspirations 'further up' — the same feverish anxiety to receive the recognition of a greater —

> Fleas there are that live on men —
> Other fleas bite these again;
> These little fleas have fleas that bite 'em,
> Thus fleas bite fleas ad infinitum.[2]

Oh, if any could have the honest humble independence to take a place apart from the castes that try to overtake each other on the high road of life; and mark the little envyings, hatreds, and jealousies, the pettiness of false pride, the presumption of worthlessness, that pass before him — all unwilling to take the low room at the marriage, all anxious to mount the highest — he would be led to think more of himself and less of others, and resolve that true respectability consisted in 'doing his duty in that state of life to which it had pleased God to call him,' without caring or seeking to go out of it.

I don't know whether or not parish clerks may be out of my province: if it were not taking a liberty, however, I would meekly beg that the rev. the vicar might devote a spare hour to teaching the clerk to deport himself with more reverend humility in his business: he lolled upon the left hand with an air of the utmost complacency, and casting a side-long glance towards the ceiling said, 'We beseech thee to hear us, good Lord,' as if it did not greatly concern him whether his prayers were complied with or not.

1. John Kerle Haberfield, the mayor for that year, occupied the mayoral seat six times.
2. A misquote of Swift or Morgan. Jonathan Swift 1667-1745.

> So naturalists observe, a flea
> Hath smaller fleas that on him prey;
> And these have smaller fleas to bite 'em,
> And so proceed *ad infinitum*

Augustus D.G. Morgan 1806-1871.

> Great fleas have little fleas upon
> Their backs to bite 'em
> And little fleas have lesser fleas,
> And so *ad infinitum*

Trinity, Hotwells

Somehow or other I had got it into my head that all the grand people remained on the hill — that the rustle of silk and satin was reserved alone for the ears of my reverend friend, James Taylor — that to the care of that estimable divine was appropriated the spiritual superintendence of every soul belonging to everybody that had five hundred a year to maintain it — if, indeed, the application of the income tax did not define the limits of his pastoral duties.

Illusion this undoubtedly was, as I soon perceived on entering the portals of Trinity, Hotwells,[1] where, though feathers did not flaunt as high, and colours did not seem as bright as on the summit — wealth having subdued its finery to a more chastened and primitive point; still wealth and rank were very visible and filled the edifice from aisle to gallery, leaving comparatively but a small space for the poor man. It was in vain that I looked round for the humble population of Hotwell Road and its purlieus. It is true there were *some* free seats; and in many instances I could see a creditable willingness on the part of those who possessed pews to share them — still the proportionate accommodation for the poor man was as nothing, his wealthier and more fortunate fellow having in this case as in others *crowded* him out.

It was originally, I believe, intended to have been more the church of the multitude than it as present is; no sooner, however, was it consecrated than half the population of the hill 'rushed like a torrent down the vale': and when reserved seats had been found for them — and I suppose they were first served — the residue of room which fell to the dwellers in the district was very inadequate, the crumb of space which remained after the 'rich men' were supplied being small indeed compared with the number who stood in need of it. Yet, when you consider that both churches are filled to overflowing, and that the spiritual welfare of the rich is quite of as much importance as that of the poor, the only remedy left is to build more; and with the former rests the solemn responsibility, since they have displaced the latter, to provide accommodation for those they have excluded, which they may easily do from the abundance of means with which Heaven has blessed them. It is in their neglect in making no equivalent that the blame in and injustice lie, and I wish both the residents and visitors of Clifton could be induced to view the matter in this light: the latter are particularly bound, when they come into a parish for a time, and dispossess those who have a prior right to the parish church to aid in giving something in return for what they take.

The congregation of Trinity, Hotwells, is of a particular character, being principally composed of persons of that complexion in the Church commonly called 'Evangelical.' I do not like distinctions, and in the Church I deplore them; but as this designation and that of 'orthodox' have become common and accepted terms in talking of such things, one is absolutely obliged to use them, which he may do, I conceive, without favour of offence. I know the dilemma to which an unfortunate newspaper editor is reduced when he encroaches upon such delicate ground; but in this case should I inadvertently tread upon anyone's toes, I alone must be held responsible for the accident, in whatever way you choose to visit it. I would beg myself to suggest, should you not have the Christian patience to bear with frankness from me, that you order your beadles to bludgeon all men they see enter in snuff-coloured coats, by which plan they will be sure sometime or another to fall on the real delinquent.

The congregation of Trinity, Hotwells, is, I have said. Evangelical, as their subdued deportment and plain dress evince: there was a manifest and in some instances a studied gravity about their looks, and I was glad to see that only one carriage, and that with a single horse, drove off from the church door at the conclusion of the service; for I do not think it is coming with an *'humble, lowly*, penitent, and obedient heart' when you 'pull up' at the House of Prayer with blazing liveries and steaming bays.

With a very natural and a very common feeling of self-sufficiency — perhaps some would call it vanity— I think myself one of the most correct and moderate judging men on the subject of the distinctions now introduced into the Church. I think we have had a happy deliverance of the old drowsy, indifferent parson, to whose supineness and carelessness the growth of Dissent is attributable — a sort of black-coated squire in the parish, only distinguishable from the lay neighbour with whom he drained the daily magnum of Port, by drawing his income in tithes instead of rents. A new spirit sprung up to stay the progress of the dry rot which proceeded from such persons, and was fast extending through the English Church; but the impulse given to this re-invigorating spirit might have hurried us into another extreme — to supplant with the excitement of Dissent the calm discipline of the Church, to hold forms and authority in contempt, and efface the characteristics of a national establishment — had not another and new movement been made to remind us of first principles, and to prove that practical charity and formular decency were not incompatible with spiritual piety: this new movement again has moved too far and too fast in many places, where we find youth and prudence — the excess of zeal and the lack of discretion — hurried on to offend the popular and hereditary Protestant feeling of England with crosses, candlesticks, &c., which create alarm and cause division. This is my confession of faith, and it is not strange that I think it a good one, for if I did not I should not hold it; I could not resist the temptation of touching on the topic, though I know it is a ticklish one. If however, anyone else entertains a different opinion, they are welcome to it, and may rest assured I shall not feel the slightest inclination to roast them for heretics: on the other hand, they are not likely to prove they are right by meditating faggots against me or the unfortunate Editor who occasionally affords me the use of a column for my 'Church-going gossip.' I do not despond at all for the Church from these divisions; I believe they are all working together for good, and that it will rise to renewed might and efficiency from all its throes. The country is being covered with new churches, and I should not discourage the emulation which prompts one portion to make an effort to rival the other in the extension and increase of such edifices. Neither should I be disposed to reject the money contributed for pious and charitable purposes, whether collected at the church porch or from pew to pew.

But what has become of Trinity, Hotwells, all this time? The truth is, I have been so pleased with my own wisdom and theological reflections that I could go on listening to myself for ever, if something had not reminded me of my business. As the church was apparently filled when I entered, I took up my position in the south aisle, and placing my umbrella against the wall and my hat on that, the sobriety of my snuff-coloured coat saved me from that intensity of gaze to which a well-dressed person in a free seat or an open standing is subjected. About the second lesson, however, my humility was rewarded by the sextoness placing me in a pew: yet I subsequently wished she had left me where I was, for my attention was from time to time distracted by one of two objects within my view, which, however well disposed, I could not help observing. One was a gentleman with three children, about five, seven, and nine years old, and never did serjeant more rigorously drill a raw recruit than did this parent these three little creatures: his eye was constantly upon them, and if they did not hold up their heads and look point blank upon their prayer-books, he was sure to see the slightest relaxation, and poke them into painful attention, — if the book or the head dropped from weariness, and their little eyes wandered for a moment from the print, he noticed it instantly, and recalled them with beck, nod, or wave of the hand to fixed gaze and formal attitude. His children seemed to engross all his devotion, and drilling them was his main occupation: it was almost in vain that I attempted to recall my scattered thoughts from this family group; for when I had succeeded at one moment, the book of the youngest falling into a horizontal position called for the interference of the indefatigable father, who only changed his line of action to see that the eldest had turned over the proper page. The other object to which I should like to have closed my eyes (and perhaps I ought to have done so) was an old gentleman immediately in front, who was given to shake his head most violently, piously he would call it perhaps, at the end of each sentence.

The congregation on the whole were very decorous and attentive, and there was quite a devotional character about them — the instances I have alluded to being rather the result of excess in this respect than otherwise. The ladies had a large majority, being I should think at least ten to one; and in the number of really handsome faces, enshrouded in plain bonnets, one could trace, perhaps better than in anything else, the progress of Evangelical principles which seem to have made most spread amongst the fair proportion of the community, and given a different direction to these feelings of youth which might, in ordinary cases and under other circumstances, seek and find excitement in the crowded ball-room.

The service was carefully performed, but the singing, both chaunting and psalms, though correct, was, I thought, feeble. One of the penalties which a 'Church Goer' pays for his migratory habits is, that he often falls in for, as it were follows, a round of collections from church to church. On the two previous Sundays it had been my good fortune to have an opportunity of exercising my humble liberality, and a sinister spirit made me secretly wish the privilege of adding to my fast accumulating and good deeds denied me on this day: a few minutes before the sermon, however, I saw two or three portentous silver plates shoved into as many pews, with a very significant whisper from the sextoness. There was no mistaking the 'move,' so I proceeded to debate the matter with myself, — 'This is the third collection,' said my left hand to my right, 'you have been called on to contribute to within as many weeks — you cannot afford to go on this way, otherwise you must give up your 'Church going' as far too expensive a kind of pilgrimage; besides, your well-brushed snuff-coloured coat is beginning to blanch at the elbows, and it is only by the most indefatigable attention you can make your beaver[2] look decent.' 'Nevertheless, I'll give something,' replied the right hand, 'I should be ashamed to pass the plate without putting something on it.' There now,' added the left, 'you see it is not real charity that prompts you to the act; it is only because you would not be thought shabby, and there is no merit in the deed; that boasts no better motive.' This rather staggered right hand, especially as he was not quite so unwilling to be argued out of his intended donation. 'I had better abstain,' thought he, 'from giving, since I cannot give in a better spirit,' and he was not reluctant to be convinced to do as his paltry penuriousness dictated; but his good genius made another effort, and determined him to give (willingly or *not*), sooner than gratify his insidious avarice. Left hand seeing this, as a last resource said, 'What is Newfoundland to you? Why give to Newfoundland, while there is ample room for the exercise of charity and the spread of religion at home?' But right hand was now fortified; 'True,' said he, 'I should be disposed to thoroughly cultivate the ground around me before I attempted to reclaim the savage and inhospitable tracts of Labrador; but confess you must that if I withheld my mite, it would not be on principle, it would be through penuriousness; and I am at least safe in giving, for I can possibly do no harm, and must do some good.' Right hand had the day, and the contest terminated in my placing a shilling on the plate as I left the church. Don't laugh, fortunate reader! my shilling may be as much as your sovereign, and should not be despised as a miserable mouse from a mountain of argument, for all offerings must be estimated not by amount, but by means. Besides, I saw more than one lofty lady, whose point lace would had purchased my whole wardrobe, raise her eyes intently towards the arched ceiling, and in every direction but towards the plate, as she passed out before me. I would not misinterpret anyone's movements, or misjudge their motives, so I attributed this sudden fit of abstraction to an inherent love of classic architecture, or, in fact, to any love but an inherent love of money.

The Rev. John Mensman[3] is one of those men who at once win you with a look, his countenance and bearing evincing simple and unaffected piety. I should not speak thus openly if I thought my honest and frank evidence would be received as fulsome, nor can it have any effect upon the object of it, for if I rightly understand his character, he looks for far higher approbation than mine or that of men. With whatever 'division' of the Church he may be classed is to me of little importance; I judge of him by his ministerial character, and from having often heard him, and so far as I am qualified to give an opinion, he not only preaches with a solemn, earnest, and deeply impressive effect, but with a true regard to the doctrine of the Church, and filial deference for its high authority. There is much solemnity without whine or drawl in his tone, and the very meekness with which he urges obedience to divine injunction, instead of weakening, rather strengthened the persuasive manner of his appeal.

1. Consecrated 10 November 1830, gutted by enemy action, 3 January 1941, restored 1958.
2. A high silk hat.
3. *James* not John Mensman was shortly to become incumbent of the new church of Christchurch, Clifton.

17 November 1843

St. Nicholas

I really think I must either turn or change the colour of my coat, for the same snuff-brown is, I fear, unfortunately for my incognito, beginning to be known. In my own noiseless quiet way, I had entered the porch of St. Nicholas[1] on Sunday last, and having exchanged a kind of cabalistic salutation with the stone statue of Alderman Whitson, as he lay book in hand in his niche by the doorway, was preparing to steal into some modest corner of some secluded pew, when I was discovered by a little round, respectable sort of man, who kept guard by the vestry, and who I afterwards learned united in his own rotund and corpulent person the duplicate posts of sexton and parish clerk.[2]

This important functionary viewed me rather inquisitively for a moment — his eyes travelled deliberately from the cork soles of my winter shoes to my Oxford grey pantaloons, without betraying any very significant sign of recognition; but when in his ascending scale of observation, he reached my coat — my snuff-coloured coat — there was a peculiar and most malicious twinkle in his small grey eye, as much as to say, 'I smell a rat,' the moment, however, my green spectacles came beneath his ken. I could see that with an internal chuckle he said to himself, 'I have caught the Church-Goer'. No sooner had he seemingly convinced himself of this, than turning with a half patronising, half deferential air, he exclaimed in a voice as round as himself, "Come along, sir, come along," and putting one of his short legs before the other, and beckoning me to follow, he pompously rolled up the aisle before me.

Now I am a most bashful retiring man, who cannot bear a high seat in a synagogue, or a prominent one in any place: in St. Nicholas the pews are arranged Amphitheatre-like, so that the inmates look point blank down on every person that enters; fancy then what a trying thing it was for me to follow this over-attentive functionary up the centre aisle, between two files of staring eyes. I would have willingly stepped into the first pew I met; but tramp went the little man before: "Come along sir," cried he encouragingly from time to time, as almost overcome with shame I felt disposed to stop or turn in anywhere, sooner than follow an ambitious little body, who, I believe, whether intentional or not, was making a spectacle of himself and your humble servant. Ten! eleven!! twelve!!! — the thirteenth pew was passed, and I was now in the act of leaving the churchwardens' also behind, still tramp, tramp, went the little man, and I began to fear he had mistaken me for the Bishop of Gloucester and Bristol, or some other right rev. father in God, and was about to show me inside the communion rails, within a few feet of which I had arrived, when, making a sudden turn, he threw open the door of a pew, that from its topmast situation might be called the *Ultima Thule*, and glad to hide my head anywhere from the multitude of eyes I felt convinced must have converged in vision to me for the last two minutes, I entered, and found myself by the superscription on the prayer books in 'the minister's seat.' The little man shut the door with an emphatic force, as much as to say, 'you're lodged,' and rolled back again.

I could not help looking after him: he was a study in himself. Equal in latitude and longitude, with a good humoured face and an important air, he seemed to move along as if not only St. Nicholas church and steeple, but the whole establishment rested on his shoulders, including the Lords spiritual and temporal. They call him, I understand, in the Annals of the parish, the 'Bishop of Parish Clerks,' and he certainly looked the Hierarch of the whole fraternity: I question if his Grace Will. Howley[3] more thoroughly enters into the responsibility of his place. He is just one of those men who if the east end of the church was being pulled down, would make a living buttress with its body, being so intimately identified with all the details of the edifice as to be on speaking acquaintance with the cherubs, and on the best possible understanding with all the statues. He is, too, let me add, in all sincerity, the very best reader of all the parish clerks I have heard in Bristol or elsewhere.

St. Nicholas church, as a building, is about the greatest architectural incongruity I know of: the exterior of the nave of the church and steeple belong two classes of the Gothic, and the internal decorations are Grecian, the ceiling, the altar, &c.; and yet with all these contradictions it is a very pleasing, light, and not inelegant structure. Still I think if I were rich, and belonged to the parish, I should be tempted to pull down the ceiling, with its little groups of sursy seraphims, and plaister of Paris clouds, together with that unsightly row of second hand bow-lights, which block up the west end. Having done so much, I doubt not I should be emboldened to attack the altar, and test the stability of those Corinthian columns of Honduras mahogany which now hold their place there. Though no sapling, I am not old enough to recollect it myself, but I have often heard my father speak of the old altar which existed before the church was rebuilt in 1762; and which, from its elevated situation — being erected over the ancient gateway, and approached by some twenty steps of alternate white and black marble — must certainly I fancy have had a very imposing appearance: but my worthy parent was one of the *laudatores temporis acti*, and would have preferred, I believe, old Bristol to new Jerusalem.

Amongst the annals of this church there is a most curious circumstance inserted. It was one of the many customs of by-gone Catholic days for the corporation to attend mass on St. Nicholas day, at this sacred edifice, and hear the Bishop's sermon, and afterwards receive his benediction. So far so good: the sermon ended, however, their worships retired to dine at the Tolzey, and while they awaited the coming of the Bishop, we are told, amused themselves with playing at dice, it being the province of the Town Clerk to procure the implements in consideration of a penny paid for every raffle — source of emolument which might still be judiciously added to the contingent profits of the post. At this pursuit they killed time, and continued until the arrival of the prelate, whose habit it was to follow them with his choristers, and mayhap take a friendly hit with their worships. I have at this moment in my mind's eye the Mayor and the Bishop at the old 'Counter,' occupied with this interesting pastime, castor in the hand of each — the chief magistrate crying 'Seven's the main, my lord;' while the head of the Catholic church emphatically added, 'But Eleven's the nick, your worship.' Couple with this picture the Town Clerk, as croupier, raking civic visit to St. Nicholas for Evensong.

The service was solemnly and impressively performed. As the vicar, the Rev. G.N. Barrow[4] ascended the pulpit, I confess I felt disposed to compare the black covered sermon which he carried to a kind of hand-grenade or bombshell, destined to explode with Protestant indignation amongst us in a few minutes. My penetration, however, for once was at fault, for the sequel proved the discourse to be neither overcharged nor intolerant. The text was taken from the Gospel of the day, Luke, chap. ix., 54, 55 and 56th vs. 'And when his disciples James and John saw this, they said. Lord, wilt thou that we command fire to come down from heaven, and consume them, even as Elias did? But he turned, and rebuked them, and said. Ye know not what manner of spirit ye are of. For the Son of man is not come to destroy men's lives, but to save them. And they went to another village.' The words were in themselves beautifully apposite, and yet so obvious as I doubt not to be selected in a majority of churches that day, forming in the present instance the basis of a just, liberal, and profitable discourse. Pointedly applicable, they were also capable of conveying a touchingly forcible admonition to Christian toleration.

1. Gutted by enemy action, 24 November 1940, now an ecclesiastical museum.
2. William K. Price.
3. William Howley, 1766-1848, Archbishop of Canterbury, 1828-48.
4. G.N. Barrow (1840).

25 November 1843

St. James's Church

After glancing round at the crowded pews for a few moments in search of some place to set me down, the sexton showed me into one which from its situation, shape, &c., was, I have no doubt, a kind of refuge for the destitute and all extra-parochial visitors. There is some such curious, common, and unclaimed locality in every church, which furnishes the *quidnuncs* of the congregation with subject matter for conjecture when the service is over, so that the door of this omnibus apartment is seldom opened without causing more than one eye to turn inquiringly towards the newcomer. The interns already in possession were an interesting looking young widow and a little boy, both I have no doubt foreigners like myself, and I had no sooner entered than several heads were inquisitively popped up over the neighbouring pews as if to ascertain the last arrival in the strangers' seat. I wish people would mind their prayers, but I verily believe such is the force of inherent habit, that if an angel were in the reading desk and a lady in hat and feathers, or even an elderly gentleman with a brown coat, to appear in the aisle, they would as if by concert, turn to look at the latter.

The morning was hearty, cold, clear, and frosty, and each person as he or she entered the church, presented that peculiar appearance which indicates so well the pungent state of the atmosphere outside. Their habiliments told too of the arrival of winter. First came Madam, with muff and tippet: then, perhaps, one or two little girls, cloaked and beaver bonnetted, followed by a tiny brother, close buttoned to the chin, and his hands buried in a pair of woollen mittens; the family cortege winds up with the father, who conscious that he has to provide food for the little mouths in front, thinks his life of value, and fortifies himself in folds of broad cloth against the contingencies of climate.

Such a group as this entered almost with me, and soon after they had taken their seats. Mamma distributed to each little mouth a large medicated horehound lollypop, as an antidote against the shrewd air of a November morning: this, however, did not prevent the elder girl coughing, which she did I suppose to prove the necessity of maternal precaution, and everyone knows how catching a cough is in church — no sooner had she given this signal of distress than her sister followed, then a family in the next pew commenced, and were answered by two elderly gentlemen from the north aisle, who were echoed in the other; presently the noisy epidemic mounted to the south gallery, and thence rapidly extending to the organ loft, set the choir going in a manner less musical than usual; the senior church-warden was the next whom it seized by the throat, though the moment the barking commenced he pulled a paper of hippo lozenges from his pocket; and lastly, as if to complete its annoying vagaries, the affliction fell amongst the children of the parochial school; and some fifty lads of tender ages and noses *retroussés*, were in a moment off in full cry with as much pertinacity as if they were having a rehearsal on Hullah's system.[1]

St. James's might have been once an imposing building; but it strikes me at present with its solid low Saxon or early Norman arches, its heavy projecting gallery, and high pews, as rather more like a court of justice than a parish church. There is always a very large congregation, this having been, if one may so speak, a popular church for many years, and in a densely inhabited parish, where they are actually obliged to pack away the inhabitants. Architectural elegance as a subordinate matter is therefore postponed to accommodation, and though one might under ordinary circumstances wish to see the unsightly gallery pulled down, the improvement would be far too dearly purchased by the expulsion of a portion of the congregation. The Camden Society are an excellent society, but more than their taste must be consulted in such matters.

At the west end is a gallery, and over it is *piled* an organ loft and organ; at the east is a Corinthian altar-screen, and I am told a picture of the Transfiguration; I give the fact subject to exception, as I received it myself, for the said pictorial embellishments defied my eyes and spectacles to make out its design. Amongst the monuments is one a mural brass, at the east end of the south aisle, dated 1632, of Alderman Gibbes, and the lady who had the supreme felicity to be his wife. It is like the picture at the Vicar of Wakefield's, where they stipulated for the portraits of as many of the family as could be painted on one piece of canvas at the price; for the heads of the House of Gibbes are represented kneeling on either side of a lectern; four sons in the same position, and descending like steps of stairs, occupy the rear of their right worshipful parent, while a like number of young ladies, presenting the same inclined plane, if indeed it might not better be called a sliding scale, muster with clasped hands behind their much lamented mother. I should say myself, conjecturing from the appearance they present, this amiable and *equilateral* family came into the world at strict intervals of eighteen months, and as there was no Registration Act in those days, were, I hope, baptized in as regular succession. Near the altar is a monument to Sir Charles Somerset, a man in mail, in all the martial array of genouillieres, jambres, and so forth: his stately lady, in pointed stomacher, ruff, and mantle, keeps him company.

Close to the communion table is Bailey's bust of the late Rev. Mr. Biddulph,[2] who long held so eminently popular a position in that portion of the Established Church included in the deanery of Bristol. For years St. James's was the centre of attraction, and the avidity with which Church people crowded from their various parishes to its portals almost amounted to a rage. There have been some men amongst those called 'popular preachers' who have been sought after with almost equal ardour; but the late incumbent of St. James was in mental calibre, decision, strength of character, and high purpose, far beyond them all: his very manner bore the marks of firmness and command, and no one can recall to mind the measured and impressive step with which he mounted the pulpit, his black bound Bible under his arm, and the solemn and serene glance, not unmixed with severity, which he cast around on the congregation, without feeling that in some degree he must have resembled the earlier fathers of the Church, and also how easy it is to account for the earnestness with which he was followed. He seemed to derive his authority and influence perhaps more from the force of character than the fascination of eloquence: it was not over one sex alone, as we find it very often the case, he maintained a pastoral and powerful influence; but the intrinsic and masculine strength of his intellect could command the respect and arrest the attention of the scholar and the sage. Anyone so implicitly obeyed was not unlikely to be affected by the consciousness of authority, and we, therefore, find him in matters connected with his sacred calling not unfrequently employing personal command as well as spiritual admonition, almost always, I should hope, for good. He was of that quality which in any situation in life would have led him to display firmness and decision.

The parish of St. James is one which must be, I should think, peculiarly trying to an incumbent: though there are many respectable residents, yet there are an overwhelming number of poor, whose claims, or rather appeals and importunities, must furnish constant, arduous, and anxious, and very often ungracious labour for a clergyman, on whom, in addition to his sacred duties, that of almoner is almost always imposed by necessity and circumstances. In such a parish we must not estimate his labours by Sabbath duties, for the least onerous are those performed in the pulpit and reading desk. The clergyman's door is seldom without some poor applicant, with his or her sad story of human misery, care, trouble, or want; and many a gusty winter's night and evening, when you might picture to yourself perhaps the clergyman seated in quiet and ease by his library fire, you should, on the contrary, look for him with more chance of finding him in some of the narrow alleys and hovelled courts of his crowded parish, following some ragged guide to the bedside of sinking profligacy, and the abode of woe and want — localities into which he is compelled to carry his purse as well as his Bible. For my part, I think the duty of visitation, the work which such a man has to do outside the walls of his church, inferior to none others in practical or parochial importance. He who mingled in his grand mission with publicans and sinners set us a momentous and solemn example in this; and it is not your fine preacher, who fills his church with an admiring audience, whose sermons are run after and repeated in drawing-rooms, and praised by the congregation before they quit the porch, who spends his week evenings elaborating discourses to create effect on the following Sunday, who does his duty best — I would not have him neglect the rich, for they unhappily are not often more independent of spiritual advice; but you may rest assured it is not in the drawing-rooms of a favoured and elect few we ought to look for the hard-working incumbent of such a parish as St. James's: he must also be found in its squalid purlieus, its alleys, and its garrets, if he would hope to give account of a faithful stewardship. It is not for ease, or indulgence, or a mere gentlemanly livelihood, or scholastic retirement, men should enter the Church; it is an arduous and solemn responsibility, in undertaking which self should be the last and least consideration.

There is usually a long list of banns in this parish, I suppose on the principle laid down in Alison's book on population,[3] that people rush most recklessly into marriage where they have the least to live on. On the day of my visit there was a catalogue of candidates, who each asked leave through the clergyman of every baker and butcher in the parish, as Lydia Languish says, to enter into the holy estate with some 'Sally in his alley.' This is generally a part of the service which appears to possess levity in the eyes of the congregation, and spinsters old and young giggle a little when it is given out; but it is in my opinion one of the most serious, and I always reflect with awe on the prospective amount of cares and anxieties into which each perhaps unthinking couple is about to rush. For fifty years I have eschewed it myself, and nothing short of a pinch of snuff sustains me when an elongated list of banns is being published.

During the second singing the beadle mounted the pulpit with a large stool, from which, and the fact of its not being a fixture, I suppose I am correct in surmising that the incumbent and curate preach from different, and have each their respective, elevations. As I approach the impressive age of sixty, my sight begins to wane a little, so that at first I could not very clearly see what the red-caped official carried under his arm, and for a moment was inclined to conclude that we were about to be favoured by one of the Rev. Mr. M. . . .'s migratory and most original sermons; as that eminent divine has a somewhat peculiar fancy for always preaching from the huge folio Bible belonging to the reading desk, which he causes to be carried up to the pulpit before him, in whatever church he may happen to be officiating in his flight for the day. Looking into St. Werburgh's some time since, I could not help feeling for the sextoness, who is somewhat fleshy and a little feeble, as she toiled painfully up the steep flight of stairs under a ponderous tome nearly as tall as herself, as though the preacher could not give out a text of three lines from a more moderate edition. Some false and wicked wag once remarked that the Rev. Mr. M., who is a professed extempore preacher, adopted this plan to conceal a written sermon from the ken of his congregation; there cannot, however, be the slightest foundation for this, for his homilies so harmonize one with the other in style and subject — such a family resemblance seems in fact to pervade them all, that I think he may safely trust to his memory in most cases — railroads. Popery, Sunday travelling, Rownham ferry, and now and then a feeling allusion to the most popular and extensive bankruptcy of the day, enriched with a parenthetical and most pointed rebuke to some drowsy auditor, forming the great salient points of all his sermons. His zealous and most uncompromising exertions on these several heads have made him the terror of the two boards of the Great Western and Exeter; and mail coach proprietors have a well grounded apprehension of his homilies, and always return from the church when he preaches with their appetites a little impaired.

I was not fortunate enough, however, to hear Mr. M. on the present occasion; the incumbent, the Rev. J.H. Woodward,[4] having preached from II. Thes., chap. 3, v.5. It was a sound thoughtful sermon, and displayed not only a knowledge of the subject theologically considered, but also a knowledge, and a thorough one, of human nature and of life; there was much taste displayed in the structure of many of the sentences, and the figures, of which he is not a little fond, were appropriate and well sustained. He did not at all appear to be insensible to the attractions of rhetorical ornament, but it was carefully and not too profusely applied; there was now and then throughout the discourse some inequality in the style, but in no one instance was he obscure, and in many there was evidence of a free, refined, and cultivated eloquence. His manner in the pulpit was animated and emphatic, but the latter quality, coupled at times with a certain air of severity, gave at moments to his discourse somewhat the tone of dogmatic dictation; this, however, I am convinced, arises from an earnest and intrepid interest in the welfare of his flock.

The income of St. James's has been lessened of late years by the withdrawal of the Fair;[5] the application of the revenues arising from which to the support of the Church was, in my opinion, the very next thing to the sale of Indulgences.

1. John Pyke Hullah, 1812-84. After investigating continental systems of teaching music to large numbers of people at one time, Hullah formed his first class in England at Battersea in 1840. By July 1842 his method had proved so successful that it was computed that in excess of 50,000 were attending similar classes.
2. Thomas Tregenna Biddulph, 1763-1838.
3. Sir Archibald Alison, 1792-1867. *Principles of Population*, 1840.
4. J.H. Woodward (1838).
5. St. James's Fair, founded about 1170 and abolished in 1838.

9 December 1843[1]

St. John The Baptist

With its long nave up Tower Lane, and its spire perched on the top of the city gate, St. John the Baptist seems as though it were purposely placed out of view. It is to its seclusion, I suppose, we owe its simplicity; for while every other church in Bristol is pealing with organs, a pitch pipe is the only instrument the parish maintains. Of Handel they are innocent, of Beethoven quite unconscious, to Mendelssohn they owe nothing — the rude little choir have been singing the Old Hundredth till they have taught it to the cherubims around; and the solemn-toned clerk, who deems it his duty to look as distressed as he can, has been for so long a period used to this primitive mode of music, that I think he would refuse to hold any communication with an organ, were such a novelty introduced.

Everything around seems characterised by the same unaffected simplicity, for I did not notice a single 'great man' amongst the congregation: what the churchwardens may be when they are in their places, I of course cannot say, for both were invisible on the present occasion. These important officials have each a pew snugly ensconced at either side of the pulpit, and their tall blue wands pointing pensively to the ceiling, appeared, I thought, quite disconsolate at the prolonged and unexplained absence of their owners: there was certainly a moody semblance of solitude about the seats in question, and from the fact of some industrious spiders — like that which laboured so opportunely at the mouth of Mahomet's cave — having spun a few fine threads transversely to the doors of both, I infer it must have been a long time since the congregation had the pleasure of looking their wardens in the face. I have heard of a church in a remote part of Somerset, and some early age of the world, where the parson did not often indulge his flock with a sermon: at length having been eloquently inclined one Sunday, he expressed to the clerk his intention to preach; the latter made an effort to dissuade him, but the rector being obdurate, the other lowered his opposition to the request that his reverence would not mount the pulpit, but hold forth his homily from the reading desk; to this, as being uncanonical, the old rector objected, and enquired the cause of the clerk's reluctance, which that worthy explained by telling his superior 'there was a turkey sitting on thirteen eggs there.' Now I don't mean to imply that there was any such act of incubation going on in the church-warden's seat of St. John's, but their absence appears to have been sufficiently extended to allow

of the incident. I think it has a bad effect to find those who ought to set the precedent of punctuality away from their posts; but as some encouragement to the parochial attendants, I think it would be as well if those officers, when it is not convenient to be present, would send their hats to be hung on their wands, as some shadowy representatives at least of constituted authority.

Like its services, the congregation of St. John's are the simplest and humblest, as well as the most attentive I have yet seen at any church within the boundaries of Bristol. There are no nodding feathers and fine satins there, and people really look as if they went to say their prayers, and not to show themselves; they appear all unconscious of grandeur — secluded, as it were, in the heart of a great city, they know nothing of show and ostentation, and if a solitary feeling of rivalry enters the bosoms of any within that ancient edifice, it is only between the two best tenors at the first and second singing.

St. John's still preserves in a very rude made and ancient sand-glass a remnant of rampant Puritanism. When tailors and shoemakers were preferred by their own choice in the time of Cromwell to the incumbencies of Bristol, this as well as the rest was taken possession of by some fanatical mar-text, the said sand-glass, which turned on a pivot, elevated by the side of the pulpit, near where the Bible was placed, so that these 'True Shepherds,' as they called themselves, measured their sermons by the primitive chronometer at their side, and many and many a time was its empty globe reversed, the preacher observing at each turn, '*Now, my brethren, let us take another glass on the subject,*' — *a treat*, I should think, considering the quality of the discourse, for those of the congregation who indulged in early dinners.

A little bit of romance attaches to this church in connection with the so-called conspiracy of Yeomans and Boucher,[2] in the time of Charles I., when the government of Bristol was held by the cruel and cowardly Colonel Finnes. Its bells were to have rung forth the signal for the rising of the Royalists throughout the city, and its crypt formed the temporary prison of the Puritan leaders; but though many a loyal ear listened during that anxious night for the startling peal, which was to arouse a disaffected city to its sense of duty, no sound issued from St. John's, and the tramp of Finnes's secret party hurrying those brave and devoted men, who risked life for their rightful sovereign, to a dungeon which led to a scaffold, was alone heard. St. John's formed at one time a portion of the inner wall of the city, which in this part at least was safe from attack, as no besieging army, would, in those days, violate the sanctuary of such an edifice. I do not believe that the date of St. John the Baptist is accurately determined: like a great many other buildings in Bristol, of whose past history we know comparatively little, and which leaves us — whilst they stand as it were in sullen reserve amongst us — strangers to their age and story.

I was shown into a pew near the door, in which was a modest looking, plain dressed young woman, who might from her appearance, have been a servant maid; but from her unaffected and obliging manner some fine ladies might have taken a lesson. I had no hymn book, but the simplicity and natural courtesy with which she offered me a share of hers more than reconciled me to what promised to be a temporary inconvenience. I accepted her offer with gratitude, for I recollected how often I had been similarly situated while in a seat by silk clad ladies without being treated with similar courtesy. As there was nothing in my snuff-coloured coat to make me superior to or tempt me to disown the simple-minded sister in a plain stuff gown by my side, neither is there anything in my homely exterior to debar me from the privilege of praising God from the same book as the finest lady in the land. When we had done I made the civil maidservant as courteous a bow for her kindness as I could command.

In the sermon I experienced an agreeable surprise. Everything was so homely around, I expected a homely discourse. It was preached by a young man, a stranger whose name I do not find in the Directory, and therefore am unable to gratify the reader's curiosity in this respect.[3] I will say, however, in all sincerity that I have not heard a sermon for a long time with which I have been more pleased. In his language there was the utmost Anglican purity, evidencing though not displaying the scholar; — his style was pleasing and perspicuous, while there was besides that obvious and earnest wish to do good, for the absence of which no amount of merit in the composition, no painful care in the preparation, can make amends. He had, I have no doubt, as some school men say, 'thought up' his subject; and while his delivery, which was much too rapid and unvaried, showed practice had much to perfect in this respect; about his matter there was that force and freshness which habit and time not only do not always enhance, but sometimes tame down.

1. This was the first date that an illustration headed the Churchgoer column of the *Bristol Times*.
2. Robert Yeamans and George Bouchier, executed in 1643.
3. James Russell Woodford, see Coalpit Heath, in *The Bristol Churchgoer and his Visit to Bath*. Incumbent G.N. Barrow (1843).

16 December 1843

The Mayor's Chapel

I was passing the Council House with my book under my arm, about a quarter before eleven o'clock on the forenoon of the first Sunday in 'dark December', when a long line of carriages, cocked-hats, and state coaches, drawn up in front of the civic edifice, attracted my attention. It was the Mayor's first visit in form to the civic chapel; so thinking it only required my presence to crown the compliment paid him in so full an attendance of his fellow corporators, I accompanied the procession.

In lieu of a carriage, being left to the primitive conveyance which nature furnished every man with at his birth, I was a little incommoded by the crowd, and in trying to get ahead of the *cortege* in College Green, my snuff-brown received from the wheels of his worship's carriage a few small contributions of that commodity which the streets of Bristol are not deficient in on a December day: as I contemplated the specks which disfigured the propriety of my hitherto unspotted garment, my choler rose for a moment in radical rebellion against all state, and with that natural disposition which I fear we all have to fly off into discontent at any fancied slight or simple accident, I was about to burst out into maledictions in my own mind against all who rode in coaches, and spattered poor pedestrians with mud from their chariot wheels: when my better genius rebuked me. 'What right have you to complain', said common sense; 'if having chosen of your own free will to walk near a state coach on a moist morning in December, you receive a speck or two on your well tended habit: if it were a Duke who passed on foot in the same place and at the same moment, he would fall in for as impartial a share of puddle, and since you choose to be at this particular point at this particular time, you must put up patiently with a spatter as you have had to do more than once in your walk through life.' Common sense is right thought I; but many an envious spirit I have no doubt has turned radical from a cause equally absurd.

"Come, push along old ge'man," said someone in my rear, suiting the action to the word, just as I had arrived at this rational conclusion, which his official rudeness however (for it was one of the macemen) for a moment I must say endangered: to carry my loyalty as soon out of peril as possible, I moved quickly forward, fancying I could find a place in the chapel before the worshipful worshippers entered, but at the very vestibule one of the Dogberries informed me in most decided terms I must wait outside until my betters were served; and as he witnessed my disappointment, a second laughed at the 'old quiz with the big book under his arm, who was in such a hurry to say his prayers.'

The state carriage drew up, and the Mayor entered with his sword-bearer, who carried a weapon he could hardly raise let alone wield for the protection of his worship, who took his stand near the door; the corporators as they descended from the other carriages in succession, bowing as they passed, drew up on either side. A sudden thought struck me — ere a single policeman could bar I boldly stepped forward, with as stately a treat as if I represented in my own particular person the entire city, and making a bend to his worship, which for execution and elegance of design was, I am convinced, never surpassed since the days of Beau Nash,[1] filed in between a corporator in bushy whiskers and another without any. This might appear impudent in me, but it really was the only chance I had of gaining admission, for it was clearly the opinion of the constabulary force on duty, that none but the souls of the sixty-three municipal representatives of the city were of the slightest value on that day.

The sword-bearer looked I thought a little suspicious at me, and it is probable had not the organ played up, and the signal to advance been given, he would have been induced in another moment or two to enquire what constituency had the honour to return a man of my apparent gravity, 'to attend to the interests of their ward in the Town Council.' Such is the force of association too, that for a moment I almost fancied myself a corporator — that the six maces as it were smiled upon me a brilliant recognition of my right, and my old school-fellow the Town Clerk[2] seemed with one of his most insinuating looks to approve the choice of the 'free burgesses of Bristol.' And here it may not be out of place to observe, that as I am most anxious to serve the city, and it has of late been difficult to find persons so patriotically given on the 1st of November, I am quite willing to undertake the public responsibility of any ward which may be vacant, presuming that however limited my abilities to serve the same, I shall yield to none in zeal, assiduity, and attention to the affairs of this great and first-rate city in general, and of the ward for which I may be returned in particular.

It was really a very imposing spectacle when the doors were thrown open, and we — I say we, for I was still of the number — advanced beneath the arched and Gothic screen,[3] the organ sending its deep and throbbing swell through the long aisle before us. But where after all were the lights of other days — the scarlet robed worthies of times gone by. The chapel was, it is true, as beautiful as ever, the carved work, the storied window, the time-worn monuments, too; but the robed and furred, and 'fat capon-lined' aldermen, whom we had so often seen sweep in brilliant and imposing line through the same portal — my wonder as a boy, and the admiration of many older heads — had disappeared with things beyond the flood. The present race seemed no more to their predecessors than a young plantation on the site of a primal forest. This was my first visit to the Mayor's Chapel since the municipal revolution,[4] and fearing I might be labouring under an optical illusion, I rubbed my spectacles twice to make sure that the moderate-sized every-day looking gentlemen by my side were indeed the successors of the obese dignitaries of a by-gone bench — that those zephyr-clad Tweed, Taglioni'd, and Chesterfield-coated persons, whose vests fitted them as perpendicularly as Maypoles, and who made no more pretence to a paunch than a Welsh curate, were indeed veritable corporators — that they belonged to that body with whose being turtle was associated, and of whose very glory venison formed an integral part! Without tangible proof, though I had occular in abundance, I would not be convinced, so stretching out my hand I touched a gentleman in front with my finger to see if he was flesh and blood, and not a phantom. The fair round belly with fat capon-lined forsooth! there is not as much flesh in the reformed corporation as would build one first class alderman of the old school; then for the ample scarlet robe which swept the square pavements with a lordly fold, you have those beggarly little skirtless abridgments in broad cloth, popularly known by the name of Taglionies,[5] and retailed at twenty-four shillings each, by Doudney and Sons, of No. 97, Fleet Street.

The best proof that the corporation must have shrunk from its originally fair proportions is, that one of the fullest attendances which I am told has been within its walls since municipal reform, were packed away in a few pews, four or five councillors taking up little more room than a single ancient corporator with gown and other appurtenances would have done.

One side of the chapel is devoted to the civic body — the women occupy the second, and the red maids and city boys amongst whom are some remarkable miniatures of our principal citizens, the other portions. The right worshipful attendants did all they possibly could to appear attentive, with a few exceptions, who seemed absorbed with their own dignity: the monastic appearance too, and mellowed light imparted a somewhat devotional effect to the proceedings, yet the day was evidently deemed by the crowd, who crammed its aisles, one of display, as if the corporation came there more for their own glory than that of a Creator, and the place boasted no higher presence than the municipal representatives of the burgesses of Bristol.

The sage brotherhood of antiquarians have not clearly made up their mind as to the year of our Lord in which this church — which was originally a Collegiate one, and an Hospital of the Virgin Mary and St. Mark — was built. It owes its origin I believe to some branch of the early Berkeleys,[6] and is built north and south, instead of east and west, for the purpose of pointing, it is said, towards the old Castle, whose amiable interns were its best benefactors, and who disposed themselves to the pious business of building churches when they were not otherwise occupied in cutting throats — making provision for their own souls in a future state, while not engaged in dispatching other people's prematurely from this.

The monuments are numerous, fine, and varied — some of them present mighty lengths of Latin, and others no lack of English; and all so abound in eulogy that one is disposed to wonder on reading them, as well as the inscriptions we see on every wall and tablet throughout the land, where the wicked were buried. I never yet saw the tomb of a sinner, or a man who had not as many virtues, benevolence, &c., as he had back teeth, from which gratifying but somewhat singular circumstances I conclude that the bad never die, or else are invariably refused the rights of sepulture; or perhaps stone-cutters are so conscientious they will make monuments for none but meritorious men, or chisel a single character for those who have not the piety of King David, and the wisdom of his son, Solomon. 'No man can be accounted happy until he is in his grave,' said Solon to Croesus, and in England there are many thousand instances in which we never know a man's good qualities until he gets there, and then we wonder we did not discover them before; but it often occurs that the amiability hid from all but their heirs or disconsolate widows, who can only be consoled for their bereavement by large legacies or second husbands.

In the Mayor's Chapel there are such heaps of Latin, elegant and inelegant, that one is inclined to exclaim with the Satirist —

> 'In yon epitaphs I'm griev'd,[7]
> So very much is said,
> One half will never be believed,
> The other never read.'

One is to a Doctor, who sacrificed himself at the age of 37 for the good of his patients — an example worthy of imitation by many of the faculty of the present day; another to Lady Throgmorton — her life extended over twenty-five years, and her virtues over fourteen lines of middling poetry: a third is to the Virtuous Dorothy Popham, as also to her husband, who, considering the Lucretian qualities of his wife, has a very equivocal crest, two bucks' heads furnished with broad and antlered honours. In the east aisle, on a raised tomb, are two recumbent and mailed figures, supposed to be the Gourneys of the time of Edward the Third, and Knights of what Hume[8] calls the most sublime and romantic folly of any age — the Crusades: having managed to carry back their bodies from the Holy Land, it is to be hoped they had the prudence to keep their heads out of harm's way while there. In the West aisle reposes a Berkeley, and in the chancel a brace of them; where is also a monument to Miles Sally, a Bishop of Llandaff, and a very fine one to Merchant Aldworth, on whose memory and many virtues a considerable amount of Latin and money appear to have been expended. There are many others but I cannot remember them: I may add, however, that somewhere in the Mayor's Chapel are the ashes of an unmitigated scoundrel named Bedlow,[9] the complotter of Titus Oates, and through whose instrumentality more than one honest man was executed — the remains of so bloody a pander to popular bigotry ought not to defile a sacred edifice.

The congregation at the Mayor's Chapel is not parochial, the Chaplain being paid for attending to the spiritual welfare of the sixty-three members who compose the Council — though some of them, it is said, are past praying for, and others won't be prayed for according to the forms of episcopacy. Several of the ratepayers, however, are regular attendants there, and unless on state occasions when those who have not got any are rather unreasonably requested to 'bring or send their carriages,' most of the corporators may be found with their own families in their own parish churches.

1. Richard Nash, 1674-1762, 'King of Bath'. A gambler and autocrat who helped found the popularity of early Georgian Bath.
2. Ebenezer Ludlow.
3. Removed in 1888 and now in the grounds of a house at Henbury.
4. The Municipal Corporations Act 1835.
5. Named after the ballet-dancing family of Taglioni in the early nineteenth century.
6. Founded 1220 by Morris de Gaunt and Henry de Gaunt, grandsons of Robert Fitzharding.
7. *Friends, in your epitaph's I'm grieved*
   So very much is said:
   One half will never be believed,
   The other never read.
   Unknown. Sometimes ascribed to Alexander Pope, 1688-1744, but not in any of his works.
8. David Hume, 1711-76, *History of Great Britain*, 1754-7.
9. William Bedloe and Titus Oates' allegations leading to the discovery of the so-called 'Popish Plots', — largely fictitious Roman Catholic attempts to assassinate Charles II.

23 December 1843

St. Philip and Jacob

The atmosphere of the first Sunday in Advent was a sort of compound of wet and air, so insidiously mixed up, that you imbibed large portions of the one while inhaling your necessary and natural share of the other. Such a day I selected for my visit to St. Philip's Church; and as I plodded through the miry streets that led to it, vainly trying to keep the rain at bay with my umbrella, I confess I could not help thinking of what an old lady told me the other day with a grave shake of her head, that the Puseyites proposed to build churches in the most inaccessible and unpleasant localities, that persons might show their devotion in overcoming difficulties and distance; for St. Philip's seemed this wet morning to me to be situated in the centre of the Slough of Despond, through which it required more than a double cork sole and conscientious determination to make one's way.

As I approached the church the Beadle was moving from door to door. There being no refractory boys about to call his peace-preserving order-enforcing talents into play, he consoled himself, for want of occupation, in scanning those who entered, and I of course fell in for a share of his curiosity: I proved, however, I think, more than a match for his penetration, for as I entered the porch he raised his cocked hat and scratched his head in perplexity. I hope he did not think — although I could not help fancying he might — I was a new applicant for the Sunday dole of bread.

On entering, I had hardly cast my eyes round with that enquiring glance which says I wonder where I shall get a seat, when a young woman, seemingly a mechanic's wife, very civilly opened a pew in which she was — a tacit but very intelligible invitation which I thankfully accepted, albeit the seat was far from the summit; for it is hard if the humblest spot in the house where God deigns to dwell be not good enough for the best of us erring mortals. If I am shown into a seat where, when I cry Lord have mercy on me, a miserable sinner in true humility Heaven cannot hear me, then I may have cause to complain, *but not till then*. As one civil turn deserves another, seeing the young woman had no Prayer Book, I offered her a share of mine; but suddenly reddening up, she declined my courtesy: there was no mistaking the cause of her confusion — *she could not read*, and I felt I had been the innocent instrument of creating pain. Poor thing! what a world did this untoward want shut out from her — what a penalty did she pay for perhaps the neglect or poverty, or both combined, of her parents, to be condemned to look alone at the exterior of every volume, whose contents were to her as those of a sealed book: how curiously and inquisitively at moments must she scan the printed page, wondering and feeling as though she would question each character and combination to communicate the microcosm of meaning and knowledge which lay beneath them, and which she could not unravel. Lord, I thank Thee, my lot and lines have not been cast amid circumstances where the terrible affliction of utter ignorance could have befallen me, for had it, what a blank would my existence have been! I am, reader, at that age when the world has ceased to have excitement for me: it never had much, for its dissipation I never could bear. I am without family, without care, pursuitless, with enough to enable me to live in ease, and no more than I can spend with ease; with some years of my allotted time to run, before I lay down my head to 'sleep with my fathers' — now take from me my book and quiet seat by the fireside at this festive season, and see in a worldly sense in what a dungeon of moral darkness and social solitude do you confine me; what, in fact, would be left me but a most intolerable listlessness, which I can hardly contemplate without shuddering?

From such a reverie I was awakened by a fretful childish whine in the same pew, and for the first time I discovered that my young neighbour was also a young mother, as she had with her a little boy, about eighteen months old, who up to that moment sat quietly by her on the further side, and escaped my observation. The mother attempted to pacify it, but failed, and as a child's cry will attract the attention of any congregation from the most eminent preacher in the world, a number of faces were of course turned towards our pew; the whine was growing gradually louder, so to help the poor young woman, who was also growing more confused in proportion, I pulled out my watch and dangled the seals fantastically before the baby's face: the effect was instantaneous; and think of it, ye poor fops of modern days, who now wear nothing but a puny thread of gold, with a tiny seal pendant from your waistcoat pocket, do you fancy your flimsy toy, your Brittgett chain — I think you call it — could quiet a child, or have any attraction for a baby eighteen months old? The little thing clutched a seal which had been in my family fifty years, bequeathed, like freedom's battle, from dying sire to son, which in size, too, might be said to rival the great one of England, and tugged away at it, crowing in ecstatic glee, until by a sudden jerk he pulled the adjunctive watch out of my hand: happily there was no damage done — mine was no miserable Geneva, but a solid piece of English workmanship, coeval with St. Paul's, and built on the same sublime and substantial scale of dimensions. Tempting as were the seals, the watch was still more so, and the little fellow had it in his fist in a moment — in the next it was in his mouth, for unfortunately he was cutting his teeth, and he used my chronometer as a choral: my chronometer, however, was not made for that interesting purpose, and fearing he might send one of his incipient grinders through the glass, I gently disengaged his little fingers from the chain, and

thereby undid all my former doings, for the little urchin shouted out in sheer passion, and the mother was obliged to bundle him up in her arms and leave the church.

St. Philip's church is a handsome, well kept, and commodious structure, and consists of a centre and side aisles: the chancel, which is deep and well lighted, would have a good effect, but the view is most ingeniously intercepted by a large pulpit and reading-desk, which might far better stand at the side: the arches between Kemy's aisle (a continuation of the north) and the chancel are very beautifully panelled somewhat like (if I recollect rightly) those of Sherborne, in Dorsetshire; but the arches in the nave are inelegant and incongruous.

According to some very old custom, the origin of which is unaccounted for in the dusty memorials of the past, it is the practise to dress up this church on the first Sunday in Advent with evergreens, and on this occasion every pillar, monument and Gothic projection was clothed in verdue: Birnam Wood seemed to have come to St. Philip's church; but peerless above all in arboreous decoration was the churchwardens' pew: over the heads of those two great functionaries a forest of laurel and arbutus stretched forth their branches in full and frondent glory, and the important pair sat in conscious dignity beneath their 'branching honours'. King Charles in the oak, as he is sometimes depicted by village painters, with a crown on his head, and sitting as complacently amongst its branches as though he were enthroned at Whitehall, instead of being hunted by Cromwell's myrmidons, might be said to afford a suitable representation of the Church-wardens of St. Philip and Jacob, seated as they were within their bower on the first Sunday in Advent. They seemed proud, I thought, and naturally enough, of their honours, and as ever and anon the door of the north aisle was opened, and a breeze stealing in amongst the superincumbent branches, waved them gently above their heads, the amiable pair appeared to fully personify the feeling of self-satisfaction.

The congregation of St. Philip and Jacob is mainly composed of substantial tradesmen and numbers of the poor of the parish, who deported themselves with the utmost decency and much seeming attention. The singing was more general in this church than in almost any I have yet been in: in fact I always find the less aristocratic the congregation the more animated the performance of this part of the service: the poor are especially, I notice, partial to congregational singing; it has the effect of at least temporarily warming them into a devotional feeling, and should not be neglected. I am convinced it is the constant hymning which fills half the dissenting houses in the country, for the poor wish to feel themselves as it were worshipping; the evil of it is that in too many instances amongst seceders it is carried to a dangerous excess, and leads to a morbid excitement more to be deplored than even the coldness of those quality who seem to think (I say it with reverence) they can praise God by deputy, and that they do enough towards harmony and devotion when they pay twenty shillings a year to an organist, two tenors, a treble, and a bass.

Like St. James's, St. Philip's is an exceedingly poor and populous parish; circumstances which impose on the pastor[1] and his curates, an enormous degree of labour, both as religious instructors and charitable almoners.

1. S.E. Day (1832).

For the better understanding of some allusions which occur in the subsequent paper, it may be well to insert here a curious invitation to Christmas, received about this time, and addressed

TO THE CHURCH-GOER

My Dear Sir, — I have not the pleasure of your acquaintance, but I have a monstrous respect for you, and read your letters with almost as much pleasure as I do my own. I have twice run the risk of insulting men in snuff-coloured coats, who have been walking the streets before me, and whom I have slapped familiarly on the back, under the impression that the peculiar coloured garment covered the shoulders of that quaint old pilgrim whose ecclesiastical wanderings have afforded us all such pleasure, not unmingled with profit, from time to time. In fact, my dear sir, you're the great point of attraction now in the paper — if perhaps I except my own occasional contributions; and I should not be surprised if the Editor, in finding his lucubrations neglected for yours, wished to exclude the 'series' from his columns; but let him do so, whether through fear or envy, and he ceases to receive the annual £1.1s.8d. from me.

But to praise or congratulate you is not the mere object of my present letter. I collect, my dear sir, from several expressions which have fallen from you in the course of your contributions, that you are a bachelor, living in what is called single blessedness, and a second floor. In all ordinary cases, that may be a very easy and enviable state — to sit by your own fireside with your feet in slippers, and a book in your hand, without any great anxiety for anybody in the world — without fearing that at that very moment your eldest son is smoking cigars, and making precocious bets and books on the 'Derby', or that your eldest daughter, whom you have designed for some substantial citizen, is writing tender epistles and making love on her own account with a poetic penniless music-master: of these fears you know nothing; and of Christmas bills for schooling and milliners, pianofortes and French teachers, you are in blissful ignorance. But let me tell you, nevertheless, there are times when even a large family has its enjoyments and comforts, of which I must say you old bachelors can have no idea; and to me a Christmas dinner eaten alone and digested in solitude, is about the most cheerless thing in the social world. Having finished your monastic feast and five glasses of Port, what a state of isolation does it seem to draw your chair towards the fender, turn your face to the fire, and spend your evening like an anchorite, contemplating the holly branch above the mantel-piece —

I am almost recompensed for my past year's anxieties, and my coming year's apprehensions, when I see my boys and girls about me on a Christmas day, and behold the rapidity with which a fat turkey and a sirloin of beef subside under their conjoint labours, when all their saturnalia, and the school tale is told, and the innocent jollity goes round, and the great log on the fire as it crackles in concert with the fun, seems to join in the family glee.

Thinking of this last week I thought of you too, and mentioned to my wife my fears lest you might pass a solitary Christmas, with no legs under your mahogany but the pair that call you proprietor: and at her suggestion I came to the determination of asking you to partake of our dinner on that day. I cannot bear the idea of your sitting down by yourself to a solitary meal, and that everybody should be enjoying themselves in the bosom of their families,

'While alone with your cup,
Like a hermit you sup,'

pondering, perhaps, notwithstanding the sunshine which seems usually to enliven your heart, on past incidents and early days, which festive anniversaries have the unfortunate effect of always recalling. Sedate and easy tempered too as the gentleman in the snuff-coloured coat now seems, 'yet once,' like Father Greybeard in the Nursery Rhymes, 'he was young,' and may have had his hopes and disappointments as other people: even his celibacy, which he affects to wear with such equanimity and apparent contentment, may be owing to another cause than apathy; there may be some matronly looking lady now presiding over a family, or perhaps passing her years in virgin frigidity, who like yourself had her early days, and warm cheek and bright eyes, to which you were not insensible; though her coldness or caprice may have infused that one bitter drop of disappointment or pain into your cup, but for which we might now see you walk to church with a wife under one arm to balance the big Prayer Book under the other.

I do not throw out these hints to inveigle your history from you; I merely indulge in conjecture which may be romantic after all — all I ask from you is the pleasure of your company on Christmas day, at No —, —— Street, (the address is left with the Editor) at five o'clock, to take your share of a roast turkey, (there are sausages) a piece of boiled beef, a plum pudding, and as good a Cheddar cheese as ever you stowed away behind the breast of your snuff-brown coat. Of my Port you will judge yourself. I promise you, too, the three youngest shall not be brought in until the dessert, and that you will not be required to nurse a single one of them on your knee. Their mamma will expect you to say the little girl is a beauty, and that my second boy has a chin and nose like Napoleon Bonaparte. You can compliment herself too on her good looks, and say that if you were not told to the contrary, you'd have sworn she was my daughter; for when you have said a few sweet things she'll take herself and the youngsters off, and leave you and me cozily by the fireside, with the bottle of Port, to crack our own quiet jokes and nuts together during the evening.

I shall therefore, my dear sir, expect you punctually at five (I am sure you are punctual), I'll take no excuse; when Christmas
'Comes in,
To sit poking the fire all alone is a sin,'
especially where this is such good company, and so unexceptionable a dinner offered by your's, my dear sir,

With esteem and admiration,
AN UNFORTUNATE FATHER OF A FAMILY

P.S. If you like music, my eldest daughter will astonish you — I do a little on the fiddle.

6 January 1844

St. Augustine's The Less

St. Augustine's[1] is but indifferently off in free seats. I occupied one of four near the West entrance. In the same seat with me was a strange character; a poor insane, fantastical, harmless fellow in a ragged grey outside coat, and who seems monomaniacal in ecclesiastical matters, for I have noticed him at almost every church in Bristol. He wears a bunch of feathers as a bouquet in his buttonhole, and always carries with him three or four old prayer books and a testament, though I conclude from his constantly turning the wrong side upwards he can read none of them. He, however, imitates all the movements of the congregation, and behaves himself with a propriety which many nominally in their senses need not refuse to take pattern by; he stood, knelt, and sat with the utmost precision, and perfectly in accordance with rubric and canons, and when the clergyman turned over the leaves of the Prayer Book he turned over his too, not always, however, with the most fortunate chance: for the Collect he got the Marriage ceremony reversed, and Prayers at Sea for the Psalms. He must have recognized me; for both of us being migratory in our habits, we met in several instances in the same church, but never before in the same pew: he was, it would seem, a bibliomaniac as well as a monomaniac, for he turned his eyes repeatedly with admiring and longing looks to my large Prayer Book — from the Prayer Book his attention was turned to myself, when suddenly recollecting he had seen me before, he pulled out a tin snuffbox from his pocket and offered me a pinch. I don't take snuff, but to gratify him I put my finger in the box, and he was satisfied. Poor fellow, I could not help thinking, from the turn his insanity had taken, being peculiarly and entirely of a church-going character, whether he had not once been a parish clerk, or perhaps a beadle. There have been military fools who follow armies, and legal fools who frequent courts; but in the aberrations of intellect it is pleasing to see it err (if one might use the phrase) in a right direction, and find 'the ruling passion' take so innocent a turn.

I have not noticed before that this is an orderly and respectable, but not a fashionable congregation; the people all seem and look comfortable — there is that citizen-like solidity about them which makes one feel warm and happy in contemplating them: perhaps it is rather a familiar and too free an idea for such a subject, but it will convey what I mean when I say they struck me as just that class of persons who had each an early dinner and a warm substantial

joint awaiting their return from church — no outlandish dishes with frippery contents and French names, but emphatic legs and downright ribs, and an honest hearty heartfelt Grace for all; not a hurried muttered mockery, which seems almost to say, 'Lord, we thank thee in as few words as possible as it is the fashion but for no other reason, for we are in haste to begin.' I do not expect to see people say a long Grace which is unseasonable, but let them do it in a decent manner, with some seeming of gratitude, or not do it at all.

I have abstained in my last few papers from noticing the clergyman's sermon at length, because it has been suggested in a letter from somebody that it is not always fair or safe to come to a conclusion on a man's style or merits from a single sermon. In the present instance, however, I must be permitted to form my opinion from a single sermon, as I never before had the pleasure of hearing the vicar of St. Augustine's the Less. I can depart from the rule the more readily as it was honestly a good specimen, giving me the idea of a sermon carefully and closely considered: there was no declamation, and his composition was easy, free, and equable, and attracted attention by its intrinsic interest more than ornament. He did not shrink from a close and analytic examination of his subject, which was in some measure a deep and difficult one, namely, as to the amount of information which God had thought well to reveal to man on the subject of his future state. This is a question on which most minds are often panting to have more enlarged knowledge; but the preacher's reasoning was eminently calculated to tranquilize and assuage all such restless yearnings, and convince us we knew as much as it was necessary or good we should know: a less firm or judicious treatment of the subject might have been attended with evil effects, but in the present instance the wisdom of the divine arrangement was most successfully and satisfactorily vindicated, in a clear, pleasing, and comprehensive discourse.[2]

1. Damaged by enemy action 1940. Closed for demolition 19 July 1956.
2. Incumbent: W. Millner (1832).

13 January 1844
St. Thomas

Very red and round berries were peeping out in little clusters from amongst very green and hardy leaves, and all looking in this respect as like old times as holly and mistletoe could make them, when I followed an elderly lady and her two daughters (all three having previously deposited their pattens by the porch) into the South aisle of St. Thomas's Church. But it was not after all the hearty Christmas Eve, 'frosty and kindly' of other days — for no one seemed cold, and all most unnaturally temperate: the children of the Charity Schools, instead of having noses rivalling in redness the berries above their heads, looked bilious, and everybody's breath was transpired invisibly instead of issuing, as we notice it on a frosty morning, like a column of thin smoke from the mouth.

"Any particular seat, sir?" said a civil lad who showed me in. "None," said I, "the nearest," and into the nearest I was shown, and had a pew of considerable size and a large bunch of holly to myself. To make amends for my own immediate solitude, my neighbourhood was well tenanted, the whole commanded by a high pew containing two grave-looking Churchwardens, who seemed all as demure as if the parish were in debt, and there had not been a vestry dinner for a dozen years.

And this is Christmas Eve, thought I, and another season of plum puddings and mince pies, parental troubles and annual payments is come round; but it is not of mince pies and plum pudding alone these holly branches remind us. They make us sentimental; they make us think of all we have lost while we have gained nothing but years, and make us invariably conclude we have not, and never will have, such times as the past: though this, I am convinced, is in great part an illusion, for it was our own youth and freedom from care and ills which made everything then seem so sunny, and no doubt in some fifty years, when the young laughing urchins and light-hearted boys now running about us become grey-headed like myself, they will also talk of past times, and invest these utilitarian, practical, perturbed days of ours with a poetic atmosphere, and speak of the bright hours of their childhood when things were different and troubles hardly known.

I well recollect my young Christmases: they were usually spent at a village not very remote, with two maiden aunts, who regularly doled out some twenty gallons of thin soup to the poor at the 'festive season,' and as invariably sent a paragraph announcing the same to the neighbouring paper. Somewhat similar in character was the charity of a gentleman in the same place, who looked upon himself, and was looked upon by many others, as a most beneficent friend to the poor, for he clothed 'at an inclement season' the six smallest boys in the parish school in new suits of the cheapest materials with the brightest buttons; and that the latter as well as his good deeds might shine before men, the tiny wearers on the day of their investment were paraded into the most conspicuous part of the church, and shared with the donor (towards whose seat they were instructed to stare with the most grateful gaze) the admiration of all present. As regularly as Christmas Day came round, there were the six boys (he selected the smallest because they excited the most sympathy and required least cloth) standing advertisements of this gentleman's unbounded charity, in the middle aisle, and the gentleman him-self in a great pew looking forth complacently on his 'good works,' which he also took care, from the brightness of the buttons, should escape nobody's notice. Verily, both my aunts and this gentleman had their reward: they gave out of their abundance in the most ostentatious manner, and men and women spoke well of them, and the neighbouring newspapers did the same — and so they had *their* re-turn. In the same neighbourhood, perhaps in the same parish, however, was some strange Unknown (for nobody could find out who he was) who sent money in anonymous notes to persons in distress, to parish charities and parish churches, and carried the secret of his identity and his many services to society with him into another world, and the presence of that God who was his sole confidant while in life. I should be sorry to do away with those large painted boards we see with benefactions and subscriptions inscribed on them in legible letters: and, for the sake of the poor, I would not cry down the custom of advertising long lists of contributions in the columns of local papers; for I verily believe you would not get one-fourth the amount you now receive for charitable purposes if the system were given up. What, for instance, can be more comfortable than the feeling of that man who opens his paper, and as he dries it by the fire in the breakfast par-lour, smiles blandly on seeing his own name amongst the foremost in a column of contributions? He secretly commends himself, and feels satisfied the world will commend him too, for he knows at the same moment is the same paper laid on many hundred breakfast tables in the city, and his munificence announced to the same extent, while innumerable mouths half filled with buttered toast mutter forth, 'how handsome — how liberal.' He taps his egg with the satisfaction, and as he does so the urn seems to simmer a song in his praise, and the silver teapot smiles sweetly and approvingly on him. Verily, *he* has his reward: he sees his name in print, and gains a certain degree of public *eclat*; but here his reward ends — his act was intended to have effect with the world, and the world gave him credit for it, but the Recording Angel's ledger is not kept for such characters, or to chronicle such hollow 'charity.'

St. Thomas's Church[1] is a pleasing and commodious structure, unencumbered by galleries: it was originally Gothic, and is mentioned as having been only second in beauty to Redcliff: with the exception of the tower, however, which was allowed to stand, it is now of the classic order of architecture, having undergone a change about the latter end of the last century, when the declamations of Inigo Jones and Sir Christopher Wren against the Gothic had still some influence, I suppose, on the public mind. It is capacious, and consists of a nave, north and south aisle, and is so seated with square pews throughout, that people have a sociable and most neighbourly way of looking in one another's faces. I believe it has a small chancel, at least I have heard it has, but I could not see it, as the pulpit, the reading desk, a row of red curtains, and a lofty churchwarden's pew literally shut it out from view, and left the stranger to make any mystic conjectures he pleased as to what was beyond them. A trifle would make a considerable alteration for the better in this building, and without the sacrifice of either money or room. I should have the entrance altogether at the West end, and, removing the impediments which obstruct the view of the chancel, give a more commanding effect to the entire.

St. Thomas's church is well attended, and the congregation, with few exceptions, may be ranked under the class called 'comfortable,' though I dare say there are some who would not take the term as a compliment: the services are well performed, and the edifice kept in excellent order, but the arrangement of the pews, which set people looking in each other's faces, imparts a certain appearance of irregularity I think to the whole. The service was performed and the sermon preached by the Curate, the Rev. W. Seaton,[2] as indefatigable and painstaking a clergyman, I am told, as any in Bristol. His style is earnest and energetic, and I have no doubt calculated to be eminently useful.

The sermon was from Revelations, and was a very useful and judicious discourse. I confess I always feel nervous when I hear a text taken from the Apocalypse, lest the preacher should get into any of those extraordinary speculations which sometimes result from a rash attempt to unravel the figures and terms of that mysterious book, and to calculate the end of the world and the approach of millennium, from its metaphorical language. I have known one worthy but weak man almost turn his brains in trying to reduce to arithmetical nicety the thousand years which Satan was destined to spend in the bottomless pit; and some preachers, we know, arguing from the same source, have attempted to predict the end of the world to the exactness of a twelvemonth, as if that event was to be revealed to the curiosity of man, which we are told the Almighty has withheld from the knowledge of the angels. It would be as well, I think, if we would in all cases abstain from troubling ourselves with such speculations, they are not necessary for our salvation, and the plain and simple highway of the scriptures is wide enough for us to walk in, without tearing ourselves with thorns, and maiming our feet with flinty stones, in trying to penetrate the recesses of that mysterious knowledge, which Heaven has in its own good wisdom wisely placed beyond our reach.

1. Used since 1956 as a centre for the exercise of the Ministry of the Word and Sacraments amongst those engaged in industry in Bristol, but now has been declared redundant.
2. The incumbent was M.R. Whish (1806), W. Seaton was perpetual curate.

20 January 1844

St. Peter's

In 1689, Samuel Wallis, erst alderman and mayor, left 20s. a year for a sermon to be preached in St. Peter's Church annually, to the Governor, Deputy-Governor, and Guardians of the Poor on the day of their election; with, however, I regret to say little apparent advantage to that public body, for judging from the riot and noise and constant contentions kept up amongst its members, they seem for the most part past praying for, and as bad as if they never had the benefit of clergy. The sermon, at least, does not appear to have done much good, and I fear, if instead of annually they had one preached to them every morning in the year, it would have little effect on the spirits who *dis*-compose the Court, and tend to establish so striking a resemblance between the neighbouring board-room and a bear garden. I have entertained myself from time to time in reading the accounts of their proceedings in the Bristol papers, and if reports speak true, I must say I never knew gentlemen on whom twenty shillings' worth of sermon is so completely thrown away; for they abuse one another with a cavalier contempt for limit that would immortalize a much higher body. Their principal business is to find lodgings for some poor people, and distribute to persons with small means and large appetites four pound loaves of bread: but their pastime is eloquence, and there is as much oratory about a few pounds of pauper jalap or a dozen broom-heads, as Cicero expended on the Cataline conspiracy.

Besides Mr. Wallis's gift there are others parochial and practical, and amongst them one of £100, the interest applied to charitable purposes, from the Rev. Hugh Waterman, Rector of St. Peter's for fifty-seven years. Fifty-seven years in the ministry of the Church, and over one congregation!

What generations must a minister, who has spent nearly sixty years in the same parish, have outlived? He must have seen the same men pass almost through Shakespeare's seven ages, and illustrate them all — have looked upon the 'baby brow', which he has sprinkled at the baptismal font, until it became wrinkled with years and cares — have joined many a smiling pair on a sunlight morning in marriage, while the merry peals rang above their heads, and read the funeral service over the same to the solemn sounds of the passing bell. The experience of such a clergyman, having his lines cast in one parish for such a period, and his profession giving him the opportunity of knowing and seeing so much of the interior of human life and the workings of human nature with

all its vicissitudes — the death-bed of poverty, and apathy, and affluent prudence (when both prudence and affluence seem hollow possessions) — must
form a great and vast volume of practical and often painful knowledge.

Another bequest is from Mr. James Birch, of the date of 1773 — £60, the
profit thereof for a sermon in the Church, and a dinner for the vestry, on the
10th of December yearly — a double provision for the spiritual and physical
requirements of men. There is a peculiar originality about most of these gifts,
but Mr. Birch's in quaintness is, I think, inferior to few. A week day sermon is
not always well attended, but a week day gratuitous dinner I'll be bound lacks
no guests: a few old women in the aisle, and one or two 'old inhabitants' in the
pews, constitute for the most part the attendance of the former, but fancy, if
you can, the full table and shining faces at a vestry dinner, and the merry voices
never silent for a moment, but while drinking to the memory of Mr. Birch,
who was doubtless himself in life one of the select, and in his bequest had a
considerable recollection of the boon companions he left behind, as well as
their weakness for parish feasts.

As I approached the porch of St. Peter's Church I saw a lady a few yards in
front, evidently bound for the same destination: I read civility in her face, and
as she walked up the centre aisle I followed without the slightest hesitation
and entered the seat with her, the sexton, who doubtless took me for one of
the family, holding the pew door open for me in his hand. The lady looked a
little surprised, but not offended, and in proof of her good disposition, placing
her toe to one of the two hassocks she moved it towards me; as a slight return
I took up her Bible and marked the proper lessons for the day. Service had not
begun, it being full quarter of an hour before the time, as I dislike coming late
into church. Indeed I feel convinced it amounts to nothing short of downright
irreverence. The last stroke of the bell is to many the signal for leaving their
dwellings, when they hurriedly perhaps throw down some book or newspaper
which they had been reading, hasten to church in anything but a proper frame
of mind, and enter some minutes after the solemn supplications of the congregation have commenced, attracting attention and interrupting the service.
The late comer bangs the door, puts down his umbrella as if he were 'ground-
ing' a musket, and in his flurry overturns two or three Bibles, and mumbles a
few words: when he rises he finds the reading of the Psalms has commenced,
and turning at random over the leaves of his Prayer Book, wonders what day
of the month it may be.

On the red cushions of the reading desk were lying, in all the glory of gilt
edges and gorgeous binding, a new folio Bible and Book of Common Prayer
a gift of several young ladies in the parish. This was the first Sunday they had
been used, and I noticed that some of the congregation looked with interest
towards them as a ray of winter sunshine shot athwart their sides and lit them
up like molten gold: I could not but secretly add my tribute of admiration to
the taste and intention of the fair donors, and contrast in my own mind the

pious propriety of this donation with many that are often made. There is no man who would sooner see the clergyman of the Church of England properly remunerated than I would — none better deserve it, and none have ampler opportunities or more generous dispositions to relieve the needy from their competence; but I am not favourable to the fashionable practise which sometimes prevails of making presents to popular and esteemed ministers.

The Church of St. Peter is an old structure.[1] It was founded at the same time as the Castle, to which it is generally supposed it belonged; but as its records are buried in the dust, antiquarians are left to their own conjecture. It is probable that a St. Peter's Church stood before the conquest, and that the congregation at one time were principally the cut-throats of the neighbouring fortress, when the preacher had to attack the hard hearts of his hearers through coats of chain armour and breast-plates of steel, though our ancestors were for the most part more tractable in the hands of the clergy than their broad clothed descendants of the present day. St. Peter's consists of a nave, two side aisles, and a chancel; the arches supporting the nave are light and handsome, and on the whole — allowing for the enormities of modern taste, whose mutilations here, as almost in every other church in Bristol, have been neither few nor trifling — it is an imposing and venerable pile. The usual black heavy mahogany screen casts its cumbrous and sepulchral shade over the chancel, and of course the ecclesiastical architects of the eighteenth century could find no place for some high pews but where they intercepted the view of the altar.

There are several monuments: one to Robert Aldworth, who, upon the strength of his good deeds while alive, has monopolized in death a very considerable slice of church accommodation: this monument in size and appearance very much resembles a shop-front, being bedizened with gilt cherubims, painted columns, and cornices. Mrs. Alderman Aldworth at one side of a lectern is smiling conjugally on her husband, and each regards the other with as much affection as love, money, and rosepink can make them. Close by is another huge monument of most elaborate carving, about the dimensions of a state bed, and with its black canopy not so very unlike one either: of the style of monument, it is one of the finest I have seen, being carved with the minutest sculpture: a recumbent figure of a lady reposes on the tomb, but that is all we know of the coffined clay beneath. Had only a dozen persons with the same immense ideas of monumental grandeur been buried in this church, there would have been no room left for the living.

In the burial ground adjoining, and beneath the green sod about three feet from the south entrance, moulder the remains of the poet Savage, who died in Newgate, after having eaten and drank, and worn out his welcome amongst the merchants of Bristol, who liked to have him at their tables — he amused them, and they fed him until his intemperance, irregularity, and ingratitude more than counterbalancing the attractions of genius, tired out his friends.

Poor, miserable, obstinate, imprudent, profligate, generous, and genius-gifted Savage, 'after life's fitful fever he sleeps well,' by the south porch of St. Peter's Church, and in a pauper's grave. Some months ago I was passing near the spot; it was a cold raw evening, and two men with a mop and water were washing the adjoining tombstones, looking for the last remains of Richard Savage, but no sculptured stone lay above the poor poet's remains. One of the two, a hungry looking unshorn man, was a scout from Grub Street, sent by some London author to collect materials for a Life of Savage.[2]

The Rector preached:[3] I was very much pleased with his manner of addressing his congregation, which was friendly, affectionate, and cordial, and his voice soft and agreeable: there was no affectation or effort at eloquence, but his language was clear, and his mode of illustration simple yet significant; there was, too, a tone of mild persuasion, a parental solicitude and exhortation, which characterized his discourse, and rendered it difficult to hear without attention, or receive without respect. He seems one of those men whose amiability and interest in his parishioners ensure them ever the esteem of their parishioners in return.

1. Destroyed by enemy action 24 November 1940. The Tower alone now stands.
2. Richard Savage, d.1743. Poet and Actor. Condemned to death in 1727 for killing a gentle-man in a Tavern, but pardoned in 1728. Obtained a pension from Queen Caroline on con-dition of celebrating her birthday annually with an ode. An acquaintance of Dr. Johnson, he subsequently lived in poverty and died at Newgate, Bristol.
3. H.C. Brice (1829).

27 January 1844
St. Werburgh's

Some time since having read amongst the list of benefactions to this church, that in 1624 'Humphrey Brown gave an estate at Elberton of £7 per annum for reading prayers at *six* o'clock every Monday morning at St. Werburgh's, £5 to the rector, 20s. to the clerk, and 20s. for providing candles during the winter season,' I fancied I should like to attend those early matins, and avail myself of the opportunity of beginning the business of the week with so pious and proper a service, on the principle '*A Jove principimus*.' Accordingly, on the following morning I rose at five, shaved myself by candle-light, and in cold water, (the latter faculty Kemble said constituted an independent man), and drawing an outside coat over my snuff-colour, sallied forth in the shrewd and nimble air towards this said church of St. Werburgh, convinced that Humphrey Brown in selecting such an hour must have been a man of early habits.

It was a sharp but bracing and dry December morning, still starlight, with a breeze abroad sufficient to fan the gas flame in the lamps, which shed their bright reflection on the bleached white flags around: save the rumble of a country market cart in some distant street, or the slow measured tread of some wakeful policeman, there was no sound to dispute the empire of echo with my iron-heeled shoes that rang sharply on the hard trottoirs. The shutters closed in each window, as I passed, made them appear like the eyes of the dwellings themselves yet sealed in sleep, and seemed to suggest such a city of sluggards ensconced under blankets inside, that I began to think John Brown's gift service would not be over well attended, and that however difficult it might be to get seats on other occasions, I was likely to experience no lack of room on this.

Just as the Exchange[1] clock struck six, for my benefit and that of the boys who waited for Her Majesty's mail bags outside the post office opposite, I arrived at the door of St. Werburgh's church — but further I could not go, for the door was closed — I pushed, but unyielding and obdurate was the panelled oak. Spirit of Humphrey Brown! thought I, this must be a mistake — the sextoness must have over-slept herself, or there is some other entrance, for surely the good man's bequest cannot be a dead letter — the £7 cannot be a hoax, nor the estate at Elberton a mere illusion. I pushed again; then paused to think if I had rightly recollected the hour; there was no mistake, I was convinced, on my part, though there must be on others. At this moment my eye caught a notice posted over my head, and which I had not seen before — Oh! this will explain it, said I — the minister indisposed, or the Church under repair; so by the light of the opposite lamp I read as follows:

'*Notice*. — Some evil disposed persons did, on the evening of Wednesday, the 15th inst., between the hours of 6 and 10, carry out of the church an old riticule basket, containing a very good black coat, a hatchet, half a pound of sugar, and a blue pocket handkerchief, belonging to the Clerk. If any person in the parish should obtain knowledge of the same, and would be so kind as to give the Clerk information thereof, he would feel greatly obliged.'

I rubbed my eyes and read again, 'a very good black coat, a hatchet, half a pound of sugar, and a blue pocket handkerchief interesting miscellany! but nothing whatever to do with your morning service. Mr. Humphrey Brown: it was a singular notice, in soothe, and as belonging to the clerk, the theft itself was almost sacrilegious. I have read parish advertisements many in my life, but this was unique. The thief that stole the clerk's hatchet may have stolen the key of the church also, thought I; but wishing to make another effort I pushed again, and was about repeating the trial for the last time when somebody exclaimed in a loud voice, "What do you want there, old chap, do you mean to rob the church?" I turned and saw a policeman at a short distance, seemingly deliberating whether he should not spring his rattle: but it is only the guilty who think of running, I stood my ground, "I want to say my prayers," said I. You should have heard the loud horse-laugh with which the impudent Dogberry received my words: the fellow roared aloud until he set the sparrows twittering in affright from every old angle in the Exchange. "What do you mean, man?" said I, a little nettled at his barbarity: "is there anything more remarkable about my wishing to worship at six o'clock than eleven." Another guffaw from No. two hundred and something, — "What parson?" replied he "is going to get out of his bed at this hour to say prayers for an old Curmudgeon like you?" "But Humphrey Brown's bequest" — (the rest of my sentence however was drowned by another peal) — "He is mad!" said No. two hundred and something to No. twenty who had joined him, "let us take him to the Station-house." "No," said his comrade with a knowing tone, "He be one of them ere Pusybites I'll be bound — they be the —— for praying early and late, they're forever at it." Then addressing me he continued, "Good man, if it be prayers you want and not to steal the communion plate there be none at this 'ere church but at Christian hours — the parson is snug in bed, the curate in his first sleep, the sextoness snoring, and the clerk dreaming" — of his hatchet and half pound of sugar, thought I, and turning of my heel departed.

On subsequent enquiry, I found there were no prayers at six o'clock in the morning, though the seven pounds are still received: there are prayers, I believe, on Wednesday evening instead. Now there is not a clergyman in Bristol for whom I have greater respect, or who is more estimable in my opinion than thou, John Hall;[2] we are almost contemporaries, your hair and mine have grown grey together, so that I am sure you will adopt anything I say in good part: I think no one is justified in taking so great a liberty with Humphrey Brown's bequest

— if Humphrey Brown left a certain sum to have service performed at a certain hour in the morning, you may rest assured he had a certain and sufficient reason for selecting that time, and no one should alter it; the inviolability of will and testament — the sacred and binding nature of a solemn bequest should not be lightly tampered with; for if it be, we do not know when the obligations of dying injunctions may be observed. Besides, I question if these alterations be for the better. Six o'clock may strike one as an unreasonable hour, but my opinion is, if you had prayers there regularly at that hour, and people were aware of it, they would be well attended.

My last visit to St. Werburgh's Church was paid on Christmas Day. I read a paragraph in the papers saying, 'the lovers of sacred music will experience a rich treat by attending St. Werburgh's Church on the evening of Christmas Day, as we are informed an anthem and other pieces of great beauty have been selected for the occasion.' I attended in the evening, and the church was crowded — there seemed, too, a swell of importance about all the subordinate functionaries; the promised anthem had turned their heads, and many had been known to postpone their plum pudding for the occasion: the pews were crammed — the aisles densely inhabited, and all turned in breathless expectation towards the organ-loft, from which I could hear ever and anon some premeditated performer clearing his or her voice, as if upon each individual singer depended the destinies of the musical world. It was an important evening in the annals of St. Werburgh's — you felt conscious there was something momentous about to take place: the 'all encasing' atmosphere of the church itself seemed sentient of the coming anthem, and I could not help thinking of some of my early rambles to Ashton Church 'a long time ago.' It was then very much the custom for the young people of Bristol to walk out there on Sunday mornings, when it was not an uncommon incident to hear the clerk regale the congregation about the middle of the service with the following announcement from above — 'If ther be any of yer great sangers down ablow from Brestel, ye'll please to cum up into the argan loft, for we be a going to sing a hanthem —*Blaw, ye, the trumpet, blow!*' There were few persons ever candid enough to proclaim themselves 'great sangers' by accepting the invitation, though no doubt it was well meant.

On the present occasion there were so many mysterious hems and preparatory sounds reached us in the body of the church from behind the red curtain which encircled the organ and the performers, that I felt a strong curiosity to get a peep within the sanctum itself; so creeping up the stairs I soon found myself in the sublime presence of choir and organist, all, however, too much engrossed with their momentous parts to mind an intruder. The 'chief musician' was all life, like a general haranguing each division on their proposed parts; the light lady Trebles, all nervous excitement, and sal volatile were enjoined to be steady: the Basses stood firm and massive as a brigade of heavy artillery, the Tenors were all on the qui vive, and the Counters stood ready for action at a moment's notice. At length the anthem commenced, and oh what a ferment was in that gallery;

not only was the organist's feet and hands, keys and pedals at work, every muscle in motion, but the exertion he used to make everyone take and execute their parts correctly was surprising: then their audible counting of time, and the no less audible directions to keep it, made that little loft the scene of perhaps more activity and hard work than had been known in the same area for years before. The audience who listened below to the beautiful music, had no idea of the huge exertions being made at that moment behind those red curtains to produce it, and create the effect which afforded them such pleasure — the panting and the pressure brought to bear on that bold anthem!

I knew a man once whose coldness and indolence kept him very often from church; still, however, to quiet his conscience he used to go and hear the anthem at the afternoon service of the Cathedral, and thus cheat himself into the idea that he had been at a place of worship. This, however, was not the case with the audience in the present instance: they not only came to hear the anthem, but with exemplary propriety remained, and conducted themselves well to the end of the service. I know no man whose appearance in the pulpit is more vener-able or pleasing than the Rev. John Hall's; there is a fine expression of benignity and kindness in his countenance, which his style of preaching, characterized by plainness and piety, fully confirms: his manner and matter are both marked by an impressive simplicity, and the great truths of religion are urged in a tone of earnest directness to the heart than if conveyed through a more ornate medium. Mr. Hall is a Batchelor of Divinity,[3] and I have heard a man of profound reading and of theological learning. He is, perhaps, one of the most indefatigable sermon writers in the church — they are all written in shorthand, which he reads with considerable facility, though I have noticed once or twice a little hesitation for a moment, which I have no doubt arose from the use of some stenographical arbitrary or another. He is deservedly popular in his parish, and I believe there is no man who more conscientiously discharges his solemn duty. I wish, however, he could be persuaded to light the candles next Monday morning at six o'clock, and comply with honest, early rising, hale-hearted Humphrey Brown's bequest for the future.

The interior of St. Werburgh's is very beautiful;[4] it consists of a nave and two side aisles, separated by light and lofty arches, with fluted columns of exquisite proportions, though the small capitals have been disfigured by tawdry gilding, added by some person who perhaps thought to improve the Gothic by a dash of Saracenic. This church, like all the rest in the ancient city of Bristol, must have suffered in some degree by time and mutilations. Notwithstanding the flat ceilings of the side aisles one can easily detect the traces of their having been at one time beautifully groined, and the illusive piece of painting at the east end intended to decoy you into the idea of an apse, is but a poor compensation for the destruction of the chancel, which I suppose once existed. There is no gallery, and the organ loft is constructed with great taste and in good keeping.

In or near this church repose the ashes of as brave and loyal a subject and sound churchman as ever served his God and his King — George Boucher,[5] a citizen of high standing in the reign of Charles I, and who was hung in Wine Street by the puritans and rebels in 1643, for endeavouring, in concert with Robert Yeomans, to restore Bristol to its rightful sovereign. He was buried at midnight, and solemn and affecting must have been the scene, which is thus described in a story of old times, which the reader has probably never read:'As the little and sad cortege which composed Mr. Boucher's funeral, wound into the small graveyard of St. Werburgh's, it was met at the gateby the Rev. Mr. Twogood, who read in solemn and impressive tone, by the light of a torch, as he preceded the body, the beautiful opening words of the burial service, 'I am the resurrection and the life, saith the Lord.' The awfully impressive solemnity of the whole scene nothing could surpass: the hour, the subject, the nature of his death, whose body they were about to commit to the tomb; the very danger that attended those who paid this last tribute of respect to the remains of the royalist martyr, all added deep and intense effect to a business always solemn in itself. The little group clustering round the grave, on which the torches shed their ineffectual lights, joined in the service as it proceeded, and when the clods fell upon the coffin to the impressive words of 'Ashes to ashes, dust to dust,' the sullen sound awoke the sleeping echoes, and the bat, startled from its hiding place, flitted round and round the torches in bewildered flight; the Grace pronounced, the body was lowered into the grave, while a groan of anguish, not unmingled with indignation, burst from many a manly breast. The interment of Master Yeomans, at Christ Church, took place at the same time, and under similar circumstances, and thus the grave closed upon all that remained of men whose devoted loyalty and heroism deserved a better fate.'

The Church of Saint Werburgh has lately undergone considerable repairs; amongst the rest, the tower has been washed with some preparation which makes it look marvellously like a structure of Roman cement raised to commemorate their late accession of fortune. Until this happy discovery of forgotten property to which I allude, the parish was not passing rich, but being lucky in the possession of two lawyers as churchwardens, those gentlemen in the course of their legal researches, one day alighted on a hidden treasure — a property, of the existence of which the parochial authorities were not before aware, and St. Werburgh — the ancient shrine of the canonized daughter of the King of Mercia, rose immediately into affluence.

There are some bequests for lamps and candles, and prayers tor the dead, with others, the usual memorials of praeterite Popery.

1. Built by John Wood of Bath, 1741.
2. John Hall (1832).
3. This was a degree of high honour in the mid-nineteenth century.
4. Closed 24 July 1876. Church rebuilt in Mina Road and consecrated 29 September 1879.
5. *See* St. John the Baptist 9 December 1843.

3 February 1844

St. Stephen's Church

From this church of tintinnabular fame, is derived the charter whereby the ancient society of St. Stephen's Ringers are permitted the privilege of annually eating a good dinner, with the additional immunity of settling in full for the same. The etymology of the term 'ringers', in the present instance, is a point of argument amongst antiquarians. In ordinary cases the substantive 'ringer', is obviously derived from the verb 'to ring'; there needs no ghost, you will say, to tell us this. Amongst the ancient body, however, now referred to, the appellation is of different origin, being derived from the active 'eat' — a curious fact in philology, which is borne out by the ancient practice of the turtle-loving brotherhood, as well as the usual mutation of words by many learned scholiasts — eat, eating, quasi *eting*, this by corruption *ering*, and by elision *ring*. Though none can more highly respect their talents as trenchermen, I should not think of trusting a member amongst them with a rope-end in a triple-bob major, or even in a 'call change', which is considered a much easier undertaking. In the large dining room of the Montague[1] I could not for a moment think of questioning their eminent capacities for their parts, but transfer the fraternity to the belfry of St. Stephen's and see what discord they'll extract from the Grandsire triples — the parish would soon hear their 'sweet bells jangled out of tune,' and wish Queen Bess throttled with her own ruffles when she first thought of conferring a charter on such bunglers.

The origin of bells I may say, as I'm on the subject, and somewhat of a bell fancier myself, is very ancient, and their use interesting; and so generally seems to have been the rage for such instruments, that from Nankin to Moscow, from the Campagna of Rome to the parish of St. Stephen, men appear to have vied with each other as to their magnitude and melody.

In Bristol on public occasions men below and birds above, are bewildered with their metallic clangour: and in earlier days after the publication of a victory over the French, I have roamed from one parish to another, hoping to find peace somewhere, and finding none, so all pervading seemed the peal with which every quarter reverberated: if caught at Christ Church when the rejoicing commenced, in vain you endeavoured to escape westward, for All Saints, Werburgh's and St. Stephen's stood between you and flight in that direction — to the east there was no point — southward you could not pass with the brisk firing of Maryport and St. Nicholas, and the moment you turned your face northward, St. John the Baptist drove you back in despair.

Bells, however, like lightning, do best in the distance, and however pleasant and poetical they may seem booming 'along the waters', you could not have a more unpleasant neighbour than a monstrous tenor swinging above your head and bellowing down your chimney, and anything more horrid than the fire-bells by night, with that peculiar, hurried, monotonous alarm which they send forth over a sleeping city, I cannot conceive.

The evening service at St. Stephen's is at half-past six o'clock.

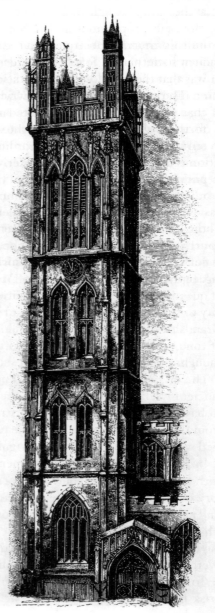

The sextoness showed me into a pew with a worthy old gentleman who seemed divided between an honest wish to worship and a strong disposition to fall asleep — no unusual occurrence amongst evening congregations, when a heavy dinner of beef and beer bears too closely on the churchhour, and soft cushions and congregational singing soothe to rest. My friend opposite me on this occasion made, I must confess, a gallant stand against the attacks of the drowsy demon; the more heavy his eyelids felt, the more desperate was the energy with which he repeated the responses; nevertheless in the midst of his most eager efforts his eyes would ever and anon close, and his lips pause apart with some unfinished word between them. Somebody says that a good man combating against difficulties is a fine moral sight, or a sight worthy of the gods, I can't say which — but a sleepy man striving to ward off his weakness is not without its interest also. At length when I saw the worthy man sinking under the dull pressure of his antagonist, one eye closing and then another, and only one partially opening at long intervals, I thought it time to come to the rescue, and offered him my snuff-box, to which he applied himself with vigour, and during the rest of the service he never once nodded. To those who attend evening prayers, and wish to join attentively in them, a light and early dinner I think indispensable; for the leaden eye-lid, the dropping head, and the heavy snore, are almost more discouraging than noon-day levity. One sometimes sees a young lady whose bright eye never droops during a long concert, even though a succession of Beethoven's endless symphonies should be played; yet during a short evening's service no ploughman after a day's labour could sleep sounder.

St. Stephen's Church is an exquisite monument to the taste of the age in which it was built. It consists of three aisles, separated on either side by seven arches of great lightness and beauty: the porch and tower are both gems of most fair proportions and elaborate workmanship. The latter, it is said, was built some time subsequent to the other portions of the structure by a Bristol merchant, named John Shipward — the only return he asked from posterity was that they would pray for his soul and his wife's, a request conveyed through an inscription on a west window which once existed. It had no less at one time than seven chantries, and boasted amongst its bequests 'a ring, (so the deed set forth) in which was set part of the very stone to which Christ was bound when scourged.' What of this extraordinary relic I cannot say, unless my excellent contemporary, the City Treasurer,[2] who has monopolized most of the 'things ancient, curious, value-worth and rare' about Bristol, may possess it as a natural appendage to his Babylonian bricks.

St. Stephen's parish is of considerable extent, and includes a large portion of the Quay, Marsh Street, and Queen Square, numbering even the bronze monarch[3] amongst its inhabitants. There are an easy, self-solacing, self-comforting set of people, who cultivate a sort of homemade doctrine — if it were not deeply mischievous I should call it namby-pamby in its nature — that 'God is

too good, too merciful to condemn any poor sinner to eternal suffering.' This is a sort of flattering unction which they lay to, and with which they salve over, their souls — a very soft and amiable mode of self-delusion.

The sermon of the Rev. C. Buck[4] on the present occasion was forcibly calculated to strip the delusive doctrine to which I have alluded of its thin covering. There were no wild denunciations —no extravagant declamatory attempts at *terrorism*, but in a clear, lucid, and incontrovertible train of argument, conveyed in language which evinced a pure and cultivated taste as well as thorough sincerity, he showed the solemn responsibility imposed upon us all, and the beautiful adaptation of justice and mercy in the Divine character — the commandments were delivered on Mount Sinai amidst thunder and lightning, more grand will be the terrors which shall surround Him when he comes to judge those who have broken them. There is much taste combined with earnestness in the style, manner, and delivery of Mr. Buck which is most pleasing, and it only requires a fuller tone of voice to give his compositions all that effect which their intrinsic merits deserve. As a hard working parish priest I have not heard of any who discharge their duty more zealously and honestly.

1. Montague Tavern, Kingsdown. Proprietor, William Pullen.
2. Thomas Garrard.
3. William IV.
4. Charles Buck (1830).

10 February 1844
St. Barnabas

On my old woman, who is coeval with myself, knocking as usual at my dressing-room door some mornings since with the warm water for shaving, I felt sensibly that my ancient enemy, the rheumatism, had made a descent on me during the night, for my shoulder ached and the dull heavy pain had found its way to my back. For half an hour I gave up all hopes of being able to go to prayers that morning, but that half hour passed, and with it a portion of my pain, I began to think there might still be a chance, and, in another hour, with the nine o'clock bell, I was up.

Notwithstanding cork soles, woollen stockings, and a strong spencer[1] over the snuff-colour, I was convinced I could not prudently venture on a long walk that morning, as I purposed, to one of the city churches; so while debating with myself on the nearest places of worship, the new church of St. Barnabas,[2] which has since the last Summer sprung up in our neighbourhood, occurred to my mind. For new fresh buildings, when I can get into old ones, I confess I do not entertain any particular fancy. They have none of the prestige of antiquity about them, no old monuments, quaint carving, or select vestries — no pious, praying petrifactions with fractured fingers and worn features — no long histories or disputed dates — but everything for the most part looks raw and palpable, *parvenu*, white and shining. A new book with innumerable white leaves is opened for christenings, burials, and marriages, with never a semblance of antiquity about it — the beadle, if they have one, has not been long enough in his situation to cultivate a red nose, and the churchwarden if the first or second of his race, and only beginning to think of laying down in his own person the foundation of a future vestry. And here let me pay a tribute to those extraordinary bodies, the 'mutton eating' glory of every ancient parish. Who has attended a vestry dinner, and seen the fraternization that exists amongst those minute little corporations — the glee with which each sings the song he has sung on such occasions for years and years — the satisfaction with which he recounts and recalls to mind the incidents of *his* year of office, when *he* wielded the blue wand and wrote himself 'Churchwarden' — the church rates he carried, — the repairs he made, — and, above all, the dinners he gave — without feeling convinced that the glory and bulwark of the British constitution are the select vestries? Then you have the proposing of healths, the object of the present toast equalled in sound feeling, good fellowship, and so forth, only by the man who is to follow, and the hearty cheer that accompanies the announcement of some name, the oldest amongst them — the man whom, the chairman feels assured, he has but to mention to draw forth the plaudits of the company — *the Father of the vestry* (hurra) — the parental head of the parish, who had oftenest drank old 'True Blue', presided at election committees, and cheered to 'Church and Queen'. And when they have exhausted each other's healths, floating in a sea of sherry, 'fondly turn to home', illustrating the polar star and all the points of the compass, until in the confusion of their cordiality you would swear that the select vestry of St. —— were all of one family, and quite ready with their better halves to enter into another ark together. Take my word for it, a new church is but half a State Church until it has reared up about it a body such as this. It is those mellow old fellows, too, who leave the bequests: nearly all the benefactions you hear of, and read of on long boards placed between windows in churches, for the purposes of the poor and religion, have emanated *not* from your cold-blooded, *sensible*, philosophical sneerers at parish jollity, but from those very warm old gentlemen whom I have described, and who have shown by many most liberal proofs that they could not only be merry and wise, but generous and feeling also.

Resolving these things in my mind, I walked forth to St. Barnabas, not, as I said before, through any particular fancy for new churches, but because it was amongst the most convenient. Two little lads in long pinafores were lounging by the door porch. 'Why are ye not in church?' said I. 'It ben't a begun yet'. Then, get in!' said I, 'and wait till it does begin.' It is melancholy to behold with what uniform economy we study (man and boy) to spend as little time as possible at prayers: twenty minutes thrown away in gossip is nothing; but five minutes in the house of God before his services commence is deemed a sad waste of our precious moments. This is particularly the case in country parishes, where you see groups making it an almost invariable practice to loiter about the churchyard until the last stroke of the bell, when they rush noisily together into a church before comparatively empty.

Following a plain staircase I found myself in the small gallery which occupies the west end, and from which there is a commanding view of the church. The most interesting sight of all that I beheld was the large number of free seats set apart for the poor — or the rich, if they choose to occupy them. The present day is celebrated for a great many supposed enlightened contrivances, political and moral; but as Dr. Primrose, in the Vicar of Wakefield, says of his wife's housekeeping, 'we do not find we grow much the richer (or happier) with all of them'; but the contrivances of the Church for her poor communicants do not certainly come under the condemnation which too many incur. Within the last few years no one has the face to think of building, or proposing to build a church, without giving up a great portion of it to the poor, and remembering the words of Christ, that the 'poor are always with us,' it is only common justice: before, people admitted the principle, but kept themselves sullenly bolted in their pews, — now, not only do they act on the principle in the matter of free seats, but most are willing to share their own. In St. Barnabas' there are a few pews in the transepts, but the rest of the building is as an open common-age, where all may come to the green pastures of the Church without money and without price; and with a great deal of good taste and feeling I saw several respectable persons mingling with the humble occupants of these seats, and thus showing a disposition to encourage their poorer brethren, and lay aside in their own selves all distinctions in the house of God.

There is no clerk at St. Barnabas, and yet the service, which is solemnly per-formed, the congregation joining reverently in it, suffers in no respect from his absence. They have an organ, and the singing, considering they have not had much time for practice, is good. I sat not very far from the organ, and about the first singing, some of the choir seeing, perhaps that I had a musical face, and willing to receive in their efforts all aid available, determined, I suppose, in conclave, to invite me in; for the red curtains were incontinently drawn, and a good-natured looking gentleman, with hair as grey as my own, beckoned me with head and hand within the pale; but seeing I could serve them and heaven as well where I was, I remained there and did my best.

The incumbent of the parish[3] (though somewhat my junior) is an old school-fellow of mine, and (though I was not aware of it) saw me it seems in church on the Sunday in question, for he met me a few days afterwards, and in an energetic but good-humoured expostulation on the impropriety of my running about from my own parish church, earnestly warned me against saying a word with reference to himself or St. Barnabas; so that as he possesses the secret of my identity, I am afraid to say in full all I should wish, and I think he deserves, of his qualities as a clergyman and compositions as a preacher — the sound judgment, the Christian moderation, and the well-timed and well-turned char-acter of his discourses: though his style of delivery is not showy it is lively, and the matter of his sermons and the diction in which it is conveyed, are good, and evince both thought and trouble expended in their preparation. I believe it is the intention to build a residence for the clergyman, for one who resides at anything like an inconvenient distance from his charge, must lose some op-portunities of doing good: the observation will, I am convinced, be well taken, as it is well meant. This church is situated in Ashley Road, parish of St. Paul — though not an aristocratic yet a most comfortable neighbourhood, the in-habitants being principally of the middle class.

1. A short coat or jacket, named after George, 2nd Earl Spencer 1758-1834, an ancestor of the late Princess of Wales.
2. Consecrated 12 September 1843, closed as a church in 1955.
3. J.J. Coles (1843).

24 February 1844

All Saints

Henry Rogers,[1] Clerk and Vicar of All Saints, I have a word to say in your ear. Some time since while seated beneath the immense mural monument which perpetuates the acts and charities of Edward Colston, in the memory of the public at large and the congregation of your church in particular, I took the opportunity of perusing the same during that interesting episode in divine service, namely, the publication of the banns between sundry candidates for hymeneal bliss, when the following inscription met my eye:

> 'For reading prayers at All Saints every
> Monday and Tuesday morning, £7 per annum.'

This, I presume, is paid punctually by the Society of Merchant Venturers; then how happens it, Henry Rogers, Clerk, that I could find none but an old woman dusting the seats on either of these days during the past week, when I proceeded (as much I will confess through curiosity as for pious purpose) to the portals of All Saints, to see if you had a greater partiality for matins than my esteemed and venerable friend John Hall, on the other side of the way. It is true some will say Edward Colston might leave any money he pleased for any service he pleased, but he had no right to impose extraordinary duties on a clergyman, for a small and inadequate sum. There is something in this certainly, and there would be much more did I not know that pecuniary recompense is the last thing taken into account by clergymen of the Church of England — to do good is their first consideration, to get money their last and least — and I have no doubt the Rev. Henry Rogers is in this respect second to none of his reverend brethren in disinterestedness or devotion; but he found no service there on these mornings when he succeeded to the parish, and never thought, I suppose, of introducing any. The facts of the case are these: the late vicar having no Monday and Tuesday matin prayers, refused through a very proper feeling to receive the allotted sum from the Society of Merchant Venturers; but on the commissioners for charities coming round and examining into the old deeds, they insisted on the latter paying the money (whether prayers were or were not said), and the latter insisted on the vicar receiving it: the vicar, however, would not consent to accept the seven pounds unless for some return on his part; so objecting to the prayers on these mornings he preached seven sermons during Lent in lieu thereof; and these seven sermons, I suppose, are still continued by the present incumbent.[2] I like a good sermon — for pulpit oratory I have a strong partiality, but I myself would prefer even one morning service in the week, regularly, to twice seven sermons from Barrow of Bourdalone. I am happy to say there is an increasing feeling in favour of daily prayers; the portals of a church should never be closed for twenty-four hours together against the public, even though but two or three should gather together within its hallowed precincts.

The Church of All Saints is of very ancient foundation, and of the original structure there still remain six massy circular piers, with Norman capitals at the west end. These are probably older than the archway leading into the Lower Green, and though two are partly mutilated and two partly embedded in a wall, they are yet interesting relics of antiquity. Placed in the very heart of the city, the old and wealthy worthies who breathed their first and last breath around All Saints made it for centuries the object of their dying munificence, so that at the Dissolution it possessed more property, in the shape of plate, vestments, decorations, &c., than any church in Bristol, and therefore was a regular *bonne bouche* for bluff Harry. Amongst this miscellaneous collection were as many curious and strange articles as could be found in the property of a provincial theatre — crosses, drinking cups, paxes, candlesticks, dresses for our Lady, Lent dresses, bells, baubles, &c. The estimable monarch Henry the Eighth, however, found use for them, and fused down the interesting miscellany into current coins of the realm. As a proof that the ancient worthies 'in Catholic days' were not insensible to the natural requirements of churchmen, I may allude to the quality of Malmsey[3] left to the Kalendaries, and the suspicious variety of vessels of 'questionable shape,' which could only have reference to clerical potations. In the early deeds, with some extracts from which I have been kindly furnished, is the following:–

(WILL.)

Baldwin Street, 4th May, 1414. A 7
Wm. Newbery gave by this his last will to Thomas
Marshall, Clerk, Vicar of All Saints, for *his life-time*,
his 'Ciphu de Mased,' with the silver covering, then being in
the possession of the Prior of the Kalendars.

I suspect this 'Ciphu de Mased' must have smelt of sack[4] occasionally, and that this said silver cover had been often in close contiguity to the noses of vicar and priors, as these comfortable gentry sat cosily in their quarters. It seems indeed to have been a thirsty establishment altogether, for a little further on amongst the items charged in a general annual obit for all good doers, I found 'three gallons of sack', 'three gallons of claret', and three of Malmsey, from which I conclude it must have been a wet service — 'a monstrous deal of sack' literally to 'a penny worth of bread', for I see the sum entered for the latter, and distributed to the poor people, is only 7d. The reader may be curious to know what ratio the prayers bore to the potations in this pious office — *to the vicar a groat, and to five priests 3 pence each!!* So that I fear the souls of the 'good doers' fared but indifferently, and that the priests were more intent upon quenching their own thirst than the fires of purgatory? There is another curious and questionable item in the same entry, 'for singing ale, two dozen' — the 'choristers' song' I dare say required it; but I confess from the unlimited tipling that appears to have gone on throughout the entire service, that the 'Miserere' must have been chaunted in a most jovial mood, and their 'potations' in the *de Profundis* 'pottle deep', somewhat like the Irish 'stations', where whiskey punch is as plenty as Pater-Nosters. These, however, are delicate grounds, which antiquarian research should not explore with too great a diligence.

The Church consists of three aisles and a chancel: and north and south there are two rows of almost shapely Gothic arches turned on columns of great lightness and beauty; nevertheless the building is rendered most incongruous by the unsightly west end, which is encroached on north and south to the width of either aisle by a house, which projects over two large massive pillars *into the church*, so that there are at this moment an attorney's office (!) and the office of a fire insurance company, in full work within the sacred precincts of All Saints, and a writ is no doubt often being filed, and a sermon preached at the same moment under the same roof — a policy effected and Sacrament administered within the same wall. This most strange confusion of sacred and profane arises from the two compartments having been once occupied by the fraternity, who had communications opened from them into the church — the Kalendaries, however, have passed away, and their apartments into the possession of Fire, Life, and Law.

The Church has been lately repaired and improved, and many of the barbarisms of bad taste and the perpetrations of Puritanism removed. In an edifice better lit the new decorations might appear a little too lively in character and colour, but closely built as All Saints is round about, the interior should not be too sombre. When I attended, the Church had been opened but a few Sundays since its reparation, and the Churchwardens from their high seat looked round about with complacency and self satisfaction, as much as to say, 'It is all our work', and very properly; it is a laudable pride, and they have done their part with exemplary diligence and good taste. But which of you, gentlemen — you, portly senior; or you, more serious junior — am I to thank for the ingenious inscription on the covers of the 'Collections of Hymns and Psalms' with which you accommodate strangers. I have long since given up carrying round with me these singing compilations, for from the multitude and variety of the editions abroad — each church having its own 'selection' — a man must have apartments in his pockets for the Bodleian Library to be certain of having a book suitable to each. In All Saints they accommodate you with one; and lest you might perpetrate any mistake as to the right of property contained therein, they 'earnestly request that this book be not removed from the pew.' Gentlemen of All Saints, what a delicate version is yours of the eighth commandment: 'Thou shalt not steal' might give offence, so with a tact I cannot too much admire, you dilute down this clause of the decalogue, and barely in the blandest manner possible, indicate that you would take it as a favour, if it were not too much trouble, if 'the stranger within your gates' would leave the little book behind him. Churchwardens of All Saints, you are the very Chesterfields of the blue wand: for you would not even offend a sacrilegious thief's sensibilities, I see. I am not surprised at anything refined from All Saints. I once dined with their silk-stocking Vestry at the White Lion,⁵ on a dinner most rare and recherche, when the 'select few' cooled their fingers and bathed their faces in rose water. However they paid for their banquet and mine too. But alluding to these books, nothing can be more inconvenient than the capricious variety of these selections. I do not agree with those who assert there should be none but the Psalms of David sung in churches: the Psalms of David are beautiful — nothing can be better so far as they go; but they do not go far enough — they do not celebrate the great event of Christianity, the Redemption: there should, therefore, be Hymns; but let us have one general authorised version, and not a legion. I lately entered a church in this city, and in each pew was an advertisement, that the version used there could be purchased at such and such places at such a price. This was doing business; and it only required the addition of 5 per cent. off for cash, with the usual allowance to the trade', to complete the announcement.

1. Henry Rogers (1841).
2. Footnote by Joseph Leech when compiling the newspaper.
   I have since learned that the matin service on Monday and Tuesday provided for by Colston's bequest has not only been revived but extended over the other days of the week: Divine Service being now celebrated every morning.
3. A strong sweet wine.
4. A strong light coloured dry wine.
5. White Lion in Broad Street, where the Grand Hotel now stands.

2 March 1884

St. Michael's

Nearly on the summit of a high hill overlooking the early portion of the City of Bristol, did our Popish progenitors select a site for the shrine of St. Michael the Archangel; and nearly on the same spot in the reign of Queen Mary, of red-hot memory, did their descendants make a bonfire of sundry poor shoemakers and weavers, who were unreasonable enough to require more than the mere word of a few monks for the existence of purgatory and the real presence. But I am willing to think that the spirit which dictated such acts is passing away from men's breasts — that all persuasions are getting ashamed of persecution, and that if we should ever again see either a Bonner[1] or a Calvin, it would be hard to find a community to countenance the ferocity of the one, or the fanaticism of the other. It was an old story of demonology that the witches were wont to make candles of men's fat, in order to see the secrets of hell — and certainly it is not by the light of such human sacrifices as once blazed on the summit of St. Michael's hill that the beauties of a system, religious, political, or social can be seen: the authors of such atrocities only make manifest to men their own iniquity, and do the cause of Christian moderation a mighty service. There is one of the legends of St. Anthony's temptation (I think it is) which I recollect reading, and which might illustrate my remarks: the devil was doing all he could one night to divert the attention of the holy man from his prayers, by flitting about the room in several shapes, and making all manner of noises, notwithstanding the repeated and stringent remonstrances of the latter who wished to impress upon Satan the absurdity and indelicacy of his conduct. But Satan (with whom most of the ancient saints seem to have been, according to monkish writers, on speaking terms) was in one of his impracticable moods, and would not be admonished; until Anthony losing all patience bethought him of an ingenious plan to punish his tormentor with a double punishment — he immediately turned his Satanic majesty into a candlestick, and a quaint and curious piece of bronze statuary he seemed, (like many we still notice in antiquarians' houses) and thus the devil, much no doubt to this own chagrin, was compelled to hold a light to the holy man while he pursued his pious studies. And so it is, you may rest assured, when bigots and oppressors light faggots and persecuting fires: like Satan in the legend, they are made by a just and most righteous judgment to hold a light to those who are in search of truth, never more distinctly seen or easily pursued than by the reflection from such bale fires.

So at least it occurred to me, as last Sunday I crossed the churchyard of St. Michael's,[2] above the last resting place of many an honest and rude forefather of the parish; over their tombstones custom has made a common footpath, and there the passenger may read as he runs, in a few short lines the history of the longest life. My 'Meditations amongst the Tombs', however, were brief, for the hands of the clock pointed to five minutes before eleven, and on the first Sunday in Lent I did not like to be late in church, as I have always looked on Lent in a more solemn light than as a mere season of salt fish: from my youth upwards I was taught by my good mother to deport myself during its continuance with less levity than a boy's spirits will always observe perhaps at other periods. Poor old lady! she fasted not as a mere formality, but as a mode of self-denial, by which she was enabled to discipline and prepare herself for a more reverential and earnest approach to Heaven in prayer. I confess I am not amongst those who sneer at self-denial, while I look upon it as not paramount but auxiliary: the routine of eating fish on certain days, with no higher or holier motive than mere custom, I cannot regard as a much more meritorious, though quite as innocent an act perhaps as wearing one's hat reversed on stated occasions: besides the 'fasting' of such formality folk consists, for the most part, not of actual abstinence, but the substitution of one dish for another,

and they fancy they have done 'something for futurity' when they have dined off Cod's head instead of veal cutlet. Thomas a Kempis somewhere says 'there was nothing he preferred to a salmon but the Psalms of David', and taking up his quaint notion I cannot think the mortification of a 'crimpt Severn and smelts' as very severe on the flesh.

Until last Sunday, I had not been inside the Parish Church of St. Michael's since the riots of Bristol,[3] when those playful little kittens — called by Lord Byron, 'the aristocracy of blackguards', and by me and most men. The People — took it into their uncombed heads to have a day's innocent amusement, and, as a practical joke, made firewood of my

four-post bedstead, gave to the flames a picture by Paul Potter, and a manu-
script book of fugitive poems by myself. I was at the time lodging in Queen's
Square, and had furnished apartments for my own accommodation, so when I
saw my 'household goods all *shrivelled* around me', to prevent further mistake,
and lest the pretty play-fellows should in their most humorous fancy carry out
the amiable pastime against my own person, I betook myself to the summit
of St. Michael's, where seated on a table-tomb, and conscious of more safety
amongst the dead than the living, I looked down from the solitude of the
churchyard on the scene below, something like Jonah over against Nineveh,
but not like him waiting in vain for the work of destruction — A dense volume
of smoke, then a spiral burst of flame from the dun mass, followed by a loud
cheer, as the red flakes showered thick as snow-fall on the crowd beneath!
Frolicsome darlings! thought I, bless your merry hearts, but you do enjoy yourselves; seeing what a little thing gives you pleasure — what an amiable and innocent way you have of disporting yourselves; what despot should ever think
of curtailing the homely pastimes of the poor — for a holy day's amusement
only hand them over a moderate sized square, a row or two of dwellings, half a
dozen warehouses, and they are as happy as the day is long — they'll make fun
for themselves. Another volume of smoke, and the flame now leaps up from
a new quarter, and the people have extended their sport in another direction.
Vive la bagatelle! who says you are not fit for freedom, — who asserts that those
merry fellows, whose cheerful voices are now ringing in my ears up from the
streets of that piled and close built city beneath, might not be discreetly entrusted with an enlarged franchise? None but some silly old Tory, who distrusts
the wisdom, prudence, judgment, and moderation of 'the many', thinks it as
well they should not have an opportunity of serving Church and State just as
they had done my 'four-post bedstead'.

But what, you will probably ask, has this to do with St. Michael's Church?
Why, the next day, or the day after, (I forget which) when the danger was
pretty well over, we might be seen one after the other emerging cautiously
from our houses, and showing symptoms of a solemn resolution to do something intrepid — and the result was a banding-together for the preservation of
what remained. I was enrolled with the Conscripts of St. Michael's parish, and
furnished with an offensive weapon: it was the first time I had 'taken up arms,
against a sea of troubles', but having once flourished them, I felt suddenly inspired with a most pugnacious propensity; for the first time in my life, too, I
experienced the sensation of a grave social responsibility. England, home, and
beauty, the fire-sides and fair daughters of at least the parish of St. Michael the
Archangel, were all dependent on my stout right arm and special constable's
staff for protection, and I felt equal to the emergency. We kept watch and ward
that night in the Vestry of St. Michael's Church, each mounting guard in turn,
while the others cultivated courage on coffee and buttered toast, inside. Not
a mouse stirred to call our slumbering heroes from their grim repose on the

Church cushions, until 'night's candles had almost burnt out', when a sound sudden, sharp, and decisive, rung in our drowsy ears, which, associating every noise with the appalling scene of the day before, led us at once to conclude the Philistines were upon us: we rushed out and learnt from our sentinel that we had mistaken the crow of an early cock for the rallying cry of insurrection. A few days afterwards I hung up my unblooded baton, and it has since then remained a monument of my first and last campaign.

The shrine of St. Michael the Archangel has nothing architecturally to boast of; it is a roomy but tame and poor building: the tower, which is the only rem- nant of the old church, though plain, is the best part. The congregation is large and still respectable, though St. Michael's is no longer the aristocratic neigh- bourhood it once was. Nebuchadnezzar might turn out to browse on the little streets that intersect the Old Park, erst a place of some repute, and I question if there be as many haunches dressed upon the hill as in other days. One of the most pleasing views, perhaps, of the interior was the long line of interesting- looking modest dressed little girls — young ladies, perhaps, is the better term — of the Clergy Daughters' School, who occupied the seats of the south aisle. This, to my mind, is one of the most amiable city institutions. If there be one class of men who more than another claim a delicate and sincere consideration, it is those amongst the clergy who have slight or insufficient means for support- ing and educating their families in a manner corresponding to their position in society. The confident and purse-proud layman, who has fought out for himself a fortune in the pursuits from which the clergyman is naturally debarred, can have no idea of the secret and sore struggles which the latter, as a gentleman and a man of refinement and feeling, must have with circumstances, and to preserve an appearance corresponding to the rank in which profession and education have placed him, while at the same time he is subject to appeals from his poor parishioners, which without manifest injury to his own family he cannot com- ply with. Oh, little do the wealthy merchant, and the wealthy tradesman, know the rigid management, the hard pinching, the self-denial, and infinite devices of thrift by which the decent and becoming exterior of many a clergyman's, many a curate's family is upheld, modestly, neatly, and uncomplainingly to public eye. And yet take up any list of subscriptions for religious purposes, and the major- ity of contributors are clergymen; while the man of wealth, the princely mer- chant, the man of ships of richly-laden 'argosies' and large possessions not to be found therein, or if he be it is but for some paltry twenty shillings, exactly the sum for which stands inscribed the name of some poor curate, whose annual stipend does not equal in amount the money expended by the former for claret alone. Verily both shall have their reward.

The two great merits of the Clergy Daughters' School are, that it provides a respectable, excellent, and economical education for the children, and is so managed that the most sensitive and (in mind though not means) independent clergyman need not hesitate to avail himself to it.

This parish has been nearly always the site on which capital punishments have been inflicted; not very far from the church blazed the persecuting faggot in the reign of Queen Mary, and on the site of the new and neat Independent preaching-house, raised as a chapel-of-ease or chapel-royal for my old neighbour, Richard Ash,[4] stood that structure 'which outlives many a tenant', yclept the gallows: founders of churches have often selected sites hallowed by the blood of saints, but in the wall of this building is actually inserted the stone pedestal of the ominous and penal upright, which reared its gaunt form for so long a time on this hill.[5] I should never myself have dreamt of using this portentous piece of granite unless in an edifice dedicated to the 'Two Thieves'.

1. Edmund Bonner, 1500?-1569. Bishop of London during the reign of Queen Mary; a vicious persecutor who caused many to be burnt at the stake.
2. The incumbent to St. Michael's was W. Knight (1816).
3. 29-31 October 1831.
4. Highbury Congregational Church, opened 1843 on land given by Richard Ash with the support of the Wills family.
5. More probable that the stone is the base of the ancient Bewell's Cross dating from 1373.

9 March 1844

Temple or Holy Cross

I think, in point of architectural grandeur and internal effect, antiquity, former franchise and historical prestige. Temple stands second[1] to Saint Mary Redcliff amongst the Churches of Bristol: its peculiar tower, its lofty arch, its slender pillars, its long drawn aisles, its deep-set chancel, and that entire air of 'other days' which pervades the whole, give to its sacred proportions a solemn character which anyone with a particle of feeling, reading, or taste, must understand, though they may not describe it.

Years and years ago I recollect going to this church with my mother, after having read the romantic history of the Knights Templar, or 'The Poor of the Holy Cross', as they originally called themselves, their feats of fasting and of battle, from the foundation of the grim and austere order under Baldwin the Second, to their suppression throughout Europe in the early part of the fourteenth century, when the cruelty, the licentious excesses, and daring impieties of the soldier-priests were exposed. I was quite a boy, and as boys will sometimes do, I fell asleep during the sermon of the worthy vicar (now gathered to his fathers). My fancy, however, was active, and in dreams I once more peopled the old church with its former founders: along the paved aisles, to my imagination, again stalked the tall figures of the spiritual warriors in the picturesque white habit and red cross of their order; these my vivid young fancy threw together with the happiest artistical effect into groups, giving all the accessories, light and shade, depth and distance, required to complete an ancient 'interior', pictorially treated on the approved principles. I was awakened to reality by the parting hymn, the first verse of which, however, I had mistaken in my sleep for the chaunt of the old crusading soldiers of the Temple. Had I known as much as I do now I suppose I should have included Brian de Bois Gilbert in my dreamy sketch, and mystified into a Rebecca, the dark eyed daughter of a rich Jew, who then lived in the Great Gardens hard by.

Every man, woman, and child in Bristol knows and tells to the stranger arriving there, that Temple tower leans a little (from base to summit the inclination amounts to nearly four feet) to one side — a trait not at all remarkable amongst men, though it is somewhat singular in stone and mortar. Old Barrett[2] referring to one of these same ingenious devices, tells us — which by the way was a tradition before Chatterton's[3] time — that the church and tower were built by a Lombard architect, on what was formerly the bed of the river — that he was warned of his mistake by somebody, who informed him that the muddy foundation would not bear the weight, nevertheless that he persisted, and when the structure was three-parts completed the tower sunk to the south, and parted from the body of the building, leaving a large gap between: the church was subsequently completed, the foundations being secured by piling and sunken buttresses. There is nothing incredible in this account, for we know the tower leans to the extent I have stated, and that it may have occurred in the mode described is not at all improbable — the celebrated tower of Pisa leans from a similar cause, a failing foundation. There is another old story told, that the church did so vibrate from the ringing of the bells that the very lamps and censers inside used to swing to and fro: something still more marvellous that this I have heard from an old friend of mine, who I fear, however, was wont to draw upon a rather fanciful imagination: he said he used sometimes when a boy, and the bells were ringing on a holiday, sit beneath the tower and inserting nuts between the corner stones have them, incontinently and cleverly cracked, as the super-structure swayed with the vibration of the bells; this certainly was one of the most monstrous specimens of a nut-cracker I ever heard or read of, and the man's *sang froid* must be great who could enjoy salt and filberts under such circumstances.

When other countries following the example of Philip the Fair of France, had succeeded in extirpating the 'Red Cross Knights', amongst those who became enriched by the plunder of their vast possessions, the Knights of St. John of Jerusalem were rather fortunate.

In Bristol the possessions in Temple fell to them, and these they held until Henry the Eighth found pressing use of them himself. The parish preserves even in its present desolation some witnesses of these old odd times of monastic power, privileges, and immunities. Who that witnesses so much poverty and wretchedness, can well fancy that once the rich houses of those haughty martial priests were here; and that later still from those shattered little paned quaint old casements, out of which now look only squalor and misery, once glanced forth the bright eyes of the richest citizens' daughters. There is no city with which I am acquainted, where particular localities have known such marked reverses as those of Bristol; but I think the decadence of Temple parish has been the greatest of all, for even less than two centuries ago Edward Colston was born here.[3] This great man's beneficence, the ramifications of which seem to have spread to all quarters of the city, also extended to his native parish, having left money for, I believe, fifty boys to be educated and clothed with an annual suit.

I have so vast a reverence for this good man's memory that I wish the latter provision of his will had a more picturesque fulfilment: but though I would not willingly laugh at anything with which the *magnum et venerabile nomen* of Colston is associated, yet I confess I cannot suppress a smile when those grotesque and monkey-clad little creatures, with knee-breeches and skirtless jackets, their lower garments in a state of most distressing tightness, and a brilliant pewter plate on their breasts, cross my track, running caricatures on defunct fashions. The more fortunate boys of St. Augustine's might, I think, spare them some of their superabundant broad cloth. Lord Dudley and Ward,[4] in his charming letters, called Pompeii 'a city potted for posterity'; and really these lads look like juvenile grandfathers of two centuries ago, who had undergone the same process of preservation, and walked out of large bottles in the British Museum for the enlightenment of our antiquarians, so obsolete and out of date do they seem.

Another religious house existed in this parish near Temple Gate. One of the most useful vestiges of these priestly times still exists in the reservoir near Knowle, from which the Fathers were supplied with good water, and which in the shape of a conduit to old Neptune, in a lane near the Church, still is found of good service to the population of the parish. It used to, and I do not know whether it may not still, be a custom for the Mayor on a certain day to visit this said conduit with the old fountain of Father Neptune, officially accompanied by certain Aldermen, on which occasions the right worshipful body were entertained with the immemorial dish of pork and pease-pudding: what connection this peculiar and particular dish had with the conduit I cannot say, or why they should have chosen part of a pig in preference I cannot determine, but you may rest assured in Bristol men will find an excuse for eating, whether it be derived from antiquity or the present age.

This parish once abounded in cloth weavers, who possessed, and for whose particular use for prayers and burial was set apart, a small chapel in one of the side aisles, where many of the craft, their thread having been spun out, rest: the trade, however, is now extinct; the sound of the loom is heard no more within its precincts, and the Jews possess their ancient Hall for a synagogue.

The cause of one of the Irish Societies, I believe that for the education of children, was this evening advocated by a Clergyman a delegate from that country. It was a fair ordinary sermon; but certainly not one which you would think it particularly worth a man's while to come all the way across St. George's Channel to preach; besides, one is in the habit of hearing so much about Irish eloquence and all that (a large portion of which, with great respect for certain friends of mine, I think is pure fudge) that we expect to find all the erratic bodies which enter our orbit from that isle brilliant stars. I was, therefore, disappointed on hearing a sound certainly, but also a plain, sermon from one who had come so far to preach it. Doctor Johnson once said of a dinner, that it was a very good dinner but not one to ask a man to: so this discourse in question was a very good one, but not one I should expect to hear preached for a special occasion, and for the purpose of moving men to acts of munificence by the eloquence of its appeal. I, however, gave what my means would allow, for as education based on religion must do good, all one can they should bestow on a country so confessedly wretched. It is now many years since I paid my first and last visit to Ireland — a *voyage* to the Emerald Isle was not then as it is now an everyday easy occurrence; it was before steam-boats ran between the two shores, and I was four days in a sailing vessel from the time I left Kingroad until I arrived in Waterford harbour. The accounts I had heard of that country, its atrocity, and barbarism made me look upon myself at starting as a bold man about to undertake as perilous an expedition as Jason when going for the Golden Fleece. I furnished myself with a case of pistols, and meditated for a moment purchasing chain armour to place under my coat. Whether it was the vividness of my imagination or their descriptions I cannot say, but I was disappointed, I won't say disagreeably so, on finding I had travelled from Waterford to Kilkenny without being once shot at; but I began to doubt my security on seeing between the latter place and Carlow the ruins of two cabins which had been burnt down by a number of 'country gentlemen', who paid a visit— made, as one might say, a warm call on the inmates the night before. This, however, was all amongst themselves, and as a stranger (as the coachman told me) I had no right to interfere with the national pastimes. There, too, I saw the bleak half-finished Catholic Chapel, planted in the midst of the dark bog, and at some distance between those barren melancholy hills peered up some equally bare and comparatively new parish church, whose minister lived in a strong stone house, with bulletproof shutters and double barred doors. O you sad looking country! thought I, with your deep pensive air of desolation, your bare blue hills and broad bogs, with no voice to enliven them but the cry of the curlew, what a contrast, near as you are, you present to your sister country. Yon gaunt apparition of a steeple how unlike the venerable village church, with its surrounding happy scenery, in England: and that bare Bastille-looking house; who that ever saw our smiling parsonages, their rose-covered fronts looking forth on the ancestral oaks of the squire's domain, would take *that*, flanked almost as it is with a police-barrack, for a vicarage. If they would learn, I should say, there are no people in the world better qualified to learn than the sharp, keen, intelligent, wily Irish peasantry. — And yet they are a contradiction: shrewd and quick to discover a joke, they are marvellously credulous, especially in matters of religion; for instance, while following the guidance of a smart and humorous fellow in frieze to one of the many picturesque 'holy wells' which abound in the South, I was struck with his instinctive penetration and tact: yet when we reached the well he told me such stories of the place, all of which he religiously believed himself, and I was amazed that so much natural intelligence and blind illusion should be combined in the same character. The holy well was a most romantic little spot, and dedicated traditionally to St. Bridget: on the bushes, which overhung the clear little spring, rags, beads, and other petty offerings from the rustic pilgrims were placed, and around its margin two or three old crones were muttering prayers, while a fresh coloured young peasant mother was bathing the eyes of a weak child with the water, accompanying the ceremony with an 'Ave Maria'. On an uneven flinty walk, which made a circle round a rude cross, several were walking barefooted and repeating prayers: amongst them I noticed two of the better order, modest-looking young girls, with neat bonnets and green veils, yet punishing their poor little feet on the flinty path. My guide, with uncovered head, approached the spot with great reverence; but the circumstances which most of all struck me as a proof of his downright credulity was, when he told me that the holy well contained a holy trout, which had been there for hundreds of years, leaving its native element only once, and that for a brief time, when a heretic coastguard man in the neighbourhood, not believing in the sanctity of this said fish, and strongly coveting it for his supper, after many secret expeditions succeeded one afternoon in netting the hallowed tenant of the holy well: he took it home, and gloating over the treat it was likely to afford, placed it on the gridiron; but in vain — the favourite fish of St. Bridget was immortal, and proof against fire; it frisked its tail quite lively above the living coals, which so convinced the coastguard of its sacred nature that, repenting his act, he conveyed the trout once more to its native element, 'and there', said my informant, 'it is to be still seen on sunny days, with the mark of three bars of the grid-iron across its back. I saw it myself a hundred times,' said he.

With the exception of such superstitions as these quoted, and which have been illustrated by so many writers, until they appear the fostered traditionary feelings — the very poetry of the peasant's nature, rather than the deplorable proofs of religious error, he is far superior in intelligence, sensibility, and sentiment to the English rustic. I don't know whether it was my want of apprehension or theirs of clearness, but, I confess, the accounts which I had heard from time to time, on the platforms of religious meetings, both in Exeter Hall and throughout the country, from those gentlemen who annually visit our shores to call forth our sympathies for the 'benighted Irish', led me to a more besotted people than the Milesian race. For turbulence, repulsive vulgarity, and self-conceit; I must, however, say, I never heard any description surpass some few of the Popish curates of the country, into whose company I casually fell. Of a different character was the ignorance of a curious old fellow, a parish priest in a very retired part of the country, and to whom I was introduced by a friend, he having promised that I should find him a curiosity. Father C. (who was suspected of having a partiality for whisky punch) was enlarging to my friend (a Roman Catholic) on the deceitful nature of some holy half-mendicant friar who had, as his reverence fancied, served him rather a shabby trick: 'this friar (I give Father C.'s own words) happened, you know, to be passing when my poor ould mother was in her last sickness, a few months since; so thinking he was a little more pious than myself, (Lord pardon me!) I kept him, as I thought it was my duty for my mother to have the best help; and there he stopped, eating and drinking the pick of the house, until the breath was out of the ould woman: when, instead of staying to say a few prayers for her repose, away he starts, before her poor ould soul could have been as far as Knocknagour' (a place on the road, about a quarter of a mile from the priest's house). What struck me most was, the precision with which he professed to measure the rate at which his mother's soul travelled, and the direction which it took.

The vicar of Temple is an absentee,[6] through indisposition; and on the curate[7] alone devolves the entire work of a populous and poor parish. The former resides in Bath, where he at present preaches to one of the many silk stocking congregations of that city.

1. Destroyed by enemy action 24 November 1940. Remains maintained by English Heritage..

2. William Barrett, *The History and Antiquities of the City of Bristol*, 1789.

3. Thomas Chatterton, 1752-70. A Bristol poet who attained considerable notoriety during his short life. He passed much information to William Barrett for his proposed History of Bristol, which although written by himself, he purported to be transcriptions of medieval documents.

4. Edward Colston, 1636-1721. Merchant Trader with the West Indies. M.P. for Bristol 1710-13. Philanthropist and founder of schools and an almshouse.

5. John William Ward, Earl of Dudley, 1781-1833.

6. F. Elwin (1816).

7. L.R. Cogan.

St. Paul's, Bedminster

Some few Sunday mornings since, I found myself perchance, or mayhap for pleasure, loitering by that friendly structure the City Gaol. I had partly designed paying the independent minister who preaches in the Cathedral, Dean Lamb,[1] a visit; but while I was yet wrapped in a contemplation of his composite character, at once dignitary and dissenter, the bells of St. Paul, Bedminster, on the other side, began to ring. Between me and the sacred edifice a deep and rapid river rolled its muddy current, as if in appropriate divorce to two such dissimilar neighbours as the city prison and the solemn temple: fortunately, however, there plied between either bank a ferry-boat, and on terms more fair and moderate than our old friend Charon's craft; for, if I mistake not, an obolus was the demand of the one, a halfpenny is the regulated fare of the other. Except in the tariff of charges, however, I thought I detected some resemblance between the past and the present; silent, solitary, and sullen the modern plies his monotonous labour, embedded between the steep banks of either side — his rope the utmost limit of his range; the only sound he hears for hours together being the heavy splash of his own oar, or the jingle of the copper coin as it falls from the passenger; he sees nothing of society but what steps into his boat at one end and out at the other, and knows nothing of Sunday but as the sound of the church bell reaches him in the watery depth beneath. I know no avocation of sullen sameness like that of a boatman at a few-frequented ferry. Lucian makes Mercury take Charon, on a dull day, from his ferry-boat to see the world from the top of Mount Pelion, and the cleverness of the conceit can best be understood by those who have noticed the monotonous life of a ferry-man though there are degrees of dullness even in this duty, and the man at Coronation Road can have no idea of the busy life further down at Rownham Ferry, where the craft actually plies between two public houses, and Thomas has a *passing* view of all classes of society, priests and deacons, sailors and sweethearts, and, in fact, all the world and his wife, when woods are green and strawberries ripe.

As I walked down the slope towards the boat, I noticed, picking her steps, a little before, me, a bustling old lady somewhat my senior. Though a venerable bachelor, my gallantry has never been questioned; so hastening on I tendered her my arm, which was accepted, and slowly we moved together down the steep ascent. I enquired if she were bound for church, and she replied in the affirmative; and after a few more common-place words she suddenly turned round, and eyeing my *tout ensemble* for a moment, said, with an abruptness that quite surprised me, "I believe I have the pleasure of leaning on the arm of the Church-Goer?" Now I dislike subterfuge almost as much as falsehood, so at once, seeing there was no candid escape from the Nathan-like directness of my interrogator, I pleaded guilty at once to the soft impeachment.

"Ah", said she with a little satisfaction, as I handed her into the boat, "then you visit St. Paul's today; I assure you, you cannot say too much in praise of our minister — he is such a nice man, a most estimable, painstaking, conscientious clergyman!" [2] I begged she would not be too ardent in her praises but allow me to judge for myself: though I confessed it was a favourable circumstance to see so discriminating (bowing) a member of his congregation so eloquent in her encomiums. Not pausing to test the value of my compliment, the old lady continued, "This is my testimony; but to the houses of the poor, and there you will hear a warmer eulogy of his kindness and attention than any I can pay — believe me. Sir, when the poor are attended to in a parish you may rest assured the rich are not neglected."

As I was not in a position to gainsay her glowing panegyrics, I enquired (to give a new turn to the subject) if the incumbent were high church or evangelical?

"This is a question I seldom ask about any clergyman," she replied, "and am seldom competent to answer; though, considering my sex and age, there is every excuse for your making such an enquiry, as old ladies, I am sorry to say, often interest themselves more in spying out what a man is than in attending to what he says."

I began to think I had got a sensible companion, as I handed my venerable co-voyager out of the boat. "If you mean", said she, as we got on *terra firma*, and toiled up the steep, "by a high churchman, one of the old indolent, indifferent, do-no good, drowsy school, who were for the most part the least religious in the parish, and who did more to injure the church and originate dissent, by their discreditable carelessness than any other cause I could mention, and only affected to differ from the serious clergyman because the contrast was so unfavourable to themselves — if by this you mean the high clergyman, nothing I assure you could be more unlike our incumbent".

Having now reached the road above, I paused to explain to her that this was not exactly what I meant by High Church; though I candidly concurred with her in her strictures on the old school — the dumb dogs — some of whom I was sorry to say still remained.

From the foregoing conversation it will be seen that the old lady and myself were like a great many others in the world; we had much to say on the subject without any very definite or clear ideas on any point; both had some notion of the existence of a golden *mean* of Christian moderation somewhere, but where to fix it neither knew: at the end of our *confab*, we found ourselves where we were when we began — we could settle between ourselves who were wrong, but it was not so easy to ascertain who were right.

In its proper place, by the entrance of St. Paul's, is a handsome font, which was found there one fine Sunday morning, but none of the congregation knew from whence it came — all they knew was, that they were not asked to contribute towards it. The clergyman and churchwardens were, I suppose, in the secret, but they kept it, and the gossips were left to conjecture as 'general as the casing air'. One or two old ladies were suspected, so said my co-voyager; the possibility of its having come from a young one was also canvassed, and subsequently the credit alternatively attached to two or three gentlemen in the neighbourhood. For two things I can only answer with anything like certainty — it did not come from me, and whoever gave it, gave it with good taste and in a good spirit; be the 'Great Unknown' who he may, he has conveyed a serious though silent rebuke to the ostentation of the age. Of the new galleried Gothic Churches, St. Paul's, Bedminster, is a fair specimen,[3] and a good deal of pains have been taken to improve it. It is a large spacious and convenient structure, capable of containing the large congregation which attends there: a handsome altar screen on correct principles has been lately raised, but the interposition of a wooden tower, in the shape of a pulpit and reading desk, greatly diminishes the effect which it might otherwise have.

A decent reverential air pervades the congregation, and the services are solemnly and carefully conducted without a clerk, some lads from the National School[4] discharging that duty most effectually. These children (twelve in number, I think,) chaunt and sing very pleasingly with the organ: they are clad uniformly in brown Holland dresses and black belts.

1. John Lamb, Dean 1837-50.
2. C.P. Bullock (1823).
3. Destroyed by enemy action 11 April 1941. Church rebuilt 1958.
4. The National Society was a Church of England body who financed parochial church schools, a very important aspect of the church concern for education prior to William Forster's Elementary Education Bill of 1870.

Christ Church and St. Ewen

Christ Church is still standing, but St. Ewen is one of those holy patrons who now preserve none of their parochial honours and possessions, beyond a pair of blue wands with a couple of Churchwardens made to match, and who at the demolition of their own sacred building fled for refuge to the nearest church, and still continue within the shelter and sanctuary then so seasonably afforded.[1] It is some fifty-five or six years ago since St. Ewen boasted a substantial shrine within the city of Bristol, it having been about the year 1787 or 8, when an Act of Parliament was obtained to justify one of desecration also. My old friend the late rector, the Rev. Mr. Watson,[2] has repeatedly told me that he recollected reading prayers in the Church of St. Ewen on a Sunday when the celebrated John Wesley, then a Clergyman of the Establishment, preached there. Part of a public and a private building now occupy the site of the old structure, and people have almost begun to forget that a church once stood there. It is recorded that from the Eastern window, which then abutted upon Broad Street, Edward the Fourth looked out on the unfortunate Sir Baldwin Fulford as he passed to execution at, I believe, the High Cross.[3]

On the removal of the old foundations of St. Ewen's some years since, several curious relics were discovered, and amongst the rest a body in an almost perfect state of preservation without the process of embalmment. The antiquarians no sooner heard of this than they flocked together like eagles over a carcass; incontinently the interesting corpse disappeared, and in a few nights more, under the superintendence of my poor old friend Dick Smith,[4] was passed into the oven of the Institution at Park Street.[5] The intention of the antiquarians was to render the illustrious dead still more proof against decomposition, but the oven having been unfortunately overheated the body was baked, and the antiquarians, to their deep chagrin, were compelled to commit once more to their mother earth the somewhat highly-savoured, over-dressed proportions of the ancient alderman.

The old Christ Church was one of the most ancient structures in Bristol, though from the accounts given of it, it seems to have had little more than its antiquity to boast of. After having stood the storms, the wear and tear of nearly eight hundred years, in 1751 a very considerable sum was expended to strengthen, repair, and otherwise beautify the building; and all to no purpose, as it appears the old garment was too much moth-eaten and fretted to be

capable of receiving a new patch, for in little more than thirty years afterwards the entire church, after having given some significant hints that it would take itself down if others did not perform that office for it, was levelled to the ground, and the present handsome and convenient classical structure erected in its place.

From the fact of its being a completely modern building, the present Church is of course deficient in that interest and prestige which usually attach to antiquity, the old church was associated with the early historical events of Bristol; but much as I love the lights of other days, I think their preservation would have been dearly purchased at the peril of those who prayed beneath. There was a period in our local annals when at the conjunction of the four streets, four churches stood, whose spires like silent fingers, as the poet says, pointed to Heaven, and attested the zeal and liberality of those who lived before us. This spot must have been at that time quite a forest of spires, when you consider that in the centre of the four also stood the old Cross,[6] over whose removal the fraternity of antiquarians do not cease to this day to shed tears, though I confess its position must have been far more picturesque than convenient: did it still exist on in its old situation, in the present crowded and crushing state of the city it must have furnished at least one fatal accident per week to the coroner, and seasonably supplied the local papers with half a column of casualties; brewers' drays would be running amok against it from morning to night — it would be cursed a hundred times a day by omnibus cads, and prove the rock against which as many flys would be found to split in a twelve month. Show me a thorough Bristol antiquarian, and if I want to melt him into grief or excite him into indignation, I have but to mention the Cross, and he is moved: even old Barrett in his book is so sensibly affected that he pauses in his dry detail to denounce the memory of the 'envious silversmith' who lived at the corner of High Street, and through whose instrumentality the Cross was removed. The worker in precious metal was not sufficiently alive to the interest of the time-honoured object, to sleep with his seven children complacently beneath it on stormy nights — he could not sufficiently appreciate the honour of being crushed by so curious a relic of antiquity, so petitioned the corporation for its removal, and the corporation, like a parcel of Goths, complied. No other piece of antiquity in the city was so completely, perhaps, identified with the ideas and even affections of the citizens as this old cross — it was sketched by the juvenile artists, it was worked in worsted by the little girls, and Southey tells us he ate it effigied in gingerbread, and a hundred times have I myself laid out my half-pence on this gothic feat of confectionery.

1. St. Ewen still has churchwardens, 216 years after the unification of the parish with Christ Church.
2. The incumbent in 1844 was J. Strickland (1842).
3. The execution of the west country rebel Sir Baldwin Fulford took place on 9 September 1463, five days after his arrival in the city from London, and was personally witnessed by Edward IV.
4. Richard Smith, surgeon at Bristol Royal Infirmary.
5. The Bristol Philosophical and Scientific Institution at the bottom of Park Street, now the Masonic Hall.
6. The medieval High Cross stood at the intersection of Broad Street and High Street with Wine Street and Corn Street. It was removed from this site in 1733 following a representation from the inhabitants of the neighbourhood, and subsequently rebuilt on College Green. In 1762 it was once again removed and finally rebuilt in 1765 at Stourhead, Wiltshire, where it still stands.

St. Matthew's, Kingsdown

Kingsdown, ecclesiastically considered, is a little kingdom or community in itself, looking down, topographically at least, on the rest of Bristol, and segregated, set apart from all others beneath and round about it. When bells are ringing in Bristol, and people are wending their devious paths to their different parishes, through dingy streets, the number of persons flocking out of pleasant houses along the hill to the shrine of St. Matthew, would surprise you. For my part I think I never saw a church of the size so well filled before, though the majority seemed to me to belong to the gentler sex. They came trooping along green lanes, dry parades, and cheerful fields, 'like a freed vernal stream;' and as group after group entered the church portals, I confess the whole seemed to me a most satisfactory sight. St. Matthew's is built on part of the site of the celebrated Mother Pugsley's field. Estimable old lady! did I not fear having Popery imputed to me, I should wish, with all my heart, peace to thy ashes! What pleasing reminiscences of lang syne do you revive, what sunny innocent faces, what bright curly heads, now gone or grizzled with age, what long Summer afternoons of play and frolic does your name recall to my vision. This moment before my mind's eye, with all the freshness as of yesterday, is that pleasant green field, with its graceful slope, and its verdure, dotted with living daisies, groups of little laughing happy urchins, rolling about in the ecstacy of their young hearts, and visions of nursery maids mingling amongst them.

There was scarcely an evening that I and my brother under the care of a nondescript creature between a kitchen maid and a nurse, were not let large on this favourite resort of 'Young Bristol;' and there is many a staid father of a large family whom I daily meet in the crowded streets, I can well remember a sunny faced little rascal, rollicking in all the freedom of full spirits amid the busy throng over which the benignant shade of Mother Pugsley we may reasonably hope was wont to watch. But these were the afternoon visitors — Mother Pugsley's well had its morning pilgrims too. Everyone can recollect the traditional virtue which attached to the pure clear water which bubbled over the two rude little basins, and the many tradesmen from Bristol who rose at sunrise to bathe their weak eyes or wash their 'one eye,' wearied with being always open, in the crystal lymph, said to have a healing quality for affected vision — and I have no doubt that the early rising, the morning walk, and the fresh air, and the clear water, if no more medicinal quality, must have been attended with salutary effects for those whose living and occupations kept them for the greater portion of the day in a crowded city. Long threatening, however, came at last: for when I was yet a child some speculator proposed to erect crescents on the good mother's ancient territory, and the foundations were actually dug out to the juvenile indignation of us all. You recollect the traitorous schoolmaster in the Roman History, who, by order of the generous Consul, was scourged back into the beseiged city by his own pupils, had the projector of crescents in Mother Pugsley's fields been delivered up to us, and a whip placed in every little hand, I believe we should have heartily served him in the same way for invading with excavators, masons, and pickaxes, our cherished territory: however, he became a bankrupt during the early progress of the work, which was given up, and the green sod rolled back to its primitive position: people talked, after this local 'Restoration,' of making Mother Pugsley's fields more attractive than ever; and of building over and beautifying the well and all that. However, the fate of Mother Pugsley's fields was only postponed not averted: enterprising masons and bold contractors, though once repulsed, returned to the charge; the children were drived out by men of plummet and rule, at the edge of the trowel, and the face of the hammer, and may be now heard squalling in nurseries where they once careered in glee.

It is a pity Mother Pugsley had not a historian; so singular and eccentric a person deserved a biographer; all we have now is the meagre outline of a life which must have been more than interesting — which was positively, in its way, romantic. It is preserved traditionally to us, that she was at once a young and beautiful bride and widow within the same week. Her husband, who was the owner of the property which still bears her name, was also an officer in Prince Rupert's army and fell near his own freehold, killed by a cannon ball fired from the rebel redoubt by Montpelier. His widow, who cherished a romantic love for her 'young soldier,' refused to be comforted by the consolations of a second marriage; and showed fortitude in resisting the troups of suitors who came to woo the double charms of an attractive jointure and a handsome face. Mrs Pugsley lived for a long life in single blessedness, the idol of all children, and the warm benefactor of little boys and girls. No abtruse arithmetician has yet endeavoured to calculate the number of presents, small wares, and sweetmeats, which during that period she made to the rising generation: the number of years which she lived, however, is better ascertained, for at the age of eighty she died, and was borne forth, by her own request, on an open bier, dressed in her marriage garments and with her wedding sheet for a winding one, the bells of St. Nicholas ringing merrily as the coffinless corpse passed under the gate, and a fiddler playing a lively tune in front. In this order, with two young women strewing herbs before her, was Mother Pugsley carried, more in a triumphal than funereal form, to the field which now bears her name; and there she lies beneath the light sod, confined by no 'scutcheoned coffin, and oppressed by no monumental marble. Bye and bye, when some citizen is excavating for a wine cellar, I expect to hear of the Widow's bones and wedding dress being dug up to make room for Burgundy. Forgive this diversion, reader;

but the old man could not refrain from having another tumble, if it were only in imagination, on the ground consecrated to the innocent frolics of his younger years.

Well, on a portion of what was once the patrimony of the Pugsleys stands the church of St. Matthew;[1] and a pleasing and convenient structure it is, consisting of three aisles, the centre one lofty and commanding, and well lit by Clerestory, and handsome cast, windows. St. Matthew's is capacious, and with the galleries, must be capable of accommodating a large number. It was well filled when I last visited it. The congregation seemed all comfortable; most of them in competence, and many affluent: indeed, if the poor were to attend, as there are few free seats, I fear they would be badly off for room. There is a handsome organ; and a row of young women, with their bonnet-strings loose, the better to afford free scope to the voice, stand in front, and are not ashamed to look the congregation in the face, or 'sing to the praise and glory of God' unless behind a bulwark of red merino curtains. Indeed I do not approve of the fashion, now happily going out, which our forefathers had of fencing in a choir with high hangings, so as to enable them to indulge unseen in all manner of unbecoming levities during divine service. I have often taken my seat in the neighbourhood of the organ loft in various churches in Bristol, and on more occasions than one have noticed during the most solemn portion of the service the bass flirting with the chief soprano, and the two tenors engaged in a professional gossip with the organist, and all screened from view by the single fold of thick stuff. There was a most becoming appearance of reverence in the manner and bearing of the congregation: indeed there was an expression of rivetted attention about some, the humblest functionary of the church deemed it his duty, I suppose, to imitate; for the beadle, who wore a long blue coat and longer face, as he crept gingerly about on the tips of his toes, turned round at the slightest noise — when one coughed he seemed as though he would annihilate them with a look, and when the winds swept loudly against the windows, he glanced distressedly towards them as though he would deprecate their unseasonable din.

The incumbent is the Rev. J.B. Clifford,[1] whose popularity amongst his own congregation is very great; being, however, founded as much, perhaps, on personal exertion, ministerial influence, zeal and character, as on his power as a preacher, it is naturally confined in a great measure to his own flock. In these days, when it is unfortunately too much the custom to make distinctions in the Establishment, the Incumbent of St. Matthew's, is, I believe, ranked amongst the extreme Anti-High Church party, as he seems to deem it, and I have no doubt sincerely, an imperative duty to introduce the subject into nearly all his sermons. For my part, though, I have as strong a disrelish and dread of the errors of Rome as any Reformer in England, yet I question the wisdom and utility of clergymen constantly harping on 'the heresies of Oxford'.

1. Consecrated 23 April 1835.
2. J.B. Clifford (1837).

13 April 1844

Holy Trinity, St. Philip's, Out

The 'moral prospects' in the outskirts of St. Philip's on Sunday morning are certainly none of the most satisfactory to those, who have been used to associate with the Sabbath ideas of cleanliness and cheerful solemnity. Along the straight line of streets which lead to the District Church of Holy Trinity, from the centre of the city, I met with, it is true, a diversity of persons, but many of them affording too little cause of congratulation either to society or themselves. Here the unwashed operative, with the beard of a week's growth, and luxuriating in the unshaved and untended laziness of an idle morning, loitered about with his face turned far oftener in the direction of a public house than the parish Church, and looking still more repulsive in the filthy contrast he presented to the thrifty and tidily dressed artisan, of his own trade perhaps, and probably with no more than his own means, bound, in company with wife and child, to a place of worship. Then by angles, for the most part adjoining beer houses on which the sun shone, basked and smoked indolent, heavy-headed, bulkish men in smock frocks, who, though they had apparently complied with what John Wesley called the fourth cardinal virtue, cleanliness, and washed their faces, were in other respects as brutalized as men could be — coarse in speech and besotted in mind. In the neighbourhood of the Church I passed several such groups, tainting the air with tobacco fumes and venting clumsy jokes. The interior of a Church is apparently a *terra incognita* to them, and the idea of entering one never crosses their mind. To their dull and cloddish perceptions the sacred edifice presents no more hallowed or softened associations than so much stone and mortar — they can hear the swell of the solemn organ, and the sound of the Sabbath hymn from within its sacred walls, as they lounge in besotted indifference outside, without feeling any emotion; they have been accustomed to hear for years the Sunday bell without once attending to its summons; and the green graves that surround the venerable building, though they may hold their fathers' ashes, possess no more impressive charm for them than so much void ground. From where they stood, however, in the present instance, they had another prospect, which to natures like theirs might have been more profitable and more serviceable than a parish Church — I mean a *County Prison*. Those who have no finer feelings to be touched, have at least fears; and I fancy the gloomy 'criminal fortress' of Lawford's gate was at times a practical preceptor not the least salutary to such people.[1]

I do not think I ever before saw so many graves open at once in the same burial ground: death, mole-like, had been working under-ground that morning, and thrown up seven red rich loam heaps, at least. I could not help thinking with myself whether these little cavities were intended to contain the mortal remains of beings, who had led the same brutish and blind life as those whom I had but just passed — who had gone through this world with intelligence barely sufficient to enable them to grope their way from the cradle to the grave.

I mounted the gallery staircase and took up my place amongst the poor children, who to a great number, principally boys, were present, watched over by two masters, a mistress, and the old Beadle, who in point of vigilance and activity was worth a host. The young urchins seemed rather amused at an old man in a snuff-coloured coat and a pair of spectacles taking his seat amongst them; and more than once, when they could escape the ken of their teachers, grinned full in my face. It was in vain I shook my head or attempted to frown them into respect, for, though on the whole they were pretty well behaved where there were so many, they had individual opportunities of playing tricks which a dozen superintendents could not prevent. Two or three indulged in those mazy and ingenious involutions caused by transferring a string from one hand to the other, and called, at least in my younger days, 'Cat's Cradle;' some perused half-penny books, and others occasionally interested themselves in pulling the hair of those who sat before them, and withal discovering such quickness as to save themselves from detection in many instances, but not in all, for the old beadle aforesaid was actually lynx-eyed — he was a perfect study; none of your modern *round beaver'd* functionaries, but one of the testy, terror-inspiring cocked-hatted old race, who have a kind of hereditary war forever waging with the urchins of the parish, and the children of the parish school. On the present occasion he was armed with a smart switch, that at various intervals during service descended rather quickly on many a curled head that little expected it; it would seem as if the old fellow could read with one eye and watch with the other, for I noticed him when apparently engrossed with the lessons for the day, suddenly glide round, and slap went the rod on the crown of some young disciple from the schools of the revered and lamented Hannah More:[2] occasionally, and I suppose to vary the action, he took up a young lady of the same establishment and shook her by the arm until he agitated her into increased attention. He certainly was most indefatigable in his interest for the rising generation, for on going out I saw him in the churchyard with his inexorable rattan still in his hand, in pursuit of a parcel of young urchins who were leading him a wanton chase round the open graves.

The church of Holy Trinity is a modern structure, capacious, of handsome design, and commanding proportions:[3] it consists of three aisles; the centre lofty, and lit by clerestory windows, is divided from the north and south by rows of (I think) six arches, turned on columns, in happy keeping with the rest of the church: it has a fine east window, the west elevation when viewed from the churchyard is not without good effect, and is surmounted at either extremity, north and south, by a small handsome open work turret, but has no main tower: by a judicious arrangement of the organ the west window is made available to the church. On the whole the design is very effective, almost too light, for a cheap built church, to be enduring. The interior appeared to me to be in anything but good repair or order.

The congregation was principally of the middle and poorer classes, but the edifice was by no means as well filled as one could wish to see it in a quarter where religious instruction is so much wanted. The service was attentively and carefully performed, and the sermon preached by the incumbent [4] from the Gospel of St. John, III. Chap., 3 v. — 'Jesus answered and said unto him, verily, verily, I say unto thee, except a man be born again, he cannot see the Kingdom of God,' was of a character well calculated for the congregation. The clergyman who has such rude materials to mould into shape and form, has no light work, but a task of toil, which some of your silk stocking mere 'Sunday preachers' can form not even a remote idea of. His ministration does not lie amidst rustling brocades and nodding feathers, but with the rough, the poor, the ignorant and uncouth; his parochial visits are not to carpeted houses, but to the hovels of poverty and the haunts of vice, where he meets with requests for alms as often as calls for advice. It is in such districts as these that a pastor has indeed to bear the toil and heat of the day, and labour until he is wearied, and yet labour still.

1. Lawford's Gate House of Correction opened in 1791.
2. Hannah More (1745-1833). A contemporary and acquaintance of Johnson, Garrick, Walpole and Wilberforce. An author of repute, she later founded several Sunday schools in North Somerset and around her native Bristol. At her death she left £30,000, the residue of her estate to go to the Church of St. Philip & St. Jacob. See St. Philip & St. Jacob, p.65 and Wrington p.275.
3. Consecrated 17 February 1832.
4. Aaron Rogers (1841).

St. John the Evangelist

An Easter Sunday morning's sun, glorious and joyful as if it too were sentient of the occasion, and sought to gild the great anniversary with its brightest beams, was shining on all around. Cotham Hill glittered like an emerald: the White Ladies themselves could not have looked whiter than the new houses that bear their name, and the windows in the surrounding villas glistened like molten gold or silver, shot forth such rays as if they had been glazed with little suns themselves.

Someone has said that there is nothing for which you cannot find a parallel but an English village scene; so I think an English Sabbath morning in those parts of England which still preserve some primitive feelings, is unlike everything else, and everything else unlike it. And what is it even in an earthly view invests it with all its poetic repose? The old grey church, its Sabbath bells, and its Sabbath ordinances: it is these that hallow even the rural beauties of nature, that infuse over tree and field and stream, an atmosphere of holy tranquility, make the lowly cot look more cheerful, and the dwelling of affluence seem more happy. Why, if you were never again to open its portals, if a prayer were never again to be said within the sacred precincts, still I fancy the old church, if allowed to stand amongst its old elms, would have a softening and moral effect — the square tower and the tall spire, the gothic window, and the grey mouldings would still preach mutely but eloquently to the people — would still have their tranquilizing salutary effect on the scene: the traveller as he saw them peeping out through the distant trees, would not look indifferently towards them, or refuse to confess that without its old church and pleasing parochial associations, English scenery would want half its beauty, would be a moral blank, an interminable green wilderness of oaks and elms, gardens and meadows.

I recollect two enterprising builders once canvassing the merits of a speculation, when one said, 'If somebody would only build a church, and place a popular preacher in it, a handsome row would be safe to let.' And I believe the principle has been proved good by experience. Erect a church in anything like an agreeable situation, and houses are sure to follow — it makes a neighbourhood, it is the nucleus of a new, though however small a circle of society, which by and by is enclosed in the parochial cincture, with parochial privileges, feelings, and foundations. This principle, however, is but partially applicable so far as the District of St. John the Evangelist is concerned, for before a stone of the present pretty and neat little church was laid, Redland, the White Ladies', &c., had begun to be favourite localities, and to furnish a 'local habitation' to those who have taken care to give the same a name, and a great variety of them, as anyone who walks from Tyndall's Park to the Turnpike, and takes the trouble of reading the titles on the doorposts will abundantly see.

There is an old prophesy (but I don't think it is one of Merlin's) that when Bristol and Redland join, there will be a plague; but I suppose the exclusive inhabitants of the latter locality would interpret the threatened affliction as merely a social one, arising out of contact with 'fat and greasy citizens' too close to be agreeable. However, be that as it may, the conjunction does not appear very distant; the Bristol people have already carried their incursions to the turnpike gates; whether these will prove another Thermopylae[1] to delay their onward course I cannot say, but should this poor life of mine last twenty years I do not despair to see a market from Cook's folly, to hear the din, and behold the dust of a city — to find ducks and green peas retailed on Durdham Down, and costermongers quietly gazing on a storm in the Bristol Channel across their counters. Then our merchants having their counting houses on the Down, might keep their villas on the Welsh coast or amid the Cambrian mountains, and come over to their business each morning in Mammoth steamers. Tyndall's park is even now *marked out* for destruction, and *ejectis Camœnis*, haberdashers and hosiers are about to take possession of the green sod on which a besieging army once bivouacked.

'The world is a great wilderness,' says Bolingbroke,[2] grumbling against his species, in his Reflections upon Exile, 'wherein mankind have wandered and jostled each other from the creation.' Perhaps the dictum of the expatriated politician is true, with one exception; and that exception is the free seats of a church: here you have no fine people to elbow you, or dispute the place with you; but the poor man makes room for you, and if you have a good coat, rather regards you gratefully for sitting where few in good coats seek to set. So in St. John the Evangelist. I entered quietly; there was no ostentatious showing the way by pew-openers; but two or three lads drew more closely together, and I sat down contentedly in the neighbourhood of some decent looking domestics and two or three servants in livery (the latter, by the way, being by far the least reverential of the party.) There was a quiet (if I make myself understood) air of attention amongst the congregation and the services were conducted in a solemn and subdued manner. There was no clerk; but whether his absence was accidental or usual I cannot say; however, the beautiful Liturgy of our Church, I thought, gained by the loss in effect; for some cleanly-dressed nice-looking children, with a purity of pronunciation one does not always meet with in children of this class, were ranged opposite the clergyman in the chancel, and repeated the responses in a clear, innocent, and unaffected manner: they also joined in the musical services with a pleasing voice, and with much precision, considering the distance they were from the organ — which is at the west end, and played by a blind man. I confess I have no great sympathy for lay clerks — those creatures (too often) of nasal drawl, long faces, and barbarous enunciation; and who, in some churches, are only of use to show that there is one person within the building who can read worse than the clergyman. In several places the parish clerks are men in orders, fitted by education and ordination for the share which they take in the holy services of the church; and though there are many ordinary clerks most respectable men, yet there are some for whom there cannot be quite so safe a security; and I cannot tolerate the idea of a beer drinking sot, who may have been 'carolling' over a can of Burton[3] in a public house the night before, inviting the congregation to sing to the praise and glory of God, the following morning. Now, children — though I have no doubt there are many of them too vicious — may be more safely presumed, from their age and inexperience, of purer life; and if we are to have the laity at all taking an official part in the services, children within the sanctuary, as Manuel ministered, are more conformable to our feelings and consonant to our views.

St John's is a pretty modern church, having been built within the last four years,[4] and consists of a nave and chancel; the latter being handsome, in correct proportions, and lit by a good east window, is perhaps, that part of the structure, in an architectural light, to be most admired. There are two reading desks, north and south at the entrance, and by rather a novel arrangement, facing each other, which extend too far towards the centre, and impair by obstructing the view. Within the altar are a pair of stately chairs; and these I now notice because I have seen them in several churches, merely to say that they have no business there: there is no more authority for such pieces of furniture than for an American rocking-chair. In ecclesiastical arrangement and architecture they are an innovation, to say nothing of the preposterously prominent position in which they place a clergyman facing his flock, looking like the 'after dinner' farmer in the couplet. The correct and most modest seat is the plain bench or sedilia at the south side; I would, therefore, advise such incumbents as have them to get rid of their stately armed chairs as soon as possible: they might suit a brown-coated old-fashioned fellow like myself, but are not fit for priests and deacons. In the body of the church the windows are too large for plain glass, and there is, therefore, far too much light let in through them. Someone, I forget who, in his book, compares Temple Church, with all its windows, to a stable lantern; and so it is with a great many sacred edifices in Bristol — they are too 'garish!' If you could get people to give you stained glass it would be all very well; but you cannot: men and women are too wise in this generation to make presents to the house of God, or invest money anywhere but where it palpably returns 3½ per cent. Though from what I have heard, my censure is far too sweeping when applied to St. John's; for I have heard of acts of personal liberality — of an organ given by one, of a clock by another, and of the altar railed and decorated by a third — that induce one to thank Heaven that all men are not wise in their generation, in one sense at least. Were I an elder in Israel — that is, were I a man having authority in the Church of St. John the Evangelist — I should open the west entrance full in front, and not have the people creeping in sideways.

St. John the Evangelist being a newly-formed district, entails upon the first incumbent[5] a greater amount of labour than older parishes, where parochial arrangements are already formed. The present minister has had to break up the ground — to establish schools, lending, clothing, and fuel funds, and all those other helps without which, amongst a poor population the spiritual consolations of a clergyman are injuriously limited. Assisted by some excellent parishioners, who have toiled constantly, though unostentatiously, with him in the good, but, to not many, grateful, work, he has had the satisfaction to see these institutions raised, strengthened, and become effective within his own time.

1. Thermopylae was the narrow pass in Greece, heroically defended by 6,000 Greeks and
   300 Spartans against the Persians, 480 BC.
2. Henry St. John, 1st Viscount Bolingbroke, 1678-1751.
3. Burton a colloquial reference to beer, after the major brewing town of Burton-on-Trent.
4. Consecrated 27 April 1841, now redundant.
5. H.G. Walsh (1841).

St. Paul's, Portland Square

It does so happen that I am not very rich; that is, I cannot afford to have my best snuff-brown coat soiled with even the venerable dust of a church pew. On the south side of St. Paul's, in a recess formed by the window, is a seat capable of containing three, and hospitably intended, like the Eastern inns of old, for the reception of strangers; its furniture were three prayer books and an old dilapidated hassock. Into this I, together with two decent looking servant maids, was shown by the pew opener. The reader must know by this time that I do not object to a free seat, and God forbid that I ever should be guilty of the impiety of refusing to worship side by side with the humblest of his creatures; but then I dislike dirt, and I see no reason why the free seat should not be kept as free from dust as any other: should the neatly dressed servant girl, who can ill afford to have her stuff or muslin gown soiled, be denied the luxury of cleanliness accorded to others, to more fortunate fellow-worshippers? Now, I am inclined to think, that the seat in question could not have had a brush applied to it for a lunar year, if not for a whole lustrum;[1] the only service in this respect which it receives being apparently from the coats of those who occasionally visit it.

From this pew I had a prospect, which I could not as conveniently have obtained from any other part — namely, a full length view of as riotous a set of boys as ever I beheld. The first intimation of the bellicose nature of the neighbourhood into which I had alighted, was from two paper pellets or lumps of crumpled whity-brown flung into the pew where I was, by a pair of pugnacious young urchins, who were keeping up a brisk war of such small projectiles outside: this affair terminated by one of the combatants proceeding to close quarters, and knocking the other's head vehemently against the exterior of the pew, and making the woodwork resound again with the contact: another young gentleman in a brown Holland pinafore got floored; while packed in a kind of alcove underneath the stairs, the better I suppose to be out of view, were the main body of youngsters, who, by their most industrious and unremitting riot, kept the school-master's umbrella in constant work from the beginning of the service to the blessing. Like Achilles' spear, the parapluie was made serviceable at either end, and one grinning urchin had no sooner got a poke of the nob which surmounted the acute termination, than a second equally deserving, was made acquainted with the percussive powers of the nob which surmounted the other. With this same umbrella practice, under existing circumstances, I have no fault to find; the lads were bad enough with all the poking they got — pulling and pinching and pushing each other, and making all manner of queer faces; what, then, would they have been without it? Indeed the poor schoolmaster (whom I pitied for having to manage such a set of irreverent young rascals,) to have been at all equal to the exigencies of the case must have been furnished with nothing short of a Russian knout. It was one of the principles of the philosophy of Pythagoras that the spheres as they moved through space made exquisite music, which we were only incapable of hearing by reason of their constant chiming: I suppose it is somewhat the same cause, its constancy, which prevents the congregation from noticing this juvenile uproar, which to a stranger is a downright nuisance, and defies his most laudable attempts at devotion. This might be prevented, I think, by placing the lads in the centre of the Church, where, being within ken of the congregation and clergyman, they would not dare to behave themselves as they do.

Now, having said so much, with the dusty pew and disorderly boys, my censures must cease. St. Paul's is a neat and comfortable Church, with a respectable and (the schoolboys excepted) attentive congregation; and the services seem all to be performed with the utmost propriety. The architecture of the edifice is, however, very peculiar: the steeple, to my mind, is unprecedented, and must have been, I think, suggested by some of the elaborate paintings on a tea-tray; it is something between an Indian pagoda and the porcelain tower of Nankin — inclining, I think, rather to the latter, and requiring only the oyster-shell lamps and silver bells at intervals to be a fair sample of the Chinese school; and yet withal it is very pleasing, the situation of the sacred edifice on the east side of an elegant and spacious square, adding not a little to its good effect. This square (Portland,) though still respectably inhabited, was at one time eminently aristocratic, before the tide of high life flowed westward. A capricious report, prejudicial to its salubrity, combined some years ago with the whim of fashion to depreciate the value of property in the place; 'But you may rest assured, Sir, this was not really the cause of its decadence,' said an eminent medical authority to me some time ago; 'for ought I know to the contrary the people might live to the age of Methuselah there as well as in any other locality; but squares are ever most subject to the influences of scandal: society therein is a microcosm — a small world; people look over on each other, and know too much of each other, and keep up a little war of jealousies and tale-bearing amongst themselves that is quite intolerable; so it was with Portland Square just previous to its decline— each made it too hot to hold the other; and so, as they took their departure people had not the candour to say it was their own gossipings which made them quit; so they laid the blame on the unoffending atmosphere, and imputed a want of salubrity to the innocent square, when, in sooth, anything there was unwholesome might be laid to the charge of those who inhabited it.' Not to draw down a hornets nest on my unfortunate head,

I must beg to say, that his strictures did not extend to the present settlers. I think it necessary to say this, as I occasionally pass through the square, and do not wish to be subject to a sudden surprise from its highly respectable inhabitants, or a hostile incursion from their cooks and kitchen maids.

The church is capacious, and traversed on three sides by a gallery; the chancel is, as usual, blocked up by the pulpit and reading desk. Talking of the reading desk, the incumbent and curate, taken conjointly, reminded me more than once, particularly during the creeds, of the double-faced figure of Janus amongst the ancients; for at the same moment one was looking towards the east and the other towards the west — one to the altar and the other in a direction diametrically opposite; an incident, I must say, not less fanciful than novel in the reading desk.

The sermon was preached by the curate.[2] The servant maid who sat next to me pronounced him, confidentially in my ear, 'a very clever man.' And here let me say a few words to you, ye 'heads of houses,' who have servants, and who sometimes think the souls of your domestics of very secondary consideration compared with a hot joint or two courses on Sundays: depend upon it the obligation you are under to pay their wages is not more binding morally on you, than to endeavour to so arrange your household affairs, even to make sacrifices of personal indulgence, that your servants shall not be prevented from attending prayers; and if you can so settle it that they can go with yourself and under your own eye the better, for I fear they sometimes leave in the afternoon for that ostensible purpose, and yet find another mode of employing their time. But to return to the sermon, the encomium of my neighbour in the black stuff gown was not unmerited: he was a plain, shrewd, and striking preacher, with some degree of originality at least about his manner, and much unaffected zeal and earnestness; his style and language were both exceedingly colloquial, but like all style's colloquial in the pulpit, from Rowland Hill[3] downwards or upwards if you like, were subject to declensions somewhat abrupt, and at times undignified; for instance, he went on describing such a one as so and so — 'and no mistake,' and concluded a hearty though homely panegyric on the Shunamite by exclaiming, 'Now there's a woman for you!' Of Gehazi he parenthically observed one evening, 'and he was not as good as he ought to be:' of a soul in a state of sin, that it was a dead soul — 'a dead body is bad enough, but think of a dead soul, my brethren;' of a prophet he said, he had no money, and they (prophets) 'seldom had much:' of the widow whose oil was increased he remarked, 'and the oil stayed,' adding, it was a merciful providence it did not continue to increase, or the 'poor woman might have been drowned.' Such phrases used in a peculiarly familiar tone, and in a kind of free and easy style, do not certainly increase the solemnity of a discourse; and D'Israeli,[4] in his Chapter on 'Jocular Preachers,' gives some samples not very superior, as 'Curiosities of Literature.' This fault, however, might easily be corrected; and, in other respects, there is great force and freshness in his preaching, and one cannot help being attracted by it. He is, I have heard, popular, personally and ministerially, amongst the parishioners — is a hard working man amongst the schools, and an able coadjutor to the incumbent, the Rev. C.P. Bullock.[5]

1. Five years.
2. Richard Simpson.
3. Rowland Hill 1744-1833. Energetic follower of George Whitfield who based his roving Evangelism on the Tabernacle he built at Wotton-under-Edge and Surry (sic) Chapel, London.
4. Isaac D'Israeli, 1766-1848. The father of Benjamin Disraeli, Isaac D'Israeli was a well known author of his period. An acquaintance of Sir Walter Scott and a life-long friend of Robert Southey. *Curiosities of Literature* referred to by Leech was published in six volumes between 1793 and 1834.
5. Leech and *Clergy List* both say C.P. Bullock (1823), however Hunt & Co's *Directory* for 1849 quote the incumbent as George P. Bullock; presumably C.P.'s son.

11 May 1844

St. John's, Bedminster

I should like to have had Malthus[1] under one arm and Harriet Martineau[2] under the other, as I walked through Bedminster causeway sometime since to the shrine of St. John. Whether it was that all the children were out at that particular moment by preconcertion, or that the population of the parish, to make up for other derelictions, do more abundantly than their neighbours to fulfil the command to increase and multiply, I cannot say, but this I know, I never saw such living swarms before in my life. They buzzed about like flies; they ran along the road and between one's legs like cockroaches; they settled upon horse and dog-cart, curricle and wagon, as each rattled by; alighted upon every projection, crept up every eminence, filled the air with their voices and the face of nature with their forms, and seemed in numerical extent and facility of annoyance to be only surpassed by the Egyptian locusts. Now, although an old bachelor — a title with which too often is associated all that is fidgety and tetchy — I do not dislike children; on the contrary, indeed, I am quite partial to a rising generation, and for one who has never seen them pass through probationary cow-pox, to whom the trials of tooth-cutting are quite a mystery — who know, nothing of measles, and to whose perception croup and whooping-cough are matters of history, I may be said to feel intensely for all their tiny troubles. And so I do; but then you may have too much of even a good thing, and Frederick the Great himself, fond as he was of the young urchins, used at times to lose his temper when overrun by them in the public places. Campbell tells us in his Life of that good and great monarch,[3] that on Saturday as he rode along the streets of Berlin, the youngsters, spoiled by previous indulgence, pulled him by the stirrups, brushed his boots, and annoyed him to that extent that he hastily exclaimed, 'go to school, you wicked young pests,' when they set up a shout of triumphant glee, and cried out, 'A pretty king, not to know this is a half holiday!'

For my part, I wonder the juvenile population of Bedminster are not murdered by market-carts, and that every time a horse hoof comes to the ground it does not commit a homicide; the creatures run, roll, and flit about in such mighty multitudes, suggesting most uncomfortable conjectures as to where meat and drink are to be found for so many mouths by-and-bye. If my mind were at all uneasy on this matter before going into church, my entry into the sacred edifices was not at all calculated to mitigate my mental unrest, for following my own guidance I found myself in a seat where three mothers were waiting with as many babies for baptism. The little beings lay horizontally on their parent's laps, rocked to quiet by a kind of perpetual motion of the maternal knees, their little pursy red faces were covered with white handkerchiefs, and from time to time they gave proofs of their existence by an abortive cry which rarely reached above the cambric: when they did exhibit anything like unusual energy, however, and succeeded in making a robust attempt at a bawl, the corner of the kerchief being coyly raised, the father, who sat opposite his better half and baby in a state of bashful affection, was invited to chirp into the pretty creature's face, a civility which was always successful, and almost as invariably returned by a convulsive chuckle from the child.

Do you know that the thought struck me at the time, of offering to be sponsor for some of the little things; but it was one of those fugitive ideas too good to last; and I was rather afraid to incur the responsibility, though, I have no doubt, the buxom widow who sat close by, as well as many others when they looked towards the place, put me down for the honours of paternity, so far as the pretty creatures in question were concerned. I suppose it is owing to the number of christenings that occur in Bedminster that the font is in such a condition as to be incapable of holding water, the lymph in the present case having been confined in a basin of common white ware.

The neat appearance of the graveyard, its pretty inclosure and embowered walk — and let me observe that a little rural church without its trees could not be more unpicturesque than Bethlehem without its palms, or Bethany without its olives — led me to expect a less ruinous interior than it was my misfortune to see on the present occasion; for one of the first objects that met my eye was a number of shattered pews in the north aisle — some broken, some rotting, and all evincing neglect and decay. I know that not long since, on two occasions attempts were made to get up a church-rate for the necessary repairs, but each time it was defeated by a body of blatant malignants,[4] who succeeded in roaring down both the rate and reason: still I think there are churchmen enough, if anyone would take the trouble to move in the matter, to keep the 'carved work of the sanctuary' from crumbling before their eyes.

Sir John Smith is the present Lord of the Manor, and as such, if nobody else will do it, ought to repair the parish church. Don't raise your hands. Sir John; don't shrug your shoulders, Sir John; don't exclaim 'absurd!' Sir John; I say you ought to do it, since the parish will not! You are a churchman, and a rich man; you derive large rents from the parish; you're the Lord of the Manor; and out of your thousands and thousands a year you would not feel the comparative trifle required to set the sacred edifice in order; therefore, Sir John Smith, you ought to do it. But perhaps you are not aware of its present condition; if not, some day or other when passing over the iron bridge, instead of passing down Coronation Road tell your coachman to drive through Bedminster Causeway; and if you let me know the day, I'll be happy to borrow the keys and take you

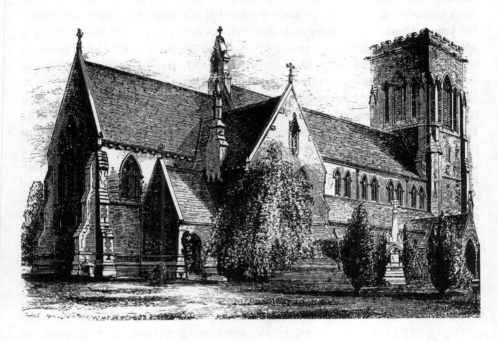

through the church, and show you the woodwork rotting, and the roof threatening, and the green mould gathering here and there; and you'll cry, 'Who
could have thought it?' and turn round and thank me for having given you an
opportunity of showing to the world what a dutiful and generous son of the
Church you are; and the old shrine of St. John's, 'which flourished ever since
the Saxon days,' will no longer be a melancholy spectacle of neglect and ruin.
Its tottering walls will be strengthened; its ancient windows and worn mullions
will be repaired; its old roof will no longer hang, like Damocles' sword, menacingly above the heads of the congregation; but nave, north aisle and chancel
will all smile in renovated decency; and then, Sir John, having done all this,
you'll feel such a rosy, comfortable, cheerful ray of approving sunshine in your
breast; and you'll be able to say to the parishioners, 'You have neglected your
duty; but I have made up for your deficiency — what you would not do I have
done.' Believe me, never did old bottle of port enliven your heart as this reflection will; and then, should the Summer breeze ever bear the sound of the old
church bells on any Sabbath afternoon to your court, they'll be such delightful
music to your ears; the troops of antlered deer, the ancestral oaks, and all the
stately architecture of Inigo Jones will sink into insignificance compared with
what you had done for the old parish church. And if the peal of St. Paul's could
say, Turn back, Dick Whittington, Lord Mayor of London,' I see no reason
why the bells of old Bedminster should not repeat in grateful euphony, 'Sir

John Smith, Sir John Smith, Sir John Smith repaired the church!' Already I see the venerable edifice restored and renovated to my mind's eye, and the good work completed; I can further hear, by the slightest stretch of the imagination, the worthy baronet exclaiming, in the fullness of his heart, ' Heaven bless the old Church-Goer, for enabling me to obtain so great a pleasure at so small an expense.' Sir John, you are perfectly welcome to the information; and I sincerely hope you will turn it to a good account.[5]

The service was performed and the sermon preached by the Vicar, the Rev. Martin Whish. Prebend of Sarum, Vicar of Bedminster and Abbott's Leigh, Incumbent of Redcliff and Thomas! I have a crow to pluck with you; how comes it to pass that you leave a parish of eleven thousand souls without a curate?[6] Is the visit that you pay them once a week, when you walk from your Parsonage on Redcliff Hill to your parish Church at Bedminster, pastoral care enough for such a population? Are the two sermons you pull out of your pocket on Sundays sufficient for the other six days they never see you — never hear your voice, and never have the benefit of your counsel? Pray, where's the resident curate that should in the meantime be working and toiling amongst them — who do you leave to visit this immense mass of men, women, and children, so much in need of spiritual superintendence? Prebend of Sarum! I do not often get warm; but, I tell you, if you preached with the tongue of an angel twice every Sunday, it would not be enough — eleven thousand people require some constant, permanent, abiding care and attention. No wonder for the place to be full of dissenters; — no wonder that as I passed through your parish on the Sunday of my visit I heard them thumping and thundering from back rooms and attics in streets and by-ways, colliers and carters making themselves heard by all who went by, through the strength of their lungs and the vehemence of their language; — no wonder, I say, these things should be, when the people are left to themselves. Prebend of Sarum, Vicar of Bedminster and Abbott's Leigh, Incumbent of Mary and Thomas! if this be not remedied, — if eleven thousand should have not something more than two weekly sermons to depend upon — if, in fact, you have not an active curate before this day month, I shall be provoked to thump my big book in downright rage, and to wish you a fixture in your stall at Salisbury Cathedral, and somebody else in your pulpit at Bedminster. Eleven thousand souls, no curate, and a non-resident Vicar! Prebend of Sarum, this will not do!

The church, as I believe I have incidentally observed before, consists of a nave, chancel, and north aisle: it has a large square tower, with open balustrades at top, and though in point of ecclesiastical architecture it possesses little or no interest, it is a venerable and, if repaired, might be made rather a pretty building, with a great character of rusticity about it: the tower was surmounted by a spire to the year 1503, when it was thrown down, but whether by man or time I am unable to say. It is dedicated to St. John the Baptist, and is, I believe, the oldest church within the municipal boundaries of Bristol.

The church was well filled by a neat and attentive congregation, who joined cordially in the services; the children acquitted themselves very creditably I thought in the singing, &c., though it would be quite as well it the clerk would speak a little more through his mouth.

As I was leaving the church someone laid their hand on my shoulder, and just at the same moment whispered in my ear, 'It will be on the table in ten minutes!' Turning round to the lady from whom it proceeded I begged to know the meaning of this mysterious announcement, when she told me it had reference to dinner, and that there was a knife and fork for the Church-Goer, if he chose to accept it. When I find my identity discovered (and I can hardly expect to preserve the incognito with my portrait in the paper,) I do not attempt to deny it, especially under such auspicious circumstances; I therefore bowed politely in acknowledgement, as I must now do to you, my dear reader; merely adding that I refer to the incident because, 'like Adam's recollection of his fall,' it 'stands alone' in my parochial reminiscence's, and it is not altogether unworthy of imitation.

1. T.R. Malthus, 1766-1834. *An Essay on the Principles of Population*, 1798.

2. Harriet Martineau, 1802-76. *Poor Law and Paupers Illustrated*, 1833.

3. Thomas Campbell, 1777-1844. *Frederick the Great* issued in four volumes in 1842.

4. It is probable that the malignants were local Dissenters protesting at the injustice of having to pay a rate levied on the whole parish for the upkeep of a church building and clergy they did not accept, at the same time paying from within their own congregation for the support of their own chapel and minister. There are numerous reports of disrupted vestry meetings in this era, and in 1868 the compulsory rate was abolished by an Act of Parliament.

5. Destroyed by enemy action 24 November 1940.

6. In the *Clergy List* 1844, four curates are listed. M.H. Whish; E. Prother; G.M. D'Arcy Irvine and W. Seaton. The incumbent as mentioned by Leech was Martin R. Whish (1806).

27 May 1844

St. George's, Brandon Hill

The editor of the *Bristol Times* handed me last week the following veritable and characteristic letter:

VENERABLE AND DEAR SIR, — We, that is the female parishioners of St. George, Brandon Hill, are extremely anxious to be favoured with a visit from your goodself, and we have been expecting one every week for these last two months, having a full share of the curiosity which distinguishes our sex. We want you to admire our church, our minister, our clerk, our schools, and our choir; and as there is a probability of our esteemed curate ere long leaving us, I, in behalf of the female parishioners, hereby invite you to come next Sunday, as we are dying to hear your report of the sermon and general appearance of the congregation, etc. We shall be very glad to see you in our pew No.—, and shall be extremely gratified would you come and take your family dinner with us afterwards. With sentiments of the profoundest respect, esteem, and veneration, I am. Venerable and Dear Sir,

Your truly attached admirer.

St. George's, — Brandon Hill, May 14, 1844

P.S. — Service begins at eleven, and dinner is on the table punctually at two.

If the exact and angular little hand in which this note is written were not sufficient to convince me of its authenticity, the last paragraph could leave no doubt on my mind, for as in all ladies' letters the point and gist are to be found in the postscript. 'Dinner on the table punctually at two.' But I fear with a *blank* for the No. of the pew, the dinner would turn out to be of the same description. 'Tis all to no purpose that you serve up your roast beef to the moment, if one knows not where to look for it; there are a great many pews in St. George's church, and a great many houses in St. George's district where dinner is on the table at two, so that, unless like Mordecai the Jew, I took my post by the gate and questioned each young lady as she left the church, I do not think I should be so fortunate as to find out the proprietor of the proffered meal. Had my fair friend been candid enough to insert the number if not of the pew, at least of the house, I certainly should have availed myself of it; but as it was, were it not for a gosling and a glass of Nuit of my own providing, I must have been satisfied with what the Germans called the Barmecide, or Banquet of the Imagination. Upon the whole I think I must put down the writer's courtesy as one of those exotic civilities called a 'French compliment.'

I am very sorry that any portion of the congregation of St. George's should have thought it worth their while being impatient for my visit: like the Irish orator's bird I cannot be in two places at a time — some must be last, and this distinction was it seems reserved, though more by accident than anything else, for St. George's church. If I had the same energy of mind and body that I had some twenty years since, and the same opportunity of telling what I thought to the world that the Editor of the *Times* has so indulgently afforded me for the last few months, I should perhaps do things with more dispatch, and go over a greater extent of ground. I should not have confined my labours to Bristol alone; I should have diverged into the green lanes of the country, and perhaps carried my enterprise into some of those back settlements where parsons it is said may be sometimes surprised in red coats, and are found more intent on the preservation of foxes than the cure of souls. Oh, you reverend gentlemen of 'the old school,' happily you are becoming extinct — a few, however, remain, preserved as it were in their own port as specimens of a peculiar race, though lost sight of in secluded parishes and rustic wildernesses out of the way, where perhaps it is as well to leave them unmolested; for though they have not disappeared altogether, their day is essentially gone by; a source of regret I should think to none, for though they might have made very fair squires, they must have proved most inefficient pastors.

Possibly the fair writer of the letter already given is getting impatient that I should have deferred my opinion of St. George's 'church, minister, clerk, schools, and choir,' all of which it appears I am expected to 'admire;' a moderately extensive demand, I think, when taken together. Well then, to begin — I don't admire your church. As a general principle I do not like the classic (Roman or Grecian) style for a church:[1] nothing is so solemn, so impressive in its outline, as the Gothic, — none so eminently suited, with all deference to the memories and judgements of Inigo Jones and Sir Christopher Wren, for a sacred building. Raise court-houses and houses of parliament, theatres, palaces, and civic chambers as long as you like after the classic models of antiquity, but Gothic (be it the Early English, Decorated, or Perpendicular) is the architecture of the Church. Don't suppose from this that I have been bitten by the rabies of Mr. Pugin,[1] I speak from my own impression and perceptions; and to my mind and eye the Gothic is eminently ecclesiastical.

There is one thing, however, in favour of St. George's — there is no situation in which such a church could be built to greater advantage; and the porch and flight of steps leading to it have a fine, noble, and commanding effect, which unfortunately, is effaced by your first view of the interior: the immense flat roof, — the wilderness of gallery, with its glare of red curtains, — the poverty and position of the altar, and the nakedness of the entire, give it far more the appearance of a dissenting conventicle than of an Established Church. Indeed, so far as the internal arrangements go, the paramount consideration appears to have been room, and in this they have succeeded, for it is capable of affording immense accommodation, and on the occasion of my visit there seemed to be both a large and respectable attendance.

I cannot say whether the shrine of St. George is situate on the site of the ancient hermitage where St. Brandon, a great many centuries ago, said prayers, ate pulse, and drank pure water, but I do not at all dispute the taste of the canonized anchorite in selecting such a spot for his meditations and residence. Some four or five years since when the improvement of Brandon Hill was brought before the Council, a member of the municipal body proposed that a Temple to the Winds should be erected on the summit: the romantic proposition was not seconded, but some of the neighbours being men of more practical ideas, by the combined co-operation of their breeches' pockets, constructed a pleasingly situated walk, with an agreeable prospect around it. I do not think, however, that the population of Bristol have availed themselves of the opportunity and privilege to the extent that one might have expected: the Sunday recreative tendencies of the local mechanic are always of a more excursive nature; and four in a fly, with a pipe in the 'bower' of a rural public and a bowling-green, and Burton in the perspective form the heaven of his enjoyment; for in his tastes and sources of gratification the English operative is, I think, the most physical or material creature in the world: his more volatile neighbours the French and Irish can make the ideal far more a component part of their pleasures.

Now with regard to the schools which I am requested to praise, experimentally I cannot say anything on the subject. I have read the sign-board, which, in letters of six inches long, yellow (I think) on a red ground, indicate the existence and locality of such interesting establishments, masculine and feminine; but I have never been inside the door of either. On several occasions I have seen young ladies, who looked the living impersonations of elemental instruction, the pretty types of rudimental knowledge, entering the edifice in question, and for the specific purpose of imparting a portion of what they knew to the young ideas of the district of St. George's; but I have never ventured to pass the threshold, though, I confess, I have often had a wish to see how such amiable professors administered infinitesimal doses of education to tender minds, and quickened tardy perceptions by birches plucked from the tree of knowledge. I think, too, myself, I should prove no mean coadjutor in such a work: I do nothing in the Differential Calculus, neither do I affect Fluctions, but I have mastered the 'Tables,' and penetrated to the mysteries of the Rule of Three: the Curate, of course, would undertake the Catechism, but I should not shrink from the concords; and, in case of emergency, should not perhaps object to part with what Geography I know to a juvenile public.

But though I cannot speak from personal experience of St. George's Schools, I have no objection, since my opinion is requested, to impart what I have heard of them — namely, that there are none more efficient in the city; and nowhere do the parishioners, in the business of parochial education, more cheerfully or usefully co-operate with the clergy. It is a subject on which no elaborate compliment can be paid, or is, I suppose, required.

Owing to the advanced age and prolonged indisposition of the late incumbent[3] the entire charge and care of St. George's have, for a considerable period, devolved on the Curate (Dr. Goodenough): [4] and the best proof that he discharged his duty to the satisfaction of those who had an opportunity of judging of it is, that on its becoming vacant an earnest memorial that he might succeed to the incumbency, was got up and presented by them to the Dean and Chapter. His discourse was plain, simple, and pleasing, as a composition; useful earnest, and affectionate in its character; and, to use the term in a literal and not party sense, it was evangelical in its tone and temper. Judging from the colour of his hair, which is whiter than my own, he is, I should think, about the most venerable Curate in the Deanery of Bristol; but Deans and Chapters, in their promotions, do *not* too often act on the principle '*seniores priories*'.[5]

1. Designed by the architect Sir Robert Smirke, completed 1823.
2. Augustus Welby Northmore Pugin, 1812-1852. Pugin, a strong Catholic advocated the genuine Gothic as the Christian form of architecture, whereas the classical style emanated from Paganism. *His True Principles of Pointed or Christian Architecture* was published in 1841.
3. R.G. Bedford, (1824).
4. J.J. Goodenough.
5. The Dean and Chapter did not act on the principle of '*Seniores Priories*' at Brandon Hill. Leech's astute comment was fulfilled, and the living which was indeed the gift of Dean and Chapter went to R.L. Hopper (1844) from Cheltenham.

8 June 1844

Orphan Asylum and Chapel

Sauntering down Ashley Hill at the time of Evening Prayers, who can help feeling an interest in the long and picturesque line of little maids, who, in their white capes and caps, disappear through the portals of that quiet and retired little chapel.[1] A 'fellow feeling' induced me to follow, for I fancy there is some, nay, a good deal of similarity between the lonely situation of an old bachelor and an orphan — both are alone in the world — both isolated, only the latter usually attracts a sympathy, which the former does not. As I took my seat amongst the quiet little congregation the 'shades of evening' left us in a sombre twilight, which I thought accorded well with the character of the place and the melancholy interest to the little maids around me. I would be the last person in the world to share in the utilitarian spirit or join in the utilitarian cry of the age; but I think there is something pre-eminently refreshing in the contemplation of practical physical charity. People may differ as to the utility and application of funds for religious purposes, but when employed to feed, clothe, and instruct the orphan, that helpless bequest which a dying parent leaves to the public — who can question its use. As the poor little things raised their voices in the Vesper Hymn, I could not help thinking that if it were possible for the spirits of the departed to witness the scene, and for us to know the gratification it afforded them, much of our charity would take a more practical turn than it does — much that goes abroad would stay at home, and to 'visit the *fatherless and widows* in their afflictions' would be an injunction more generally attended to.[2]

Service over, I returned with the children to the Asylum, and was kindly permitted by the Matron — an active and civil young woman — to go over the house; and was almost tempted by her eloquence to add my name to those donors of £5 emblazoned in blue and gold in the hall — and some day, when an old maiden aunt of mine dies, I mean to do so. I learned the whole economy of the house; and furthermore, that while all the young ladies of the country were getting up bazaars and running about with collecting cards for the 'Poor benighted Feejees,' the Orphan Asylum was in debt, and the charity sorelycrippled for funds!

"And this is the way of the world, my dear Madam," said I, sitting down in the Matron's room to a cup of tea, which she kindly offered me, "this is the way of the world; in charity the most distant objects generally loom the largest."

"'Tis a melancholy fact, Sir," she replied; "Do you take cream and sugar in your tea?"

1. Hook's Mill orphanage; the new building of 1827 replaced a building of 1795 when the orphanage was established.
2. Chaplain: H.S. Livius, Rector of Welborne, Norfolk.

The Rural Rides

THE RURAL RIDES

THE RURAL RIDES
BY THE CHURCH-GOER;
TO THE EDITOR OF THE BRISTOL TIMES,
AND HIS READERS, AND MY OWN,

These Presents Greeting,

My Dear Friends, — The old man, whose prosings you endured with such praise-worthy fortitude some months ago, is about to make a second experiment on your patience. The most indulgent natures are those oftenest imposed upon: and the only plea the CHURCH-GOER can advance in mitigation is, that on parting from you last June he intimated that it was just possible he might bore you again. You seldom find that people keep their word for good with half the tenacity that they do for evil, and in fulfilling his promise the CHURCH-GOER feels he might have been forgiven a less implacable memory.

My Dear Friends, – Thus far had I gone in the third person, but finding it a stiff and awkward mode of communication between two old friends — feeling I could not express myself with half the cordial freedom that I wished towards my kind and indulgent readers, I set it aside for the intimate and easy familiarity of the first and second person. Well, how are you? It seems an age, a hundred years, since we last met, or rather parted, by the orphan asylum (I think it was) on Ashley Hill, and my eyes if not moist were 'heavy with the weight of unshed tears.' Old and vain, however as I am, I cannot pretend to think that you were equally affected at the separation; but still I am convinced, from a thousand little proofs of your good nature which you gave me, that you did not see the old man depart without feeling at least a commiseration for his loneliness, or turning to have another glimpse of his snuff-brown coat before he was quite out of sight; and I thought (was I mistaken?) a whispered 'God speed him' reached me as I trudged on my silent way. If it was not so, do not undeceive me, for I would not have the illusion removed — I would still hope that something like a kindly impression had grown up between us during our acquaintance, though we never literally looked each other in the face. For my part I am ashamed to say with what heavy heartedness I took my leave on that occasion. Could you have heard, instead of read, my last 'farewell,' you would have perceived a little huskiness in my voice, but let that pass: suffice it to say, that after a last fond lingering look behind I took my homeward path, my only solacing reflection the hope that we might meet again; though I secretly determined not to trespass too soon or too hastily on you a second time, if I could find any other employment for an old man's leisure. But my brief literary existence I found spoiled me for the little minutiae of an old bachelor's daily life, and the trifling tasks in which before my public career (I like a large phrase) I took pleasure. The geraniums were my only resource, cutting time was at hand, so I set about slipping *Grampions* and *Great Dukes*, *Conservatives* and *Nitidums*, *Victory's* and *Duchesses of Buccleugh*, with a desperate resolve to forget the charms of composition now given up; but to no purpose; I had tasted the weekly excitement of preparing, and the weekly gratification of reading, my own writings in print: and Pelargoniums I found possessed no pleasure for me like this. I tried to read newspapers and books, but other people's efforts had no attraction for me like my own. I hope my candour will not cause me to suffer in your estimation, dear reader; but I am frank with you, for where there is no confidence there can be, I think, no friendship; and I run the risk in my 'Confessions' of being thought less wise and more vain than many may have deemed me, that you may see I do not affect to be what I am not.

I think I have said enough to show you that the life of an old bachelor, who had no graver business to employ his time than rearing geraniums, is not a very eventful one, and that the discontinuance of my weekly task was to me a sore deprivation — it left me from Saturday to Saturday without an object, and living in my lodgings, and looking down during the long evening on a little garden, was all the variety that life seemed to have: besides old men are usually garrulous, and my weekly paper was a pleasant way I had of getting rid of my small talk.

Nevertheless, I question with so many motives if I should have resumed my pen were it not for another incident which I shall hereafter explain. I got no hint to begin again — none of these small but substantial proofs of public approval which serve at once as significant testimonials of the past, and encouragements for the future. I hope I shall not in consideration of my natural delicacy be pressed too hard for my meaning; but I may be pardoned perhaps for saying that, whilst I have read of slippers and surplices presented to popular curates, not even a pair of cork-soled shoes have found their way to a certain snuff-coloured coated person, whom I might mention, 'as a slight testimonial of the regard in which he was held.' Not even did the editor of this paper, who disposed of three additional copies every week to as many old ladies, whom I might name, and all through my contributions, think a little token in the shape of a gold pencil-case deserved.

It seems, however, that if the public in general, and a newspaper proprietor in particular, were insensible to my merits, a coterie of various aged ladies were not quite as oblivious of my existence. A month since, as leaning listlessly in my arm-chair, and tired of a solitary life, I repeated from Larry Sterne,[1] 'Surely — surely, man! it is not good for thee to sit alone — thou wast made for so-

cial intercourse and gentle greetings,' when my landlady (kind soul) opened
the door with a preliminary tap, and handed me a note in a plain fine-paper
envelope, with the prettiest little seal and prettiest little device, too minute,
however, for my eyes to make out. "Thank you, Mrs Smith," said I, and she
left the room, and I turned over the tiny epistle twice or three times, amusing
myself with conjecturing the contents without breaking the wax. It was a most
ladylike missive, genteel in the character of its shape and superscription. It is
not a tailor's bill, nor anything like it, thought I; besides my snuff-brown coat
was paid for before I put it on my back — it is not a druggist's circular, it does
not smell of civet. Could it be a love letter? Foolish old man, who ever dreamt
of falling in love with a person posting from half a century to three score years?
When I was ill six months ago, someone (from my heart I forgive them their
dismal joke) enclosed me an undertaker's card: but this could not be a repetition of a hoax more thoughtless, I hope, than wicked.

I broke the seal, and read —

'. . . DORCAS SOCIETY.[2]

'Venerable Sir,

'Perceiving that for some time you have completed your church peregrinations, we beg to renew (which we do cordially) the invitation given you some
two months since, to visit our sewing soirees. Our next meeting is at Mrs. . . . ,
. . . Place; an easy chair, a soft pair of slippers, and a cup of souchong are heartily at your service. We will make you as comfortable as we can; your society is
what we mainly covet, but if you bring a book with you, and read what is most
agreeable to yourself, and you think most useful to us, our obligation will be
the greater.

'Earnestly praying your attendance, I beg, venerable Sir, to subscribe, (for
self and fellows) your's sincerely,

MARIA . . . . Hon. Sec.'

It could not come more opportunely. 'Surely, surely, man, it is not good for
thee to sit alone,' and with such an offer of good society you shall not.

The following Monday evening — seven to the minute — found me, after
crossing a trim little garden in front, and with my snuff-coloured coat brushed
to perfection, and my shoes smartly polished, before a green hall-door answering the number in my note, with the brightest brass knocker and handle, and a
smart scraper shining with black lead, and looking so neat that I could not find
it in my heart to soil it with my cork soles. I knocked; and the door was immediately opened by a pretty, nicely-dressed girl, evidently of the class called
'parlour maids,' and here let me pause for a moment to say a word in praise of
this order of domestics. No significantly arch smiles if you please, kind reader;
a man of my sober age and habits can do so I hope without provoking a joke.
I like your parlour maid, with her clean gown, neat cap, and agreeable face,
better than a hundred footmen with their servile pertness, and their awkward

calves packed into white stockings, and their snub noses thrust up into the air with starched neckcloths; and when this pretty little maid, looking as refreshingly pleasant as a May morning, opened the door, civility and respectful welcome beaming from her face, I felt myself at home. "Whom shall I say. Sir?" said she, modulating her voice to ask an abrupt question in the softest tone, as taking my hat and cane from me she hung one on a brass cloak-pin, and placed the other in a neat umbrella stand. "The CHURCH-GOER, my good child," said I, and you should have seen the delighted welcome that kindled in her eyes; and, oh, the delightful satisfaction I felt to think that even the old snuff-colour was not unknown to her. I do not pretend to judge what fame may be to your fighting or forensic hero, but this to me was glory: even she had heard of the CHURCH-GOER: possibly she had heard her mistress speak of me, possibly she had picked up the paper in the parlour on a Saturday morning; but still it was evident the name was no stranger to her: it was worth writing quires for such a reward, and in the triumph of that moment, in the little celebrity to which that simple girl paid her smiling homage, I envied neither William Pitt nor the Duke of Wellington their reputation.

"The Church-Goer, ma'am," said she, opening the little drawing-room door, and a good-natured looking person about — but there, I am no judge of ages — rose with a bright smile of cheerful welcome and alacrity to receive me. "Miss . . . and Miss . . .," said she, introducing me to two young ladies, who with myself were the only visitors who had yet arrived. "It is so good, so kind of you," she continued, while the younger of her two companions — who might be one or two-and-twenty, with pretty eyes, and brown hair which fell in ringlets in front — rolled a large easy chair for me near the table: "it is so very good of you to come, and no amusement to offer, and no society but a few ladies."

"Madam," I replied, "if I were a fine young gentleman, instead of a sickly old one, I should make a gallant speech, and tell you how far preferable to me is the society and refining influence of a few cheerful, sensible, agreeable women to the boisterous excitement of male company, or even the literary rivalry of male conversation; but being as I am I beg . . ."

"I do not know what you are going to beg," interposed my hostess, good-humouredly interrupting me, and glancing at a French clock on the mantel-piece, "but I must beg your pardon: the fact is, it is now five minutes past seven, when according to rule our proceedings commence, though only two or three should have arrived. Before we begin work, however, some of us usually read a short Psalm, and perhaps you have no objection to 'act the Clericus,' as our curate calls it."

I took the large old Bible from the same pretty hands that rolled the chair for me, and as our entertainer specified a 'short Psalm', I selected the shortest, the 117th. I shall not attempt to describe our little group at the moment; but to me, as I made a poor attempt to perform the parson's part for those gentle and kind beings so much my juniors, I felt my situation if not patriarchal almost parental. Fancy me in an easy chair and soft slippers, bending over my big book with, I had almost called them, my little family around me: or if you cannot realize our evening's coterie without aid, perhaps a rough sketch may further assist your imagination.

THE CHURCH-GOER

DETERMINES AT THE DORCAS ON DOING SOMETHING

Knock after knock at the door announced every ten minutes a new accession to the number of our visitors: they were ladies of all ages, but I was the only Lord of the Creation amongst them, and the attention and praise they bestowed upon me was enough to turn any old man's head. They worked away meanwhile, and laughed and talked of the respective merits of their respective Ministers, of visiting societies, the affairs of the parish. Evangelicals, Puseyites, Popery, the probability of the curate's being married, of stone altars, and love matches, until they talked themselves out of breath, and then inquired if I would be kind enough to read something interesting and useful. I said that before leaving home I had made an extract from a work which I thought possessed some interest and advantage for ladies. The Roman population did not call on Mark Anthony to read Caesar's will with more energy than my fair companions did on me to proceed with my extract. 'Some delightful little scrap, as one of them ventured to anticipate, 'from the Old Fathers.' I did not undeceive her, but read as follows:

'Making tea is a very simple process, and consists merely of pouring boiling water upon the leaf. In making both tea and coffee, I believe it is better to use water which has only just boiled, than that which has been long over the fire. The latter, I fancy, has something vapid about it, but of this I am not certain. Soft water I have always understood to be preferable to hard. It is scarcely necessary to say that in order to make good tea, it is requisite to provide a good material. The process I should recommend, as most certain to prove satisfactory, is as follows. Have a kettle in the room. As soon as the water boils, pour some into the tea pot to heat it; then put in as much tea as will produce the desired strength, not by long infusion, but almost immediately. Pour the water hot from the fire upon the tea. Put the quantity you like of sugar and good cream into your cup, and pour the tea upon them, stirring it as you pour, and all one way round, which causes a smoothness and amalgamation very agreeable to the palate. I am now supposing you to be drinking tea for the sake of the tea. Under other circumstances you must do as well as you can. During the season of fires, I think a kettle much preferable to an urn, as ensuring a better condition of the water. With respect to the look of the thing, that is no consideration with me in comparison with the real advantage. As to the trouble of reaching it, that is not much; and there is nothing good to be had without some trouble. Letting tea stand long to get the strength out, or putting it near the fire to stew, is a very erroneous practice. The quicker it is made the more delicate is the flavour. Long infusion makes it coarse and harsh. For this reason the second cup cannot be expected to be as good as the first; but I recommend a habit to be acquired of taking only one cup on ordinary occasions. I think more weakens the digestive powers. A habit of sipping, instead of gulping, will make a small quantity produce as much enjoyment as a large one, and the difference as to health and elasticity of tone is immense. This question of quantity I recommend to the consideration of ladies, some of whom are apt to think that there is no harm from liquids except from strength.'

"And this, ladies," said I, bowing, "terminates my extract." They looked surprised. They evidently calculated on a chapter from St. Augustine, Ignatius, or Jeremy Taylor,[3] and the lady of the house hardly knew whether or not to consider it a hit at her Souchong which we had just had: I begged, however, to remove at once any such impression. I selected the subject, I said, because I thought it of every day importance, and especially to ladies; and a good cup of tea was not quite so common as some people imagined, so that any useful information of the manufacture of so agreeable a beverage could not be said to be without its advantage.

They took it all in very good part, and the lady of the house saying the period of the evening usually set apart for business having now arrived, she should call on the fair Secretary to read the minutes of the last meeting. The young lady thus appealed to, taking a small roll of paper out of her work box, proceeded to read as follows, and not a little to my surprise:

At a meeting of the . . . Dorcas Society, held on the . . . day of . . . . at Mrs. . . . house, in . . . Row,

Mrs. . . . in the Chair,

Proposed by Miss . . ., seconded by Mrs. . . . .

Resolved, 1st. . . . That this society perused with great satisfaction, and saw with regret the termination of the Church-Goer's visits to the various Churches of Bristol.

Proposed by Mrs. . . . ., seconded by Mrs. . . . .,

2. . . . That this meeting do recommend their venerable friend to extend his peregrinations to some of the country churches in the neighbourhood, which he might conveniently do on horseback.

Proposed by Miss . . . . seconded by Miss . . .,

3. . . . That our venerable friend be respectfully requested to receive as a slight testimonial of our respect, the trifling sum of £25, to be expended in the purchase of a horse for such and said purpose.

Proposed by Mrs. . . . ., seconded by Mrs. . . . .,

4. . . . That our esteemed friend be affectionately admonished to purchase none but a quiet animal, on which he may, without his friends feeling anxiety, entrust his precious and valuable person.

As you suppose, these resolutions took me completely by surprise: I saw, however, I could not, without hurting their feelings, refuse a compliment paid in such a spirit, so without further parley I consented to receive the money, and promised to comply with the request.

Having resolved on starting a horse, the next question was where, when, and how to buy it: the fact was I knew no more about horses than I did about a north-west passage; and as for points and all that, I might as well have gone to purchase a rhinoceros, so far as my judgement extended to symmetry, sinew, and shape. And still I knew it was not every horse that would suit me; in fact there were very few that would. It would be rash in me to say I was never six times on a beast's back in my life, but I think I might safely assert my feats of equestrianism never extended to the full dozen, so I must have a sober, quiet 'bit of flesh:' none of your flying Childers, or Godolphin Arabians,[4] or 'grey Momuses,'[5] to carry me some fine Sunday morning like a Maxeppa[6] or madman through a congregation, crying out "Stop 'im:" yet I must not have a poor broken down brute either, for falling was quite as bad as running away. The best thing was to go to 'the next bazaar sale and select for myself, and with this intent I took up a newspaper to see if there was anything offered that might suit me.

The first 'lot' that caught my eye was 'a well bred bay gelding, a superior hunter; has been hunted with the Queen's stag hounds, and at Melton — equal to twelve stone across any country.' This would not exactly suit; I wanted something to carry me to church, not across any country. The next was, 'a grey Irish gelding, rising five years, 15h.3in., rides well on road, and promises to make a good hunter.' This would not do either, I did not like his nation; if the horses were like the men, they were too mercurial for a person of my sober habits: besides, he might be disposed to 'repeal the union' between man and beast, and think it a very meritorious thing to leave an elderly Saxon on the road side. 'Lot 3, a bay horse 'Driver,' a good hunter.' I'd as soon think of backing Bucephalus. 'Lot 4, a bay filly, by Colonel.' Too young, I didn't like disparity of ages between horse and rider. 'Lot 5, a pair of forest ponies.' 'They may be Dr. Ashley's perhaps, and one of them might do,' was my first thought, but Triptolemus Yellowly[7] crossed my mind immediately after, and I read on. Lots of hunters of all qualities and capacities followed: some first rate fencers, and others competent to carry the Irish giant across any country, but the 'Church-Goer' in a 'bit of pink,' and a pair of top boots, was an idea not to be dwelt on. The advertisement, however, stated that there were 'several other good and serviceable animals to be offered on the day of sale:' so hoping I might find one to suit amongst the undistinguished 'ruck,' I attended on the following Thursday.

Collected round a little green rostrum at the upper end of the bazaar, was a small knot of men — some dozen gentlemen, and about the same number of horse dealers. They looked at me, and possibly discovering something very unequestrian in my appearance, one or two of them smiled. The 'first lot,' a tall grey horse, was being led out at the moment by a groom; he was walked up to the rostrum, and three or four knowing looking dealers, in top boots and sporting cut coats, proceeded to examine him, passing their hands down his fore and hind legs, and peering into his eyes, and pulling his lips asunder to look at his teeth: the brute was then trotted up and down, a man scampering after him and cracking a long whip. This was or had been a hunter, so I waited for the next, which was a savage looking powerful black, that kicked up its heels the moment it was trotted out, putting me in mortal terror of my life. I need not tell the reader this was not the kind of creature I wanted. Lot 4 was a gaunt, grave, Roman-nosed quadruped, that looked as if he had spent the bloom of his youth at funerals. At this moment it struck me that there was something so very respectable and honorable in the face of my friend in the rostrum, I had better at once place myself in his hands; so going round and plucking Mr. Leigh by the skirt of the coat, I told him in a few words my business, and my willingness to confide my cause to him. "Very well, Sir," said he smiling; "there are many more lots to come; see what you like yourself, and I will say to the best of my ability as to whether the animal will suit you or not." Satisfied with this assurance I stood patiently by, while hunter after hunter, and carriage horse after carriage horse were being knocked down. At length Mr. L. cried out, "Lot 20", and looking across at me he said in a low tone, "perhaps this might suit you, Sir." The head of a little roan animal protruded from the stall, followed by a round plump carcass admirably in keeping. Had my friend Leigh, like some deity in the artistical contest of the Gods of old, made a steed, he could not have fashioned one more to my fancy: it was neither a horse nor a pony, but it was between both — a kind of intermediate stage, commonly known, I was subsequently informed, by the name of 'Cob'. It was plump and stout, but slow, for when the man cracked the whip the only symptoms of increased activity, which it evinced was by wagging its little tail rather briskly above its round fat quarters: it seemed as if it thought it undignified to use any less staid or sober pace than a walk, which it did well, though all the cracking would not induce it to do more.

"Gentlemen", commenced Mr. Leigh, "a roan cob, called in the catalogue John Bunyan".

'John Bunyan,' thought I, 'I'd buy him for that name alone,' not that I am an unqualified admirer of my friend of the Pilgrim's Progress, but there was something so odd in the selection of the nomenclature. I moved forward to examine 'John', but gave way to three dealers who pushed in before me. One felt his legs, another examined his eyes and teeth, and as they did not seem to have any fault to find, I began to fear I might possibly be outbid in Bunyan. "Give him another turn," said the most knowing looking of the three, and John got another turn: on reaching the rostrum again Mr. Horsedealer looked significantly at that region of his side under which the lungs are supposed to be, and then after a momentary contemplation gave poor John two such sudden sharp and decisive thumps in the ribs (meant I afterwards learnt to try his wind) that the little horse (and who would not?) coughed as often in reply. Now, though it is quite natural for man or horse, when either gets a couple of punches in the side, to cough; the horsedealers shrugged their shoulders, and made way for me. "It's all hard meat," said Mr. L., as I laid my hand on the crest, and it was hard enough. The little horse let me handle him quietly; there was something of friendly salutation in the wag of his tail, and I almost thought (perhaps it was fancy) he gave a knowing side wink at me, as much as to say, "We'll get on well together — we were made for each other."

John was put up for £10: 'twelve,' 'thirteen,' 'fourteen,' were offered in quick succession, and I soon found that though the dealers could shrug their shoulders, they could still bid. "Fifteen," said I; a gentleman in a white cord trousers, "sixteen;" a titled lady's groom from Clifton, "seventeen:" "eighteen," said I once more; "nineteen," from the gentleman in the white cords. I paused for a moment. "It's just the horse for your purpose. Sir," said Leigh looking over at me: "then twenty pounds for John Bunyan," exclaimed I; "twenty-one, though it's fit for nothing but an old man," added the gentleman in the white cords. "Then an old man," said I, understanding his hint, "bids twenty-two."

"No advance on twenty-two," demanded Mr. L., after a moment's silence and looking round. "Is there no advance on twenty-two? — the horse is worth thirty," and then after waiting another minute, "if there's no advance I must knock him down for twenty-two — going, going for twenty-two," and he held the little hammer poised in the air — "gone for twenty-two," and the hammer fell with a sharp knock: then turning to me he said, "You've a bargain. Sir". "What name. Sir?" said the clerk. I hesitated for a second. "Oh, a gentleman in a snuff-brown coat," said I, handing in four five-pound notes and two sovereigns. "John Bunyan — a gent in a snuff-brown coat," repeated the clerk in the same business-like, imperturbable tone. The gentleman in the white cords congratulated me on my bargain. "John Bunyan, Sir," said he, "is a stout little horse, and if he carries you in is able to carry you out of the Slough of Despond." I thanked the gentleman in the white cords for his joke, and proceeded to admire my purchase.

John Bunyan was just the horse to my mind: he was slow, sure, and singular; he would not run away with me; he would not fall with me, and there was no mistaking him — and the last was not the least consideration. Poggio[8] tells a story of an Italian, who allowed all the persons at an inn to depart before him; for, not knowing his own horse, he let others retire with theirs, satisfied that when the rest were gone he might safely presume the one left behind to be his: and I confess, were I the owner of an ordinary animal, so uncritical an eye have I for symmetry, I should often be in the predicament of the Italian, and find it difficult to recognize my bay or brown (let us suppose it,) amongst many bays or browns. But with John Bunyan there was no danger of this — there was an identity and idiosyncracy about him in character, colour, shape, and size, which distinguished him from nine hundred and ninety-nine animals out of a thousand; he was like no other horse but himself.

His very slowness — some call it laziness — enhances his value in my eyes: he has a most imperturbable solidity of carriage, nothing puts him out of his way; he has but one gait, and he seems resolved that nothing shall accelerate him out of it. His staple pace is a walk; and if the historian should have to record a solitary deviation from this at a future day, I am quite certain it will never exceed a slight canter. However, as I said before, his celerity is quite sufficient for my ordinary requirements; and I hope the foul fiend will never make me, as Poor Tom says in Lear, [9] 'proud of heart to ride a high-trotting horse;' for, mounted and ready for the road, John Bunyan and his master have no ambition to cut a more imposing figure in their 'Pilgrim's Progress' to country churches than the following profile presents: *(In the newspaper the 'mounted' engraving appeared here.)*

1. Laurence Sterne, 1713-68. Author of *Tristan Shandy*, first published 1759.
2. Dorcas societies were formed by women of a church to make and provide clothing for the poor.

3. Jeremy Taylor, 1613-67. Cleric and devotional writer.

4. Godolphin Arabians; named after Francis Godolphin who in 1733 bought one of the first three arab stallions imported to Britain from which strain most racehorses are now descended.

5. Momus was the Greek God of ridicule; the connection here is not understood.

6. *Mazeppa*; a poem by Byron (1819). Mazeppa was bound naked to a wild horse.

7. Triptolemus Yellowly is a character in Sir Walter Scott's *The Pirate* (1821).

8. Gian Francesco Poggio Bracciolini, 1380-1459. Italian humanist.

9. Shakespeare, *King Lear* Act III scene iv. A typical Leech misquote. 'Tom' does not speak at all, but is spoken of: 'Who gives anything to poor Tom . . . made his proud of heart, to ride on a bay trotting horse over four-inched bridges, to course his own shadow for a traitor.'

Chew Magna

My first ride — my first essay on John Bunyan was, you may be sure, too important an event to be lightly regarded by me. My razor might be heard going on its strop an hour earlier than usual; and my estimable landlady got no less than two pairs of bellows to bear upon the kitchen fire, in order to urge the kettle to an expeditious boil, that I might have my breakfast if possible by half-past seven. My snuff-colour, neatly folded and scrupulously brushed, lay with my riding gloves on a chair in the parlour; and my new whip hung imposingly over the mantel-piece. It was an important morning: the cat, as if conscious of something unusual, purred restlessly around me; my landlady gave me a paper of cayenne lozenges, to keep the night air from finding its way to the interior of my body on my return; and when I started for the stable, the servant maid came running after me with her mistress's respects and a huge pair of brass heel spurs, which her late husband had used in the Royal Gloucestershire Yeomanry Cavalry, and she (poor soul!) thought might be of use to me on my present expedition. I, however, had no notion of employing such murderous implements against John Bunyan's sides, and sent them back.

On entering the stable, John promptly intimated his knowledge of my arrival by a friendly neigh of recognition; and turning round his little plump head, while his manger chain rattled through the ring, he seemed to say, as he eyed me significantly, "Oh, you're come are you? — I'm quite ready to start."

Dear Lady Patrons of the Dorcas, you should have been there to see me mount, not like the mad-cap Prince of Wales, but soberly from the summit of a stable stool. I wish you were, for I was anxious that you should see the piece of horse flesh in which I invested your twenty-five pounds — (the odd three, I should have told you before, having gone to the purchase of a saddle). He looked so sleek in his coat, his hoofs so brightly blackened, and his mane so smartly trimmed. Indeed, I was myself so wrapped up in admiration of him, that it was not until he stopped at the corner of the next street, as if expecting some intimation of our intended route, that I thought of selecting one; for up to that moment I had not dreamt of our destination, or of the church with which I meant to make a beginning. Somewhat at a loss, I looked around me to collect my thoughts, when the distant Tower of Dundry, which may be seen from almost any part of the city, caught my eye. "For Dundry, John Bunyan," said I, turning his rein in that direction; but I had not got a mile when I resolved on extending my incursion as far as Chew-Magna.

Reader, have you ever mounted Dundry Hill? It is no joke to climb, but having climbed it you do not lose your labour. John seemed to drag his fat sides and
my own up the ascent with some toil, and I think if, like the prophet's ass,[1] he
had his parts of speech, he would have expostulated with me on the injustice of
remaining on his back under such circumstances; but on the preceding night,
while I had my feet in the hot water, a twinge or two about the region of my
right ankle gave me a hint that I must not take many liberties with my lower
limbs, and I thought it better to press a little hard upon my new purchase, than
run the risk of being knocked up at the very opening of the campaign.

I'm a poor hand at describing scenery: and to tell you the truth, to me most
descriptions of scenery are nearly unintelligible — a mere luxurious chaos of
hill and vale, trees and rivulets, an indistinct vagueness of verdure and sunshine
scattered over the page which I cannot realize, though doubtless the author
has it all in his mind's eye at the time of writing. I always wish for the pencil and
the canvas of the painter as the only medium for conveying my ideas on these
occasions, though if the wish were complied with I should still be in the same
predicament as ever, as the highest pictorial efforts, of which I am capable, are
the portraits of John Bunyan and myself. Nevertheless, I have a reluctance to
'babble o' green fields'[2] from a consciousness of my own manifest want of talent in that way. I do not know when I was more struck by the beautiful diversity of any landscape. A fertile and hamlet-dotted vale interposed between me
and the wooded ridge of hills on the side of which stands Ashton Court, and
which are so abruptly divided from the corresponding heights of Clifton by
the grand and picturesque ravine that forms a passage for the river Avon: the
giant barrenness of St. Vincent's rocks, which first strike the eye from Dundry,
give to this gorge a savage character, which is almost increased by the contrast
of the adjacent villa-crowned eminence of Clifton. This favoured suburb, with
its stately Bath-stone-built crescents and terraces gleaming in the morning
sun, was a marked object in the noble view, and seemed to me, removed as I
was from the city at that moment, and in the centre of rural life, the palace-
like monuments of commercial greatness and social refinement.

But it is from the summit that the vastness of the panorama, stretching far
and away on all sides of Dundry, may be seen in its fullness of grandeur. From
the formation of the ground you can almost look quite round you: retracing
the view from the heights above Bristol to Ashton, you continue your survey
over a wooded vale, bounded by Wraxall and Backwell Hills, and others contiguous to the Channel. From Bishop Sutton in the south the eye passes on
over an elevated outline 'further east,' until it pauses upon that singular freak
of folly and senility, Beckford's Tower,[3] in the neighbourhood of Bath; so that
the vision, if it be not by this time exhausted with admiration, may still pass on
in almost uninterrupted survey and a circle to the point from which it started,
and rest once more upon the blue summit of the Monmouthshire hills which
may be seen rising in the distant background behind Vincent's Rocks.

How long I should have continued absorbed in the splendour of the sight, I cannot say, had not John Bunyan — who I am sorry to see does not seem to have an eye for the 'sublime and beautiful,' and who appeared in the present instance to have preferred some cockspur which grew in a neighbouring hedge, to the noble view which engrossed his rider — reminded me of mundane matters and of myself and my journey, by drawing me into a rough thorn bush, having forgot his owner's interests altogether in the urgency of his own. I remonstrated with him for conduct which to say the least of it was neglectful, and expressed my surprise that a quadruped of his apparent gravity should not be superior to the vice of covetousness and the charms of cockspur.

Having left Dundry Church on the right we now began to descend, and though the hill on this side is hardly as steep as on the other the declension nevertheless was none of the easiest, and John Bunyan picked up a stone, which I was obliged to dismount to hammer out of his hoof. The view still continued beautiful, and the villages of Winford and Chew Magna almost beneath my feet, and Chew Stoke a little more in the distance, with their pretty Church towers and cottages peering up amongst the trees, added not a little to the truly English character and picturesque quiet of the scene. The Greater Chew, my destination, seemed so snugly ensconced and secluded at the base and beneath the shelter of the giant hill — so remote at once from railroads and cities — that I expected to find everything in a state of primeval simplicity amongst them; and I amused myself with speculating as to which might be the parson's or squire's residence amongst the snug country houses upon which I looked down.

Marvellous is the sagacity of a man's horse at times: for as we entered the village by one of the two public buildings of the place, the 'General Shop,' I perceived that John Bunyan turned his head round and round, and I had little trouble in discovering that he was on the look out for the inn; and as he was kind enough to undertake the task, I left it entirely to his own discretion. There were two I saw close together, with equally inviting sign-boards — one, the 'Bear and Swan,' an odd conjunction, with appropriate device; the other, 'the Pelican,' — I could only hope not 'of the wilderness'. John chose the former, after a moment's scrutiny, and walked into the yard as boldly as if he paid the rent and taxes.

"Whoin be I to gie 'un corn, sar?" said the stable-man, taking the bridle from my hand, and leading John into a two-stalled stable.

"I'll give it myself, my good man, when I return from church," said I, "not that I at all question your probity, or deem that justice might not be done the beast at your hands; but I find in life, whether it be with the human or the brute creation, the highway to the heart lies between the turnpike gate of the teeth, where those who mean to pass must pay toll. Now, my good friend, for obvious reasons, considering how much we are likely to be together, it is desirable for me to stand well in the esteem and opinion of my horse, who rejoices in the name of John Bunyan; and to this end, and to cultivate the closest possible friendship, I wish, when I conveniently can, to convey the corn to his manger with my own hands."

"Yes, sure, measter!" replied the man, with rather a bewildered look; but I was equally sure he did not understand one word of what I said.

A smart little 'Mary, the maid of the Inn,'[4] with black hair and round face, met me with a curtsey of welcome at the back door as I approached.

"What time do prayers commence, my good girl?" said I, following her into the little bow-windowed parlour to which she led the way, and confiding to her custody my riding-stick.

"Eleven, Sir; and three in the afternoon;" and again, after a pause, "Do you dine. Sir?"

'Service at eleven and three,' thought I, 'and dinner between both; and since the vicar is not very likely to send the sexton running out after me from church with a parole invitation to eat my mutton with him, I must even suit myself here.' But speaking of dining between services reminds me of an interesting anecdote of his parish, which I heard only last week from the rector of Upton, in Gloucestershire.[5] There are eleven old people who for twenty years have attended morning and afternoon service in that church, and who come from a distance of two, three, and four miles; but instead of returning to dinner 'between duties,' they have been in the habit of each bringing their little frugal meal of bread and cheese in a handkerchief, and eating it in the church, under shelter of which they remain seated from one service to another; thus by this simple and praiseworthy plan availing themselves of the advantages of the full Sabbath prayers, which, if they returned home to their dinners, from their advanced ages, and the distances they would have to travel, they would hardly be able to do. Mark this, you rich, who with the Sabbath bell sending its afternoon call to your drawing rooms, and you who live almost under the shadow of the church tower, yet disregard and neglect the great privilege within your reach; read this, too, you poor, and you who might, without any sacrifice of personal comfort, attend both services, and are yet rarely to be found at either; here is a beautiful and impressive lesson of affectionate devotion set you by these eleven simple peasants of Gloucestershire, who deserve a church, and who will one day rise up in judgment against those who have had in every respect a thousand-fold superior advantages. I don't know when I was so much struck myself with an instance of pure and unaffected piety.

But to return to my dinner, or rather my order about my dinner: I said I should have eggs and bacon at one o'clock. Now, I named eggs and bacon, not because it is a very paramount dish with me, but because I have always in my imagination associated it with the country inn, and the clean white table-cloth — the *munda supellex*[6] of my little five-foot favourite Horace who, by the way, knew more of comfort and the art of giving a small dinner party than all the Walkers in the world, besides, I have a most cheerful idea of the dish, which, for the most part you can hear in the parlour hissing through its process of cooking in the kitchen. A modern monkish poet, who seems to have entered into the matter with all a churchman's gout, thus describes the delicate details:

'While the fragrant turf smoke
Curls quite round the pan on the fire,
And the sweet yellow yolk
From the egg shells is broke
In that pan,
Who can,
If he have but the heart of a man,
Not feel the soft flame of desire?'

"You can have eggs and bacon. Sir," said the girl, who evidently from her tone did not seem to think it quite a Sunday dish, "but there is a leg of mutton roasting at the fire."

"The leg of mutton will do, my child; give yourself no further trouble, unless perhaps it be convenient to procure a spoonful or two of currant jelly."

The bell had not been long ringing when I entered the churchyard. An inscription, on the front of the organ-loft, informs the curious, who may also become if they like the incredulous, that the church was repaired and *beautified* in some year of our Lord, which I forget. But the question is, as to what our ancestors some two centuries ago meant by beautifying — I fear myself that their ideas on this point consisted in crowding it with cumbrous wood-work, mutilating columns, washing over corbels and carvings, and surrounding unsightly monuments with immense iron railings. Chew Magna does not show more than the average amount of vandalism to be seen in most of the many beautiful churches of Somerset. I fancied I could trace the bad taste of the latter part of the seventeenth century, (a period which appears to have been rather fertile in bunglers), in many parts of the church, which consists of a nave, side aisle, and chancel. In an architectural point of view the tower, which is a handsome one, is perhaps the part of the edifice which I most prefer, and which from the Western approach has a most pleasing effect. I do not know the date of the erection, but the structure appears principally of the perpendicular Gothic.

The congregation was not very large at the morning service; but in the afternoon the church was full. The protracted old age and indisposition of the last incumbent entailed a large amount of labour and trouble on his successor. However remote from cities the country has its own abounding and crying vices, and I am told the laxity of morals, the besotted blindness, the spiritual indifference, which at one time prevailed in the parish, required all the energy of an indefatigable, active, and intrepid clergyman to correct. I do not intend to offer any offence to the memory of anyone, (and the last incumbent was, I believe, an amiable man), but I think the rural parish, from the indolent and sluggish nature of the peasant's mind, for the most part requires more activity, if possible, on the part of the minister than even a town congregation, and this is a quality which is not always to be found united with old age and indisposition. Earnest and untiring exertions, and a bold determination to do his duty, on the part of the present vicar, have, however, reclaimed Chew Magna to a state of order, discipline, and public propriety, which renders it, in all that makes a parish socially and spiritually respectable, second to none in the diocese. And there is no clergyman, you may rest assured, who is determined to do his duty, who will not find his labours, however up-hill and hard they may be, eventually crowned with success.

The sermon in the morning, which was preached by the vicar,[7] was a plain, practical, useful discourse, eminently suited to his hearers, with no attempt at theological abstruseness or studied eloquence; and the congregation was on both occasions most attentive.

On returning to the little inn I found my leg of mutton ready for me. Do you know, I like a comfortable, quiet meal of this kind in the country. I know it is a dictum of a modern author, who is thought quite an oracle in these matters, that a man should avoid dining alone, for solitude begets thought, and thought begets indigestion; but I don't believe him: a man may 'chew the cud' of 'sweet,' not 'bitter fancy,' while masticating his mutton, with impunity. There is no necessity for trying to square the circle, or troubling oneself with the theory of parallels, or mentally investigating geometrical angles while you are at your dinner; but I think a little, quiet, easy, pleasing rumination at meal times, leads rather to health than otherwise. I confess, as the tidy waiting maid, with her white apron, rivalling the table cloth in cleanliness, placed the dish before me, I felt so entirely satisfied with my own company, I should not have thanked Prince Albert for his. The room was small, and commanded from its little bow window no more extensive prospect than the green street door of an opposite neighbour: the ruins of Bolton Abbey, in half a dozen different phases, and a few pictorial efforts of native talent, adorned the walls. Whether like *Dick Tinto*,[9] in Scott, the village artist had run up a score at \, and painted himself out of debt I cannot say; but he certainly had done a great deal for mine host and immortality: there was a dead hare, and a live woodcock, with other attempts, but eminent above all was a portrait of an old toper of the village, with a pipe in his hand, and upon whose face the painter had fastened a perpetual broad grin: this 'counterfeit resemblance' alone was quite company enough for me, for look up when I would from my plate he kept giggling down from his frame upon me.

"What do you drink. Sir?" inquired the maid of the Bear and Swan. I paused, but was about to say water, when she interposing, observed, "Our home-brew is counted good. Sir."

It is curious how man allows himself to be led by suggestions, as in the case of the mutton so in the matter of the beer, I suffered myself to be influenced by my smart little attendant. When others are willing to cater for me I see no use in taking the trouble for myself. Half the charm of taking mine ease in mine own inn, especially in the country, consists in the simplicity of fare precluding the perplexity of choice. Besides, contrary to the habit of a larger portion of the world, I have the fullest confidence in the fraternity of hosts, and the sisterhood of hostesses, and in indifferent matters of this kind I always defer to their greater experience.

The mutton removed, the maid of the Bear and Swan placed a plum pudding before me. "This was not in the contract," said I, as the savoury steam rose up in rapid whirls and shaded for a moment the grinning toper on the opposite wall from my eyes.

"Sir."

"I don't think I shall eat any."

"Sir," said the maid of the Bear and Swan, placing my plate, "Mrs. Weeks is celebrated for her plum puddings."

"Then," replied I, again consenting, "I for one shall not be said to slight her reputation."

As the remains of the plum pudding went out, a tall, portly gentleman came in. He had seen me, he said, (with a bow) in church, and if I purposed waiting for the afternoon service he should be happy to see me again, and to a cup of Souchong afterwards. "I am a past churchwarden," he added.

It will only make half an hour's difference thought I, aloud; and John Bunyan is a good walker.

"And it is a moonlight night," said the past churchwarden. This decided the matter, and I accepted his Souchong.

1. Balaam's Ass, Numbers Ch.22 vv22-31.

2. "a' babbled of green fields". *Henry V* Act II scene iii.

3. Beckford's Tower. William Beckford, 1759-1844. An eccentric book collector and writer, Beckford inherited a fortune and squandered much of in on his building schemes. His 'Fonthill Abbey' Tower of three hundred feet was erected in great haste by men working day and night, and upon completion immediately fell to the ground. Undismayed, Beckford built another, which also fell after he had sold the estate. Beckford's Tower was yet another building, at Lansdown, Bath where he had moved after disposing of the Fonthill estate in 1822.

4. Robert Southey, 1774-1843. Poet, historical and miscellaneous author. *Mary the Maid of the Inn* (1797).

5. Upton St. Leonards, Gloucestershire. H. Parsons, (1833).

6. *Munda Suppellex*; from Horace, *Epistulae*, meaning 'clean household goods'.

7. E.A. Ommanney, (1841).

8. Dick Tinto is a poor artist, the author of the note from which Peter Pattieson compiles the story of Sir Walter Scott's *The Bride of Lammermoor* (1819).

5 October 1844
Keynsham

I was in the act of placing a little Worcester sauce on my chop on Saturday morning last, when the *Bristol Times* was laid on the breakfast table by my land-lady, who (kind soul) is so solicitous about my minutest comforts that for the most part she will allow nobody else to wait upon me but herself. The first thing I turned to was of course my own composition, and do you know I was quite frightened at the first glimpse to see the space over which it spread — almost two columns! Reader, I sincerely beg your pardon for the infliction — this was certainly imposing on your good nature: I cannot palliate the offence, I can only promise it shall not occur again. I cannot even now account for the length to which it extended, but I suppose it arose from the overwheening notions we all have of our own compositions, and the reluctance we feel to draw our pen through anything we have written.

It was, therefore, with a sincere resolution to cultivate the virtue of brevity I placed my left foot in the stirrup-iron, and slowly extended my right leg over John Bunyan's saddle, on the following Sunday.

Most persons visiting Keynsham would have taken eighteen pence in their pocket, and a place in a second-class carriage. But I was born before an inch of 'permanent way' was laid down, and when I can get the turnpike road, with leafy hedges and green fields on both sides of me, I have no wish to be shot through dark tunnels like a pea through a pea-shooter. My time is not so precious that I cannot afford to loiter an additional hour on the way; nor is it a loss either, for you generally meet, or rather met, with some conversable creature in a stage coach, from whom you departed a trifle wiser; it might be on Mangel Worzel, or it might be on the Elgin Marbles. Now you have time to pick up nothing in a railroad carriage but a heart complaint: you get in, and look around you for a colloquial face in an absolute company, and if you are fortunate enough to find one amongst persons who appear all cast-iron, like the permanent way beneath them, you clear your throat, you give a preliminary cough or two, and you have just time to make a remark on the salubrity of the season, when the train stops, the door is unlocked by a man in Lincoln-green, who shouts 'Who's for Nailsea,' or 'Nottingham,' as the case may be, and your vis-à-vis alights, and your gossip is nipped in the bud.

The road to Keynsham, though pleasant, fortunately for the reader presents little to reflect upon. The only incident which merits a special record is, perhaps, the fact of John Bunyan having been frightened by the up-train,[1] just at that point where the railway approaches the turnpike close to Keynsham. I was balancing myself in the saddle, repeating part of Keble's 'Christian year,'[2] while John with his regular foot-fall, kept time to the cadence of the verse, when 'whirr!' — out from the side of the hill shot the bright copper boiler with its train of polished carriages, like a monstrous tea-kettle eloping with a string of monstrous tea-caddies. John snorted and elevated his tail a little, and then pausing as if deliberating whether he ought to expend any of his energies on a start; but he took the more sensible course and stood still, though I could perceive he was greatly alarmed. It was evidently the first time he had seen a railroad, and I thought I would endeavour to convince him of the unreasonableness of his fears; so turning his head in the direction of the still retreating train, and patting him encouragingly on the neck, I told him it was a locomotive engine — an invention of modern science for superseding his species; that it made a great deal of noise, but contrary to the adage did a great deal of work also. He seemed reassured, and by the time we entered the Lamb and Lark[3] had completely recovered his equanimity.

As I entered the churchyard the bells had only begun their work, so I paused for a short time to 'meditate amongst the tombs.' Picking my steps over bunches of dock-leaves, nettles, and fern, and the little mounds beneath which the 'rude forefathers of the hamlet sleep,' I perched myself on the headstone of some estimable defunct who lies at the east end of the burial ground, and who departed this life, according to the stone-cutter, sincerely regretted by his family especially, and the parish of Keynsham generally. I was trying to get off by rote the ambitious epitaph of a poetical chandler who reposed nearly opposite, when my attention was attracted by two very antiquated crones, who came hob-

bling towards me over the graves which, in the course of nature, they ought to have long since filled; both had apparently attained to four score years, and one was considerably taller than the other, and as she bent over her crooked stick, reminded me of the penny portrait of 'Mother Hubbard:' her companion was a little crabbed-faced old creature, and carried a large gingham umbrella that seemed as if it had been made in the time of the Norman Conquest, if not for Noah. They made their way with pain and difficulty to nearly the spot where I sat, when the taller of the two, turning aside the long rank grass with her stick, pointed out a little rudely placed row of stones to her fellow crone. "Here," said she, in a voice faltering with age, and wiping her old eyes with a large snuffy brown cotton handkerchief, "is where my baby (poor dear!) lies. I placed these stones myself, and Mr.— grumbled a good 'un."

"Poor dear!" croaked her companion, moving a few steps nearer the church and pointing with her umbrella to a little green mound, "and here's where my little da-ar-ling is buried."

Good gracious, thought I, and could these sapless old creatures, with half an inch of hair on their upper lips, and looking as hard as walking mummies, have ever been young mothers with blue-eyed babies at their breasts! I shut my eyes to try if I could picture either to my fancy as a fresh, soft-looking young woman; but their old quivering voices, which seemed to me as if two of the last generation had arisen to have a gossip among the headstones, kept off the illusion: the very babies of whom they spoke, and whom they recollected with a tenderness that age hardly impaired, had they lived would have been grandfathers or grandmothers at that moment. Yet such had, of course, been the case: these old crones, with their horny eyes and their hard features, had, no doubt, their day of rustic attraction, when they

'Danced with the lads of the village,
No cheeks glowed more ruddy than theirs!'

Though now they may be sent to point a warning moral to vain beauty's 'chamber,' and 'tell her though she should paint an inch thick, to this complexion must she come at last.'[4] The old women hobbled back again towards the church, wiping their eyes with their brown pocket handkerchiefs, and sighing their vain regrets for babies buried sixty years ago.

A few persons were standing listlessly by the porch, and just as I came up a gentleman about five or six and thirty years old, and to all appearances *a* clergyman, passed by them into the church. I should have put him down for *the* clergyman, only that no one noticed him — no one put their hands to their hats, or saluted or bowed to him, or paid him any of those respectful little recognitions which almost invariably pass between a church pastor and his parishioners. This hurt me; for I began to think, if it was the clergyman, vicar or curate, there did not exist that hearty, cheerful, cordial, family feeling which should be found in every English parish between the minister and his flock. Again I thought, perhaps he may be a stranger — a clergyman brought over from Bath for the day; and even this thought carried little consolation with it. Half the beauty of the English parochial system consists of its pastoral character — in a clergyman being at once the spiritual head and guide, friend and teacher of his parishioners, amongst whom he should live and move and interest himself, as if it were his own family; but this, strangers, who come like shadows and so depart, cannot be expected to be. We will suppose a number of unemployed or invalid clergymen in Bath, having no regular duty, but lying about on the 'Guinea Coast,' as an old reverend friend of mine used to say; and one of them gets a note on the previous Saturday from the Rev. Mr. Blank, of some neighbouring parish, requesting that he would do his (Mr. B's) duty for him on the following day. So he takes out of his desk some old sermon, which has seen service on forty similar occasions before, and rolling a soiled gown in an old newspaper, takes the railroad, perhaps, and arrives at a strange church just as the bell is about to cease; preaches his sermon to people he never saw before and may never see again, and pocketing it and his guinea departs once more as soon as the 'duty' is done. Now, this is a cold, heartless, matter-of-business sort of thing which I do not like. The clergyman of a large parish ought to make it a point either never to be absent or to keep a curate, not to leave his flock to such uncertain and occasional aid. Indeed, in every case a clergyman with a large and lucrative parish ought to keep a curate; for this having a chance man to fill a gap, and preach to people whose habits and characters he knows nothing about, is a bad plan.[5]

Keynsham is a large church, consisting of nave, north and south aisle, and chancel, and was originally viewed as a parish church, a fine structure; but now it presents, in the interior at least, a miserably dilapidated appearance,[6]

The first object that struck me on entering was the parish fire-engine, with other anti-*phlogistic* material conspicuously placed in the north aisle; from all I saw it could not have been kept there to cool the fervour, by playing on the persons, of the incumbent and his flock, and for all other purposes the parish I think might have more properly provided a shed for such lumber outside the sanctuary. When a fire occurs (and I dare say such things so occur sometimes in Keynsham), I cannot reconcile to my ideas of the reverential awe which should invest the house of God at all times, the circumstance of a number of fellows breaking in, with the noise of hobnailed shoes and loud voices, on the midnight solemnity and silence of such a place, and dragging with shouts an uncouth looking fire-engine from out its sacred portals.

There was no person that I could see to show me into a seat; but to obviate the necessity for a sextoness there seemed to be locks upon none of the pews, and even hinges did not appear to be a very abundant article in use: from some remnants of white paint which I saw about, I conjecture the church underwent that process some half century ago, but several deal boards had since been added in quite a state of nature: a few private pews were lined with green baize, but the rest were for the most part dilapidated and dusty: the once handsome and elaborately carved oak ceilings of the north and south aisles were in a state of decay: where the panelling had fallen out, in some places common deal had been substituted, but in others the 'carved work' had fallen down so fast, that they had seemingly grown tired of filling up the gaps: an unsightly stove chimney

Keynsham Church prior to restoration in 1861.

traversed two or three of the windows of the north aisle in a diagonal direction, and the frayed and faded glory of the pulpit fringe and cushions, accorded with all around. Even the books in the reading-desk shared in the general dilapidation — the Bible could not be said to have two whole covers, and the Book of Common Prayer seemed devotedly determined to share its fate. In fact, everything spoke of ruinous neglect; and my own feelings, as I looked round on the signs of indifference and decay, and the scanty and scattered attendance, and witnessed the feebly and coldly performed service, were melancholy and dispiriting in the extreme.

Now, though I am as great an admirer as most people of architectural propriety and order, yet, knowing that these things are in a great measure matters of taste, for mere informality or impurity of style or offences against the recognised laws of ecclesiastical arrangement, I should not think of finding fault with or censuring anyone; but for ruin, neglect, and uncleanliness there is no excuse. I am sorry to be compelled to speak my mind, but I must say that when I see the appearance of carelessness in the sacred edifice, I have but a poor opinion of the affairs of the parish: you cannot help thinking that as the church is, so the parishioners are, and that if the condition of the one be allowed to grow bad, the state of the other cannot be a matter of extreme anxiety. I must say myself

Keynsham Church after the completion of restoration in 1863.

that were I the clergyman of a large and wealthy parish like Keynsham, sooner than not have my church in a suitable state — in a state becoming the solemn purpose to which it was consecrated, I would ask for a rate every month until it was granted;[7] or if my importunity did not succeed, I would go about with a bag, and beg from door to door for the means of keeping it in repair, and you may rest assured no parishioners would be found to resist long the intent and zealous anxiety of any clergyman: where there is a hearty will you may depend upon it success will not be long wanting. If there were none else to keep the church clean, I should make my own servants do it.

I don't know the census of Keynsham, but it is I believe both a large and populous parish; the congregation, however, was miserable: there were a few respectable families of the immediate neighbourhood, and a few poor men, most of them seemingly from the Union Workhouse. I'm told that the place swarms with dissenters, and I am not much surprised. The humble population of every parish require pains to be taken to keep them in the church: they must be visited, they must be looked after, cheered and encouraged, or they will soon be snapped up by active schismatics. It is not enough for a clergyman to rise from his breakfast table each Sunday morning, and proceed with a sermon in his pocket to the parish church, and return again in the afternoon to go through the same course, and see no more of his parishioners until the next Sabbath: to employ the words of the commandment with all reverence I should say, 'Six days shalt thou labour,' as well as the seventh, and your duty ought to draw you almost as imperatively to the interior of the church. This may be irksome and unpleasant to some people, but the man who is not prepared to postpone his personal convenience, pleasures, and even comforts, to his duty, is unfit for the awful responsibility of his post. It is not for ease or income we go, or at least ought to go, into the church — it is a stewardship from Heaven for which we will have to account.

The whole service was performed and sermon preached by the clergyman whom I saw enter, I should therefore conclude the vicar keeps no curate.[8] Whether he be by his unaided exertions able to do full and faithful justice to all the duties of his sacred office, is a question for his own mind and judgement — whether he can without help visit his poor every week, superintend his schools, and attend to all the incidental and parochial exigencies. Any clergyman who finds he is not equal to this of himself ought to have help.

There is no organ, the choir consisting of a double bass, two wind instruments, and the children of the Charity Schools.

The sermon was from James v. 16, 'The fervent prayer of the righteous man availeth much.' There was no fault to be found with it; it was a very fair and sound discourse; though I thought the seeming lassitude with which the preacher got through the service at the reading desk hardly accorded with the earnestness which he inculcated from the pulpit.

1. Brunel's seven foot gauge line for the Great Western Railway was opened between Bristol and Bath only four years earlier.
2. John Keble, 1792-1866. Divine and Poet, the 'true and primary author' of the Oxford Movement. Author of *The Christian Year* (1827).
3. The Lamb and Lark, Keynsham. Landlord, Charles Amos. At this time the inn was also the local Excise Office.
4. 'Now get you to my Lady's chamber, and tell her, let her paint an inch thick, to this favour she must come; make her laugh at that —' *Hamlet* Act V scene i.
5. The incumbent was W.W. Quarterly (1825).
6. The church was renovated 1861-3, see illustrations.
7. It would appear that the predominant Dissenting population had refused the church rate (an annual levy on the parish) towards the upkeep of the church. The rate could only be levied if the majority of the parish were in agreement.
8. The *Clergy List* shows a curate for 1844 and 1846, W.G. Hawtayne.

THE CHURCH-GOER
A CHAPTER OUT OF PLACE, BUT A WORD IN SEASON

My good reader, sit down and join me in railing at all Newspaper Editors in general, and the Editor of the *Bristol Times* in particular. Last week, when I walked into his office as usual, with my 'Church' in my hand, legibly written and pinned at the corners to keep the sheets together, I found him sedulously engaged in preparing to 'enlighten the public' with a pot of paste and a pair of scissors: he had a number of long slips of paper before him, to which he was transferring a multitude of small square paragraphs, carefully culled from a heap of his contemporaries which lay mutilated and reticulated by the table at which he sat.

"Still at work, Mr. Editor," said I, taking a seat opposite him, "posterity will be indebted to you for a large amount of paste and paper, to say nothing of scissors worn out in their service, which I sincerely trust they will repay you in that sterling coin stamped with the head of Fame."

"Yes," said he drily, and glancing at the paper in my hand he continued, "I'm afraid we can't find room for you this week."

"Not find room for me after having gone to the trouble of writing twenty-five pages," said I, in something like a tone of hurt pride if not indignant surprise.

"Why," said he, "we can't get more in than our paper will hold: and there are the Clergy and Glos'ter feasts this week, and the consecration of Christ Church, Clifton, and a medical meeting, all to be reported, and of importance, too." he added, cutting and pasting away as coolly as if he had not mortally wounded my vanity with the last observation.

'So, so,' thought I, 'of importance,' and mine I suppose is not.' Talk of the apple of a man's eye being sensitive, but there is nothing you can touch to create so keen an anguish as his self-love: what mortal is there that does not think well of his own compositions, and the Church-Goer is no more than mortal, though he wears a snuff-brown coat? Here was I, fancying that the only part of the paper read, or deserving of being read, was my column, and that I was fast making this man's fortune for him, coolly told that the *post prandium* orations of a number of country gentlemen and parsons were of importance, plainly implying that my elaborations were not. A kind of cold consciousness began to creep over me. Can it be possible, thought I, that stuffed with praise and pheasants I have been all this time overrating myself, and that the address of a Gloucestershire man, who has dined on stewed beef and vegetable marrow, is more looked to than my peregrinations?

"Oh, very well," said I aloud, stricken and humbled by the discovery, as I folded up my composition, and placed it in the pocket of my brown coat, "I see my papers are not of so much importance to you or your readers as I thought they were, and I shall not therefore trespass again on your valuable time and space."

The Editor laid down his paste-brush and looking up in my face very good temperedly said, "Don't be foolish: your papers are very well in their way, and when our space is not occupied with more urgent matters, I shall be very happy to insert them, as there are a certain number of old ladies who look for them; but you ought to know just as well as I do, that if you wrote as well as the Archbishop of Canterbury or myself, I must print the reports of such meetings before anything else, and the smallest squire in Gloucestershire thinks his speech in returning thanks for having his health drunk, of more importance than all you or I will ever write — he'd never forgive me the omission, and what is of vastly greater moment he'd stop the paper —"

"Copy, Sir," shrieked a little fellow with a black face, and a sharp treble, thrusting his head into the sanctum, and cutting the Editor short.

I was just on the point of saying with Don Giovanni in the opera, "So this is your friend, the *Devil*, have the goodness to introduce me," when St. John's clock struck ten, and as I was so far on my way to Clifton, and had nothing else to do, I thought I would walk leisurely up to Christ Church, and look in at the consecration.

Many like myself were bound for the same destination, but though I walked deliberately (for I had not John Bunyan between my legs) I reached Clifton Park before eleven o'clock. "Have you got a ticket, Sir?" inquired a policeman, as I was about to enter the west porch. I told him I had not, for I was not aware a ticket was necessary.

"I'm sorry for it," said the man civilly enough, "for my orders are not to admit anyone without a ticket."

"And you may rest assured," replied I, "that I have too great a regard for your cloth to ask you to exceed them," and I turned away to wait until my friend James Henry,[1] by the Grace of God Bishop of Gloucester and Bristol, made his appearance, as I knew I might affect an entrance under shelter of his lawn sleeves. I make it a point never to fret or chafe at a little rebuff or refusal like this; besides it is usually done at consecration — the church won't contain the whole of the world, therefore you can only admit a part, and of that part those who pay for the edifice are naturally preferred. However, there were an old lady and a newspaper reporter, neither of whom seemed to possess my philosophy, as both protested, if not very angrily very loudly, against what they called the disgrace of keeping the doors shut against the public.

"It's of a piece with everything else they have done," said the old lady; "the positions in the church have been all regulated by the amount paid, and now the tickets are disposed of on the same principle. It is all very well to keep out common people, but to refuse a gentlewoman! —"

"And not admit the press," added the reporter; "I never heard of such a thing before."

"Very sorry ma'am, very sorry sir," quietly replied the constable from time to time. "I can't help it; those are my orders; if I were told to keep out the Archbishop of Canterbury, I must do it, or be fined a week's pay."

Eleven o'clock, however, struck while they were yet altercating, and the transept doors being thrown open we all entered, including the elderly gentlewoman and the reporter, whose voices I could still hear grumbling until they were borne out of view and hearing by the crowd.

This is an age of affectation, and in nothing perhaps more than in architecture: everybody pretends to have an eye for the sublime and beautiful in this. I heard at least a dozen persons discussing point after point of the building on the day of the consecration, and as people never shine so much as in finding fault, the captious of course had the majority. Now, technically I know little or nothing about architecture; I know and feel when a building pleases me, and I was pleased, and greatly pleased, on the whole with the new church: with more money spent on it of course it might have been made more beautiful; for instance, the interior of the nave looks bare and cold for want of the disengaged columns and the recessed mouldings around the windows, which give such richness and finish to those of the chancel: but people must cut their coat according to their cloth, though I question if this was altogether a wise act of economy.

"Pray, Sir, can you tell me," whispered an old lady, as I crushed into a seat by her side in the north transept, during the reading of the deed of consecration. "Can you tell me who's to have Trinity, Hotwells?"[2]

"Can't say, Ma'am," said I, "for up to the present the Bishop has neglected to consult me."

I saw the old lady did not know well how to receive my answer, and I cared little myself how she took it, for I saw she was one of those gossips who mistake such tittle tattle for religion, and chose the church more for its minister than for itself.

"There is not a pew to be let here," commenced the old lady again after another pause. "I'm told the first ten or twelve pews have given over one hundred pounds each to the church, and a friend of mine, who gave thirty, is halfway down the nave."

"Well Ma'am, said I, all cannot have the first pews, and it is only fair the highest sums should have the highest seats."

"Oh certainly, certainly," replied the old lady, who didn't think of disputing any point — "quite delightful I'm sure — so popular; and the poor people I'm told, too, are to be allowed to pay half-a-crown each for their sittings in the aisle — did you hear that?"

"No Ma'am, and I hope it is not true."

"Indeed, dear me," said the old lady again, with the same indisposition to all contradiction; and after another pause, "Did you hear Mr. Taylor[3] was to forbid the consecration today?"

Fortunately the service of the day commenced, or I should have been talked out of all propriety and patience by my gabby neighbour, who was one moment repeating the responses with wondrous energy, and the next staring round on the congregation with restless pertinacity, taking occasion at times to inquire of me where they made stained glass, and if I did not think the old church at Clifton would be deserted now.

1. James Henry Monk, 1784-1856. Bishop of Gloucester in 1830, Bishop of Gloucester and Bristol 1836. Monk had a severe skirmish with Sydney Smith, who ridiculed his Toryism in his *Third Letter to Archdeacon Singleton* on the Ecclesiastical Commission *See* pp. 194 and 217.
2. James Hensman moved from Trinity, and was incumbent 1844-7. Trinity Hotwells went to Humphrey Allen, previously curate at Hay, Breconshire.
3. James Taylor. *See* p.34.

26 October 1844

Winterbourne

Tom Paine[1] says somewhere something to the effect that 'laws are like turn-pike-gates — the highway of life was free enough before their enactment, but then came cunning and chicane to set up their artificial barriers to make one pay toll at every turn.' Loving reader, do not be alarmed for my principles, I have not read the graceless Republican for twenty years; but when I was a young man his works were making a noise in the world, and I turned over one or two of them through mere curiosity: I have not, however, placed my eyes on a page of his for many years, nor should I have thought of him now, had not the toll-bar at the 'Blackbird's' evoked the long-dormant passage to my recollec-tion. But, whatever Tom Paine's ideas on the subject might be, John Bunyan's are decidedly of a character quite orthodox: he has a respect for turnpikes and would as soon think of levanting from a livery stable before his oat bill had been liquidated, as of passing a toll-house if the pike had not been paid. On reaching a gate he will pull up of his own accord, as much as to say "We must not cheat the Trust," and appears altogether so intelligent on the point that although of course, he does not ask for a *ticket*, I have been induced at times to fancy that he must *think* of it. Indeed, if ever a horse had politics, John (albeit his name-sake, I believe, was not) must be a Conservative: he has an innate respect for constituted authority, and if there's a *Crown* Inn in the village he turns to it. His very sturdiness seems the result of principle, and I sometimes think he is slow not so much from choice as contempt of the go-ahead habits of modern times and horses.

John Bunyan paused at the Blackbird's Gate, and taking the hint and three halfpence from my trouser pocket I paid the man in full of all demands, and requested a ticket in return. "You needn't mind it, Sir, I shall know you again," said the man.

"My good man," said I, "I find the world in general so treacherous of memory in all money matters that I prefer, as the law contemplated, having a voucher for my payments. Besides, you must have a much keener eye for physiognomy than I can easily give you credit for to be able to recollect every face and form that pass in the twenty-four hours. I for one should be very sorry to give you the trouble of bearing me in mind until my return, since by taking a ticket I may save you any such effort of memory."

"Trouble!" repeated the man, with an impudent familiarity which made my blood boil. "La'bless thee saul, no trouble in life, I'd a know thee again in half a century if I never saw'd thee in the meantime. Trouble, bless thee! Why, man and boy, I've been at this gate for twenty years, and I never know'd the likes of thee go by before, and if I was to sit for twenty year I'd never set my eyes I 'spect on such another. Trouble, bless thee! thee'rt too remarkable an auld chap to forget soon, 'tis only once in a century such a rum 'os and rider pass the Blackbird's".

"And I hope," said I indignantly, "'tis only once in a century I shall have the misfortune to meet with such an impudent fellow at the receipt of custom."

I had hardly gone a half-dozen yards, when a gentleman in black, on a bay horse, came trotting up, and having paid the pike was about to pass me, when suddenly looking down at John Bunyan's legs he said, "Are you aware your horse has picked up a stone. Sir." I certainly felt John a little lame for the last few steps, but knowing no other cause I attributed it to the corn. Thanking the stranger, I dismounted, and remedied the matter, and this little roadside courtesy having served, as it were, for a mutual introduction, we continued our way in company, our conversation taking of course an atmospheric turn.

My companion wore a black coat, as I said, and a white neckcloth, the presumption therefore was, he must be a parson — a well-mounted parson. But then he might also be a medical man, or a man in mourning. At that moment, however, as if to relieve my doubts, the corner of a quire of post paper, stitched in a blank wrapper, protruded from his coat pocket.

I determined to make a bold stroke. "You'll lose your sermon, Sir," said I.

He put his hand hastily behind, and coloured slightly. A random shot, thought I, and yet a true one.

"One good turn deserves another," said I. "You saved my horse a lameness, I saved your flock the loss of a sermon."

"It may appear strange," said my new friend, "but I do not think the loss of a sermon such a serious deprivation to a congregation as your remark would seem to imply. I don't think it would be any harm, if half the sermons that are made were dropped (as mine was near being) on the road before ever they were preached, and never found, if it could only make people attend more attentively and devoutly to the beautiful and piety-breathing prayers of the Church."

"But what's to prevent them attending to the prayers and the sermon too?" said I.

"What's to prevent them! Why their own itching cars and unstable hearts — their love of novelty, their restless, craving curiosity. Could there be greater preventatives than these — can the poor human heart have greater enemies? How many congregations barely *endure* the service that they may hear the sermon? If the prayers only got the attention that the preacher does how many thousand times more good would they not do? One page of our beautiful liturgy, uttered in the spirit that God requires, and the Church directs, "with a lowly, penitent, and obedient heart," would fall like refreshing dews on the soul, and leave us in a holier, happier frame of mind than a hundred discourses. The best and most elaborately prepared sermon is to my mind a poor, bald, and meagre composition, compared with the touching beauty and true piety of a single sentence of the Litany."

"But, my good Sir," said I, "if the world gave such prominence to the prayers of the Church, there would be no encouragement for the popular preacher."

"The popular preacher!" repeated my companion with emphatic severity. "The preacher of the populace, do you mean — those ordained incarnations of clerical vanity and assumption, that too often go under that denomination — the men that are mighty with followers, who will be drawn to God's house not by the humility of their own hearts, but by the fluent tongues and sounding declamation of popular preachers? Why the idolatry of some congregations, who crowd the churches and chapels of *popular* preachers, is palpable and glaring as noon day — they set up an idol in a gown and band, and worship him."

"My dear Sir, you surely would not blame a man whose eloquence has the effect of drawing people to his church — the direction of your argument is to set a merit upon dullness."

"Pardon me. Sir, but this is an unfair inference. There is no man who has a higher respect for true eloquence that I have; but, without pausing to inquire whether the popular preaching of the day comes strictly under this designation, I would say that eloquence in a preacher, unless accompanied with humility of heart — unless it spring alone from the high and holy desire to impart and produce good — is nothing more than human egotism. The oratory of the platform and the pulpit is a different thing: the ambition to achieve a reputation for eloquence in the one is pardonable, in the other it is positively impious; and I'd sooner be the veriest dullard that ever set a congregation to sleep, than the man who worked for the reputation of a popular preacher; for the clergyman who works for his own *eclat* is unfaithful to his service."

I saw my fellow equestrian was what the world calls a High Churchman; and meanly as he thought of eloquence, possessed much of it naturally himself. I was anxious, too, to find out what sort of a composition that was in his coat-tail pocket: he was a censor of other people's sermons, I was curious to know what kind were his own. I thought I'd try and find out where he was going to preach.

"I think I have the pleasure," said I, "of speaking to the rector of —

"No where," said he with a smile, "not even a curate; I am, in fact, one of those supernumeraries which there will be, so long as parents make more parsons than the Church can find posts for."

"But you are going to preach now?"

"For Mr. Salter, at Iron Acton;[2] and as my road lies this way," said he, bowing and turning off to the right, "I wish you a good morning."

Mr Salter, thought I, when my companion was out of sight, is, I suppose, from home; I wonder does he give my friend this supernumerary a guinea for his sermon. An easy way of earning twenty-one shillings has your clergyman unattached; for one sermon will answer for twenty places if he would not, indeed, do as I saw a singular and very original-minded clergyman of Bristol once do. He was asked to preach in a neighbouring parish and I happened to be one of the congregation at the time, when to my surprise — and I will confess amusement also — he preached an article from the last *Quarterly*! He prefixed a text, it is true, and with this slight addition the essay became a sermon; and a very peculiar sermon it made, for it was all about spinning-jennies. But if a clergyman has to preach twice or three times a day, he may be pardoned for borrowing, begging, or stealing; for it is out of the question that he can write them all. If a man be sure of different congregations, then he may make the same sermon serve each, as the vicar of a large parish in Bristol used to do: he had two or three churches and a chaplaincy, and at each he used to preach, if possible, once on the Sabbath, so managing his sermons that by shifting them a little he made a few go far. He used, however, to make a mistake in his count sometimes, and it has more than once occurred that he has preached the same discourse twice in four Sundays to the same congregation; for on a particular occasion I recollect an old vestryman saying to me as we left the church, 'This is twice we have had death in the pot this month,'[3] alluding to the miracle of Elisha, on which the worthy old vicar had just preached. To prevent too close recurrences, and for the purpose of saving their own stock, some incumbents are in the habit of pressing into their pulpits every strange clergyman who happens to visit their parish, or anybody in the parish — a peculiarity my friend the Rev. James Taylor displays at Clifton, I am told, to such an extent that anybody who walks out with a white neckcloth and a black coat runs the risk of being asked, with a bland bow, to 'do duty next Sunday.' It is said that two chancery barristers and a doctor of music had the offer of his pulpit in this manner.

On entering Winterbourne I noticed a good many going into a barelooking Dissenting chapel, with 1829 in immense figures in front; so, as the inscription was in that part of the building where the denomination of the sect assembling there is usually placed, I concluded this was number 1829 of the two thousand varieties of dissent. Amongst those going in, I noticed several ambitiously-dressed young women, and the Taglionis[4] of their country beaux were certainly a cut above non-conformity.

It was originally my intention to have availed myself of an invitation which, the reader will probably recollect, I received from Winterbourne when I was making a round of the city parishes, offering me hospitality, &c., if I would visit their church. It is true the note was anonymous; but as the churchwarden was the most likely man to have sent it, I determined to ascertain who he was and call on him. There was a comfortable square-built house a little in from the road. "My good man," said I to one of a number who were going in the direction of a lane which led to the church, the bells of which I could hear, "whose house is that?"

"The parsonage," said the man.

"Where is the churchwarden's?"

'Twas at the other end of the village. I was very thirsty after my ride, and in immediate want of a draught of something or another; and as it was so far to go to the churchwarden's, I thought I'd try the rector.

"But," said my modesty, "you don't know the rector; and it is cool to ride up to a man's hall-door and ask for a drink, when you don't know him."

"Yet hospitality," answered my thirst, "was an old duty imposed upon the church and the clergy, and I do not see why the Reformation should do away with one of its best attributes. To be sure the refectory no longer exists, the dole is done away with, and the buttery hatch is only known to antiquarians; still that rectory does not look as if it were altogether unconscious of a barrel of home-brewed, and the gate is invitingly ajar; besides, what's the use of a Doctor of Civil Law if he does not practice civility. What do you think, John Bunyan?" said I, touching John with my heel, and John decided the point by walking straight up to the gate. A neatly-dressed young woman with a white handkerchief folded in her hand, and her Prayer-book placed formally in that, was coming down the walk from the house.

"Is the rector at home, my good girl," said I.

"No, Sir," said she, making a curtsey, and in a tone of civility, that quite emboldened me; "he's gone to church."

"I'm very thirsty," said I, "would you be kind enough to let me have a drink?"

"Certainly, Sir," said she with the utmost alacrity, as if she really felt a pleasure in compliance; "if you'll be good enough to come this way."

I fastened John Bunyan's bridle to some rustic paling and followed the young woman to the kitchen, resolving by the way that the rector was the model of a country clergyman to teach his servants such kind civility; for the domestic is ever the reflection of the master.

"Will you have cider, Sir?" said she.

"Thank you, my dear, I'm afraid of cider" said I, recollecting my rheumatism; "have you got any water?"

"Plenty of water, Sir, but you had better have beer; I have got the key," and she took it out other pocket. This placed the coping-stone on my good opinion: admirable man, thought I, Rector of Winterbourne, thou must be, not only to have such obliging domestics, but when you go to church to considerately think of leaving the key of the beer behind to refresh the wayfaring man. I had the beer, and told the young woman to tell Dr. Allen the 'Church-Goer' had called; but lest she may not have presented my compliments, I take this public opportunity to thank my yet perhaps all unconscious host for his hospitality. His domestics are well bred, and his beer well brewed.

The bell had not ceased ringing when I reached the church, and the sextoness civilly inquired if I wished to be shown into any particular pew. I mentioned the Church-warden's, and was immediately conducted into a square pew; but the gold-topped wand (gross, unpardonable neglect!) was wanting. In a minute or two that gentleman made his appearance in a pair of primrose gloves, and bowed to me very courteously, and I returned the salutation with all the grace in my power. Though it is still printed in my picture, I did not bring my great Prayer-book with me on this occasion. There were a number, however, both of these and Bibles in the pew, of which my neighbour politely handed me one; on opening it, however, I found it was French. I affect, it is true, a smattering of the tongue; yet as I wished to be able to say my prayers without the aid of a dictionary, I thought I'd try English, so I laid it down and took up another, which proved to be Italian. Italian I knew nothing at all about; so I tried a third, which came up Latin, and, by the way, was flanked with a Greek Bible. This must be a detachment from the Bodleian Library, said I to myself: one would think that the tower of Babel was in the neighbourhood, and that this was the family pew for it — a sort of Polyglott seat, as one might say, where a man might be accommodated in every language but the one he understands. By this time the churchwarden had noticed my embarrassment, and very kindly relieved it by borrowing an English Prayer-book for me from the next pew.

The tower and spire of Winterbourne are justly much admired for their lightness and elegance; and in other respects it is a fine and creditable specimen of an English parish church. It consists of a nave with north aisle, and chancel: the nave and north aisle have I perceive been lately rebuilt, and in a manner and by means that reflect credit on the parish and all who took part in the work.[5] I can recollect years ago visiting this church, when there were, if I mistake not, a row of cumbrous and unsightly semi-Doric, semi-anything columns dividing the nave from the north aisle: this portion of the edifice was found to be in a dangerous state, so it was rebuilt last spring, and in the renovations the early decorated style is chastely carried out, and the 'Dorics' replaced by piers and arches of a suitable character. The heads of the new windows of the north aisle are very pleasingly varied, and the timbers of the oak roofing being exposed to view, give a subdued and ecclesiastical character to the interior. I noticed a number of new free seats tastefully constructed, being open benches, finished off with the Gothic termination, and carved poppy head. I said that the repairs were creditable to the parish, and the alacrity with which a rate was granted, and that a large one, redounds to the honour of the parishioners, and is a strong proof of the friendly, I had almost said family, feeling which must exist between them and the rector. It is a fine and wholesome sign when men come forward freely at the call of the clergyman and churchwardens to tax themselves for the repairs and restorations of the church. The zealous interest which an incumbent takes in his parish, begets for the most part a corresponding zeal and interest in the people, and the earnest activity of the one is responded to by sympathy and support from the other. I liked, too, the appearance of the attendance at church — it had all the character of a truly English rural congregation: the hale and hearty Gloucestershire farmer, with his wife and fresh-coloured sons and daughters, and a very considerable number of the agricultural labourers forming the staple of a large congregation, there being also as many of the gentry as lived in the neighbourhood, though in respect of a resident aristocracy I believe the parish is but scantily furnished. All present joined cordially in the services, and the singing, though homely, was hearty, the children of the schools being lustily aided in it by the honest farmers and their wives.

When the Rector[6] entered the pulpit (on ascertaining it was he from my neighbour the churchwarden), I resolved from all I had previously seen (to say nothing of my reception at the Rectory) to be pleased, whatever kind of sermon he might happen to preach. However, he did not stand in need of my clemency. He took his text from 1 Kings, xviii., 21 — 'How long halt ye between two opinions? if the Lord be God, follow him; but if Baal, then follow him.' It was just the sermon for an English rural congregation, plain, practical, and frank; no firing over their heads with forced and fine things unsuited to simple apprehensions; no cumbering the mind with doctrinal difficulties. It was delivered to profit, and not to surprise or perplex, evidencing a double knowledge on the part of the preacher — a knowledge of his subject, and a knowledge of his hearers.

I perceived the offertory was observed, and with one or two exceptions (for I confess I did follow the collectors a little closely with my eye) cheerfully contributed to: two or three ladies, however, did turn away their heads as the little embroidered bag was held over their pew doors, as if Pope Gregory[7] (I believe that's the old gentleman who now presides in the Vatican) were stitched up in it.

After leaving the church the Rector passed me on the road with a buff bag in his hand filled (principally with coppers I should say from the sound): and I confess the cheerful penny offerings of that simple congregation sounded quite as gratefully in my ears, as the jingle of the rich man's guinea.

1. Thomas Paine, 1737-1809. Born in Norfolk, Paine rose to fame in America as author of *Common Sense* during the wars of independence, and later wrote *Rights of Man*, advocating civil and social rights for all.

2. John Salter (1828). Rural Dean.

3. 2 Kings 4, 40.

4. Taglioni. A kind of overcoat in use in the first half of the nineteenth century. Named after a family of ballet dancers in the early nineteenth century.

5. The north aisle and nave were rebuilt in an arcade of four bays in 1843.

6. William B. Allen (1835).

7. Gregory XVI 1831-46.

9 November 1844

Yatton

The Editor of the *Bristol Times* has made it a kind of agreement with me, whether I travel on John Bunyan's back, my own feet, or by a railroad, that the 'counterfeit resemblance' of my 'matchless steed' shall in any and every case surmount the column, to give a character, as he calls it, to my papers. This will account for my equestrian appearance being kept up, though I paid my visit, in the present instance, to Yatton on the 'permanent way' of the Bristol and Exeter line. My reasons for departing from my usual mode of pilgrimage were various: my first was, that John was unable to travel — I suppose, loving reader, you will not require another.

"A second-class ticket for Yatton," said I to a young man who was stamping away in the office; but the young man, either not heeding or hearing my request, continued to stamp away with unabated energy, until thinking he might not have marked my words I repeated them, and received in return a rebuke for my hasty tendencies. "You must have patience, Sir," said he, "I have been endeavouring to cultivate that virtue all my life, my good youth," was my reply.

"Yatton," cried the green-clad conductor, throwing open the door of a carriage so marked. "Who's for Yatton?"

"I am," said I, stepping in and taking my seat with a limited family party, a large hand-basket containing something savoury, and a railroad labourer. It is surprising how instinctively and immediately, when thrown within a small compass with any number of persons, one will commence speculating on the quality, degree, and destination of each as if it could possibly be a matter of interest or importance to him who or what they were, by whom he chanced to sit for an hour or so in a railroad carriage or a stage-coach. It was upon this principle, I suppose, that I began immediately wearying myself with conjectures as to whether the family party meant to have a family picnic, or were carrying a ready-cooked dinner to some country acquaintance: nay more, I speculated on the probability of the object in the interior of the basket, which so excited my olfactory sympathies, being a roast fowl, or duck subject to a similar process of cookery. I thought I'd ascertain the point "The smell of your roast duck," said I to the head of the family party, (a mechanical looking sort of man) "almost gives me an appetite for a second breakfast," and I pointed at the same time to the basket.

"'Tisn't a duck," said the man.

"Then it is a —"

"Goose," added he, before I could finish my sentence.

I looked at him to see if he meant this literally, or as an equivoque. He was not the cut of one to perpetrate a pun; yet there was something in the way he said it to determine me to make no further attempts to cultivate an acquaintance with the family party; I therefore kept my opinions to myself until we reached the Yatton station, when on descending from the carriage I discovered that my friend, the navigator, (as the public are pleased, through some curious fancy, to call those rough landsmen who cut out railway lines,) had alighted also.

I am a very indifferent judge of distances, but I should think it is about half-a-mile or so from the station to Yatton; so seeing my neighbour to all appearances bound on the same destination, I fell into company and conversation with him. He had on a coarse white flannel blouse and a cap of dressed sheepskin, and in other respects, so far as dress was concerned, differed little from his race, but that his laced boots were not quite as heavy as usual, and were well blackened: he was of a far more intelligent, and I had almost said delicate, countenance than the generality of his rough tribe; for he really had a soft pair of hazel eyes and silken lashes that a lady might envy; and I soon found out that he was, in a moral sense also, a striking exception to the usually besotted and brutalized beings which railroad enterprise has called into a class existence throughout the country. From the sum which he said he earned, over 14s. a week, I conjectured he was engaged in that description of work which required rather more skill than the usual pick-axe and shovel slavery. He said he was from the part of the country where we then were, but had been working up towards Swindon for some time, and was then coming down to see his mother. I have always taken an interest in this railroad race, which an iron age has produced; I have taken an interest in them for their own sakes, and the sake of society; for while I deplored their moral and religious degradation, I could not help thinking of the dangerous elements and materials of disturbance which British wealth and British speculation were originating over this fair land, to make, perhaps, future and fearful levies for the anarchist and revolutionist when, or even before, the completion of our railroad projects left them comparatively unemployed.

Pleased to find amongst a class which before I thought the most insensible and embruted body in Great Britain, one who retained his good honest English and Church of England feelings amongst such associates and sad examples around him, we continued to walk together until near Yatton, when my companion, wishing me a good morning, turned up a bye road which he said led to his mother's cottage. He told me he had not seen her for twelve months, and I can easily contemplate the pleasure of that reunion to both.

On entering the church-yard, which I did over a wooden stile, from the village, I found, as one generally does in a country parish, a number of rustics loitering about. There was one old fellow, however, seated by the base of the ancient cross, and at the moment engaged in winding up or setting his watch by the village oracle, to whom I applied myself, as being the most conversible son of the soil there.

"Fine morning, measter," said he on seeing me approach; "what be the time by thee?" and he pointed to the bunch of seals which descended from my fob. I told him.

"Dost thee keep rayle-rowad time?" was his next inquiry.

I answered in the negative.

"Ha," said he, with apparent satisfaction, "I be delighted that there's be one as don't go by those run-away ingines. All the village are a-going mad, shoving on their watches ten minutes to be by the rayle, as they say."[1]

Here's an old 'worshipper of the rust of antiquity,' thought I — one of the fossil remains of the real rustic, who distrusts or despises everything new. I'll be bound he'd sooner take three hours and travel in his own market-cart to Bristol, than be indebted to Brunel or the 'rayle,' as he calls it, for taking him there in one-sixth the time.

I asked him the name of his clergyman.

"Our parson?" repeated he, as if he knew him better by that title, "Mr. Clarke;[2] and as worthy a man as ever wore a gown."

"Charitable, I suppose?"

"If he has an enemy I'll eat un," said the rustic, closing his watch in its outer case, and dropping the old-fashioned affair into his fob; "if a man ben't a favourite who visits and helps the poor, edicates their children, and knows and advises all his neighbours, why it would be hard to please us country volk."

"But you have said nothing about his preaching: how do you like him in the pulpit?"

My neighbour scratched his head, and seemed rather brought to a pause by the question. "Whoy," said he, at length, "if thee ask me what kind of a preacher he be, I like a loud preacher — one to make the old church ring agin, like Parson B., a fine speaker that knocks the dust out of our hearts and the ould velvet cushion. Mr. Clarke is a good preacher for some; but I am old and getting hard o' hearing; and he goes so fast I can't always understand him, as it were, you see."

"Well," said I, "I shall hear him today, and judge for myself. This is a fine old church of yours; do you know when it was built?"

"I can't say, measter," said he; "I am no scholard, or learned in auncient things; but I dare say he is a thousand, or maybe five hundred year old."

Well, thought I, that is as near as some antiquarians go in their researches.

"There are some ould effigies of a great family of the Newtons, that lived once in these parts," continued my informant, growing communicative; "one is a Jidge, and lies on his back on a painted tombstone, with a fine lady by his side, and his two dogs at his feet; I suppose they were buried with him. But there's the small bell," said he, rising, "and the parson does not like us to be late in church."

The first thing that struck me on entering the south porch was a board conspicuously hung up, on which were the words — 'TAKE OFF YOUR PATTENS,' painted in plain letters, a very necessary injunction in a rural parish, considering the dreadful clatter the iron-shod damsels sometimes make.

All the natives looked at me, but nobody offered me a seat, so I helped myself to the first I saw, and which I occupied in conjunction with an old ploughman and a boy in an ambitious livery coat. A stranger in a retired rural church, especially if he happen to wear spectacles and broadcloth, is an event too remarkable in the annals of the parish to be lightly overlooked, and my friends around me stared at the new comer as if they would have said, "I wonder who you are, and where you come from, and what brings you here." A man who was standing at the intersections of the transepts, nave, and chancel, and pulling away at the bell-rope, presenting rather a prominent figure in the scene, appeared indeed as if he would almost ask the question; even the school children, who, headed by the master carrying a music-book in his hand, entered in long file through the south door of the chancel, and who came pat, pat, clatter in their wooden shoes up the aisle, immediately descried the stranger, and looked over their snub noses at me as if I had two heads. Well, thought I, it would seem as if Yatton was not often favoured with the visits of an illustrious stranger; I must get out of the way as soon as possible after the service, lest the church-wardens be for waiting on me with a deputation to present an address.

As soon as the clergyman entered the reading-desk, however, the people turned their eyes from me to their prayer books. The service had hardly commenced when I saw the force of my rustic friend's remark in the churchyard. There is an old joke of an Oxford spark saying he would give any man the Creed and beat him before he came to the end of the Litany. I really believe from the rate at which he read, that the incumbent of Yatton might do this with ease: I attempted to keep up with him, but finding the pace impossible I closed my book, and listened with resignation. Now I hope no man is above mending a bad fashion, and from the high character I have heard of the incumbent of Yatton, I sincerely hope and am sure he will not take it amiss of me when I recommend him to read slower. I do not for a moment think he sets a subordinate value on the prayers, or that he thinks the time devoted to their recital thrown away; but I assure him that too rapid a mode of 'getting through the service' on the part of the clergyman is calculated to produce indifference on the part of the people, who are already too much inclined to contract a kind of lax and gabbing habit of making the responses. I cannot bear to hear the beautiful prayers of the church, which so abound in fervent appeals, in deep devotional and penitential expressions, and awful epithets, being skipped through by clergyman and congregation, as if they were performing a mere daily task, the primary object of which was expedition.

While I am in my captious mood I shall endeavour to dispose of all my fault-finding at once: I would, therefore, recommend the minister to rebuke his flock for a practice, which they have in common with most rural congregations, namely of turning their backs to the clergyman when the *Te Deum* and *Jubilate* are being performed and the psalms sung, leaning deliberately on their elbows, and looking up at the organ-loft as if they were listening to the music in front of a fair booth, instead of 'singing to the praise and glory of God.' The organ is a large,[3] and for a country church, an elaborate instrument. It was once surmounted by three allegorical and musical figures, comprising King David, with gilt harp strings and knee buckles, and two Vicars Choral of Honduras mahogany, whom he is in the act of accompanying; but these have of late, like Darius, 'fallen from their high estate,' and occupy lower posts full in front of the gallery.

The text was a short and comprehensive one — 'The wages of sin is death.' The same fault that I find with him in the reading-desk applied to the preacher's manner in the pulpit. His delivery was rapid, irregular, and unequal; and, owing to these causes nothing, but the most careful attention could enable me to comprehend a sermon which was in itself simple, solemn, and unaffected: preached with more deliberation the discourse would have been everything one could wish — a good plain country-church sermon, suited to the education and condition of his audience.

But after all what a man is or does in the pulpit is as nothing comparatively with what he is and does in his parish: and I am told that morning, evening, and mid-day, the incumbent of Yatton may be seen issuing from the picturesque little Gothic Rectory on the south-east side of the churchyard on his errands of instruction, his rounds of visitation, and charity. It is these duties that contribute more than your set Sunday sermons to make a parish moral, and the people of wholesome and healthy habits. The country parson that talks by the ploughman and reaper in the field, and the labourer in the homestead, may do more good than Massillon[4] could with all his eloquence.

Yatton is amongst the best of the many beautiful churches that abound in this part of Somersetshire. It is, I believe what is sometimes called a quarter-cathedral, and is a prebend to Wells: it is cruciform in its design, with a square tower springing up at the intersection of the aisles: the south porch is a good specimen, and the west end would reward an attentive examination, if it were not that the eye is offended with the quantity of sheep's soil with which the main though closed entrance is, as one might say, hermetically sealed. I am not able to speak as to the date of the church, which is dedicated to St. Mary, but I believe the ancient family of de Wick were, if not the founders, at least eminent benefactors. There are two old monuments in the north transept, recessed in the wall, which are supposed to belong to this family: not far from these is another very splendid altar tomb of white marble belonging to and bearing a recumbent figure of Judge Newton,[5] with another of his lady. There are other monuments, but I had not time to examine them. The congregation, which is a good one, is almost wholly composed of farmers and agricultural labourers.

1. Bristol local time was ten minutes nineteen seconds after London time.

2. D.M. Clerk (1832).

3. The organ, built for Bath Abbey, was bought from the Bishop's Palace at Wells in 1842.

4. Jean Baptiste Massillon, 1663-1742. French Divine and celebrated court preacher.

5. There are four tombs; Sir Richard Newton (d.1448); the Judge, Sir John Newton (d.1488); their wives. They lived at Court de Wick in Yatton.

23 November 1844
Henbury

Southey, in the Life of the author of the Pilgrim's Progress,[1] says, that John Bunyan at one time took great delight in bell-ringing. My horse would seem to have inherited a taste for the same tintinabular melody from his illustrious namesake, for when we reached the Down we found the echo of all Bristol's bells there before us; and the swell of sweet sounds, borne on the breeze from twenty towers, swept by us in a full flood-tide of magnificent music. John pricked up what remains of his ears, and turning his head towards Bristol, stood still and listened with a look as intent and intelligent as a horse could assume: his little nostrils dilated, his eyes expanded, and he seemed as if he would drink in the sonorous air at every sense, like the wild ass of the desert. I am not surprised at even a quadruped's appreciation of the sublime and beautiful on this occasion, so great and resistless was the body of sound, so powerful as it passed, mingling with the neighbouring peals of Westbury, that it appeared as if nothing could have arrested its course until it dispersed over the broad waters of the Severn.

The view from Henbury Hill gives a man some idea of the manner in which the suburban citizens of Bristol live. I could not help rising on my stirrups, and taking a survey of the surrounding scenery and the neat, and even elegant, villas that peeped out from amongst the little plantations on all sides, reminding one of roast beef and real comfort, of the number of families preparing for Church, and the number of joints being then got ready for the spit against their return. I could almost venture to tell the programme of the day's proceedings within each of those pretty free-stone residences — two services attended, an early dinner eaten, and an English Sabbath wound up with closed window curtains and candles, and Handel and hyson[2] in the drawing-room.

Having given John Bunyan's bridle to the ostler at the *Salutation*, and turned from the stable-yard, I felt for the first time in my life a certain degree of diffidence in approaching an English parish church. There is nothing in a state of nature there: everything about the village is trained to look exclusive and aristocratic — the walks are tended and the hedges trimmed to the highest point of precision. In summer the flowers seem to grow formal, and the very birds moved about from twig to twig, and chirped to each other, with distant propriety. Even the same air of extreme politeness appeared to pervade the parishioners in death: their burying ground was laid out for the best society,

and the head stones might have been arranged by a Master of Ceremonies, so punctilious was their juxtaposition.

This overpowering gentility appalled me. I should not have ventured to laugh loud in the village, lest I might awaken aristocratic echoes, and without a previous introduction I should not have dared to ask the first man I met, the road.

I had been in the habit of late, when I visited a country church, of helping myself to a pew when the sextoness was not at hand. 'This will not do at Henbury, Mr. Church-Goer,' said I; 'you are no longer amongst bumpkins, you must not take these liberties here — every pew is like a preserve: you must not put your hand on the first door you meet, for if this green cloth lining, these soft cushions, these rich carpets, these mohair hassocks, these morocco-bound, gilt-edged Prayer Books and Bibles lying about, be not sufficient to protect the seat from rash intrusion, you must be very dull or very daring indeed.'

Meditating these things I stood in dread and doubt by the porch, looking at the tall thin cypress trees which stood like 'melancholy mourners o'er the dead,' and yet was afraid to enter. 'Tis true I might have taken my place amongst the poor, as I had often done before, and been under an obligation to no one; but to tell you the truth I am not fond of this. Not that I object to sit with my fellow-creature because he or she happens to be less fortunate than I have been; but I often find when a man in a sound suit of broadcloth sits on the same bench with the poor in a parish church, the people around, who never think of previously offering him a pew, are only too ready to invent an unworthy motive for him, and attribute the act to 'the pride that apes humility,' the most contemptible pride of all in my opinion. I therefore, determined if possible to procure a scat in some pew sooner than draw people's attention from their prayers, which is another effect that I find a man in fine clothes, sitting on a free form, has upon some congregations. Twice I crossed the threshold, and twice I essayed to catch the sextoness's eye, but one genteel family after another entering attracted her attention each time, and I retreated once more to the churchyard awed by the exclusive air of all I witnessed within, and the sounds of a quick succession of carriage steps being let down outside. 'Twas after my second retreat, and while I drew timidly aside to allow more fresh and favoured visitors to pass, that a gentleman walked by me; as he reached the porch, however, he turned round, and after looking at me for a moment advanced, and in the civilest and politest manner possible said he should be very happy if I would take a place in his pew. I thanked him, accepted his offer, and was in another moment installed in a good seat near the pulpit.

Here I have been doing Henbury all this time a great injustice, thought I as soon as I was seated: in the plenitude of my silly nervousness I have been making for myself a bugbear out of its gentility, forgetting that the essence of true gentility is civility. I have at this moment no idea who my unknown and courteous friend may be; but I take this opportunity of publicly, as I did privately, thanking him for his attention.

For so highly respectable a parish as Henbury is, I must say the parts of the service allotted to the congregation are coldly performed. They would lead one really to conclude they had no 'belief', for during the Communion Service they left the Creed altogether to the Clergyman, and he repeated it in so low a tone that it was quite impossible from where I was to hear him, though the clerk, I confess, had voice enough for himself, priest, and people. Then for singing, the ladies for the most part, at least as far as I could see, seemed too genteel to do that for themselves, thinking it quite enough to pay an organist, and give a number of charity boys an annual coat (with buttons) of grey with trousers to match, to do that business for them. Some years ago I recollect loitering into the Church of St. Roch, at Paris, on a week-day morning, and seeing an old woman seated reading by a row of iron railings that cut off a small side chauntry from the body of the church, and on which were stuck a number of little lighted bees-wax tapers: I was thinking what it could mean, when a young lady entered, and walking up to the crone gave her a coin, whispered something into her ear, and walked off, upon which the old woman took another taper out of a little box by her side, lit it, and placed it with the rest. This explained the matter: the young lady had not time or inclination to say her prayers, and she deputed the old woman who made a livelihood by praying all the livelong day for ladies who were too proud or too idle to pray for themselves. There is not one of the fair flock who kept their mouths closed during the singing of the Psalms at Henbury on Sunday, who would not think the pretty Parisian Papist a great fool for her pains, in supposing that Heaven would be satisfied with her orisons second-hand; but after all, I do not see the great difference it

makes whether you are vicariously prayed for or sung for — whether you give
an old woman a half-franc to do that for which you ought to do for yourself, or
fancy you do enough for a solemn part of the service when you clothe a dozen
charity children in rough cloth and rows of buttons for singing, and keep your
mouth shut yourself. And the curious — I had almost said provoking — part
of it generally is, that there is hardly one of those young ladies who are silent
in church, who will not, in their own drawing-rooms at home, and before their
own pianofortes, sing Handel and Mozart's music for you by the hour, and
dash through 'Giorno d'orrore,' a Pastorello from Benedict, or the last Italian
air, with a determination most magnanimous. Oh, that those pretty warblers
would only consider how much sweeter their soft tones would sound in the
old parish church than by one even of Clementi's best instruments at home;
they can have no idea how harmoniously their beautiful voices would blend
with the old organ and those of the charity children, in a simple psalm under
the solemn cope of the ancient nave, or they would not keep their pretty lips
so inactively together, or their little tongues so mute within the closed ivory
barrier of their white teeth. I have been to oratorios and concerts many in my
day, for in early life I was fond of those things, and I still play a little on the
flute every evening; but never have I heard anything please me or reach my
heart with half the touching beauty of the 137th Psalm, when sung one summer
Sabbath morning by a number of sweet female voices in the little rustic church
of Madley, Salop. Whether it was my particular frame of mind, the time, the
season, or the association, I cannot say; but I shall never forget the touching
tenderness with which the tones of their voices then fell upon my ear in the
beautiful lines —

> 'O Salem, our once happy seat,
>   When I of thee forgetful prove.'

So it seemed to me, for the moment, did the captive daughters of Judah
mourn their exile, and sing when far from, yet yearning after, their own beloved and beautiful Zion.

This requires little musical learning from young ladies: all it wants are willing hearts and cheerful voices: in fact, I am no advocate for elaborate displays
in parish churches as a custom; when the congregation are obliged to leave all
the work to the organ loft. The more simple the singing, so that man, woman,
and child may join with heart and voice, the better.

The fair portion, however, of the congregation seemed to be the least inclined to open their lips or exert their lungs, for many of the other sex did
both, and with good will; and one hearty old gentleman whom I noticed near
the reading-desk, whose years exceeded mine in number as his hair did mine
in whiteness, sung away out of a large lettered Prayer-book, with an old English
and orthodox energy quite refreshing. He appeared to me the Sir Roger de

Coverley[3] of the parish: he had a word of affability and inquiry for everyone, and everyone had a bow of respect and deference for him. How far the following patches of the character of Sir Roger may be applicable to the estimable person to whom I allude, I leave to the ingenuity of the reader to find out: 'As Sir Roger is landlord to the whole congregation, he keeps them in very good order, and will suffer nobody to sleep in it besides himself; for if by chance he has been surprised in a short nap at sermon, upon recovering out of it he stands up and looks about him, and if he sees anybody else nodding, either wakes them himself, or sends his servant to them. Several other of the old knight's peculiarities break out upon these occasions. Sometimes he will be lengthening out a verse in the singing-psalms half a minute after the rest of the congregation have done with it; sometimes when he is pleased with the matter of his devotion, he pronounces 'Amen' three or four times to the same prayer, and sometimes stands up when everybody else is upon their knees, to count the congregation, or see if any of his tenants are missing. As soon as the sermon is finished, nobody presumes to stir until Sir Roger is gone out of the church. The knight walks down from his seat in the chancel between a double row of his tenants, that stand bowing to him on each side: and every now and then inquires how such a one's wife, or mother, or son, or father do, whom he does not see at church; which is understood as a secret reprimand to the person that is absent.'

I can well recollect the first time I visited Henbury Church on a fine summer's evening: it was with a friend, a stranger, to whom I wished to show the neighbourhood. The little village,[4] the surrounding country seats, the brook, the bridge, the old church, with its low flat tower, the picturesque gothic school close by — upon all the soft air of peace, comfort, and repose seemed to rest, reminding one of what I think Mary Howitt has said,[5] that no other country in the world has a parallel for an English village. We crossed the pretty churchyard with its cypresses, and looking as quiet in its 'russet mantle clad,' as if none but those who 'slept in the Lord' slept there, to the sextoness's cottage, to solicit permission to see the interior of the church. The good woman took down the key, and throwing her bonnet loosely on her head, civilly complied with our request. The 'dim religious light' through the painted glass, fell with its varied but subdued hues on the little chancel, sculptured altar screen, carpet, and communion cloth, while a parting ray or two from the setting sun, glancing obliquely through the more western windows, lingered on one or two of the many white marble tablets that around recorded the worth of those who had gone, and the affectionate recollection of those who remained behind. A silent church is at all times a peculiarly solemn scene, but Henbury church seemed to me on this evening particularly so: all three indeed, even the sextoness, appeared to feel I thought the 'influence' of the hour and place, and we walked noiselessly about, as if instinctively understanding each other's impressions and unwilling to disturb either them or the holy quiet of 'God's House' with the fall of our footsteps, or the sound of our own voices. The fretted roof, the long drawn aisle, the pointed arch, and the lofty column of the cathedral, have all their awe-creating power; but the soft repose of this beautiful village church was of a different character, and had a more soothing and almost as solemn an effect, which was not at all diminished but rather enhanced by the pretty evensong of the robin and green linnet without. And yet, in point of architectural proportions or detail, Henbury has nothing to boast of: the columns and arches that separate the nave from the north and south aisles (which had been beautifully, and I believe newly ceiled with oak), are of a clumsy and incongruous character, and the main chancel does not lie in a straight line with the rest of the church: but the refinement and liberality of the parishioners, evidenced in every part of the building, hide all original defects; all that good taste and munificence could do has been done by the neighbouring gentry, and the sextoness pointed out one or two stained windows which had been brought from Italy as presents by wealthy parishioners. All this does credit to the place and the people: pride becomes a virtue when the beauty and adornment of the parish church is its object.

The charities and schools connected with the parish are excellently managed and liberally supported; and I have heard that much is done by the rich to alleviate the condition of their less fortunate fellow-parishioners.

I have brought the only charge I had to bring against the congregation: that is a want of *heartiness* in the performance of their part of the service; in other respects, for so large a number, I never saw a better ordered or more attentive congregation in my life.

The sermon was a fair specimen of mediocrity,[6] delivered in a tiresome and monotonous tone: there was nothing remarkable one way or the other about it. I have tried to recollect the text, but have forgotten both that and the matter.

I have received the following letter this week. It is the second invitation that has reached me from the same quarter, from which it would appear that the good people of Thombury are upon *thorns* about me. The writer has to apologise to the readers of the *Bristol Times* for two things — first, for seducing me into a villainous pun (a practice I am not addicted to generally), and secondly, for using so much Latin, while he might find plenty of English to suit his purpose: one of his years ought to be above such weakness:

TO THE EDITOR OF THE BRISTOL TIMES

Your occasional correspondent 'The Church-Goer' envelops himself with so thick a mist, as to the spot where he may be found, that I cannot ascertain where the piece of intelligence which I wish to convey to him should be addressed; for, notwithstanding the hints he drops the public of the notable insignia of 'a snuff-coloured coat,' 'a pair of spectacles,' and 'a large Bible,' still I cannot by these innuendos guess the No. and street of his habitation. I, therefore, must throw myself on your goodnatured readiness in obliging the public by inserting in your favourite columns the communications to him that otherwise would waste 'their sweetness on the desert air.' As you are the known happy medium for conveying to him 'pheasants and venison,' I am confident you will not hesitate to communicate to him a piece of intelligence equally interesting to himself and society at large, inasmuch as it regards the moral and religious welfare of the reading and reflecting public. Reckoning on the familiar habits he seems to be on with you, of 'being accommodated with the gift of a sheet of paper,' 'the loan of a pen,' and 'room at your desk in the office,' I am convinced you will readily comply with my request. The purpose of this petition is, that he will forthwith avail himself of the assistance of his good friend John Bunyan, and gratify a longing and expectant parish with his presence, as it will extend his ride out by a little more than a mile beyond the place where he has promised to partake of 'eggs and bacon, after hearing the sapient discourse of the Rev. Divine at *Alveston*.' When he is told that the neighbouring parish has been for some time on the tiptoe of impatience for his arrival, he will not fail to gratify so reasonable a desire. And as by the means of his friend John, the radii of his visiting circle are so much extended, he can with ease perform the journey, the inspection of the fine old church and castle of Thornbury, will amply repay the trouble of enquiry; and when he has been gratified by hearing the Vicar's sermon, and gained all the antiquarian secrets of the Castle, formerly belonging to the unhappy wight,[7] whose head the cruel king ordered to be chopped off, he will of course honour one of the many candidates for the favour with his presence at dinner. Should not the high and mighty Vicar give the invite, there is the mayor of the borough who once called himself a Quaker, but now attends his church duly every Sunday; he will most hospitably entertain him. As he has only one gala day in the year officially, 'The Church-Goer' must not expect any great splendour, for as he only sports 'Coffee, toast and butter on Christmas day in the morning,' he will not find

'Prætextam, et latum clavum, prunæque batillum.'

However, should these expectations fail, I'll take care to wait for him and Johnny Bunyan at the Ship at Alveston, where, as you have declared you don't like 'cold water or horse ponds,' we'll be snug and enjoy ourselves.

'Animæ quales neque candidiores.'

Yours truly,
ECCLESIAE AMICUS.

Thornbury, Nov. 11th, 1844.

I'll dine with you upon one condition — that you promise not to quote a single line of Latin during dinner.

1. Robert Southey, 1774-1843. Poet Laureate 1813-43. Southey wrote a life of John Bunyan in 1830 for a new edition of Pilgrims Progress.
2. Hyson — a Chinese green tea.
3. Sir Roger de Coverley was the literary ideal of the eighteenth-century squire created for the Spectator by Joseph Addison and Sir Richard Steele.
4. Blaise Hamlet, created in the picturesque style by John Nash for John Scandrett Harford in 1810.
5. Mary Howitt, 1799-1888. A prodigious writer throughout her long life. Leech must have been referring to her earlier works which included *Sketches of Natural History*, (1834); *Wood Leighton, or a year in the Country*, (1836); *Birds and Flowers and other Country Things*, (1838) and *Sowing or Reaping and what will come of it*, (1841).
6. Incumbent: H.H. Way (1830).
7. Edward Stafford, Duke of Buckingham, 1478-1521, executed by Henry the VIII. It was Edward Stafford who caused Thornbury Castle to be built.

30 November 1844
Stapleton

Knowledge is a most Protean thing: it is to be met with under so many shapes and such various forms, that one ought to pass neither object nor individual indifferently by, lest the desired quality be contained in one or the other. For my part I think I have picked up more information by the roadside than in books. Riding or walking, on foot and on horseback, what all affect to desire, and many sincerely seek after, may be encountered day and night, in town and country.

Fully impressed with this conviction, I never hear the approaching sound of horse's feet in my rear that I do not instantly set about preparing an appropriate salutation, wherewith to accost the rider the moment he overtakes me, in the hope of detaining him to be my companion, for a time at least on the way; and I seldom meet a foot-passenger going the same direction as myself, without wishing it were the fashion to ride double, that by giving him a seat on John's croup I might have the benefit of his society for a mile or two. Indeed I have upon some occasions lately — more in the sociability than gallantry of my nature, I confess — meditated mounting a pillion for the temporary accommodation of the fair country pedestrians, whom, Prayer Book in hand, I often meet in my rural rides — bound for the same destination, the same old parish church as myself. But this is an age of scandal and levity, when an elderly gentleman cannot indulge in a common wayside courtesy, without being subject to have his motives and movements both misconstrued. This sneering, innuendo, imputation-passing custom is a gross tyranny — it terrifies a man from following the impulses of his better nature, and frightens him from the performance of roadside civilities as pure and disinterested, as innocent, as anything can be. For instance, what prevents me, the proprietor of a strong and steady nag, purchasing a pillion, and offering the first young, old, or middle-aged woman whom I met a seat for a mile or two, or in fact for as far as she happened to be going my way, on the soft cushion balanced so comfortably behind me? What prevents me, I say, doing this, and having a pleasant companion, and a little agreeable conversation, instead of a lonely ride in monastic solitude along the uninteresting road, as I often have? A scandalous and a remark-making age. If anyone met me jogging along on John with an honest countrywoman posed on a pillion behind me, and both of us chatting to our mutual entertainment, it may be edification, would my grey hairs or my sober port, think you, protect me from impertinent observation and rude reflections? No, no. The Church would be scandalized through the Church-Goer: I'd be made the subject of caustic conversation amongst my friends, and perhaps of a sly paragraph in the newspapers. And yet what harm is there in it. It is true that anyone seated behind, to keep herself steady and balanced, must grasp him who rode before rather tightly round the waist: but 'evil to him who evil inferred' from the fact of a rustic arm — be the same plump or lean — passed for so innocent a purpose round my snuff-coloured coat. It was only last Sunday week, as I rode to Henbury, that a gentleman's servant drove by me in a gig, and suddenly pulling up a few hundred yards in front, invited a decent looking young woman, who was going to church, to a seat beside him, which she accepted without the slightest hesitation or embarrassment, but simply I could see as a natural roadside courtesy. Why have I not a pillion, said I, to make a tender of the same civilities, and be thanked in the same way? Had John Bunyan the conversational powers of Baalam's beast,[1] he might have observed in reply, "Because you are afraid." And he'd be right. I'd start a pillion tomorrow if it were not for the scandalizing propensities of the age. It would be only an act of common gratitude if I did so. John was a gift from a number of good-hearted ladies to me: there was a small balance in hand after his purchase, and if I expended that in a pillion for them, it would still be an inadequate return for their kindness.

In my present ride to Stapleton, however, I was not in want of company. Near Ashley Road I heard the sharp trot of a horse behind me; and as the rider came up with me I was ready with my salutation, and wished him "a good morning, and a pleasant journey." "Thank you," said my new friend who had short cut whiskers and a white neckcloth, a half serious half secular air, and spoke in a formal and rather nasal twang, "I can hardly be said to be going on a journey, if it may not be said to be a journey of grace," and he added, by way of supplement, something between a groan and a sigh.

"Oh, indeed!" said I, knowing not what else to say; but on perceiving that my companion was not very expeditious in renewing the conversation, I added, after a slight pause, "Then I have the pleasure (though, from his appearance, I candidly confess I hoped I had not,) of addressing a clergyman?" "No," said he, looking up as though he would thank Heaven for a happy exemption; "I preach the Gospel."

Humph, thought I, that leaves anything but a flattering converse to the poor clergy; but I determined to let it pass, for I dislike argument of all kinds, and particularly on religious subjects. It is a profitless waste of mental strength, in my opinion; and so disinclined am I to all dialectics, that I make it a point never to dispute a matter with a man: if he talk nonsense I have my own notion of it, but I leave him in undisturbed possession of his.

Now my new equestrian neighbour looked as though he was sharp set for controversy, armed on all sides like Lucian's[2] Philosopher or a hedgehog with 'thorny points of doctrine,' prickly as one might say, with texts of scripture — with quotations innumerable at his finger ends, ready at hand to be pushed forward at every move of the game of argumentation, with all the practised adroitness of a draft-player. Schismatics are always arguing with each other on election, perfection, predestination, etc., and they show an expertness — I will not say a reverence — in the use of scripture, which is quite surprising. Set two tailors or shoemakers of adverse sects down together at a trial of skill, and though both should be bunglers at their trade, they'll astonish you by their dexterity as disputants: Mr. Stanton[3] or his French antagonist never moved their pawns, knights and kings about on the chess-board with more ingenuity than these will check-mate each his neighbour in turn with texts of scripture. Confront two opposite schismatics and their feathers are up in one moment, and the next they are closed in deadly dispute. I used the word 'deadly' figuratively, but I almost might employ the term in a literal sense also: for I recollect some years ago dining with a leading non-conformist, where I was, I believe, the only churchman present, and as I said little or nothing, the company generally were not aware of my creed, and were in fact barely cognizant of my presence. There were more than one Dissenting minister at table, and the conversation was altogether of a polemical — they would call it of a religious — character. One of the ministers — a little sharp-set dogmatic disputatious-looking man — had, I could collect, a pamphlet war with another dissenting teacher of a different sect some time before: to this frequent reference was made, and the little man 'fought all his battles o'er again with extreme ardour and vollubility for the company until at length, rising by degrees in the exultant warmth of his narration, he exclaimed with a tone of real triumph, and half-affected regret, — "But it was my pamphlet that did it: he never got over that, poor man! I believe it killed him, for he died soon after!" Here was sectarian charity doubly illustrated; here was one man dying from the effects of mortified pride and bitterness, and the other, though affecting to deplore, exulting in the death as an evidence of his own triumph. For my part, I have no genius to religious controversy; and I cannot conceive how people will go on hair-splitting, and accumulating volumes, and hating and abusing each other about thorny points of doctrine amongst dissenters, and in the church about little points of discipline, as they do. People that do this can have minds for nothing more enlarged: while they fritter away their attention on little things, they have no conception of the grandeur of the Christian religion.

Putting my companion down for one of those narrow-minded controversialists ever ready and ever eager to do battle for any and every minute point of doctrine, I determined to shake him off as soon as possible, preferring my own thoughts to such a companion, for he seemed one of those gloomy, sullen faced individuals who'd scowl a fine morning out of countenance, and rebuke the birds for singing, and the very flowers for growing.

My companion, however, perceiving I had no inclination to renew the colloquy, perversely determined to do so himself, for after a preliminary groan or two he said, taking up the thread of our former conversation, "No; remembering the fourth commandment, I should not be found doing no manner of work; if I had not a call to preach the Gospel as the Scriptures says. Wo is me if I preach not the Gospel."

I said I concluded that he was a Dissenting Minister, but he intimated that he was not exactly a minister, but I think he said one of the 'Itinerant Brethren,' a sort of lay preacher, one of a class who make incursions from Bristol in hundreds every Sunday morning to the surrounding villages, where in dissenting chapels and hired rooms they sermonize, much to their own gratification, and they doubtless think the edification of those who hear them, to poor people who are too good to go to their parish church. My friend was bound for the neighbourhood of Frenchay, and had paid I suppose the hire of a horse that he might have the pleasure of launching a six days discourse on a patient audience.

"But *you* cannot have the same excuse for working your beast on the Sabbath," continued my friend after a pause, "and art therefore wilfully breaking the commandment."

"But I may have a call," I replied; 'if not to preach to hear the gospel — I'm going to church."

The Itinerant brother shook his head, and I saw he would not admit this as a valid excuse. "Ah, said he, you're going to hear an unconverted man in a house with a steeple to it."

"Then I suppose," said I, smiling, "you think I would do better to accompany you to Frenchay, and listen to the discourse of which you are now brimful."

"Undoubtedly," said he; "you would then hear one who has been born again."

"But what proof have I of that?" said I, amazed with the complacency with which the gentleman advertised his own holiness, and decided on the unrighteousness of others.

"By their fruits you shall know them."

"A very good criterion," said I, "but the only thing I have the pleasure of knowing about you is the charity which prompts you to conclude that others are unconverted; and the humility which induced you to declare that that change has taken place in yourself: may I ask when that important event occurred, and under what circumstances, for you seem so sure of it that it must have been a very marked incident in your life?"

"It will be five years ago, come the 14th of February, that I went to a revival meeting: I was not ten minutes in the room when I was led to cry out into groaning and crying for my sins, and in ten minutes more I was on the penitential form, a converted soul."

Heaven help us, thought I, if none are saved but those who pass through a few moments of feverish and morbid excitement, in which the fears and fancy are both worked upon by a power so wild and ecstatic. Here this man goes into a room where one man is loudly praying, while others, terrified by the horrors of hell which he is hideously depicting, are as loudly groaning and crying out on all sides: he kneels down, and is, what no weak mind can avoid being, acted upon by the surrounding excitement, and, after groaning with the rest for a short time, works himself up to a pitch of enthusiasm, when he fancies he is saved, and acting on this impression he advances to a form set apart for those who have attained to this point, and ever after thinks himself converted, and qualified to denounce as 'in danger of hell fire' all whose more sober and disciplined natures would never allow them to fall into similar excess. I should be the last man in the world to make light of conversion, or the Christian life of which it is said to be the beginning; but I believe that morbid and wild excitement — that momentary passage of nervous enthusiasm, that ebullition which some sects specifically call 'conversion,' and which is physically unattainable by calm or dispassionate natures, or, in fact by any but wild, weak, fitful, and ignorant persons — no more resembles the new Christian life, to which Christ referred in his nocturnal interview with Nicodemus, than a paroxysm does a settled principle.

I hinted to my companion that one of the fruits for which I looked was charity — charity in our estimation and judgment of others: and though I might be going to hear a clergyman, who had not graduated through a revival meeting to the penitential form, I might ride my horse quietly to hear our beautiful services in a country church, without being said to commit a sinful breach of the Commandments.

"Beautiful service!" said he, with a most depreciating tone: "words, words, dry words — set phrases strung together by ungodly Bishops."

"You ill-conditioned Vandal!" said I, foolish enough to lose my temper for the first time I believe for ten years; but I could never stand patiently to hear our beautiful Liturgy abused. "If I were not more charitable than yourself I'd ride you down; the few who have adorned nonconformity with their talents and their piety, have pronounced our Liturgy perfection. Robert Hall[3] has passed a panegyric on it as just as it is glowing; and John Wesley said, "I believe this is no Liturgy either in ancient or modern language, which breathes more of a solid, scriptural, rational piety, than the Common Prayers of the Church of England: and here you a — a cobbler of shoes for aught I know, —"

"A tailor and habit maker," interposed my companion.

"Well, a tailor and habit maker, can find no more mannerly description for it than 'set phrases strung together by ungodly Bishops!'

And so saying, without wishing him good morning, being now at Stapleton, I turned into the Bell stable-yard, I am ashamed to confess it, in something like a passion.

I was so wrapped in 'virtuous indignation' on entering that I forgot for a moment or two to dismount; so there I sat in the saddle muttering 'strung together by ungodly Bishops,' until the ostler overhearing me, and thinking I was inquiring for 'our respected Diocesan,' said, "the Palace? please. Sir, you just passed it." This recalling me to my senses I dismounted, and hastened out of the yard without looking before me, the effect of which was that I nearly upset his Lordship of Gloucester and Bristol,[4] who happened at the moment to be entering the churchyard wicket on the same destination as myself.

Neither I nor his Lordship were a bit too early. Had I been too late, however, I should put it down to that Itinerant Brother and his attack on the Church. The malignant to speak of the Book of Common Prayer as he did! Why it was only the other day that a churchman, who was born a Dissenter, attributed his change (when speaking to me) to that very Liturgy so reviled. It is an interesting fact that deserves to be related. He said he had been reared as a strict Dissenter, and never recollected to have seen a Book of Common Prayer in his father's house, and never entered a church until he was eighteen, when one Sunday morning, being in the country, mere curiosity induced him to enter one, and for the first time he heard our inimitable Liturgy, which came upon him with its piety breathing and comprehensive petitions, the simple and beautiful majesty of its addresses to the Almighty, the contrite humility which pervades its penitential confessions, and the fervour with which it enables faith to express itself — all these, presented to him for the first time in the full force of freshness and novelty, made such an impression on him that from that day forward he was a churchman, declaring that he could never again bear to listen to the bald and erratic extemporisings of Dissent.

In a pew near me was, I believe, a marriage party — their first appearance in public after that interesting ceremony; which first appearance I wish they'd make in the market place instead of in church, for there is scarce a young lady in the congregation who said her prayers on such occasions, but keeps peeping and peering towards the pew full of white lace, white gauze, and white gloves. There is a churching pew and a christening pew — there ought to be a marriage pew also; a place set apart in some retired and secluded spot, in which the young people might 'blush unseen' for the first time after the honeymoon; it might be appropriately decorated with all the chubby cherubs collected from the altar screen and mural monuments around.

Stapleton Church is a very plain, unpretending, semi-Roman kind of structure. It is dedicated to the Holy Trinity, and consists of one aisle and a low tower at the West end; the outside is poor, but the interior is very neatly, and seemingly newly, done up, the walls and ceiling being marked out with courses in imitation of masonry, the latter having the effect of an arch. The building is very pleasantly situated, and in summer when the casements are left open, and the refreshing breeze and song of birds allowed to enter, it gives you an admirable idea, surrounded as it is with cheerful villas and sylvan scenery, of an English village church. The congregation are numerous and respectable. I have nothing more to tell you than that the Rev. W.R. Bailey is Perpetual Curate on Stapleton,[5] and was the preacher on the present occasion.

1. Numbers 22, vv22-31.

2. Lucian's Philosopher was Menippus — the cynic philosopher baffled by the contradictions of philosophy. Lucian lived between c.115-200 AD.

3. Howard Staunton, 1810-74. Chess champion of Europe in 1843. Published books on chess and Shakespeare. The popular 'Staunton' chessmen are named after him.

4. Robert Hall, 1764-1831. A Baptist Divine, Hall had several connections with Bristol.

5. Stapleton was the Bishop's Parish Church when the Palace was at Stapleton.

6 .W.H.R. Bayley (1841).

14 December 1844

Fishponds

Fishponds (so called, it is shrewdly conjectured by some eminent philologists, from its having been once the residence of fish) is a most miserable looking place — so cold and cheerless, indeed, that a man instinctively buttons his coat and quickens his pace as he passes through it. I met nothing whatever to interest me on the road, save two detachments of the rising generation proceeding with a pair of bull-terriers to regale themselves with a dog fight, and indulging by the way in anything but delectable conversation. My good fellows, thought I, I wish I were the Rev. Wm. Mirehouse for once in my life, and I'd find other occupation for you on Sunday morning; for Mr. M. is a magistrate as well as a minister, and 'doubly armed' against vice — with the Bible in one hand and the Statute book in the other — he makes the treadmill sometimes second his moral admonitions, and his flock are less inclined to break the Commandments, when they know that breaking stones at Lawford's Gate[1] is likely to follow.

The day was 'frosty but kindly,' and as I felt John's gait rather slow for a quick circulation I dismounted, and walked by his side. This would have been pleasant enough on any other road, but I looked round me in vain for the characteristics of English life and comfort, which can be seen, though presented in a different dress, as well in winter as in summer: the woodbine and clematis had disappeared, but there were no hedges of holly and evergreens, looking as robust in their hardy verdure and close compactness as if they had agreed to stick together in stout defiance of frost and snow: the red roses, like beauty in the blushing bloom of youth, had gone, but there was not even a tall spinster-like chrysanthemum to take their place: we can no longer expect to see the soft geranium looking out in rich and varied clusters from the open lattice, but hardly a less cheering sight is the ruddy reflection of the cottage fire, gladdening and greeting the traveller's eye as he passes the window, and telling of a pleasant and cheerful interior, of the smooth-sanded floor, and the polished hearthstone.

I saw none of these things around me to relieve the signs of cold and careworn winter, and was wishing myself, prayers said and service over, on my way back, when I thought I was like a great many in the world more anxious to escape from the sight of want than ready to relieve it. Heaven, for its own wise purposes, implants in us all a disinclination to witness misery, with the intent that when we meet with it we may do all in our power to relieve it; but this instinct, I fear, far oftener prompts us to escape from the sight of, than assist, suffering; as if, when we turned our backs upon and banished it from our minds, we did not leave it behind in all its dismal, abiding, benumbing reality.

But though we fly from the sight of want we cannot escape it; it will follow us in such a season as this personified in a thousand shivering, pinching, and hungry forms: crouching in doorways from the biting air, chattering its teeth near crossings, sheltering itself by corners from the cutting blast; it appears to us with its blanched features and its ragged figures, imposing upon us responsibilities from which we cannot escape but at our peril, and forcing itself upon our notice in such a palpable shape as to leave us without an excuse to Heaven. A hundred other monitors call our attention to misery: our own sensations and our feelings are in themselves so many hints to duty: we feel the keen air through our own thick close-buttoned moleskin, and yet we pass the half-clad, houseless creature, while the loose coin in our waistcoat pocket beneath remains as it were to rise up in judgment against us: the frost bites our fingers through our warm gloves, while the stockingless feet of the poor, purpled with cold, cannot move us to practical pity.

This is the season of all others which leaves us without apology for neglect. There is hunger and want in summer as well as in winter; but hunger is an internal suffering, and in the warm summer weather many a fasting pauper may pass us without carrying the witness of want in their faces; but the half-clad creature trembling in the streets when the thermometer is below zero, is too obvious an object to be overlooked: it won't let us plead ignorance or glaze over our neglect with the excuse that we had not seen it. If we, warmly clad and well fed, feel the effects of cold so severely, we can have no difficulty in forming an estimate of the privation and pain of those who at this inclement time have the weather as it were conspiring with the world against them. I looked into the police office as I was passing by the Council House on Tuesday last, and amongst the first cases brought up were two poor wretches for stealing coal; pinched with cold and misery, and tired of shivering before an empty grate, they could only have turned thieves through sheer necessity, and, similarly circumstanced, I fear I should myself be disposed to covet a lump of my neighbour's Newport Red Ash; they are now, however, provided with food and fuel in the City Gaol.

I was some evenings ago sitting by my fire in a warm dressing gown and worsted slippers; I had had my two glasses of sherry, and was watching the little jets of gas as they burst out in fitful brilliancy from the black lumps between the bars, while a plate of walnut shells, the debris of my dessert, crackled and blazed up in cheerful unison with the first of English comforts, a sea coal fire. The only sounds that reached me from outside were the clear ringing echo of the passenger's footsteps on the dry frosty flag-way, and a kind of gusty cry of 'Muffin — hot muffin,' so that disengaged as my ear was, I had little difficulty in hearing a single knock at the door. It was of a peculiar character, or I dare say I should not have noticed it; it was timid and low, as if the benumbed fingers which held the knocker hesitated in their office; a second followed, a little louder it is true, but the increased force I could see evidently cost the author a severe effort, as if he or she, or whoever it might be, raised the hammer high and faltered with fear as it fell. I rung and told the servant to answer the door, which she did, but it was hardly opened when it was shut suddenly and sharply again. On bringing up my tea soon after, I enquired who it was that called, for I took an interest in the knock. 'A woman with matches, Sir,' said she, with a somewhat indignant tone; 'it is like their cool assurance; they have grown as impudent as can be since the frost set in, and knock at the door as if a body had nothing to do but answer them!'

Thus, thought I, the frost that supplies the robin with boldness to perch on our window sill, and crave the crumb from our table, drives the poor shivering creature to the habitation of his or her fellow also, for relief; the keen cutting elements that indurate the ground and embitter the very air with cold, conquer the fears and diffidence of both and compel them, though not without some doublings, to approach the dwellings of man. Who refuses the mute appeal of the pretty feathered mendicant, as in its dauntless distress it almost enters our breakfast parlour? but the innocent audacity that interests us in the little bird, is called 'impudent assurance' in a fellow-creature, and the heart that would bleed to injure a feather of the red-breast, does not hesitate to slam the door in the pinched face of the poor starving match-seller, whom want has nerved to the desperate deed of knocking at it. This poor woman, after trembling for an hour or two in a thin scanty cotton covering by a cross way, and unable to attract the attention of the warm-clad passenger as he hurried home out of the keen cutting air, despairing, too, of a casual customer, and unwilling to return empty handed, it may be to a quenched hearth or a sick child, glanced round in doubt at the adjacent dwellings, and after looking for a while wistfully at the cheerful reflection of my fire, through the red merino window curtains, timidly thought of trying what chance of charity there was from one seemingly so warmly lodged and well favoured with the world's comforts. Poor woman! Her reception was such as not to allow her to be again easily drawn away from her crossway, by the 'tempting aspect' of my house at least.

'Free seats for ever!' thought I, as I entered Fishponds Church, and saw nearly the whole area of the edifice devoted to the poor and the stranger. It is capable of containing between seven and eight hundred and there are out of that nearly six hundred unappropriated sittings. Indeed, I could only count about sixteen pews, which, being placed closely together, at the east end, accommodated the *elite* of Fishponds — yes, *elite*, for, poor as Fishponds is, it cannot be without its elite. The rest of the building is occupied by the non-elite of the place and the pauper children and old women of Stapleton workhouse. It was one of the simplest and humblest congregations (with the exception of the sixteen pews) I have ever seen. I sat on a form with several old women, and paid as much attention to the service as two or three hundred children with colds in their heads would permit me to do. Pocket-handkerchiefs, I perceive, are not provided under the Gilbert Union Act,[2] but I think at this inclement season they are indispensable: most of them being foundlings, caught cold on the first night of their exposure, and have never since recovered from it: I should, therefore, suggest a sermon on behalf of an instant supply — an appeal to which the interns of the sixteen pews aforesaid ought to liberally respond for their own sakes. The cold, however, did not keep the young urchins from singing, for on the psalms being given out, an invisible violoncello in the gallery squeaked the key note, and they commenced with good will, and, considering the rude materials of the choir, got through with credit. Though nearly all the children sang with more or less effect, I noticed that the chief vocalists were arranged in two equal lines in front, these files only being furnished with Prayer Books.

As I found it the case in most country churches which I have visited, the congregation turned round to loll and listen; so that half the audience, namely, the children, were looking eastward, while the other half, by confronting them, had quite an opposite aspect. Not to be singular, I did the same as my neighbours, and had, therefore, an opportunity of examining the various lineaments of the little boys and girls — the latter in their grey freize cloaks, and the former in jackets of a like material[3] — and I think I never saw such an epitome of the human face in all its diversity of features: eyes of all colours, noses of all shapes, hair of all hues — some would be well-looking, others threatened to be positively ugly — some showed intellect, some evidence of obdurate stolidity — some promised to be agreeable, others were already repulsive. I believe the principle portion of them are foundlings, or illegitimate children; and, I confess, I could not help looking at them with some interest, and conjecturing how many of them had been found tied to knockers, how many packed in linen parcels by hall-doors, how many picked up by policemen on their beats, how many remitted in baskets by rail, and how many found with recommendatory letters tied with silk threads round their necks. I looked upon each little *enfant trouve* as a walking duodecimo edition of romance,[4] if one could read it, with its secret tale of sin and suffering. There were few of them but might have turned out a Tom Jones in the hands of another Fielding.[5]

Fishponds is a 'plain and unaccommodated' place of worship; there is no sexton; no robing-room; the Rev. W. Mirehouse changed his surplice for his gown in the reading-desk, and opened the pulpit door, and performed other little minutiae for himself. He had hardly given out the text — the 4th verse of the 144th Psalm, 'Man is like to vanity; his days are as a shadow that passeth away' — when two or three old gentlemen immediately commenced muffling themselves up with assiduity, buttoning their great coats, pulling on their gloves, and making such other preparations, seemingly for a long sermon, that

I began to grow apprehensive. But it was not a long sermon; and I do not know when I have heard a much better one; some parts of it were positively eloquent; and the pervading characteristics of his style were forcible and figurative. His manner, however, was more open to exception than his matter: it was free, and at times far from ungraceful; but it was for the most part infinitely more magisterial than ministerial, and accompanied with a tone and look so authoritative that you would have thought he was reading malefactors moral lesson from the bench of Lawford Gate, instead of addressing a congregation from the pulpit of Fishponds. One almost expected that he would conclude his discourse by declaring, 'If you don't do as I tell you, I'll commit you for three months.' There was a dogmatic shake of the head, too, and his voice, though modulated to meet other feelings, never sunk to the softness of affectionate admonition; and, as he thrust his hands into his pockets and throwing himself back against the board behind him, looked his audience full in the face, and, addressing them with the directness of Nathan, told them that every moment was, as it were, a messenger from another world come for their commands and taking back what they had to give, never returning to afford them an opportunity of recall; though I could not help being struck with the unfettered ease and energy of his action, I could never for a moment in my mind separate the justice of the peace from the parson.

The church is a plain, poor structure, naked both within and without: but it serves the great purpose for which it was built, and compared with which architectural orders and adornments are but as dust in the balance — namely, to afford spiritual accommodation for a large and populous district; and it is peculiarly gratifying to find that the wants of the poor have been the first consideration in the structure. It was built within the last twenty or thirty years, and consists of a nave and small chancel: there is some stained glass in the east window, through which the cold white light of winter entered with a little prismatic warmth. At the east end is a gallery, inhabited by the children of the charity-school, and the invisible violoncello player before referred to.

The churchyard seems to be almost wholly used as a Golgotha for the neighbouring poorhouse, as the long ranks of little red clay-mounds, with a small inscribed footstone to each, indicated. I seldom saw a more desolate and cheerless-looking resting-place for the dead in my life; not a shrub or altar-tomb, that I could see, rose to vary the dismal and monotonous dreariness and flatness of the place. I walked round it after service, and there were two old women standing by a patch of newly-broken earth, which had lately received some mortal remains; though little was the care devoted to other graves, this had evidently received less. The two old women were whispering mysteriously as they stood by it.

"Whose grave is this, my good folks?" said I.

"The poor young woman who was buried at midnight, without prayer said for her poor soul," said the elder of the two, slightly shuddering.

"Yes," added her companion, "and they might have found 'tempry sanity' for this poor wildered creature as well as for another."

My curiosity was excited, and seeing it was an incident one does not every-day meet with in a country churchyard, I begged they would tell me all about it, which was, as well as I could gather from them, to the following effect. It was, in fact, a rude version of a rustic Ophelia's story. It appears that her name was Esther Tilly: she was the daughter of a farmer living in the adjoining par-ish, or somewhere on the borders of Horfield and Stapleton, and having fallen in love with a young man, a kind of farm-servant named Williams, her father forbade her the house, and she went to reside with a relative, still continuing her love, 'not wisely but too well,'[6] for the young man Williams: some flaw, however, some trifling interruption to their mutual attachment took place, which, joined perhaps to her other troubles, had the effect of 'driving her to desperate terms,' and one evening, after writing a letter informing her lover other determination, she proceeded to a little pond in her parent's orchard, and throwing herself in, she was seen by someone at a distance to float for a moment, until

> 'Her garments heavy with their drink,[7]
> Pulled the poor wretch
> To muddy death.'

An inquest was held, and the jury, arguing I suppose according to the clown's logic, 'If I drown myself wittingly it argues an act, and an act has three branch-es — it is to act, to do, to perform; argal, she drowned herself wittingly,' found a verdict of *felo de se*, and the body was buried that same night by torchlight, between the hours of 11 and 12 o'clock, without the solemn rite of Christian sepulture, and with all the haste that accompanies a hurried work of horror, beneath the broken earth by which we then stood. But it was not in their end alone that the story of the poor country girl and the 'pretty Ophelia' agreed: their burial was marked by a singularly similar incident, for, on the body being lowered into the ground, the young man, Williams, bursting through the circle of torch-bearers, threw himself on it in the frenzy of his feelings reminding one of a similar act of the excited Hamlet at the grave of Ophelia —

> 'Hold off the earth awhile,
> Till I have caught her once more in my arms.'[8]

The story appeared to me a peculiarly sad one; and I confess I could not help wishing with the old woman that the jury had charitably interpreted the act as one of temporary insanity. In the case of a fine lady some would not have as summarily decided on the state of her mind: and I think with the clown that 'great folks should not have countenance in this world to drown and hang themselves any more than their even Christian;' and it would have lessened the horror of a sad tale had Hope, like a charitable angel, been allowed to hover over the unhappy remains.

'They threw quick lime too, into the grave,' said the old woman, seeing me gaze down on the rough red cheerless-looking earth at my feet; 'and cast her body in as if she were a dog or a particide (parricide), instead of a poor distraught girl.'

I said nothing but turned away, for the cold began to creep up my legs; the cutting blast came across the bleak churchyard, and, whistling through the loose stones of the ill-built wall close by, piped an appropriate dirge above the grave of the poor suicide.

1. Lawfords Gate House of Correction, opened in 1791.
2. Thomas Gilbert, 1720-98. As a poor law reformer, Gilbert took especial interest in the reform of the poor law in England, and it was through his influence that the Poor Laws of 1782 and 1787 came about, enabling parishes to group together to form workhouse 'unions'. The workhouse children that Leech refers to are from Stapleton Workhouse which was built after the major Poor Law Reform Act of 1834. However, such was Gilbert's influence in this field, even fifty years later Leech still uses the term.

   Thomas Gilbert's 1787 Act also included legislation enabling parishes to raise funds for the 'union' workhouses. Part of this legislation was the introduction of double toll at turnpikes on Sundays, and Leech refers to this on his visit to Blagdon.
3. The introduction of a cheap and coarse uniform was one of the many innovations of the 1834 Act.
4. Duodecimo was a popular size for novels and cheap books. Now the term refers to books of a size of 7½ inches by 5 inches, but originally it was so called because on machines available at that time it would have been printed on a sheet comprising twelve leaves making twenty-four pages.
5. *Tom Jones* by Henry Fielding, first published 1749. Fielding based his novel in Somerset, close to his birthplace of Sharpham near Glastonbury.
6. '. . . Nor set down aught in malice: then you must speak, *Of one that lov'd not wisely, but too well'*. . . . *Othello* Act V scene ii.
7. '. . . Till that her garments, heavy with their drink,
   Pull'd the poor wretch from her melodious lay
   To muddy death.' *Hamlet* Act IV scene vii.
8. '. . . Hold off the earth awhile, Till I have caught her once more in mine arms: . . .' *Hamlet* Act V scene i.

28 December 1844
Thornbury

Amongst the various luxuries of this festive season within the borough of Bristol, one cannot conscientiously number that of sleep. From 8 p.m. on Christmas eve, to 12 o'clock, I was regaled with a succession of 'Glories shone around' from a number of small voices at my door; and when these ceased, a trombone, a clarionet, and first fiddle. With two o'clock and the last cadence of *Auld lang syne*, I fell asleep, and awoke at eight. On descending to breakfast my landlady presented me with the compliments of the season and a plate of muffins; both (poor soul!) a little over-buttered.

Henri Quatre[1] could not think France happy till every peasant had a fowl in his pot. Whether it was through a feeling allied to that of the illustrious monarch, namely, a wish to provide feathered food for their friends, I cannot say, but all the way between Bristol and Filton was lined with fowlers — shop-boys, for the most part, who, furnished with fusees,[2] dealt destruction round them in the most independent style imaginable, and scared both John Bunyan and his rider out of their 'seven senses.' John, for the first time since I had the happiness to make his acquaintance, acted in a manner unworthy his sober and sedate character, and jumped from side to side at every pop, perilling my personal safety and his own too. It was in vain I assured him that it was an im-memorial practice amongst the 'prentice boys of Bristol on Christmas morn-ing to kill the time and small birds before breakfast, and that the detonations which he heard were the result of this ancient practice: John still bounded about at every report, and, sooth to say, I was hardly more easy in mind than my respected quadruped; for, independent of the danger arising from his fitful agility, I felt I was exposed to another still more imminent, from the fusilade of my young friends, who fired into the bushes with the most superlative indif-ference as to the parties who became the recipients of their spare shot; for, upon one occasion, the spent lead that brought down a blackbird in its career, fell in a shower, fortunately not fatal, near my horse's feet.

Were I not in a hurry, I should have been disposed to loiter on Almondsbury hill, which overlooks so noble a prospect, with the broad waters of the Severn bounding the view; but the bells beginning to ring in the old and picturesque little church, with its lead-covered spire, in the hollow, told me I had no time to lose; so I pushed on without pause to the Ship at Alveston. Here, for the first time, I got a peep of the fair church tower of Thornbury, with its beautiful

ballustraded top but as I looked down on the 'old burgh' with its old houses snugly nestling amongst old trees, no sound reached me, no bells boomed out their Christmas peals, and I began to think I had arrived too late, not only for the procession, but prayers. What, thought I, after riding twelve miles to see them, have they presumed to march to church without my being there to see. I pushed John to a more energetic walk than usual, and as I pulled up at the Swan porch, the first question I asked of my landlady, who promptly made her appearance, was, 'If prayers had commenced.'

"No, Sir," said she, "they do not commence today until half-past eleven, on account of the Mayor; the usual time is eleven."

Now, the reader, from sundry invitations sent me, may possibly by this time be acquainted with the cause of delay. It appears that Thornbury (proud place) has a Mayor and Corporation, and the principal and almost only duty which the great civic functionary has to perform during his year of office, is to provide coffee for his co-councilmen and the incumbent of the parish, at his residence on Christmas morning; and, having discussed that and a quantity of hot rolls, to walk, preceded by some poor men and women, through the town to church. In consideration of the Mocha[3] and munchets the service is accordingly delayed, as we have already seen half an hour. It never struck their worships — it never occurred to the incumbent, that by beginning their breakfast 30 minutes sooner, the parishioners who have not the good fortune to partake of cake and coffee at the Mayor's expense, need not be obliged to postpone their dinners half an hour, to say nothing of the very secondary position in which it places the celebration of the solemn service of the church.

But it was more than half an hour, for I stood with my back against the wooden column of the Swan porch, still waiting the apparition of the civic procession, some minutes after the hands of the Town-hall clock pointed to half-past eleven; and I began to think that his Worship had added a *demitasse* of ratafie to his *dejeuner*, when a person who happened to come up at the time, and of whom I made some enquiries, assured me this could not be the case, as the Mayor was an impregnable teetotaller.

At length a rush of little boys with red noses announced that a movement of that momentous body, the Mayor and Corporation of Thornbury, had taken place, and that the functionaries had really finished their breakfast. First came a file of old women, in gowns, aprons, and bonnets alike; then a string of elderly men, in brown coats, with very bright buttons (the Corporation of Thornbury wish their good deeds to *shine* before men), and black hats with very broad brims, the gift of the Corporation, the recipients being left to find inexpressibles for themselves. The ancient Romans showed their glory by the line of captives that followed their cavalcades; the Corporation of Thornbury display their charity by the number of paupers that precede their procession. They are not the people (bless their hearts) to

'Do good by stealth and blush to find it fame.'

People may call your worships 'Pharisaical functionaries,' but depend upon it there's nothing like letting all the world know your benevolence: once commence the silent system of almsgiving, and half the close-fisted in the country will take credit to themselves for the acts of charity done by others in secret, and the public will be cheated out of its compassion by swindlers. The poor passed, two tall staff-men swaggered on in front of the party, and then came the Mayor, in a broad brimmed hat, and black surtout, and a brown cotton umbrella, having the Rev. Townsend Stephens, canonically clad, on his right, and a detachment of brother aldermen filling up the rear. They were a good-humoured, good-natured, good-looking set of gentlemen, and as they wiped their mouths after the Mayor's muffins, none could seem more happy or contented: but they were piteously shorn of their pomp no state carriage, no gold chain and silver gown, no insignia or precious metal, unless indeed a decent sized silver mace (I forgot the mace), and a white wand (which I also neglected to enumerate).

I don't know what there was remarkable or worthy of remark in my contour or brown coat; but as the procession passed the Swan, they all, including his Worship and his Reverence, stared at me as if I had two heads, and there was a whispering and seeming consultation amongst them, which I fondly put down for a friendly contest between the Mayor and the Rev. Townsend Stephens, as to which should have the pleasure of asking me that day to dinner. Here, however, I was mistaken, for independent of a piece of Glo'ster and a brown loaf,

— but of this by-and-bye. I followed the procession, and had the inexpressible delight of hearing two fellows in fustian jackets (I pledge my word for the fact) exclaim as they crushed by me in the crowd, 'The Church-Goer is in town.' Talk of celebrity — that's what I call glory — to find that one's reputation, one's title and likeness had travelled twelve miles from Bristol, and that the very bumpkins in the street syllabled my name, "Take heart, old gentleman," said I, striking the breast of my brown coat encouragingly, "*Non omnis Moriar* — let the Duke of Wellington look to his laurels, I'm blessed if I don't have a bay or two to my own brows." I felt myself growing, expanding — my snuff-colour seemed suddenly to become too small for me, and I let out a button or two to prevent a catastrophe — "You old goose," said commonsense immediately after, "what! grow vain at your time of life — nobody ever recollected you yet at half-past ten on a Saturday morning."

My moral reflections brought me and the procession to the churchyard, and I leaned over the wall to look at the little cortege as it wound up the gravel walk. There was one poor man amongst the recipients of the brown coats who had some affliction of the legs, and as he toiled along, a prominent and somewhat painful object in the affair, I felt disposed to regret that the civic body should have thought it necessary for their pity-moving purposes to exhibit him in the procession.

Spirit of Handel, what a crash! Before I had crushed my person within the porch, and while the black surtout and brown cotton umbrella of his Worship were still in view, I was literally overwhelmed with a dashing voluntary: such as the organist only plays once a year when the Mayor gives coffee and muffins to the Minister, cloaks to the poor, and winds up his good works by walking to church. It was a voluntary, indeed, given with all his will, and full of fugues, and canons, and quavers, and other fantastical flights, which seemed to skip with a sort of solemn frolic, and hunt each other with a kind of musical glee up to the old oak roof, through the middle and side aisles, and around the monuments and holly bushes with which the church was full and forest-like, until at length eddying in combined echoes about the civic pew they seemed to not in ecstatic joy. But great as the voluntary was, the '*Gloria*' which immediately followed left it far behind in *eclat*. Ranged full in front of the gallery the singers exerted all their powers to equal if possible the occasion: in the centre was the conductor, with a roll of paper in his hand, and Mendelssohn could not have wielded his baton with half the dignity of my friend (for I will call him my friend); he was keeping common time it is true, but in 'uncommon' grand style: with each bar 'the down beat' descended on the book before him with a sound which was heard by and above the whole choir, although the principal bass was so deep that he seemed to sing down his cravat — the trebles left nothing to be desired in their quarter, and if I neglected to say the tenors did their duty, I should not be doing mine. Nor was the organist disposed to lose his share of the day's credit: no man could be more industrious, and were it not for an indescribable idea of extreme labour, arduous toil, and intense exertion which the entire conveyed, I question if I could too rapturously express my gratification at all I saw and heard. As it was, the congregation I could perceive were delighted, and the very evergreens around, as they bowed their branches, appeared to concur in the general opinion of approval. A little fellow near me, who was perfectly entranced, looked me full in the face whenever a passage more forte than usual occurred, as much as to say — so at least I read his looks — "Well, you have heard a pretty considerable quantity of music in your lifetime, old gentleman, but did you ever hear anything like that?" I don't think I did — the effort was a most praiseworthy one: the only fault I had to find was, we saw rather too much. I suppose the man with the baton would revolt if we put him out of sight; but I confess, picturesque an object as he is, I'd be disposed to place a red curtain in front of him and his roll of papers. One must not quarrel with this display at Christmas; but, as a general principle, I'd prefer a simple psalm, in which all might join, to such laborious affairs. I have heard once of a hard-headed countryman, who, when taken for the first time to a cathedral, turned round to his friend when a grand piece was finished, and said, with a sort of severe simplicity, "Do you call this praising God?" An ill-natured person might be disposed to repeat the question after some of our occasional country church exhibitions. But these performances, in my opinion, if not too many, are rather a subject of congratulation: they argue a creditable pride on the part of the parishioners and parish authorities of the church, and prove that neglect and indifference do not characterise the congregation. All present, I thought seemed pleased with themselves, their choir, and their beautiful pile; and even the incumbent looked around as if he would say, "At this particular moment I don't envy His Grace Dr. Howley, Archbishop of Canterbury."

The church was well filled — and I might almost say crowded; but I dare say this was a Christmas-day congregation, for I actually overheard one young girl say as she left the church, that she had not been there since the previous Christmas-day: I have no doubt, however, she was a dissenter. I found my way into a pew near the door, where there were two young men, who did not behave themselves particularly well; and a dreadful draught that gave me a cold, from the effects of which at this present writing, I am suffering in my head and shoulders.

I think Thornbury one of the handsomest country churches I have ever seen; it has quite an imposing cathedral-like appearance. It has two side and a noble centre aisle, the latter lit with a fine and lofty row of clerestory windows. The arches which divide the north and south from the principal aisle are of great symmetrical elegance, springing from clustered columns of graceful lightness. The chancel does not at present look to the best advantage, owing to the east window being stopped up: it ought to be opened. The stone pulpit is worthy the edifice, and in style, construction, etc. shows the good taste of the period in which it was placed there. I never heard, and I don't recollect ever seeing the Rev. Townsend Stephens[4] before in my life, so that my opinion is only worth one day's experience. I hardly remember ever hearing a better reader; and his sermon, from Luke ii, 10, 'And the Angel said unto them. Fear not, for behold I bring you good tidings of great joy, which shall be to all people,' he delivered in a distinct and sonorous voice, and with a clearness and correctness of enunciation which must have made the discourse plain and distinct to everyone within the church. He had other advantages, too, which are seldom thrown away, even amongst more Evangelical ministers and hearers — a good head and shoulders, and he stood something like six feet, honest measure, in his shoes. His sermon, whether a holiday one or not, was a good one; and, on the whole, in pulpit and reading desk, the Rev. Townsend Stephens may take a very respectable stand amongst country parsons; and now you have the whole of my knowledge of the Vicar of Thornbury. I say this because I need not tell the reader, nor the Rev. Townsend Stephens either, that what a clergyman is in the pulpit and reading desk is a very small portion of what a clergyman ought to be: I must be able to trace him from house to house and from cottage to cottage during the other six days of the week, seconding by precept and example his Sunday sermon; labouring, nay toiling, in the sacred, aye and awful service upon which he has entered; for pleasant as the rural parsonage, with its rose-grown trelissed front, may seem, there is a fearful responsibility and condition attached to its tenure, namely, the care of many hundred souls, — the Tithe Commutation Act is not the only knowledge necessary to the man that enters on such a charge. I make these observations in a general way: I know nothing about the Vicar of Thornbury beyond what I saw and heard of him on Christmas-day, and what a man told me on the road, that personally he was exceedingly popular amongst his parishioners.

The reader is perhaps aware that the people of Thornbury had been pestering me with invitations for the last three months, and I was promised innumerable dinners. You'd have thought (I certainly did) from the pressing epistles that reached me, that a hundred families at least were burning for the honour of having my legs under their mahogany, and that the sound of John's hoofs would hardly be heard in the street before as many hatless heads of houses were seen running out to lay hold of his bridle and hands on each other, in fierce contest for the pleasure of providing entertainment for man and horse. Nevertheless, I declare to you, good reader, that from the time I passed the first house on my entrance until I arrived at the Swan, I was not accosted by a single creature who had even a luncheon in his looks: and then, as I was leaving the church after prayers, there was not one friendly hand (though I walked slow to afford them an opportunity) to touch me on the shoulder and say, "A roast rib and plum-pudding precisely at two." Where, may I ask, was the poet, and where the old gentleman abounding in Latin and fine professions, who was to meet me at the Ship at Alveston — where the Mayor — where the Corporation, where the Churchwardens, where even the Rev. Townsend Stephens; he could have leant over the pulpit and said to the clerk, "see that old gentleman (I know he saw me) in the snuff-coloured coat going out of the porch: run after him and tell him my turkey will bear one moderate appetite more." But no such thing; I reached the Swan without the hospitality of the town offering the slightest interruption to my progress.

"Some luncheon, lady mine," said I, bustling into the warm bar. A kind soul is mine hostess of the Swan. "Do stay and dine with us. Sir," said she, with the most good-natured *empressement*. Thank Heaven, thought I, there is one hospitable heart in Thornbury; but stay I could not — I would not. Dine at an hotel on Christmas-day! that in my opinion was the acme of destitution; so I had some good brown bread, cheese, butter, and general gossip by the bar fire with my excellent friend Mrs. —, she'll excuse me but I really forget her name, or rather I never knew it.⁵ Reader, if you ever visit the Swan, there's a wooden armchair in the bar, with a high back, I sat in that — respect it; and look at a large slate some four feet square behind the door; it is a monstrous piece of antiquity, and did good service before drib and day-books were invented. There are some 'old scores' on it still, which mine hostess said she feared would never be paid. Under her guidance I made a visit to the Sessions-room, which is attached to the house and where the local magistrates dispense infinitesimal doses of law and justice to a grateful public. It contained at the time an immense new Swan, carved out in wood — quite a *Rara Avis* I can assure you, and which my enterprising hostess informed me was in a few days to surmount the vestibule of her hostelry, to which the 'silver cygnet,' I need not tell the reader, attached a title. I expect there will be quite a sensation in Thornbury on the day of its elevation.⁶

John Bunyan is at the door, but before I go, a word about the Castle. I suppose everybody knows its history, and I have more to do with Church than Castle building. It was begun in the reign of Henry the VIII by Edward Duke of Buckingham, but never completed, as that poor gentleman lost his head because he did not know how to keep a civil tongue in it.⁷

It is a curious statistical fact that as I left the town there was not a single creature that I could see in the streets; all but the poor Church-Goer were within doors, wrapped in the blandishments of roast beef and plum pudding: nevertheless, I forgive thee, Thornbury.

1. Henry IV of France, 1553-1610.
2. Fusee/Fusil, a light musket, the original weapon carried by fusiliers.
3. Mocha — a choice coffee from S.W. Yemen.
4. Maurice Fitzgerald Townsend Stephens, vicar 1823-72.
5. The landlady's name was Mrs. Gayner Frances.
6. The wooden swan still surmounts the porch of the Swan at Thornbury.
7. *See* Henbury note 6.

11 January 1845

Westbury-on-Trym

My acquaintance with Westbury is of long standing. My worthy father, who resided in a close and crowded part of Bristol, and was confined by the situation which he held amongst the 'cribbed and cabined' habitations of man during six days of the week, almost invariably in summer used to walk out to morning service in some of the neighbouring country churches, and on these occasions he took either me or my poor brother with him. My mother used to say it was not right for the head of the family to be absent so much from his own parish church, but he always answered that he never was in a more happy and devotional feeling or a more cheerful frame of mind to enter a church porch, than after he had walked two or three miles through a beautiful country, in the morning sunshine and amongst singing birds. My mother and my sisters, who always attended in their parish church, seeing it was useless to oppose his innocent hobby, at length abstained altogether from expostulation, which was never very urgent, and my excellent parent continued his summer morning walks as long as he could walk, and I verily believe I inherit my roving propensities from him.

Westbury was amongst his most favourite excursions, and I can fancy I still see the hale and hearty old man (I wish he had transmitted his health with his habits to me), as like the boy Ascanius with Father Aeneas, hand in hand I trotted on by his side, across the Down, while the echoes of Westbury and Bristol bells were meeting mid-way, as it were, with their noisy salutations. "Come, boy," he'd say, after loitering a minute or so to look with pleasure in every lineament on the Channel, 'marking the embarked traders on the flood:' "Come, come, step out, or we'll be too late;" and then he'd take out his old silver watch, 'the same which now I wear,' and which still retains within its capacious cases the same piece of silk with the motto of 'Fear God, honour the King,' which had been embroidered by my mother for him when they were courting. My father, who was as well known almost as any of his parishioners to the incumbent, used to receive the Sacrament frequently at Westbury, and while he remained in for that part of the service I was allowed to ramble about the churchyard, and I recollect regarding Ruddle's tomb with a sort of awful dread, no doubt occasioned by the story of his murder. There was also another tale of horror with which my young blood used to be frozen, about the ghost of Pen Park Hole, which frightened Captain Sturmy out of his wits and life, and which I used to hear at an old farmer friend's in the neighbourhood, whom we visited in our rural rambles. But goblin stories are gone out of fashion now, and the respectable old-fashioned ghost, who inhabited old ivy-gabled churchyards, after frightening generations of rustics has itself been frightened away by the railroad whistle.

As I passed the high wall of Westbury convent there was a comfortable looking gentleman, doubtless a Roman Catholic priest, entering at the gateway, and such was my curiosity I should have willingly given my saddle and bridle, to be allowed to enter with him, and have a quiet dish of gossip with the superior. What a curious effect has a lofty piece of masonry on one: if that wall were down, and a line of open iron railing occupied its place, I should not have felt so ardent a desire for admission to the interior: but such an impassable, not-to-be-peeped-over a barrier, though it shuts out everything else, opens a field for a world of speculation makes me imagine all manner of beauties in black gowns and white veils, each with a history as long and interesting as a three-volume novel of Colburn and Bentley's[1] publishing. A commonplace notice of any of those picturesque virgins is quite out of the question — nothing short of blighted love and implacable parents could have brought one of them within its boundaries: then there is the vesper bell, and the matin bell, and the midnight chanting, and the morning hymn, and a hundred other imposing associations which make poetry and Popery almost synonymous, and furnish romance writers with half their stock-in-trade. Yet I have no doubt that, if some day my friend the Abbe O'Farrall were to take me under his arm and protection, and introduce my heretical snuff-coloured coat within such orthodox precincts, I should perceive a large share of that influence and atmosphere which belongs to flesh and blood pervading the place, and find that some portion of the old world feeling had crept over its walls; and perhaps be shocked to see their 'maiden meditations' suspended for the moment by the physical attractions of a leg of mutton and trimmings, or the Mother Abbess engaged in a game of cribbage with the next in authority. And yet I think the original idea of a convent was not altogether without good, and we must recollect it was not wholly unknown to the early Christian church, for I fancy St. Ambrose was a stickler for something like the institution.

As I entered the little turnstile to the churchyard the bell ceased, and before I had crossed 'God's acre,' as our Saxon forefathers called the burying ground, I saw four or five rough looking fellows hurrying out of the porch and putting on their hats as they did so; the haste with which they ran from the sacred building, jumping over graves and tombstones, as if they would not be detained a moment longer than they could possibly help in the neighbourhood of the 'House of Prayer,' attracted my notice, and I soon perceived they were the ringers. These fellows verify more than any other class I know the adage 'the nearer the Church, the farther from Heaven.' As the organ pealed after them and seemed to call them back with swelling and solemn voice, they did not even turn round. I'd almost have forgiven them if they had cast one hesitating look behind them; but no — away they went, running and leaping all the way down to the now silent village, perhaps to a skittle alley or beer house. And yet if there be any 'hempen homespuns' who ought to feel a touch of sentiment, or at least sensibility, it is these bell ringers. Their very occupation is full of poetry, and ought to partake of religion; their's is no everyday handicraft — antiquity, which softens everything, seems to hallow the avocation, and they never pull the ropes that they do not awaken the voice of other days — the voice that spoke to centuries agone and generations past. The insensate clods! the very vicissitudes of death and marriage, which they are called on to signal or celebrate, ought to touch their natures, if the solemn beauty of the Sabbath peal had become too much a matter of course to have any influence upon them. Amongst other modes of seeing in the new year, I have one which is somewhat peculiar perhaps to myself: for a slight consideration I am allowed by the ringers to accompany them to the belfry to see out the old and in the new year: and on Tuesday week, about a quarter of an hour before midnight, I met my friends by appointment at the porch of a certain church in the city, which for the present shall be nameless. The lanthorn which the tenor carried up the 'spiral staircase, narrow and damp,' shed a sort of sickly, almost sepulchral flicker on the winding steps and dark wall, and threw just enough of light on the rough faces that followed, to make them look as if they came from another world. On arriving at the belfry the ringers took off their coats, and each laid hold of a pendant rope, and, in a moment more, a peal, solemn and dirge-like, sounded upon the ears of the hundreds who, in their surrounding houses, were watching to see '44 out, and send the 'knell' not of a 'departing hour,' but a 'departing year,' through the mists of passion and of sense' that arose from a crowded, a careless, and a careworn city. It ceased — the conductor held an old silver watch in his hand, and I took mine out of my pocket: it was within a minute or two of twelve, and not a sound was heard but the breathing of the ringers as they paused from their work. That minute was the most eloquent silence I ever *heard* — a thousand sermons preached from the pulpit below in the church, could not have touched the heart like that minute's silence in the tower. As the second hand ticked, ticked round its little circle, the last pulsations of the dying year, I looked upon the little group of faces, upon which the lanthorn shed its light: the men stood statue-like with the ropes in their hands — I glanced back upon the dial of my watch, two seconds more, and the little hand was on the hair-line which divided '44 and '5. I fancied — it was a mere fancy — that the shadowy form of the old year as it departed to its brethren 'beyond the flood,' glided by us at that solemn moment. While I was yet occupied with the thought the bells swung round a welcome, more boisterous and wild I thought than merry, to the new year. Aye, here it comes in, thought I, as with the last drop of the ebb begins the flow; but God only knows, as the dim tide comes flowing up to us from futurity, what events it bears upon its surface, and over what ruined hopes and wrecked happiness its surges will roll. Millions will pass from amongst us during the twelvemonths we have now ushered in with such a clamorous peal, and yet of these doomed millions not one person seriously believes that he will die. His relative or his neighbour may die, but he is not to die: there is nothing in which we willingly give precedence to other people but in death. 'After you. Sir,' is the comfortable feeling, is not the complaisant expression in all these matters. In my own mind I was at that moment verifying the truth of my own thoughts, for while I was thus reflecting *for others*, I never once fancied that I ought to think for myself. 'And you, smooth old gentleman in the snuff-coloured coat,' some monitory spirit seemed to whisper in my ear — 'have you ever dreamt there is the slightest — we'll say the *slightest* possibility of your being one of the unconscious millions for whose coffin the oak planks are now seasoning?' 'Certainly not,' thought I; 'no, no; I am going to live, of course, and write Church-Goers for years to come. No, no, no; what could have brought that uncomfortable thought across my mind? — We'll change the subject.' But the subject would not change for me: if stuck like a barbed arrow, and fastened on me until I began to fancy it a presentiment. The chimes were in their last merry strokes for the new year, but there was a thought pealing in my mind above them all; and as we descended the little spiral staircase, our business done, it was strange that the toll for the old year was more vividly in my recollection than the welcome for the new. A trifle, however, will sometimes turn us from our best thoughts; and mine were endangered by one of the ringers who preceded me calling out to another behind, in a voice which had a hollow echo in the old tower, "Bill, I'll have a drop o'beer to begin the new year with: what sayest thee?" "I don't care," answered his companion, "if the old gent. 'll stand treat." "Begin the new year with a muddle! — the old gentleman will do no such thing," I replied.

Westbury Church formed at one time part of a collegiate establishment, consisting of a dean and five canons. William Cannyngs — a name illustrious in our annals, and associated so intimately with the noble pile of St. Mary's, Redcliff — was Dean of Westbury in the 15th century, having taken holy orders after filling the civic chair of Bristol five times: a precedent which, I believe, has not been followed by any of his successors, though it was a notable, if not very usual wind up, I confess, the chief magistracy. We don't hear of aldermen now-a-days turning priests — throwing off the ermined robe and gold chain to assume the gown and cassock, and turning to long fasts after feeding on turtle. But there is no authority that I am aware of, that has yet been audacious enough to assert the father or friar could ever equal, in opportunities of eating, a Mayor of Bristol; though to give the clergy their due, there have been some very eminent professors of the art gastronomic amongst them: two or three abbes, of whose sermons we never heard, having handed down works on cookery to posterity. Nor has the Anglican church been altogether without its 'ornaments' in this particular. I happened some time ago to be with a friend in Wiltshire, who was a churchwarden, and with whom I went to a visitation dinner. I sat near a well-conditioned divine, who no sooner found out I was from Bristol than he earnestly enquired 'whether we got much turtle there now.' I said I believed we had; though I only spoke from public report. "Ah, Sir," said he, "it will never again be what it was in Burnham's time; Burnham, Sir was great for balls; he made them as firm as flint, and yet as light as a feather." Everybody who has ever eaten turtle knows what the little savoury bread balls are, and know who Burnham was. I was a little amused with the grateful zest with which my rev. neighbour cherished the memory of a former master of the Montague.[2] But a still more curious incident was in store for me: not far off was a haunch of mutton: my neighbour was helped with a fine longitudinal cut; he looked for a moment admiringly on his plate, and as he emptied a spoonful of salt on the side, his face was complacency itself. He looked, however, for something; he glanced up the table and down; he called the waiter and whispered something; the waiter went away, but did not return. We were mid-way up the table, and after a pause my neighbour rose, and directing himself to the Bishop of Salisbury, who presided, said, in a tone at once emphatic and aggrieved, "My Lord!" Sarum lifted his calm eye towards my neighbour. "My Lord, *they have forgotten the sweet sauce!*" Sarum had no turn for jokes; yet there was a quiet comical condolence in his voice as he said — "*Indeed*, Doctor!" Now, this may appear a trifling thing to make an episcopal appeal about; but when one considers what a serious improvement the supplementary sweet sauce is to a haunch of Southdown, and how easily obtained it is, one can hardly blame even a divine for deploring its absence. If they went so far as to provide the mutton for 'episcopal stomachs,' as Mr. Turner elegantly designates them, I see no reason why *alter deficit*. Had William Cannyngs filled the place of Sarum, he would understand my friend's feelings: a past mayor would not have been insensible to the importance of sweet sauce. When Sydney Smith[3] first got the prebendal stall in our Cathedral, he was lodging in College Green, and as his fame as a convivialist was not then as noised and known abroad as subsequently, he was allowed to dine at home more frequently that one would suppose; and his dinner was always a beef-steak, and that beef-steak he always bought himself. I was then, as I am now, my own purveyor, and there were few days when he was in residence that I did not meet him at Burge's,[4] in Denmark Street (his favourite butcher and mine), overseeing and selecting his own cut. After Sydney had described a circle with is finger round a certain pin-bone, and emphatically told the man of fat to 'cut there, and cut boldly,' as the Roman augur said, Burge turned to me and asked, "and where will you be helped, Sir?" "I'll follow suit," said I, "the cut next to Mr. Smiths's; I can't go wrong with such a precedent." The Canon's droll eye twinkled, his large, pouting, and somewhat luxurious lip moved with that comic twitch which spoke the man, as he said, "You're a wise man, Sir; this is one of the cases where you can't err if you follow the church, and you'll find your obedience rewarded with a good beef-steak."

The wall towers to which I alluded as encircling the college of Westbury, were standing up to the time of Charles the First; but they were razed by Prince Rupert during the brief period he had possession of the city, that they might not be made a nest for the republican hornets. This precaution, however, did not, I think, prevent Oliver Cromwell, subsequently turning the church into a barrack for a troop of horse. The sacrilegious roundheads, however, behaved themselves pretty well from all I can see; at least they left us in tolerable integrity a beautiful church — a church capable of being made still more beautiful. It preserves most of its collegiate character: it has side aisles divided by two rows of lofty and commanding arches, from the centre or main one, which is lit by clerestory windows.

The churchyard, which has a pleasant picturesque situation, is not barren of 'memorial, monument and tomb.' Who does not recollect the tomb close by the public path, 'To the memory of Richard Ruddle, who was coachman to Sir Robert Cann, Bart., and was robbed and murdered by Bennet and Payne, 27th October, 1743.' As a boy, when I used to walk to Westbury with my father, this to me was a source of awe and dread; and I used to pass shrinkingly by the tomb of the murdered man, for the village gossips had invested both it and the whole story with innumerable associations, all frightful to the fancy. Bennet and Payne, or one of them, was hung in chains near the Down for this act, and swung creakingly over many a passenger's head as he hurried with frightened steps across the turf on the long winter's night. There was a story that they not only murdered and robbed, but ate the bodies of those they killed: however, the baronet's coachman seems to have been made of 'sterner stuff' than their ordinary victims, for he was fortunate enough to obtain Christian burial in a state of corporal integrity; and the parish authorities, when the church lately underwent repairs, seem to have selected this of all others as an object of 'repaint' and restoration.

A good many attend the church, but it is not a good congregation. I mean the congregation, independently of the neighbouring respectable families who must come to church, does not comprise many of the humble and poor parishioners: where they go I cannot say, but, on making some enquiries as to the religious statistics of the parish, I received the following curious and incongruous catalogue: — 'We have a Baptist chapel, a Methodist chapel, a Popish chapel, half-a-dozen private ranting-rooms, and about twelve beershops!' But whether the poor go to the dissenting chapels, the ranting rooms, or the beershops, this I know, they don't seem to go to church. Is there no reason for it? The vicar, or incumbent, or perpetual curate, or whatever other description my friend, the Rev. R. Carrow,[5]

Parvise over South Porch

rejoices in, preaches there once a month, and then does or says nothing to make people uncomfortable; and the curate being also the chaplain to the Infirmary, has little leisure left for parochial visiting, so that the poor are very probably left in a very independent state to themselves, and the beershops. This is a pity, the parish is of great extent, and should have the undivided use of the curate at least, who should make it a point once in the week to 'darken the door' of every poor parishioner. Mr. Mais has, I think, £20 a year as chaplain of the Infirmary. I would, therefore, suggest to my friend, Mr. Carrow, to add this sum on to the present stipend, so as to confine the services of Mr. M. altogether to Westbury, and, in consideration of this, we shall willingly dispense with his monthly sermon. The curate is an excellent and pious man, but he is not an animated preacher; he means well, and there is a strain of devotional sincerity about his sermons, but he never could hold my attention for many minutes together. Many years ago, I was a regular attendant at the Cathedral, and I recollect one day sitting next to my old friend Dean Beeke,[6] when a rather 'slow' man (I forget who now) was preaching. When he had plodded away to about the middle of his discourse, my Very Rev. neighbour nudged me with his elbow: I turned my ear towards him: "Do you know what I am thinking of?" said the Dean. "I don't know. Sir," I replied. "I'm thinking," said the Dean, who was a great calculator, "how many bricks it would take to stop up that window." It is something the same with me, I'm ever disposed to wander when I'm at Westbury, and am too often, I am ashamed to confess it, mentally engaged in cutting down the pews. There is a want of life about the congregation, too, and I think if my estimable friend, the curate, would only try to put some spirit into them, the effort would have a similar and salutary effect on himself at the same time.

1. Henry Colburn and Richard Bentley were two of the largest nineteenth-century publishers. Bentley advertised himself in 1843 as 'Publisher in Ordinary to her Majesty'. Colburn and Bentley were partners from 1829 to 1832.

2. Montague Tavern, Kingsdown.

3. Sydney Smith, 1771-1845. Smith held the third prebendal stall from 1828 to 1845. Starting his career as a curate in a living near Salisbury owned by Michael Hicks Beach of Williamstrip, Gloucestershire, Smith later became a controversial figure, famous for his social charm and reforming zeal. He once found himself arguing against the Archbishop of Canterbury and the Bishop of London over the necessity of having a National Church. Bishop Monk, referring to Smith's appointment as a canon-residentiary of St. Paul's said he got his canonry for being a scoffer and jester.

4. James T. Burge — subsequently moved to Nicholas Street.

5. Richard Carrow (1810). Curate J. Mais.

6. Henry Beeke, 1751-1837; Dean of Bristol 1814-37. Beeke had a wide reputation as a financial authority. Nicholas Vansittart, later Lord Bexley, when chancellor of the exchequer (1812-23) frequently consulted with him on financial matters.

18 January 1845
St. George's, Somerset: or Easton in Gordano

To the steam-boat passenger coming up the river. Pill, with its sickly yellow hovels and beershops rising out of and surrounded by slime and mud, and its group of tarry sailors and tattered women leaning over dirty half-doors and crumbling walls, is unpicturesque and unpleasant enough; but until you traverse its narrow broken streets, which, but for courtesy, might better be called kennels, and see the traces, not so much of poverty as of filth, vice, and intemperance which abound, you have no idea of the commonwealth of dirt and degradation which a community of sailors can raise around them. Quin, the player,[1] when indignant with the people of Bristol, once said, that when the swine possessed with devils ran down the steep into the sea, they never stopped until they landed at Pill; and, considering the favourite element of these four-footed animals, I can hardly conceive anything more suitable to their tastes, so far as mud and mire go.

Even John Bunyan, accustomed as he has been for the most part to carry his rider through wholesome hamlets and pleasant villages, seemed not a little surprised on finding himself up to his fetlocks in a sort of amphibious mixture, which partook in equal parts of land soil and marine mud; and, as he glanced round on the crowded hovels, which strove to look gay, but smiled ghastly in yellow ochre, he seemed to think — "Well, I have been in a great many places, but this is something new — decidedly new to me."

I passed through Pill without attracting the attention of more than a few diminutive infants, who made an abortive attempt to pelt me with potato skins; and reached the hamlet of St. George's, more directed by my own instinct than anything else. I put up at the post office — the post office and the hostelry being one. The stableman had his hands in his pockets, and looked as if he expected me. I enquired the hour at which they went into church; and he said he thought it was half-past ten — he believed it was half-past ten — indeed he was almost sure it was half-past ten.

"My good friend, you don't seem to speak from very great practical acquaintance with the fact," said I, "judging from the diffidence with which you pronounce on the time. I can hardly conceive that you sing in the church choir."

His reply was — "How could he go to church, when gentlemen came with their horses? — there must be somebody to attend to them."

"Thank you, that's quite enough," I replied, and I felt a twinge at the moment; but whether it proceeded from conscience or the rheumatism, I did not stop to investigate.

"The nearest way to the church, my good friend?" said I.

"Over the stile at the corner, and across the field. Sir." Parson Mirehouse, could you not contrive to get the stones in the walk that leads to the south entrance broken a little smaller? in its present state, to one with tender toes a short pilgrimage to Compostella with peas in his shoes is not a much greater penance. Like myself, I found all that went before me were obliged to walk on the wet grass. I met a gentleman in a dark grey wrapper in the churchyard, who inquired if I could let him have a seat. "With pleasure, sir," I said, leading the way, as if I were the lay impropriator himself. I looked around, and, close by the pulpit, I saw an immense seat, which at first I took to be the churching pew, but eventually it turned out to be the freehold attached to the manor-house; the manor-house being void so was the pew, and to this I led my friend in the dark wrapper. I am sorry from the appearance of the church — the emptiness of the seats, both free and appropriated — to say that the musical invitation of the tenor bell seems to meet with sorry compliance from the surrounding neighbourhood — the said bell and its five companions sounding their pressing and pious call each Sunday morning in unwilling ears. In the great gallery at the east end there were one bassoon player and four singers, and none else; free seats for nearly four hundred in the nave were occupied by some half dozen adults and a handful of children; and even the pews boasted but a poor sprinkling.

How is this? Easton-in-Gordano is a large place, and ought to furnish at least one church: Pill alone might supply a congregation. I know there is nothing, humanly speaking, inviting to a clergyman in such a place as Pill, with its rough inhabitants and uncleanly community; but these disadvantages must not, and I am happy to say seldom do, stop or deter a clergyman from his duty.

Sailors are said to be either great reprobates or great fanatics: this may be because they are wholly neglected or left to erratic enthusiasts. For my part, I see no reason why sailors should be less susceptible to the good felt by, or the teachings found to influence, other men. Their calling is one of peril — in the midst of life they may be truly said to be in death — their home is on the most majestic element: they are surrounded with sublimity, and who ought to be more alive to the power, and glory, and mercy of God than 'they that go down to the sea in ships, that do business in great waters; these see the works of the Lord and his wonders in the deep: for he commandeth and raiseth the stormy wind, which lifteth up the waves thereof; they mount up to heaven, and, go down again to the depths?'[2] It is Young,[3] I believe, who says, 'an undevout astronomer is mad;' but, for my part, I cannot conceive how a seafaring man, who does not feel some religion, can with more truth be said to be in his senses. It may seem not quite so unnatural for us landsmen, enveloped in mists that our own little passions have raised around us, busied with many things,

and hardly raising our eyes above the level of ourselves and our daily occupations, to claim some excuse for not seeing the wonders of creation that spread
themselves around and above us: but there is nothing, so far as human ken can
go, to hide the grandeur and expanse of God's works — this 'universal frame'
— from those that 'do business in the great waters;' and I am convinced, if the
poor Pill pilot would go and hear one of the Rev. Mr. Mirehouse's many good
sermons, or, in case of his not going, or 'not being able to go,' as the phrase is, if
Mr. Mirehouse would be content to forego the comforts of his carpeted drawing-room on certain mornings or evenings of the week, and go down and teach
him in his hamlet 'by the Avon's ooze,' such teachings, I'll be bound, would not
be thrown away. The poor pilot or fisherman, when out in his skiff or yawl at
night in the Bristol Channel, with the stars shining above him, and no noise
but the rush of the waters as they surge by him, and break against the bows
and sides of his boat, would be sure to think what he had heard, over again in
that sublime solitude, while looking out for some foreign vessel or watching
his nets. He could not help it: the words he heard would be sure to occur to
him in the solemn silence of the night, and steal insensibly to his recollection.
In the peopled steamboat you cannot feel as that man in his lonely skiff would
feel: it is to him alone in that situation I should say it is given to apprehend,
if anyone fully can, the fearful grandeur of the passage, 'And the spirit of God
moved upon the face of the waters!'[4]

I wish, indeed, that the Vicar of Easton in Gordano could or would turn the
population of Pill to a little more account, or that at least some could be found
to fill the church. It is melancholy to read in large letters on the front of the
gallery, that about twelve of fifteen years ago, and during the churchwardenship
of two persons, names now forgotten by me, and the Rev. Henry Mirehouse
being vicar,[5] the church was enlarged, and free seats for 480 persons added;
and then look at those seats, and see that some dozen people, exclusive of the
schoolboys, have availed themselves of the privilege.

If I were a clergyman I could not bear to look at the gaunt backs of empty
forms Sunday after Sunday from the pulpit. I'd go out into the highways, and
almost force people to come in. Mr. Mirehouse is a Magistrate, but stay! may
not this magistracy have something to do with these empty forms? I may be
called an officious old fellow for interfering with what some may say does not
concern me; but as a general principle, as the phrase is, I am averse to having
the magisterial and clerical character combined. It may be a weakness of mine,
but such is the case. The affectionate confidence with which a flock should approach the parson is, I am of opinion, counteracted and deterred by the fear,
or at least awe, with which they regard him as a Justice. There is everything
that is amiable, merciful, and paternal in the ideal of a country clergyman; he
is the father of the parish, and there should be nothing to deter his people
from seeking his advice and counsel both in sin and sorrow: whether the terror
with which in their weak minds they invest the Justice, 'clad in the panoply

of legal power,' presiding on a high bench, and punishing with earthly penalties his own parishioners, is compatible with this affectionate confidence and
respectful familiarity, is a question for others: I don't think it is — I don't like
the 'composite order' in this respect— I don't like to see the 'statutes at large'
side by side with the old divines in a clergyman's library. In fact, I don't think
a man can serve the Church and the Lord Chancellor, without letting what he
owes to one clash with what he ought to be in the other. I know it is a sacrifice
which many men do not like— this abandonment of power and authority; but
if I were the Vicar of Easton in Gordano, I'd throw up my commission and see
it those four hundred and eighty free sittings did not fill a little better. This
and more frequent visits to the pilots and fishermen of Pill might have the
desired effect.

I can't congratulate the Vicar of St. George on his architectural taste, for
it is since his incumbency that the old church has been pulled down. I recollect the old church very well; and for the same money expended on the new
it might have been enlarged or repaired, in which case we should not have a
fine old Gothic tower with a half schoolroom, half conventicle, built onto the
east end of it, as at present, but a parish church. The existing edifice is a cold,
staring, comfortless, bare, barn-like building, with a few old, barbarous monuments, repainted and reset in its modern walls; amongst the latter are a series
to the multitudinous family of the Morgans: over the manor pew is a remarkably odd one, to 'the charitable and virtuous Mrs. Mary Morgan,' who died at
54, and made such good use of her time as to have three husbands during that
period: the virtuous Mrs. Mary's first husband was 'the hon. Band of gentlemen pensioners' — I beg pardon, *one* of the hon. band of gentlemen pensioners, the second a Lewis, and the third a Morgan. Mrs. Mary, the virtuous, was
no monogamist; beneath are three red-headed cherubs, looking as lively and
life-like as rose pink and Prussian blue can make them: I hope they are not
meant to be at all allegorical of her three spouses, for they are the very acme
of preternatural ugliness. In the chancel, which is a poor thing, there is a cumbrous half-length figure, in canonicals, of Roger Soudon, vicar of that parish
a century and a half ago: Roger evidently had ambition, but his executors had
no taste. The entrance to the gallery and tower, which is through the church,
is quite exposed: indeed nothing could be in worse judgment than the whole
edifice. Whoever the Vandal architect was that knocked down the old church,
I might have forgiven him if he had not built the new one.[6]

The Vicar is an admirable reader, impressive without ostentation, and
when I heard his sermon I wondered there were so many empty seats; his
manner is solemn and earnest, without severity, and he talks home with the
directness not merely of earnest admonition, but strong common sense, to
the reason, business, and hearts of his hearers. I should like to try the effects
of such a sermon from a man who had not a suffix in the shape of a J.P. to his
name.

I think the singing would be very fairly done, and the congregation would join, if the old fellow with the bassoon in the gallery would allow them; the instrument emits supernatural growls, which have quite a frightful effect on one's ears. If I were the Vicar, I'd sell the 'horse's leg,' as the country people call it, and buy a new drapery for the pulpit with the proceeds.

1. James Quin, 1693-1766. A Shakespearian actor and contemporary of Garrick.
2. Psalm 107 v23.
3. Edward Young, 1683-1765. *The Complaint; or Night Thoughts on Life, Death and Immorality* (1742).
4. Genesis 1.2.
5. Henry Mirehouse (1819).
6. It was mostly rebuilt again in 1872.

1 February 1845
Portishead

I have an old and long standing acquaintance with Portishead, before it numbered as many houses as it does now I knew it, for few summers have passed for the last twenty years without my visiting it, for a greater or less time. My favourite resort is the hotel[1] at the point, though I have occasionally chartered a moiety of a cottage to myself for a month or so, always selecting the site so that I could shave with my face towards the channel, and if I was able to throw a rose bush or an arbutus into the picture it was all the better. Depend upon it, this choice of a prospect is a great secret of cheerfulness and comfort, your first look out upon the morning should be as free and open as possible: the first influences and impressions on the waking senses are the strongest for the day, and your serenity of mind, for the following twelve hours at least, often depends upon whether you have opened your eyes upon a tall gable, a tiled roof and a water cistern, or green fields broad waters and blue mountains. People frequently build their bedrooms to look out on their back yards, in which case shaving and dressing is gloomy work; but both are a positive pastime if you have a sunny sloping lawn to soothe your vision. Just fancy the 'Damascus steel' passing smoothly down your chin, soap slowly turning like snowflakes over its brilliant blade, or a bunch of jesamine and cluster of roses peep coyly round the corner of the casement in upon your toilet, and a bullfinch or linnet on the topmost spray of the opposite larch exerts all its melody as if in compliment to you. Portishead Point was always suggestive to me of a dilatory dressing hour and I could never resist the lazy making influence of the Welsh mountains and the intervening channel in its morning calm, when each craft on its surface seemed like a painted ship upon a painted ocean. I used to say to my estimable acquaintance and worthy old soul, Miss Pring, that amid such a scene they ought to know no wickedness, for all nature, as well as my excellent friend Dr. Shipton,[2] was preaching peace to them, and there ought to be no corruption known as Possut, but what occasionally visited it in the shape of the old corporation.

But Miss Pring said I was joking, for she knew me to be too good a Tory to talk that way but in jest. And so I am a good Tory, and amongst other things most admire the conscientious determination with which the scarlet brotherhood adhered to the matter of dinner, and the sage ingenuity with which they combine to make three courses and game go along with business. Their ostensible object in visiting Possut was to see that nobody stole their estates, or moved their landmarks. All the Chamber constituted the deputation, and as many of them as were not afflicted with gout took the view from the nearest eminence. Those that could not take a view taking their fellow corporators' words for the fact, and all taking their wine.

I like those country estates whether they belong to a corporation or a close vestry, for they give you so good an opportunity of having a rural dinner and fresh vegetables, once in the year. I myself belong to a vestry which had at one time ten acres in a certain parish, about five miles from Bristol, and to which we paid an annual visit of inspection, winding up with a dinner at the village inn: we got into difficulties, half our ten acres was sold, still we went out in four carriages, for, like the Sybil and her books, though the quantity were less under the expense of inspection were the same: the five acres further diminished, until at length all that was left us was a cottage and a dozen gooseberry bushes, which however, we continued to visit with the same pertinacity and good faith, keeping up the same number of courses, and all it will be recollected at our own expense. At length there was not even a gooseberry bush left, and still we went and dined, and having no property of our own to inspect we inspected that of our neighbours.

Whoever the former proprietor of John Bunyan may have been, I think he never took my trusty steed for the benefit of the sea breezes to Portishead, for John looked round him with the eye of one to whom the scene was quite new, and it was not until he saw the Gordon Stag swinging from its lofty post that he appeared to have any idea of the existence of an inn there. I wish someone would put up my family heraldic achievements to swirl, to swing and creak in the wind, for it must be a great gratification to the thirsty traveller to know that he may drink his beer, and pay for it, under the protecting shield and complicating quarterings of some mighty house.

Having left John to the ostler, and the ostler to the sale of two ducks to some gentleman who seemed to select the Sunday as the most suitable day for this venal transaction, I turned churchwards. I was in very good time, and had some leisure moments left to loiter about the burial ground, and read the tombstones. I was some months ago in a little village churchyard in Hampshire, and could not help being struck with the extraordinary similarity of style in all the poetic epitaphs so that I was convinced they were all the work of one hand, and concluded the parish stonecutter not only engraved the letters, but made the verses. While I was engaged in my perusal, a patriarchal old farmer made his appearance, and I enquired if such was the case, but he said, "No, no, it be the curate as made the powtry, and beautiful powtry it was: there was not a dry eye in the parish for a fortnight after the new headstone was put up, there was a power of weeping — it was so effecting". "Indeed," said I. "Yes sure master," he continued, "And after the two babes yonder, and the broken posies, we were in tears for a good three weeks: oh, he's a beautiful poet." 'The two babes' was a headstone commemorating the death of twins, which the curate compared to flowers untimely nipped, and the melancholy idea was further illustrated by two fractured emblems at the top, which the stonecutter had 'bodied forth' in a shape something between a dahlia and a drumhead cabbage. Yet this was an amiable quality in the curate, and a most innocent vent for his poetic fancy, for if he had not put his verses on tombstones, he might have printed them in a book, or the local paper, the consequences of which one can hardly speculate on. In connection with this story, I wish to know if it is the curate or the vicar of Possut who supplies the poetry for the departed of that parish, as in either case I should recommend them to 'revise their proofs' for however harmonious the numbers, and lucid the sense, the orthography is not of the first order. It is true that Pope,[3] with all his melody of verse, was an excreble speller; but that was in the reign of Queen Anne, when the public were not as critical as the nineteenth century, when we abound in normal and national schools. For instance, near the south porches a lofty headstone with loftier verses, to Mistress Vowles, in which some words are spelled wrong, and the passenger has impotently attempted to correct them: 'Extremes' spelt 'Extrems' by the stonecutter, is amended by someone inserting with a black lead pencil an 'a' between the 'e' and the 'm'. Another hypercritic succeeds, who writes 'both are wrong, place an "e" between the "m" and the "s", and that will be right!' all this conspicuous enough on account of the white ground of the headstone.

There is a lofty cross, with a flight of five or six steps and in good preservation. I like these old crosses in country churchyards, though it is as much as a man's life is worth to say so in these days when so much speech subjects him to danger of being burnt or mobbed as a Puseyite "they are monuments of popery," said my old aunt Peggy, who has lived to be eighty, and never made this notable discovery until within the last five years, when she began to subscribe to the *Record*. "They are relics of popery and ought to be pulled down." "So are nearly all your cathedrals my dear madam, and three fourths of your parish churches, and you don't pull them down." But let us change the subject: it is a dangerous one for an old gentleman who is not at all ambitious on being a martyr, but if I should be converted into one which should certainly be against my will, and as Coleridge[4] says, 'If an inscription be put upon my tomb, let it be that I was an enthusiastic lover of the Church; and as enthusiastic a hater of those who betrayed it, if they be who they may.'

While yet absorbed in my meditations amongst the tombs, the peal in the beautiful tower above my head ceased their mellow tones, and the little pertinacious, sharp toned, talkative bell outside the church, and nearly over the chancel arch, commenced a flippant and importunate clatter to convoke all the stragglers in it was the third and last time of calling, and the few loiterers, who like myself, remained outside, no sooner heard its small though not still voice, than they rushed towards the south porch. If this bell be not a modern erection, I was thinking that it might be, like the cross, a relic of popery, and what was called in catholic times the sanctus bell.

The last occasion on which I was in Portishead church was rather a peculiar, certainly an interesting one. It was a summer's morning: I had strolled down from the point and on passing through the churchyard I noticed a little group of people there, and a somewhat unusual stir. I enquired the case from a person at the door and she informed me it was a marriage, and the 'grand contracting parties' were expected every moment. Never having been a principal or even second in such an office, I easily prevailed upon her to admit me and I took up my position in a pew by which the bridal procession must pass. It was a beautiful morning and as the sun streamed in through the windows, it seemed to have lit up the church with a flood of golden light for the occasion. I had not long to wait, for the doors opened in a few minutes after I had taken my place, and the marriage party entered, and oh, what a rustle of gauze and satins, and what a flutter of light hearts beneath them, and what a troop of bright faces. I felt almost in as earnest an ecstasy as if I were going to be married myself; and as I glanced towards the bride, shrouded in her long veil, and surrounded by her bridesmaids, it was as if upon something sacred. There was no levity in the scene: it was bright and sunshiny enough, but it was toned down to the solemnity of a holy rite and holy and solemn it was, joy above and around the little group, but it was joy subdued and surrounded by religious awe; and I felt at that moment a purity of sentiment, and I think I may say a proper and solemn sympathy in the scene befitted it. The morning sun shone in on the little crowd that clustered around the altar, and the surplice of the clergyman, and the dress of the bridal party, glistened in its rays, so as to remind one of the description in the Apocalypse of the martyred throng around the throne, 'who washed their garments and made them white in the blood of the lamb'. For a minute after the minister had taken his place, not a sound was heard but the rustle of the bride's dress as she took up her position on the left: and then how beautiful and impressive arose the first words, 'dearly beloved, we are gathered together here in the sight of God, and in the face of his congregation, to join together this man and woman in holy matrimony!' Hear this, you Whigs (I could not help saying it in my own mind), or rather you Whigs could you ever have heard it before you devised your odious registration of marriages act,[5] with its staff and marriage joiners or fourth and fifth of Victoria, or your second and third of William IV, or whatever you call it, with its cold blooded machinery — what do you think of your civil contract performed in a small back parlour by some parish dresser and dyer, out of a large ledger, compared with such a solemnization in an old parish church, 'in the sight of God, and the face of the congregation,' and amongst the graves of their fathers and within the carved work of the sanctuary. Can you ever expect that the union formed in their cold-blooded Act of Parliament can have either love or religion about it, or that a life-long association, commenced under such irreverent circumstances, can be cheered by affection or blessed by prosperity.

The soft whisper of the bride's voice as she promised to love, honour, and obey, would almost have encited me to march to the annihilation of all the registration acts in the Empire. It is nothing to me that people say that young ladies do not always keep these promises; the service is not the less beautiful for this, for if they break them it is ever the man's fault, for I agree with the recent philosopher 'that though man seems to be designed for the superior being of the two, as things are, I think women are better creatures than man.' I was so charmed with my morning adventure, that the only thing to complete my happiness was to have been asked home for a cut of the wedding cake, for I could not think of course of coveting the clergyman's traditional kiss.

On the occasion of my last visit, however, the weather was not as propitious as on the nuptial morning. It was cold and boisterous, and the wind whistled round the little church, and shook the windows of the north aisle, like a strong man, trying to make a forcible entrance, and so I could not help looking back at the time-worn mullions and staunchions in some apprehension. At every noisy gust my neighbour wrapped his blue cloak more closely round him, until at length he seemed as comfortable as broadcloth and a clear conscience could make him.

Portishead is a pleasing little country church, but with the exception of the tower, however, which is lofty and well proportioned, there is little to remark about it. It consists of a nave and chancel of nearly equal length, and a wide north aisle, with three unpleasant looking pipes protruding menacingly from the wall at the east end, and put up there, I suppose illustrate the term of 'church militant,' or to keep the audience in order in absence of the churchwardens, for there is a large pew erected against the wall of the north aisle for these well-beloved officials, but there is no trace of one or the other; and I was thinking that perhaps of earlier times when Chancellor Raikes[6] has tried to set churchwardens against minister, and minister against churchwardens, his charge has had the effect of getting up a row between them and the reverend Mr. Woolley[7] or perhaps they were late the night before marking up the lessons for the following day, and overslept themselves; or perhaps they had a cold, and got the loan of the newspapers from their next door neighbour the curate. At the west end is a small gallery, the front of which is covered with signboards, one announces that the gallery was repaired in a certain year and my old friend Dr. Shipton was vicar, and Shipton curate, and two persons (names not now remembered) churchwardens; As the whole gallery is hardly worth saying so much about, the repairs which could not have involved more than the expenditure of ten pence for nails and a pot of paint, it hardly called for so elaborate a commemoration. Close to this is a blackboard, on which were intended to be inscribed for the benefit of the congregation the hymns, or rather the numbers of the hymns to be sung on every Sunday; but as the custom has for some time been given up, the last named, which was made many years ago, still remains to mislead the public. But the most remarkable and the most imposing of all these inscriptions on the gallery, is one which tells the parish and posterity, as plainly and as conspicuously as white lead and lamp black make it, that 'This organ was presented to the parish church by James Adam Gordon Esq. 1800 and something'. My first thought was that it had been 'this grinder had been presented' it would have been more correct, as it appeared to me to be one of those easily played upon apologies for a musical instrument: had Mr. James Adam Gordon given them one as big as Naish House, with a stop diapason, and goodness knows how many other musical complications, he could not have made more ado, or put up a mightier signboard to commemorate the gift, than he was for this pygmy grinder: but grinder did I say; it may not have been even that, for anything more than a false front of mahogany, for I never heard its voice the whole time. I could see nothing behind the Honduras which did not go back more than a few inches. When the psalms were given out I listened to hear the first tones of the free gift, for, thought I, though it be a grinder, it must be a remarkably good one; for Friar Bacon[8] did not wait longer for a speech from his brass head not a note. To be sure the children did their best work, and did it well, but no thanks to the grinder for that: there it was with as little music in it as the churchwardens pew, and James Adam Gordon getting all the glory all the while, though had he presented the parson with a musical snuff box, it would have been quite as useful, so far as effect went, to the parish. I am no great lover of this ostentatious liberality, which takes the value out of the gift by blazoning the boon in black and white before men, it was somewhat the same sentiment that made Alexander offer to rebuild the Temple of Ephesus after it had been burnt down, if they would allow him to inscribe his name in front: but if men will really insist on having their reward, let them give value for it, call things by their real names let them call an organ, an organ, and a grinder, let it be designated by no more grandilioquent a title than a grinder. Had I taken the mere word on the signboard I should have gone away mentally obliged to Mr. Gordon for a first rate instrument and thus been cheated out of more gratitude than the gift deserved. I do not accuse Mr. Gordon of fraudulent attempt to get more than his due, but there he was all this time in his seat in the chancel, looking up at the inscription to his own glory, and countenancing the perpetuity of the piece of intelligence not strictly correct. Until the grinder recovered the use of its voice, if I were he, I should have the board pulled down, or else (and this is a much better suggestion) I would substitute an actual organ, capable of being played upon, for a thing at present of not more use, though presented by James Adam Gordon Esq. than a structure of ornamental gingerbread.

Though, perhaps, if I were to deliberate on the matter, I would not advise organ or grinder, so long as the children and congregation go on as they do, thanks to Mainzer, Hullah,[9] the sol-fahing system has certainly done something for country church music, and when you can get a charity school by a little drubbing and drilling to go together, and to keep anything like time and tune, and the congregation are imperceptibly emboldened to fall in, a double bass or bassoon, or even an organ, are as well dispensed with, as the last especially often tempts people to shelter their laziness under its amazing body of sound.

This evenings psalms were given out by the rector, who read them through well, though with the slightest smack of what Mrs. Siddons[10] calls the 'provincial te-ti-tum'. This plan, which I begin to see adopted in many country churches is a great improvement on the old system of allowing the parish clerk to perform the duty, to the discomfort of all present who do not like to hear the sublime and beautiful version brawled through the ruddy nose of some licensed victualler. The congregation in winter though good, is not large; in summer, however, the church is crowded, though Portishead has not yet attained to that almost invariable appurtenance to watering places, a popular curate a kind of public depository for silver teapots and embroidered slippers. The congregation is parochial in winter; in summer it is more of the migratory order. The vicar read prayers, and reads well, though his endeavour to do so was a little too manifest.

The sermon was preached by a stranger, as my esteemed neighbour in the blue cloak informed me. I like a sermon from a visitor for several reasons: when a clergyman leaves home he usually puts two or three of his very best in his portmanteau, to provide for casual calls, as he is far too reasonable to expect anything but that his own parishioners put up with his bad ones. Another thing about the parson on voyage, you are always sure to escape a series. I cannot bear a series; though I know some excellent men who are never out of a continuation of this kind, but are sure to be always at the beginning middle or ending of a succession of some of the books from Genesis to Revelations. There is another kind of continuation which I admire even less than those, and that is — when a clergyman after he has given three quarters of an hour on the subject shuts his book and tells you he will finish the subject on the following Sunday. There is an apposite story told by Wharton in Boswell's *Life of Johnson*, of a Mr. Swinton, a chaplain of Oxford Gaol, who was greatly given to dispersing his subject over two or three Sundays. And upon one occasion when preaching the confirmation sermon, on the repentance before the two men who were to be hanged the next morning, he observed at the close that he would give them the rest of what he had to say on the following Sunday. Happily the congregation are not in many instances destined to be hanged the next day, but there are many other instances besides suspension likely to leave some of them only half enough on the subject in mind. The discourse on the present occasion was solemn and impressive, but rather heavily delivered. I listened attentively, but could not help hearing my wanton friend in the dark wrapper by my side snoring rather rapidly. I took the liberty of touching him on the knee, for I know of nothing that more disconcerts a preacher than such somniferous sounds. The present patron is Mr. Gordon who purchased the Advowson at the time of the Revolution, or Reformation, or Reform Bill, or whatever you call it. [11]

1. The Royal Hotel, built 1830.

2. J.N. Shipton, D.D. Instituted at Portishead in 1791, but moved to Othery, in 1832.

3. Alexander Pope, 1688-1744.

4. Samuel Taylor Coleridge, 1772-1834.

5. Registration of Marriage Act, 1836.

6. Henry Raikes, 1782-1834. Chancellor of the Diocese of Chester, 1830-34.

7. T.L. Wolley (1838).

8. Roger Bacon, 1214?-1294.

9. Hullah's System, see p.55.

10. Sarah Siddons, 1755-1831.

11. The Reform Bill. The living was shown in 1822 as being the gift of the Corporation of Bristol. However, between that date and 1846 it was acquired by James Adam Gordon.

Slimbridge

It was not my original intention to have travelled so far from home, but being on a visit with an old friend in the neighbourhood, I thought I would walk across and see the old and, as I had heard, beautiful church of Slimbridge.

While on my road I heard the cry of hounds, and very soon in front of me passed a hare, and about four couple of awkward young dogs. It surely cannot be my lord,[1] thought I, who has chosen the Sabbath for a hare-hunt: nor indeed was it; the dogs were hunting on their own account, and for their own amusement, as I subsequently learned. They were not interns of his lordship's kennel, but young dogs 'out at nurse,' as I think the term is, his lordship compelling every renter of £50 to keep one of those awkward overgrown puppies for the space of a year, until they are qualified for the pack; thus there are few of the tenants, who might not claim the honour of being foster-father to a foxhound. These creatures have the most extraordinary habits: though scattered amongst the farmhouses through the country, they will to the number of six, eight, or ten, meet as it were by concert at some central spot, and, as I said before, commence hunting on their own account, killing hares for themselves, the biggest bully always having the best bit: with the shades of evening they 'homeward plod their weary way,'[2] leaving the world to darkness and the hares, not, however, it is thought by the naturalists round about, without a perfect intelligence to meet again in the morning, when, having had their breakfast (and each is said to eat as much as a pig), these loose-living creatures go out according to appointment for another day's dissipation.

It was with no slight relief of mind I saw his lordship was not answerable for this Sunday's sport, and I should have felt comfortable under the conviction that he was saying his prayers in the great pew amidst the ashes of his ancestors, if it were not my misfortune to pass the pool of Slimbridge, when I witnessed that his lordship was engaged on a Sabbath day in duck hunting on his own estates, and amongst his own tenants. My lord! my lord! are there not six days when you might decoy ducks to your heart's content, and not set such a pattern to those who look up to you as their exemplar as well as their protector? If you choose to run the risk of the spiritual responsibility of such an act yourself, it is your own business, and if done out of the public sight, I should have nothing to say to it or you. But there are some deeds the mischief of which are not confined to the doer; and what, think you, are likely to be the

moral obligations and Sabbath impressions of your tenantry, when they see one powerful by possessions, ennobled by birth, inheriting the accumulated honours of a lofty and long line of ancestors, offending in this open manner, not merely against the solemn code of the decalogue, but the received impressions of society? — should we be surprised if they too deserted their parish church, and turned Sabbath duck-hunters? Mind, my lord, I ask for no proof of active religion from you; I do not say you ought to go to church twice on a Sunday, and ring the Castle bell before retiring to rest on the Sabbath night, and call the servants into the baronial hall, and take down the iron clasped family Bible (for Berkeley Castle, after all men say, is not, I am sure, without such an heirloom, though thrust away somewhere amongst old helmets and hauberks) and have your chaplain read prayers for them there — though such things have been ere now, and that amidst ancestral halls and towers as time-honoured as your own. But there are certain outward observances of order which belong to the list of 'duties' which society expects from property in return for the rights it possesses; and one is, a decent example from the great to those dependent upon them.

There were some peasants standing by the south porch. I asked who the parson was. They said a Mr. Goldspur or Goldsburgh,[3] I think: but that he had another living (oh! these 'other livings!') in Somersetshire, where he resided: there were, however, two curates, which they seemed to think a very good substitute for one rector. "And here they be" exclaimed my informant, pointing towards a square house adjoining the churchyard, and very like a tea cannister, though it turned out to be the parsonage, and from which two clergymen were approaching in their gowns and bands. The loiterers bowed to them as they came up, and I, lifting my hat, made a low obeisance, as I always do to those wearing the livery of the church. As soon as the clergy entered, I led the way for the churchyard loungers, and found myself in one of the finest country churches I have been in for some time. I took up my place in one of the stalls of the chancel, where there were some other persons sitting, and from which I had the opportunity of seeing a very primitive congregation and not a very large one. Both curates occupied the reading-desk, dividing the duty, and in the service there was the utmost solemnity and simplicity combined. The singing, however, consisted of a solo from the clerk, to which the congregation listened with breathless attention. I tried to join him, but being at such a distance our voices did not blend, and I gave it up; and indeed he did not seem to want any assistance, for he warbled away as happy and independent as a bird. I afterwards learned from two interesting little girls, daughters of the village tailor, who sat near me, that a violoncello was in contemplation; and I think there was something said about a flute, but on this point I am not clear. The elder of the curates, also a Minor Canon of Bristol preached,[4] and pleased me so much that I mentally vowed he should have the next living of which I became patron. There was matter in the sermon, made plain to the homely comprehensions around him, such as they might carry with them to their hearths, and recollect over again as they sat round their wood fires in their cottages. The building bore internal and external signs of extensive restorations and repairs, not quite completed: there was a lofty, commanding, cathedral effect about the pile; and when service was over, I could not help loitering behind the congregation to look around me.

While doing so the elder curate came out of the vestry, and kindly offered to show me the church. I willingly availed myself his courtesy; and found him better informed in ecclesiastical architecture than any amateur I think I had ever before met with. The restorations were made mainly under his super-intendence, and he had with his own hands, worked often till one o'clock at night in that silent and solitary old church, without seeing the ghost of even a bygone Berkeley, cleaning and bringing out the delicate foliage of the capitals of the columns which supported the two rows of arches dividing the north and south aisles from the centre. New clerestory windows of a beautiful design had been inserted,[5] and a new pierced parapet carried round the church. The edifice is, I believe, about the time of Edward the Second: the chancel, which is the oldest portion, being the decorated, and the other parts principally of the perpendicular order.

Some old fresco paintings had been discovered, and I could trace portions of one over the chancel arch. The rector had given nearly £1000 towards the restorations.

There was no nonsense that I could see — no Camdenian extravagance to frighten nervous people. I confess I have no sympathy for those outre gentle-men, who are for introducing into our churches anything for which our church services have no use, or our ritual does not recognise, merely because they were there in Catholic times, for I do not see why they should be such admir-ers of 'the old faith' in little things, and not in great; or why they should insist on crosses and candlesticks, and keep their wives.

My reverend friend invited me to the parsonage to lunch after I had seen the church; and merely to see if curates were conscious of cold roast beef, I consented, though my country friend's beans and bacon were almost due.

1. William Berkeley, Earl Fitzhardinge, 1786-1857.
2. Thomas Gray, 1716-71. *Elegy in a Country Churchyard* (1750).
3. John Goldesborough, rector 1811-46, also perpetual curate of Redlynch, Somerset from 1813.
4. James Eccles Carter, also author of *Notes, Historical and Architectural, on the Church of St. John the Evangelist, Slimbridge*, 1845.
5. By Francis Niblett.

Chew Stoke

A DISAPPOINTMENT

I had gathered from my respected and respectable friend. Mistress Jenny K—, that Morning Service commenced at Compton Martin at eleven o'clock, so I started fully resolved to say my prayers on Sunday, February 9th, in this favoured part of Somersetshire, if I possibly could.

The reader may be curious to know who my esteemed informant is, and I have no objection to take him a little into my confidence. I have for years been in the habit of marketing for myself. It is a custom I have acquired, and I should not think it Saturday if I did not purchase my own provisions, and have a gossip with one old good wife or another, whom I can recollect for years, for there are many homely honest faces there that have been familiar to me for almost a quarter of a century, under (I verily believe) the same black or grey beaver bonnet; and to my mind neither face nor head gear seem to have changed since that time. My oldest and most esteemed acquaintance, however, is Mistress Jenny K—, 'the mother of the market,' and there is not one of my readers, who is in the habit of catering for themselves, who will not easily recognise my worthy friend, even under my meagre description. She is 'Jenny K—' to most other familiars and friends, but my father, who was an old-fashioned man, never permitted any of his family to call people by their bare Christian names, and fully convinced of the propriety of his advice I have continued to observe it, and to 'Master' and 'Mistress' everyone beyond a certain age, however long I may have had the honour or pleasure of their acquaintance. Mistress Jenny's 'standing' is always the first I visit on a Saturday morning, and I verily believe I should not be comfortable for the following six days, it I missed her honest face and portly person from the side of the piled-up butter, eggs, and pork (the latter fair as the fairest lady in the land), and all adorned for the most part with a sprig of evergreens or a bunch of flowers, looking as new as a May morning, and redolent with the freshness and bloom of Moreton Farm.[1] Mistress Jenny, too, is, I believe, as glad to see me as I am her, and from a good pair of lungs and a sound heart comes the welcome which she gives the 'old gentleman,' as first wiping her honest hand in her apron she lays hold of mine with a cordiality of grasp, which tells me that truth and sincerity are not yet clean gone from the world. Mistress Jenny ought to be a Queen, only I would not miss her from her place in the market, to furnish the best court in Europe. She is fond of a little chat, and so am I, and we have many a long 'spell' together; I am her only newsmonger, and I tell her when a King dies, or corn rises, or an old citizen whom she has remembered like myself for years, is gathered to his fathers. I never, however, thought it necessary to communicate the *important* secret to her that the 'old gentleman,' who had the couple o'pound of butter and the little basket of fresh eggs from her almost every week, was the Church-Goer; and it was, therefore, with some little surprise I heard her upbraid me last Saturday with never telling her I was the 'ould gossip that went round on a bit o' a pony to the country churches.' "But never mind," she continued, "I'll forgive thee if thee'lt come to Compton Martin tomorrow, and hear Parson Brown,[2] and I'll give thee and the little horse as much provender as either can stow away."

"It's a bargain, Mistress Jenny," said I. "What's the hour of service?"

"It was eleven last Sunday,"

"Then, I'll be with you at half-past ten. And now what's butter today?"

Mistress Jenny subsequently offered to drive me out the same night in her cart, and give me a bed at the farm if I liked. But where I go, it possible, there I wish John Bunyan to go also, so I started a quarter before eight on Sunday morning. I need not talk to the reader about the ascent to Dundry, for I think I have tired him on that point before; but it was much colder now than when I climbed it in summer, and I kept my nose deep in my comforter until I had passed Chew Stoke a half-a-mile: and here I began to think it was nearly time I heard the peals of Compton Martin: for there stood the church full in front of me on the side of the hill, and the Gothic parsonage peeping out from amongst the leafless trees, but no sound of Sabbath-going bells reached me. "Can you tell me, my excellent friend," said I to a good-looking farmer who passed me, "the hour of Service at Compton Martin?" "It was half-past nine *this* morning. Sir," said he, "as Mr. Brown had to go over and do duty at (I think he said) Nempnett."

"Then I have had my ride for nothing," said I, "for it is now half-past ten. Service was at eleven o'clock last Sunday; pray how do the parishioners become acquainted with these changes, if Prayers shift from one hour to the other in this way?"

"He sends round the clerk to our houses on Saturday or some other day during the week."

"Well," thought I, as I paused in doubt as to what I should do, "Mr. Brown, it you have two churches to serve you ought to keep a curate: but I suppose as the clerical phrase is, Compton Martin 'is too poor to carry double.'"

My friend seeing my indecision, said, "If you turn back you will be in time for Prayers at Chew-Stoke, Sir." I thanked him for the advice and turned back, and soon heard old Bilby's[3] beautiful bells pealing out from Chew tower, which stands so picturesquely amongst, and 'bosomed high' by, patriarchal yews. I passed the brook and great village grinding-stone, where they sharpen every-thing that grows blunt, (but their wits), and the parish poor-house, which was just such a one as the poet Crabbe describes,[4] and looked like a monument to the 43rd of Elizabeth;[5] and the parsonage, which is a nice old little Gothic dwelling. Altogether Chew-Stoke is a truly English picture of rural scenery, situate in a well-watered, well-wooded, and well-sheltered vale, and would, I think, make a most pleasing subject for a pretty painting, with its venerable church, its 'yew trees' shade,' its richly battlemented tower, and its clear stream running by its green lanes and amongst its gardened cottages.

Ancient Parsonage House at Chew Stoke.

Having got a temporary standing for John, I proceeded to the church. As I entered the churchyard the bell ceased. Not to be too late, I hurried towards the south porch, and — *met the congregation coming out*! Bless my soul, thought I, here's another disappointment! "Are prayers over my good lad?" said I to the first of a school of boys in blue coats, breeches, and black stockings and bands. "No, Sir," replied the lad, "there are none today; the parson's taken very bad."[6] I next saw the rector's son Mr. Wayte, Jr., to him I applied, and he con-firmed the unfortunate intelligence; his father had been seized with a sudden indisposition, which rendered it quite impossible for him to quit the house: he regretted if I had come to church that I should be disappointed. I need not say, that I felt still more for the cause, and expressed myself to that effect; though Moore's 'Irish Gentleman in search of a Religion,'[7] was hardly more perplexed than I, by my two ineffectual attempts to quest of prayers on one Sunday. However, as I had ridden so far, I did not wish to go back without seeing something; so I asked permission to view the church, which was granted me. The tower is the best part of the edifice; the interior is plain and poor, though there are one or two good windows in the south aisle, which is separated from the nave by a row of arches, the pillars of which are dreadfully chopped away and mutilated. Near the altar, in a kind of open cupboard, are two old tombs (1651), 'Annotations on the Bible;' the Book of Malachi was open, which was the last, I suppose, that required elucidation. From the boards placed against the walls, it would seem that the departed parishioners of Chew Stoke have not forgotten the poor, the bequests, for such a place, being very considerable; the school before alluded to, for educating and clothing a number of boys, being well endowed. The church is dedicated to St. Andrew.

There is a rude organ loft, and a little instrument you may grind or finger. The west entrance is closed, and the lower portion of the tower converted into a vestry-room. In this little apartment is a plain mural tablet to the memory of Bilby, the celebrated bell-founder, who, as well as his son, cast some of the finest peals in the West of England. He resided before his death in Chew Stoke, the peal of which, at least some portion of it, is, I think, a present from him; he lived close by, so that for years he had the pleasure of hearing his own handiwork each Sunday morning.

While I was yet reading Bilby's monument, the schoolmaster came in and invited me to accompany him to the school and examine the boys. It was just the thing of all others I desired, so I readily accepted his offer, and by way of preparation began to turn over the Church Catechism in my own mind, for, like many other things, my youthful learning evidences a manifest tendency to rust. On my way to the school I met a young woman with her Prayer Book and pattens in hand, and as she was going churchward, I thought I'd save her a hundred yards or so by telling her there would be no service today, and the reason why. She seemed concerned, but said smartly enough, it was well she was not going to be married, or she should be sadly disappointed.

When I had got nearly the whole way to the school, and halfway through the Catechism in my own mind, we were overtaken by Mr. Wayte, Jr., who said he was going to read as much of the morning service as a layman might to the children, and I could join: I said, with pleasure; but first I should like to examine the children, as the master was evidently desirous I should do so. Mr. Wayte, Jr., however, did not seem to understand me; or if he did, was not anxious for my interference, for having reached the school, he mounted the desk at once, and commenced with a hymn. There were two or three other persons besides myself and the children (some thirty boys and girls) present; and for rude simplicity at least nothing could exceed our worship in that low-roofed apartment, amongst old forms and moth-eaten and knife-marked desks. It would have been more impressive, however, had it been shorter, for my young friend read the Litany, though both I and the schoolmaster were anxious to commence the examinations. The layman, however, was obdurate, and when prayers were over, it was too late to think of anything but Mistress Jenny K—, and Moreton Farm, and my promised dinner.

My friend the good looking farmer informed me that Mr. W. Jr. was intended for the Church, "when they smoothed un down a bit, and knocked off a few more knots or so."

Neither boy nor girl could I see about the homestead at Moreton Farm on my arrival; so being conscious of a hearty welcome, I helped John to a stall in the byre myself. How quiet and completely at rest seems everything about a farmyard on Sunday: the plough laid down on its side, and the cart thrust away under the shed, and no sound but the munching of the housed cattle as they chewed the cud, or the occasional flutter of the barn-door fowl, as they pecked among the scattered seeds and chaff. John provided for, I had little difficulty in finding my way into the kitchen, and there, seated on the semi-circular high-backed settle by the capacious fireplace, with her esteemed and worthy goodman, I found my friend Mistress Jenny K— (in her old market beaver bonnet.) The back of the settle was turned to the door, so I came on them unawares, and it was not until I had taken a survey of both and the apartment, that they were conscious of my having entered. There was a fine sea coal and log fire down, which blazed and crackled, and shed a ruddy lustre on everything around, in that cleanly, comfortable, and well-kept kitchen, making the rows of polished pewter plates, on the dresser shine with a brilliancy that beat her Majesty's best silver service, and lighting up a hundred curious culinary articles, in the surface of which you might see yourself, and which hung upon hooks, and rested upon shelves round about. But pleasant as everything looked, Mistress Jenny and the goodman were the most interesting objects in that little cheerful apartment; before them was a small round table, on which lay a Bible and large Prayer Book, from which the farmer was reading, while an old setter dog, stretched on a mat which had been placed for him in the ingle or great recessed fireplace, seemed to watch them with an almost intelligent affection and interest.

I took the outstretched hand of Mistress Jenny, while a welcome, broad and manifest, beamed from her good-natured face. If an 'honest man's the noblest work of God,' as they say he is, my friend Farmer K., who rose from the settle as soon as he saw me, taking off his spectacles as he did so, and laying them down on the still open Prayer Book before him, is not very low in the list of created things. I did not care to enquire whether they had been at church that morning, or whether Mistress Jenny, tired from her journey to Bristol and back again, and her long stand in the market on the previous day, chose rather to have her prayers at home with the good man by the fireside, than walk across in a cutting easterly wind to Compton Church; for had they, I might perhaps have lost this, as perfect a picture of domestic comfort, grateful contentment and attachment as I think I have ever seen. "Now, bless my heart, if it aint glad to see thee," said Mistress Jenny, looking at me with a face beaming with gratification, as I took up my seat in the corner of the ingle opposite them; "it was kind of you to keep your word," then raising her voice so as to be heard in another apartment, she called out, "Patty, lay the cloth."

I had just tasted of my friend's hospitality when the snow began to fall heavily, and the little pensioner robins came to the casement, and, perching on the sill, and peeping in through the glass, waited like tiny mendicants at a monastery gate for their accustomed dole, and to them Mistress Jenny dispensed her bounty with no niggard hand.

It was a pleasant contrast was the snug little apartment, and its clean swept and bright hearth and my cozy ingle corner, with the scene outside; but I confess, as the great flakes fell obliquely across the window, I could not relish the idea of re-climbing Dundry Hill on John Bunyan's back in such a naughty night. My simple friends would have me stay, but as I knew it would be a night of intense uneasiness to my landlady (good soul) it I did not return, I even faced the road with as bold a heart as broadcloth could give one, and, long before I came to the summit of Dundry, what between the dreariness of the scene and the continued fall of the snow, and John's feet constantly 'balling' (I think they call it), I thought I should have met with the fate of the 'Babes in the Wood,' and have my obsequies sung by the shrill grey plover on that lonely hill. Indeed, the leafless trees as I passed beneath them seemed to stretch out their gaunt white arms as if to warn me back: but. Heaven be thanked, I got home safe in time to relieve the anxiety of my landlady, and have a cup of warm tea.

1. Moreton Farm in Compton Martin.

2. Parson Brown is either a mistake by Leech, or he may have been a curate, although no curates of that name are listed in either 1844 or 1846. The incumbent of Compton Martin and Nempnett was W.H. Cartwright (1843).

3. The Bilbie family, famous Bellfounders, 1698-1814. The Chew Stoke Bells: 1718 By Edward Bilbie (2) 1698 By Edward Bilbie (1) 1731 By Thomas Bilbie (2)

4. George Crabbe, 1754-1832. The poem Leech refers to is probably *The Village*, 1783.

5. The great Elizabethan Poor Law Act, 1601.

6. William P. Wait (1819).

7. Thomas Moore, 1779-1852. *Travels of an Irish Gentleman in Search of a Religion*, 1834.

Abbott's Leigh

John Bunyan (the Pilgrim) in his Experience, and I think in his Progress,[1] talks of being 'put to the plunge!' The low state of the water at Rownham Ferry, on the morning of my visit to Leigh, imposed upon John Bunyan (the quadruped) the necessity of following the precept, if not the precedent, of his pious namesake. The boat was moored in the centre of the stream, now shrunk to the width of little more than a mill course, and a plank on either side enabled me to pass over dryshod; but John was compelled, not however without much apparent reluctance on his part, to take to the water and ford it. As the current ran rippling between his legs and up to his belly, he seemed frightened, but once on *terra firma*, he shook the water from his sides, like dewdrops from the lion's mane, making the stirrup-irons clash together, and ring again like hammer and anvil, as he did so. Two public houses, like Sestos and Abydos, stand on either bank, and I have no doubt occupy the site of some ancient hostelries, where the physical comforts of those who have to cross that way were for centuries provided for.

Some milkmen, returning from Bristol with empty cans, made their passover with me, and old John, the boatman, having nothing to do but receive the money, had a word of gossip with each. When not colloquially engaged, my old Charon turned his attention to the contents of a well-thumbed *Weekly Dispatch*, and thus by snatches collected and communicated knowledge such as it was. When I inquired if he got time to go to church, he turned his pimpled face towards me, and, with a kind of under-growl, seemed to express his wonder at anyone being so 'soft' as to ask the question. The ferry belongs to the Dean and Chapter of Bristol: it is the same by which the 'mitred Abbots' of St. Augustines used to pass over of old to their country house at Leigh, and I think the Collegiate Corporation, when they let the tolls, ought to have made it a stipulation with the parties taking them that sufficient men should be employed to enable each to attend prayers once at least on the Sabbath. Anciently if the boatmen did not get mass, he sometimes got the Abbot's blessing *in transitu*; but there is little chance of a casual benediction now, as neither Dr. Lamb[2] nor any of his half-dozen Canons pass that way, or use the ferry, unless perhaps once in the seven years, when Sir John Smyth[3] gives a dinner party. In Roman Catholic times there was a little chapelry at Rownham, that Religion, with all its corruptions, never neglecting to provide a place of worship, where a handful of persons were likely to congregate together. Were a church there now, I think I should be disposed to pause on the way, for the hill is almost enough to frighten one from pursuing the journey, and the immense fence of stone and mortar, with which my excellent friend, Peter Maze, has girded his dwelling, by shutting out the prospect on one side, does not at all add to the attraction of the ascent. It is all very well for his recluse neighbour, the solitary Baronet, to shut himself inside his high walls and strong gates with his deer and pheasants, but my old acquaintance, the honest merchant, ought to let the world see a little more of him, and allow us to turn our tired gaze from these gibbet-like structures intended for the Suspension Bridge,[4] to the green and sunny slopes that encircle his residence.

The reader, who has often walked to Leigh, will surely recollect *Beggars' Bush*, the ancient whitethorn on the roadside, once the shelter of the mendicant pilgrim from the noonday sun, and now supported by a friendly prop in its venerable and declining old age. Near this he will also recollect, if he be as old as I am, a bridle road diverging to the village.

This road occurred to my mind as I passed Beggars' Bush; so, wishing to refresh the pleasant memories of 'auld lang syne,' as well as to save time, I thought to turn John's head that way, but was disappointed, and indignant, to find the footpath to the village closed to the public. This is another of the incidents by which we trace the progress of enlightenment: pleasant 'primrose footpaths' through green fields, and which had existed from almost immemorial time, and were not merely refreshing to the wayfarer, but dear to the villager, are suddenly discontinued; stiles built up, and the pedestrian thrust out on the dusty road, and warned off by boards, threatening all manner of terrible punishments and prosecutions 'according to law' to the trespasser. Trespass! it is only of late that it has become an offence: it was no 'trespass' when for centuries the peasant child hunted the butterfly, and the village maiden plucked the cowslips along its path. And when I hear of late years the poor accused of becoming less respectful, I sometimes think it is the rich that have grown more selfish. I can easily see how these apparently petty matters may particularly affect the city mechanic, who, coming out to enjoy the country air in his old and pleasant haunts, after six days toil in a crowded town, suddenly finds on some Sunday his favourite pathway closed against him, and turns into the next beer house, it may be to grumble in sullen discontent against the great who 'begrudged him,' as he will tell you, even that little enjoyment.

Whose fault it is I cannot say; but as I went forward I met with one of the ancient villagers, who informed, on my expressing my surprise and displeasure at what I saw, that it was the common report of the parish at the time when the footpath was closed, that it was effected mainly by three of the Suspension Bridge Commissioners, by virtue of some mischievous and latent clause in the Act of Parliament, whereby these men were empowered, not merely to mar the scenery which Heaven and nature had made so beautiful, but to thrust people out of their pleasant haunts in the green fields. My friend mentioned the names of the trio, and I was not at all surprised to learn that they were three of the greatest brawlers for popular rights, liberties, and so forth, in the neighbouring city; for we find that the loudest to talk are the last to feel for the humble.

I should, I believe, have ridden brimful of indignation to the very church door, if it had not been for the soothing effect which its peculiarly sweet peal of bells had upon me, charming away my choler as they chimed across the intervening landscape to meet me with their soft Sabbath greeting. After they had rung for about a quarter of an hour their pleasant music ceased, and the large bell alone took up the task, tolling forth for the like period as though for a funeral. On arriving at the church I inquired of the clerk, an old man, why this sepulchral-toned bell, of all the six in the tower, was employed to call the parish to the cheerful service of a church which invites us to 'come before His presence with thanksgiving, and show ourselves *glad* in Him with psalms;' and he informed me that it had been done now for some years, at the desire of the vicar, who wished that on his road from his town residence he might hear the bell, and regulate the pace of his steed accordingly. I may here remark, that I passed him on the way: he was on a little bay horse, and in a brown study, so I did not interrupt him, especially as John was a far better walker than his quadruped.

From the road immediately overlooking the little village there is a beautiful view; the broad waters of the Severn expanding like a sea in the background, and the red stone tower of the church, with its fine old patriarchal yew tree standing out amongst pleasant dwellings to the right. Close by the gable of the quiet little country inn, the *George*, are the parish stocks. It is very odd, but I seldom see a pair of stocks without wishing to put someone in them, as it is with regret one sees so interesting and venerable a relic of the past penal code become a dead letter, and fall into perfect disuse. So much for modern prison discipline, treadmills, and silent systems, and solitary confinement, and so forth, have done away with ducking stools and stocks, and other time-honoured monuments at once of the wisdom and wickedness of our ancestors. Occasionally when I have seen these little round holes, which seen to invite a pair of legs to occupy them, looking so disconsolate at having nothing to do, I have been almost tempted myself, like Lord Camden,[5] to take a seat, if but for a few minutes, to keep them in practice, did I only know where to get the key, as I perceive there is a padlock to the one at Abbott's Leigh; the clavicler of the parish church being also, I suppose, the clavicler of the parish stocks. I should like to know from the village antiquary to whom the pair of legs which last adorned this wooden structure appertained, as it has not apparently been put into requisition for years; though if I were by when the Lord Bishop of Gloucester and Bristol rated the churchwardens of this parish at the last visitation, I think I should have suggested its present unemployed, but still effective condition, and the eligible opportunity it presented as a favourite medium for the enforcement of episcopal penalties, and the punishment of remissful wardens.

In the churchyard, which occupies a most picturesque situation, are the steps of an ancient cross, and the fine old yew tree before alluded to. Close adjacent is the parsonage house, most judiciously placed, and commanding a noble and beautiful view — just such a house, were I a parson, where I should like to live, and have my pleasant little library looking down on the Severn.

The church is a plain though venerable looking structure; and the interior, with the exception of the chancel, is in a primitive and almost rude state of simplicity: it consists of a nave, two side aisles, and a chancel, which last has considerably more pretension to decoration than the other parts of the building. At the west end there is a gallery, and in that gallery, there are a big fiddle, a flute, and, I think, a bassoon, together with sundry persons who perform on these musical implements, severally and respectively — I wish I could add respectably; but the singing, which on the whole is only indifferent, is silently surrendered by the congregation to the parish choir, who, of course, do their best; and if people will not sing themselves, they must even be satisfied with the way in which those do the business, to whom, in their spiritual laziness, they have deputed it. The mural tablets, I perceive, have lately been cleaned, and the letters newly picked out with black. Who the devout Old Mortality was who performed this work, I cannot say; but he deserves thanks for preserving the memories of the departed from the obliteration of time; and his example might, I think, be meritoriously followed by other churchwardens. In the chancel are monuments to the Norton and Trenchard families, who successively owned and occupied Leigh Court.

The parishioners of Leigh seem to go into church at all hours — a circumstance which was attended with some slight but still annoying interruption to the Vicar, on the occasion of my visit. During the reading of the Psalms a bevy of servants came in, making a considerable noise, upon which the Vicar unfortunately, though naturally, raised his eyes from the book to see who the offenders were, and, in so doing, lost his part by mischance, and, in trying to regain it and recover himself, got hold of the wrong verse; as the clerk read the right one, they were very wide apart, so the Vicar to prevent further confusion, as the simplest remedy said, "Let us begin the Psalm again!" and again we began it, though we were nearly all at the end before; but we could not have a good thing too often. Now people ought to come in themselves, and make their servants come in earlier; and, if I were the Rev. the Vicar, I should preach a sermon against late attendance; though I could perceive he attributed the interruption in the present instances to the wrong cause, namely, the fidgety habits of the school-boys, who stood in front, for on subsequently going into the vestry he had one of them called to him to the door, and there apparently read him a lecture on the impropriety of his conduct, and condemned him to stand up by the pulpit rail during the communion service: immediately before the sermon, however, the little fellow was released. Had he condemned the three servant-maids to durance, there would be more equity in it. I would suggest to the clerk, that instead of encumbering himself with the arduous and double duty of knocking the boys on the head and repeating the responses, he should transfer the long stick with which is ever and anon appealing to youthful sinciputs,[6] to some assistant, and apply himself entirely to the reading department.

The Vicar preached. The Rev. Martin Whish,[7] who as well as being incumbent of Redcliffe and Thomas, prebend of Sarum, and rector of Bedminster, is also Vicar of Leigh, has been for so long a time connected with Bristol, and must be so well known as a preacher, that it is almost a work of superogation on my part to describe him. His style is somewhat singular and eccentric; you have hardly had time to admire some beautiful and remarkable bit of divinity when you are struck with some odd incidental, colloquial remark, delivered, it may be in a rapid parenthesis, or slowly propounded in a solemn period. I have heard him, after involving himself for some time in abstruse reasoning, which I confess was not very clear to me, suddenly cut it short by telling his congregation that 'that was a knock-me-down argument,' but the only thing it seemed to knock down was a young lady's gravity who sat opposite me, and who, by way of preserving her propriety, was obliged to turn to the Thirty-nine Articles at the end of her Prayer Book. As I said before, however, in almost every sermon which I have heard him preach, there have been some scattered passages of much originality and beauty, but which, unless to an attentive listener, are often lost in the irregularity of the rest. The great curiosity, however, is the sermon itself, so far as paper and ink go. I should think that he has not used a complete clean quire of post since his entrance upon the ministry, the greater part of his discourses being written on fly leaves of letters, backs of circulars, and Christmas bills, of unequal size and all shades. Nor is this the only singularity of the Vicar of Leigh's sermons: the pages do not appear to be written consecutively, for he will turn over half a dozen leaves at a time to one where the corner is turned down in a huge equilateral triangle, and from this he will read back, like a Hebrew book, and then make another skip and dive midway into the discourse.

The Vicar of Abbott's Leigh is a very kind hearted man, but although the Bishop and, I believe, the Clergy of the Diocese, have been working at him for years, they cannot either coax or bully him into keeping a sufficient number of curates; and Abbott's Leigh, which is nearly four miles from Bristol, is without a resident minister, or even a regular clerical attendant, there being in two hundred and eight successive Sundays no less than one hundred and eighty strange clergymen: the parishioners having in fact on no given Sabbath morning any more definitive idea of who's going to occupy their pulpit that day, than of who's to preach at St. Paul's Cathedral — they have no notion from which cardinal point of the compass the minister is to come who is to preach to them, or what stranger the neighbouring city will send forth.

1. John Bunyan. 1628-88. 'Experience' possibly refers to *Grace abounding to the chief of Sinners* (1666). *The Pilgrims Progress.* (1678).

2. John Lamb, 1789-1850. Dean of Bristol 1837-50.

3. Sir John Smyth, 1776-1849. Sir John succeeded to the baronetcy on the death of his brother Hugh in 1824. He died unmarried in 1849 when the baronetcy became extinct.

4. The foundation stone for the Clifton Suspension Bridge was laid 27 August 1836. A wrought iron bar 1,000 feet long and one and a half inches in diameter was slung across the gorge as temporary means of transfer for man and materials. By Leech's time of writing, work had stopped due to lack of funds. The bridge was completed in 1864 as a memorial to Isambard Kingdom Brunel — the original designer. Leech later became deputy chairman of the Clifton Suspension Bridge Company.

5. John Jeffreys Pratt, second Earl and first Marquis of Camden, 1759-1840. George Charles Pratt, second Marquis of Camden 1799-1866.

6. Sinciputs — a fore part of the skull.

7. Martin R. Whish (1806).

View of Bristol from Clifton looking towards Rownham Ferry.

Lympsham

Lympsham, is one of those places you would hardly find if you did not look for it. It is thrust down so far into the westward out of the way, that unless, like me, you had a special invitation, 'twould never suggest itself to you. A railroad runs through the parish, but there is no terminus nearer than Weston; and as for stage coaches or guard's horn, I don't know when or if ever there were such things heard there.

I have no doubt that the printer has placed me on horseback as usual at the top of this paper, but the truth is I found my way from Weston to Lympsham in the interior of a fly. It was one of those occasions when John Bunyan is allowed to remain idle in his stall, and eat his hay and corn without doing anything for it. The morning was cold and squally, with occasional sleety showers, and the snow was still laying about unthawed in the ditches, so that it was not until I reached the top of Uphill, when the sun breaking out from the chilly grey clouds for a few moments seemed to call my attention to the scene, that I could muster courage enough to let down the glass and look out; and certainly it is a sight almost worth catching cold for — the Channel seemed as broad and bright as if it were not three parts mud; and Brean Hill and many a bold headland, ran out like great bullies into the sea, as if to meet and repel it. But everyone must know the ground as well as I do. I cannot fancy there is one who takes up this paper, who has not at some time or another been for a month or so in summer to inhale the fine sand and sea breezes in this locality, and ride donkeys to every eminence in the neighbourhood, for the benefit — of those who hire them out. On the right of the road, then, I need not say, are Uphill new church, and Uphill old — the former built by Mr Wilson, of Bath,[1] the latter by the Devil. I only state the general account in the country; and as half the history, especially of heroic ages, is founded on tradition, I am not the man to impugn such authority; I may add, however, that Mr. Wilson's design seems to have greatly the advantage of that of his Satanic majesty, who, judging from the specimen here given, certainly does not seem to shine in architecture, though Southey, in his *Painter of Florence*,[2] represents him as possessed of taste. The new structure is a very handsome one, and does credit to the author: it was built principally by private subscription and from the sale of pincushions, the proceeds of more than one bazaar having gone towards its erection. The Father of Lies does not seem to have had any extraneous or friendly aid of this kind in his undertaking; but if the story be true he accomplished the work himself, by his own individual exertions, and in opposition both to the patrons and the parish, who wished, and for a long time persisted, in building the church at the base of the hill, but the work they did by day was regularly removed at night, by their obstinate and indefatigable foe, further up; until at length, tired of so unequal a controversy, where their antagonist had labour for nothing, the mortals gave in, and Belzebub had the day and his whim. To prevent the recurrence of so unpleasant a circumstance and so unseemly a dispute, the new church has been erected on the summit, and at present a very good understanding, from what I can learn, seems to subsist between all parties.

Uphill is a little Pisgah [3] in its way for prospect: on the north (I think it is the north, but I really am a very bad judge as to the points of the compass) you look back upon Weston, wearing quite an air of elegance in the distance — I say nothing of a nearer view: and on the south, stretching far beneath, is one of the most extensive tracts of campaign country I think I have seen, with the river Ax winding for miles through it, and looking like some huge shining serpent as, glistening in the occasional sun gleams, it glided along in its tortuous course. Immediately under you is Bleadon, and thence, some mile or mile and a half distance, may be seen amongst a clump of trees, the handsome embattled, but leaning tower of Lympsham Church. If I had time when passing Bleadon, I think I should have looked in to my friend Parson Williams,[4] and told him how freely people talk about his parish, and how frequently they refer to it in familiar comparisons: the very sparrows which perch upon the old cross seem to twitter their remarks; and rooks that crowd cawing about the pinnacles of the church are nowhere else so significantly loquacious. A set of open mouthed, talkative, scandalous fellows are these same rooks; and I sometimes think, as they wing their way from parish to parish, and alight in garrulous coteries on the summit of one tower after another, they amuse themselves in canvassing the merits of the ministers of the various churches at which they call.

Lympsham is divided from Bleadon by Hobbe's Boat Ferry,[5] so called from the fact of there being no ferry there. The river, it is true, once ran by, but an act of parliament was passed empowering it to take another course, of which privilege it promptly availed itself. Having got within the parish, along the main road, and from every bye-road, came coburgs, cars, and all kinds of rural vehicles, passing me and well laden with people of their way to church; while the bells, ringing loudly and clearly, gave an air of animation to the scene which one does not generally witness on such occasions in the country. There were no phaetons nor fine carriages, with bright liveries or smoking bays, it is true, and my fly was the only thing that would bear even a limited comparison to a landeau; but from many a market cart, now applied to Sunday uses, might be seen blooming faces and rustic finery, of the fascinations of which the fair proprietors had no poor opinion. There is no man who has a greater abhorrence of, or contempt for, the impertinences of the road than I have: and I am happy to say, as I raised my hat gravely and respectfully to each church-going group or party as I passed, they returned the salutation in their frank and friendly manner, which showed they had no suspicion of any impudent freedom on my part. 'Tis evident, said I, no stage coach passes this way, with bagmen to abuse the pleasant courtesies of life, for people are not ashamed to reciprocate simple civilities from the inoffensive wayfarer.

The church, churchyard, schoolhouse, and pretty parsonage of Lympsham lie all together, and seem, in their smiling contiguity and repose, one sacred homestead: there are no stiff walls about them; and a light rustic paling or a wire fence, or a row of evergreens, is the only thing that divides one from the other, or all from the public. The parsonage is an exceedingly pleasing and picturesque object in the view, with its long front and its pretty porch and its oriel windows, its old trees, and its little glimpses of greensward between; while there is an air of elegance and competence beside so tempting, that were comfort all a man sought for in the ministry there are few laymen from this to that who would not be quite willing to exchange places with the rector of Lympsham. He was standing under his own porch in gown and band as I drove by; and on the fly pulling up, he came towards me; but seeing it was neither Sarum[6] nor Chancellor Law[7] that alighted but an old man in a brown coat, he drew back again.

Nothing can be more creditably kept than the churchyard; it is literally pretty. Just as you enter, there is a little round flowerpot with a laburnum tree in the centre. The graves are not ranged together in stiff and formal rows; but they lie apart with a pleasing irregularity, and that rustic simplicity and repose which, in many country churchyards, rob the Grim King to our imagination, of half his terrors. In my mind, attention to the churchyard is only second to attention to the church; and the peasant who does not take a deep interest in it, is devoid of proper sensibility. Every Sunday, as he passes through it to church — every weekday, as he passed by it to his work — the thought ought to occur to him, that here he will one day rest, and within this very place when the last summons is heard, he shall awake. With the rural parishioners, this is the case more than with any other: there are few vicissitudes amongst them — few removals — few goings away; and the strong probability is, that they die where they have been born and lived, and that almost everyday during their existence they see the spot destined to be their resting place; and it is only natural to think that they should care about the little solemn inclosure — 'God's acre' — in which they are one day certain to have so enduring an interest

At the east end of the churchyard is the parish school, and as I walked round the burial ground I was tempted by the juvenile buzz that reached me outside to peep into this little hive. Independent of the regular master and mistress, there were some young ladies of the parish amusing themselves with a perfectly harmless attempt 'to teach the young idea of how to shoot. This school, which is a plain neat cottage-like building, was erected by the father of the present Incumbent, and bears upon it an inscription somewhat to that effect.

A comfortable looking man in a black gown showed me into a pew It is not usual for country parishes generally to have sextons, but a sexton in a gown was certainly more than one expected to see in a little secluded place like Lympsham: but it was only in accordance with everything else I witnessed at, in, and about the church. Everything was done decently and in order, and there was manifest evidence of all those little attentions, which it is our bounden duty to see cared for in connection with the sacred temple and the solemn worship.

I do not know when I have been in a country church with so large a congregation: it was not merely the pews that were filled, but the forms placed in the aisles were closely occupied also. I could not help thinking it was some special occasion. Indeed, several, I could see, were strangers like myself, for they looked about uncertain where to go, and more than that, when they got a place they seemed uncertain what to do — a circumstance from which I concluded, as it subsequently turned out, that there was an unusual muster of Dissenters: few, if any of them, had Prayer Books, and all seemed ill at case, though they affected to look with critical and judicial faces towards the clergyman. The Rector is one of the most active men I have ever seen in the reading-desk or pulpit, and, from what I learn, out of it too: he not only read the service and preached, but he led the singing and chanting, both of which they did, and did well, without an organ: indeed, I never before heard such hearty general congregational singing — everyone took their share, and a man with a bass voice somewhat more than his share. If anything there was too much singing: for the musical part of the service, I have often thought, is more exciting than edifying — it touches the ear more than the heart, and after it has subsided it is some time before the minds, especially of those who have taken an energetic part in it, are brought back to that calm and equable frame in which it is necessary to be in order to feel the simple, subdued, and chastened piety which breathes in all the prayers of the Church.

The text was taken from 1st Cor., c.iv.2, 'Moreover it is required in stewards that a man be found faithful.' He opened with a most happy figure from the Revelations, alluding to the Angel who was presented as standing in the sun, and whose brightness was lost in the surpassing effulgence of the great luminary. So, he said, it ought to be with the minister of the church: he himself, and personal considerations connected with him, ought to be lost in the greatness and grandeur of the message with which he was commissioned; but there were times when a clergyman might be pardoned for speaking of himself, and the present was, in his opinion, such a one. He then read some passages from the Ordination Service, to show the solemn responsibilities he incurred in undertaking the care of souls; and next proceeded to allude to some painful circumstances which had occurred in the parish, and with regard to which some portion, at least, of the congregation then present and the clergyman would not appear to be quite of one mind; but as he did not state what the difference was, and referred to it with evident pain and reluctance, and not without considerable excitement, I was left quite in the dark as to its nature, and was wearying myself with conjectures as to whether they had got up one of the surplice quarrels in the secluded village of Lympsham, or if there were a difference about tithes, or what. It was plain, however, that the 'mild Arcadians' of the place, remote as they were, were not sufficiently so to escape all cause of strife. He pointedly alluded, too, in the course of his discourse, to some whom he had requested to attend there that day, and in contradistinction to his own flock, which latter he enjoined to hold fast by their old faith. Those whom he addressed as invited, I had little difficulty in seeing, were my friends with long faces and without Prayer Books. Having dismissed this unpleasant subject, which he did with manifest relief to himself, the rector proceeded to preach on conversion, the necessity of which he enforced, but distinguished between it and conviction; and argued against its being a sudden or momentary change, induced by wild enthusiasm and excitement, but a gradual working of the heart, and maturing to good. He treated the subject with much force, judgement, distinctness, and penetration; and as an extempore preacher, I have not heard a more fluent one. He has much natural eloquence; and rapid and animated though he be, with language (and suitable and good language) at will, he seemed at times as though he could not give utterance quick enough to

the 'thick coming fancies' which crowded upon him. There is a kind, affectionate, friendly, and earnest manner about him, too, which gave you the impression
of a man speaking to and amongst his own family; and from all I could learn this
is completely the character of his intimacy and ministerial connection with his
congregation. "He is the child of the parish, I might say. Sir," said a gentleman
to me: "his father held the living before him, he was reared amongst us, he has
grown up amongst us, he has been about in the cottages almost since he has
been able to walk, and there is hardly an old inhabitant upon whose knee he has
not sat when a boy; and thus (and backed by liberality, charity, and ample means,
as he has been) has grown up that amiable and affectionate feeling which has
made rector and flock as it were one family," which ought to exist everywhere.
Like most fluent extempore preachers, however, the Rev. Mr. Stephenson[8] has
no idea whatever, apparently, of measuring time, for his sermon on the present
occasion was full an hour and a half!

A trial which no man has a right to make of his hearers' patience. He made
five or six main divisions of his subject, and four or five subordinate divisions
of each of these again, with an exhortation to each: once or twice he told us
we must not think of time, and certainly he set us the example by seeming
perfectly unconscious of its course himself: in fact he was borne impetuously
along by his own fluency and feeling. Considering the cause a little more length
than usual was indeed admissible; but the sermon I heard on Sunday morning
would, without exaggeration, have made three very good ones.

On leaving the church I was quite full of curiosity to know the cause of the
marked, though to me unintelligible, allusions of the minister in the early part
of his sermon. There was clearly a hitch somewhere; but where that was, I
could not, for the life of me, guess. An elderly lady, who sat in the next pew to
me, passed me in the moment of my anxious inquisitiveness. I apologised to
her for interrupting her, but I said I was desirous to know what unpleasant occurrence had taken place to interrupt the peace of the parish, and provoke the
references the rector had made in the beginning of his discourse. "Why, Sir,
they have been roaring — they have been ranting here, and turned Lympsham
upside down with roaring for their sins."

"Then," said I, "your parish has been visited by some of those wild and erratic visionaries, which have sprung from the morbid extravagances and excesses of schism."

"Yes, sure. Sir," was her reply; "they have been preaching and groaning and
revivaling in a room, until as Jem told me, the candles went out of their own
accord; and they thought the Old One was in the room."

"Judging from the zeal of your own parish minister, madam, I should have
thought that Lympsham was the last place where such extraneous aid could
have been thought necessary."

"Yes, sure. To come to our parish, too, of all others! Indeed if they visited
Bleadon, one would not be so surprised."

In short, I learned from this earnest and elderly gentlewoman, that the parish had been suddenly struck as if with a religious panic. The morbid and wild feeling had been introduced by an itinerant, who got possession at once of some vacant room and a simple people's reason — a circumstance not unusual in this age and country. Already all the dissenters in the neighbourhood, and several of the simple portion of the Church congregation, were attacked by the epidemic; and the most singular thing of all was, that the very church schoolmaster and mistress were amongst the number; and not content with forcing and frightening themselves and others at this room into a state of ecstatic terror, they spread the mania amongst the children under their care, who went home to their parents frightened out of their little wits and crying, and on being questioned as to the cause of such unusual conduct, literally said "they were converted:" to so melancholy and morbid a pitch had people's minds been worked. But it appears that this spiritual phenomenon was not altogether unknown in this part of the country. About twenty years ago the same feeling passed like wild fire through nearly the same district, including Lympsham, Berrow, East Brent etc., and turned people's senses for the moment, as it has almost done on the present occasion. It was a critically unfortunate circumstance, too, that just at the moment that it now made its appearance, the Rev. Mr. Stephenson was confined to his bed by a very serious illness: and only arose to find his parish, in which his heart was wound up, agitated by a religious fervor and ferment. The Sunday when I heard him was the first on which he had preached since his illness; and he had, as I subsequently learned, sent round to request the attendance of his dissenting parishioners, as well as his church congregation; and this accounted for the curious and awkward apparitions I beheld. I heard there were several local preachers there; and I have little doubt that, being a stranger, I was also taken for a 'supply' to some neighbouring chapel.

I cannot say what the Rev. Mr. Stephenson has done with the schoolmaster and mistress, and to a nature like his, it must give great pain to act, as I certainly should act in the case; for such people are clearly incompetent to the control of children when they cannot control themselves. For persons too, attached to church schools to run after every wild visionary is unpardonable.

I have left myself little room to speak of the church, for I always go off at a tangent on this subject. However, there is not much to be said about the church: it has a chancel, nave, and north aisle, and is neatly kept: there is a pretty painted east window, and a good roof to the side aisle, with bosses bearing heraldic devices, etc, are very badly painted in a paltry, domestic dwelling kind of style. I have heard that the Rector intends this year to expend a considerable sum of money on it; and if the repairs are made with judgement and taste, the interior of Lympsham Church may be as attractive as the environs. The tower, which is a handsome embattled one, owing to the base having given way at one time, inclines as much as two feet from the perpendicular.

I may here say that I attended prayers in the evening also, when the attendance was nearly as good as in the morning, and the sermon better.

There was an affecting circumstance which came under my notice on the occasion of my visit, and I can hardly refrain from mentioning it before I conclude this paper. There was an old man standing pensively by the west door as I entered, and he afterwards took up his place near me in the church, when I perceived him look with a wistful and sad, a regretful but a humble, glance, towards the reading-desk. I felt impelled by an indescribable interest in him to inquire who he was, when I learned he was the late clerk. He had been dismissed for some error, cider was unfortunately on one occasion too plenty for him, and he had 'fallen from the high estate,' which he had occupied for twenty years. He was regretted and pitied by the Rector and parishioners, and there was a touching air of sadness and penitence about him, and something like an appearance of conscious degradation, as he saw another occupying the post, and reading out of the great prayer book which was his for near a quarter of a century. Poor man, he still went to church, though I have no doubt every Sunday renewed the pang.

1. St. Nicholas, built by James Wilson, 1844.
2. Robert Southey, 1774-1843. *See* Thornbury, p.204.
3. Pisgah — a mountain ridge in ancient Palastine.
4. David Williams. *See* Bleadon, p.297.
5. Not quite correct in Leech's text. A clyse was built at Hobb's boat under an act of 1802. The river was not diverted.
6. Edward Denison, 1801-54, Bishops of Salisbury 1837-54.
7. James Thomas Law, 1790-1876, Chancellor of Lichfield 1821, and Special Commissary of the diocese of Bath & Wells 1840.
8. Joseph Henry Stephenson, M.A., succeeded as rector in 1844 and continued until 1901. The living belonged to his father Joseph Adam Stephenson who was rector from 1809-44. For a few months in 1844 the rector was W.W. Rowley who turns up later at Weston-Super-Mare as the 'admired Mr. Rowley who has gone to get married.'

22 March 1845
Stoke Gifford

I have never been at Stoke Gifford Church, so I asked a friend where it was, "Just by Stapleton" was his reply, "only a pleasant walk." Trusting to this information, and as my medical man had told me to take a little more walking exercise, I thought I would leave John Bunyan at home to chew his corn and the cud of fancy, and depend upon my own legs for the nonce. Instead of a pleasant walk, however, I found I was misled into a toilsome journey.

The first couple of miles were agreeable enough, for at Baptist Mills I met a little fellow who was going as far as Stapleton, and who made a very innocent and prattling companion as long as our roads lay together. I fell in with him in a very simple way; finding myself involved in the mazes of some bye-roads, I inquired of him if he could inform me the way to Stapleton; he said he was going there himself, and that if I had no objection there was a short and pleasant path through the fields, across which he would be my conductor. I readily accepted an offer made with all a boy's frankness, and in another moment we were gossiping away with as much freedom as if we had been friends since the flood. Unquestioned he told me his little history in one breath; he was serving his time in Bristol to a draper, his relatives lived at Stapleton, and he was on his way to spend the Sunday with them; he spent most of his Sundays in the country, going out in the morning, and returning again at night.

Here was a youth pent up in a close shop six days in the week; just fancy the secret pleasure with which when he awakes on the seventh, he recollects it is Sunday, and that there is that morning a release from the captivity of the counter, that he has not to creep down from his bed to a dusty shop, and pin up, with cold fingers, an infinity of small articles and tempting finery in the windows, polish the brass plate in front, and all that. In winter a run across the fields to raise the ruddy glow on his cheeks, and a day's restoration to his own family, where instead of being with strangers, he feels he has an interest in each heart, make a happy change enough to the emancipated apprentice; but in the sultry summer season, how positively delicious to escape from a great crowded city, which is heated like an oven, and the flags beneath one's feet feel like a hot dresser; then every hawthorn tree with its clustered white head, every pleasant hedgerow with its crown of honeysuckles, seem to welcome the draper's lad to green fields and fresh air, and you might think he was flying from a doomed city from the fact of his never looking back to the dense mass of bricks and mortar which he is fast leaving behind him for one day at least.

I was compelled once or twice to admonish my little companion to walk slower, for he skipped along as if my legs were as young and my heart as light as his. I asked him how he liked the early hours of closing, and he said *his* master did not observe them; they still kept open until about eight, they went to bed about ten.

"Then what do you do with yourself in the meantime," said I, "do you go out?"

"No, the lads were not allowed to go out; they had a room where they sat, and sometimes read, and sometimes romped."

I enquired where he got books. He said he had a few of his own, that was all; a fact from which, I think, the religious and philanthropic, who are ever puzzling their brains for new methods of spending money and doing good, might take a hint. I would suggest 'A Drapers' Lads' Lending Library,' a title as beautifully alliterative as it is benevolently comprehensive.

"Then, as you are not allowed to go out in the evenings, my little friend, do you never taste fresh air but on Sundays?"

"Oh, yes. Sir, when we go out to match patterns," was his reply. "I like to be sent out to match patterns, especially if it is far off," continued the lad with much earnestness.

I had now got all my tiny fellow traveller's history, there was but one curiosity left to gratify. I confess he was such a hearty, frank, little fellow, I hoped he was a Churchman, so I asked him if he knew the Rev. Ricketts Bailey;[1] he said yes, he heard him preach nearly every Sunday. "Then do you go to Stapleton Church," said I.

"Yes, and the Bishop goes there too." For the sake of saying something, I inquired whether he would sooner be a bishop or a draper.

"I'd sooner be a draper," was his sincere but somewhat singular reply. Having parted with my young friend at Stapleton, I continued my course in the teeth of a very sharp wind towards Stoke Gifford, and had several opportunities of regretting, before I got to the grand entrance gate of Her grace the Duchess Dowager of Beaufort, having been silly enough to leave John Bunyan behind me. The dust careered along the road in a kind of circling dance, and whirled round and round me like a winding sheet, until I thought I should be smothered. As I pulled the gate bell with one hand, I was obliged to hold my hat with the other. I received from the porter the usual distinct directions as to my road, to go straight on until I came to something, and then to turn to the right, and then to the left, and then to the right again, and so on, until my ideas of dexter and sinister were completely confounded; so thanking him, and muttering to myself the safe maxim, *via trita via tuta*, I followed the beaten tract before me. I don't know the number of statutable miles that Stoke Gifford may be from Bristol, but I should think I must have walked two or three through the Park, before I got even a glimpse of the village, though I paused every half mile to look out for it, and deliberate with myself whether I should not turn back, so tired did I feel. It was in one of these breathing moments, as I gazed round me, half bewildered and whole vexed, that an envious gust of wind came and whipped off my hat. I don't think I ever gazed with more perplexity and distress at anything than I did after my truant headgear, as it went rolling away, eloping, I might say, from its natural guardian with the east wind, spinning along and skipping up in the air with a wild levity that ill became the covering of so sedate and so grey a head. To run after it, or think of following it was out of the question; tired and 'winded' as I was, I could not have run ten yards, at that moment, to overtake a mitre, much less a twenty-four shilling beaver; all I could do was to look after it in help-less distress. I felt there was nothing for it but to leave it to its mad career, and pursue my road or turn back without it; it was taking the direction of Filton, and I had made up my mind to see it leap the next fence like a fox hunter, when it was suddenly turned by one of those capricious gusts which seem made to blow round a corner, and came circling back towards me, rolling like an iron hoop on its rim, though at some distance around me, as if, like a repentant prodigal, it was ashamed of its conduct, and hesitated to approach the indulgent owner it had so rashly deserted. It was a fortunate gyration so far as I was concerned, for before it could start on another onward race, or be carried off again, it was luckily inter-cepted by the trunk of a tree, where it was detained until I was enabled to come up to it. Having recovered the runaway, with the loss of a small portion of its fur, I placed it firmly on my head, and to prevent a similar or second escape, tied my old Indian silk pocket handkerchief over it and under my chin. The wind could no longer affect my hat, but as if in rage and disappointment at being foiled, it vented all its wrath in numberless other little ways, blowing furiously in my face, tossing the skirts of my coat wildly and indecorously about and above my head, and sweeping clouds of dust in my eyes. The winds since the days of Virgil were blustering bullies, but I determined not to yield, and made my way manfully to the road in time to see a light blue landeau fly drive by. "Whose is that?" said I to a farmer who joined me at the moment. "The parson's," was his reply; "Mr. Parker's."

"Then where does Mr. Parker live?" said I. "In Bristol,[2] he comes out every Sunday, in the morning one Sunday, in the evening the next."

"Then you have only one service in the week?"

"That's all."

Well, thought I, this is an easy way to manage a parish, one *fly*-ing visit, extended over two hours, and one service in seven days. So it was, however; the Rev. Mr. Parker lived at Kingsdown, and contracted with a flyman to carry himself and a written sermon, once a week, to a parish six miles off, to the spiritual supervision of which he is supposed to attend.

Stoke Gifford is an old and primitive-looking little parish Church; it consists of a nave, chancel, and north aisle, with a little tower on the south side. It is, altogether, with its sober churchyard, a rude, simple, and not a very cheerful object.[3] There are a few houses scattered about, and these collectively are dignified with the name of a village. The congregation are quite of a rustic character; and the edifice was so well filled I thought it a pity that where the population seemed ready to attend, they should have but one service on the Sunday. At the west end is a platform, from which the village choir perform with their own voices and two flutes; there are also several 'great singers' amongst the congregation, who seem to join with amazing unction and energy.

The Queen's letter was read rapidly through after the Communion Service, and thrown down, when finished, with a flourish on the table; but not a word said about collection or contribution, that was all left to the imagination. The text had reference to the observation of the Sabbath; and the preacher got through the sermon, from beginning to end, in a most fluent and off-hand manner. He had a dash at 'the bloody Chartists and the beastly Socialists,' and a cut at the 'wily Papists and subtle Tractarians;' he told us about Luther's ink-stand and the plains of Marathon, and recited in sonorous cadence Lord Byron's poem on the death of Sennacherib;[4] I mean those sounding verses about the 'Assyrian coming down like a wolf on the fold,' and the relics of Asshur, I beg pardon, 'the widows of Asshur being loud in their wail.' He was very energetic in his denunciations of those who broke the Sabbath, and very properly too; threatening with the judgments of heaven even those who saw a friend on Sunday. He, however, made a reservation in favour of works of necessity; under which head, I suppose, having a fly, horse, and man, from Bristol and back again, ten miles journey every Sunday, was included. Immediately in front of me was a family in deep mourning, who had evidently that day appeared for the first time in Church since the loss of some very near relative; upon this subject the preacher touched, towards the end of his discourse, and with some taste and good feeling, much more, I candidly confess, than was evinced in the foregoing part of his sermon; here there was a pleasing solemnity, as unlike the rattling part that preceded it, as two things could be, even though the former was enhanced by the poetic account of the slaughter of the Assyrians.

1. W.H.R. Bayley, perpetual curate of Stapleton (1841).
2. Edward Parker (1834) lived at St. James's Place, Kingsdown.
3. The church was restored c.1894-7.
4. George Gordon, sixth lord Byron, 1788-1824. *The Destruction of Sennacherib* (1815).

Long Ashton

There is a sensible and thrifty proverb which enjoins us to provide for rainy days; and last summer, when I meditated on these papers, I paid a visit to a few country churches and made memoranda of what I then saw and heard, in the anticipation that I might be sometimes prevented by stress or by weather from taking my usual ride during the winter.

Last Sunday was one of those soaking days that no man with rheumatism would think of going any further than his own parish church, so I went to my bureau and extracted my entry for the Parish of Long Ashton. Ashton church rather abounds in monumental curiosities both inside and out. Against the wall of a little chapel on the north side is a white marble monument to Dame Anne Smyth in a very ambitious and somewhat antithetical inscription in Latin, which after very sticky panegyric thus concludes that she died on the 9th September 1733. Go thou and do likewise. I think there is an old story somewhere in the Pluck Papers, of a man at Cambridge who went in for his Catheticals and could not answer a word. At length his examiner enquired sneeringly if he could quote any one single passage of scripture. "I can," said the other, "and Judas went and hanged himself," "very good," said the examiner, "do you know a second," "yes," was the reply, "go thou and do likewise." So by the writer of Dame Smyth's inscription we are enjoined to imitate the example of that excellent lady and die on the ninth day of September at the early age of 33. In the same little chapel is a very fine canopied tomb with the recumbent figures of Chief Justice Choke[1] and his wife who have got a lion and dog at their feet and something more angelic in the shape of a pair of cherubs at their heads. There is also one of those old English inscriptions which have more powerful earnestness of entreaty about them than a hundred lines in Latin. The church is a handsome and pleasing structure and the utmost attention seems to have been paid to its preservation and cleanliness. It has a nave, north and south aisle, two side chapels and chancel. The last is separated from the main body of the church by an exquisite gothic screen richly elaborated in flower and fretwork. On either side of the east window in a curious old English character are, I think, the belief and Lord's Prayer or, Commandments, I forget which. They were for a considerable time concealed but have lately been discovered and restored. The side aisles are separated from the centre by rows of pointed arches which spring from clustered columns of light and pleasing symmetry. In the chancel are some pews lined with scarlet, the only occupant of that part of the church at the time of my visits was my friend Peter Maze, and as the doors lay invitingly open and as the cushions looked seductively soft, I had a great mind to go into one of them for the nonce as there were none of those comforts in the little square seats in which I was shown. There was a cumbrous quantity of woodwork in the shape of pews which are so high and huddled together that much of the effect of the very pleasing and light church was destroyed. At the west end is an organ loft and red curtains of which were drawn aside on the occasion of my visit, that the man who blew the bellows might look down at his ease at the congregation and exhibit a movement similar to that of a man at work at the windlass of a well. There are a peal of fine bells in the tower, some of them are ancient and have old legends on them, one or two however have been cast by Bilbie. On one of the latter is a memorial 'Sir John Smyth, Baronet, for whose name I will now bespeak'. And certainly in the absence of all other panegyrists it is better to have a friendly bell than have nothing to say in one's praise.

Long Ashton is not only a pleasant and picturesque village, it is also a populous and respectable one. There is an air of English comfort and elegance as well as neatness about the cottage-like villas that compose it, and one looks down from the sunny slope on which it stands on a considerable tract of pasture lands, and meadows, interspersed with pretty plantations and residences. It was said to be a favourite resort with the monks and friars of Bristol in old popish times, and I can easily understand how it may have been attractive to

the monastic ideas of pastoral beauty and repose. Indeed, forty years or perhaps more ago it was a most popular Sunday retreat with people of Bristol, and I recollect going there many a time with my worthy father on the bright sunny sabbath and meeting several of our neighbours there also. I think I have in some other places alluded to the curious announcement made by the old clerk on these occasions, and his endeavour to enlist all the accidental musical talent that might be in the church from the neighbouring city. The old fellow stood I have now in my minds eye in the gallery, the most prominent and important personage in the village choir and addressed himself in the following words to those beneath 'if there by any of there great sangers from Bristol down ablow, y'ell be pleased to come up in the organ loft for we be a going to sing a hanthem today, blow ye the trumpet blow'. My father used to contribute, much as he could to the harmony of the parish from his place in the body of the church, but he would never that I can recollect be induced to confess himself to being a great sanger by accepting the clerks' invitation to ascend the loft.

I recollect too that it was on one of those visits to Ashton with my honoured parent that I first saw a country funeral, and the impression which it made, not an impression of dread or dark melancholy but of subdued solemn interest has never wholly afterwards effaced from my mind.

It was one of those golden evenings when a good man, if he were to have a choice, would above all others select as that which to be laid to sleep in the village churchyard with his fathers. And all it wanted was the incident of a rustic burial to heighten the interest of such a scene. Nor was this want long in the present instance, the service over, we noticed as we passed out from the church a funeral approaching, and only a portion of the congregation appeared to have been previously aware of what was about to take place, the remainder witnessed the effecting ceremony. As the mournful little procession slowly drew near, now and again hid for a moment from view by some interposing tree, I could not help remarking, young as I was, the contrast it presented in its simplicity to the obsequies of the more opulently crowded city, with all the sable display which the French so characteristically call 'pompes funebres'. The nodding plumes and long procession can barely attract the passing glance of the bustling man of business, and obtain an uninterrupted passage forward through the throng and tumult of active trade and human life. On the contrary, the plain country burial, as it seems by proportion to be inferior in pride and circumstance, does seem to surpass in interest that of the town. It must take a man of more than common note to elicit even a remark in the crush and selfishness of the crowd; men are isolated from each other and knowledge of each other, but in the small country community their acquaintance, if not their sympathy, seems as that of one family. If the minister asks for the prayers of his primitive flock for 'one who is dangerously ill' they, know who it is. The vital spark has hardly quitted the early tenement ere the intelligence spreads to the village, and the first mournful tones of the passing bell are no sooner heard than each observes 'oh, it is for poor so and so', and by the extent of the group that gathers around the open grave, you may often judge the estimation with which the deceased was held by his or her friends and neighbours. In this instance, though the body was followed but by one female mourner and three or four villagers and a few boys, most of the congregation (an expression of deepest sympathy if not deep interest in every phase) awaited its arrival by the entrance gate, around the spot to which the old grave digger had brought from underneath the tower the ancient bier and the spade, the latter bright from constant and recent use in God's acre. These were placed on the stone pavement which led to the church porch, and the simple funeral having now entered the little gate, the bell which had been tolling the last few minutes in the tower above our heads ceased its deep tones, and the body having been deposited on the bier, and that subdued bustle attended on even the simplest form of burial being hushed, the clergyman (I think it was Mr. Collinson[2] since gathered to his fathers) approached amid the most profound silence of the uncovered group, and repeated these words, the touch and beauty of which, aided as they are by circumstance the most solemn repetition that can ever impair; 'I am the resurrection and the life said the Lord: he that believeth in me though he were dead yet shall live; and whosoever liveth and believeth in me shall never die'. We then followed the body to the newly dug grave which had been prepared for its reception, a clergyman reading the remaining part of service which derived its impressive solemnity more from its touching import, and the effect of occasion than from any studied intonation of voice and manner. The effect on my young mind was that of awe and wonder, for it was as I have said the first funeral I had ever witnessed, and death had never come so home to my youthful apprehension. After a few whispers as to the adjustment of the webbs, the body was lowered into its little and last receptacle and the handful of earth as it fell on the coffin lid blended with the words 'ashes to ashes, dust to dust'.[3]

The mournful business over, the group departed slowly and pensively for even the most thoughtful cannot shake off at once the effect of such a scene, and each as he moved off seemed to prefer his own thoughts for companions to any other for the time. I could not help noticing too, during the ceremony, that however light and full of life and love all nature seemed it perfectly harmonised with the mournful business then taking place in that little country churchyard. The birds were carolling their vesper song from the branches of the surrounding trees while the burial service was being read beneath, and yet there appeared no ill-timed levity in their song, and it the landscape glowed in the sunshine and verdure, there was also a pastoral repose — the peaceful hush of the sabbath holy hour over all, which accorded well with what was passing. The scene was at once solemn and soothing, taming to human pride and monitory to the human heart. I have dwelt perhaps too long on the reader's patience on this the reminiscence of the first country funeral I have seen, and I shall only detain him to say the remains of the interment which I had casually witnessed were those of a young man, a master I think of the parish or charity school who had died of consumption. I think I have already said that the usual congregation at Ashton Church is large and respectable, and the service was got through reverently and in order. On the day of my visit the Vicar offered up on behalf of John somebody or other (I forget the name), his grateful thanks to the almighty God for his recovery from a dangerous illness to which he had been cured in Bristol Infirmary. This was a pleasing trait and act it is true of only common thankfulness, and yet one too often neglected.

The Vicar[4] read prayers and preached. He was a good natured, good looking, comfortable man, and his sermon which abounded in pastoral illustration was a quiet easy discourse, for he seemed far too good tempered to wish to trouble his own, or his hearers minds, with any very exciting or uneasy topic in the middle of the month of June. As I was leaving the church I met with a person, who, while he spoke generally of the vicar with satisfaction, complained that some short time before when the parishioners had wished him to pray for rain, he declined on the grounds that he had not got his hay in, and could not therefore sincerely pray for that which he knew must do him harm. Whether the story be a true one, or whether it be an old one I cannot say, but the party to who I allude assured me it was a fact and I merely give his words.

1. Sir Richard Choke, d. 1483? 1486?
2. John Collinson, 1757-93, vicar of Long Ashton 1787-93, and author of *The History and Antiquities of the County of Somerset*, 1791.
3. It is interesting that Leech should choose Long Ashton to place his allegorical burial story, as it was at Long Ashton that he was buried forty-eight years later.
4. G.R. Blackburne (1841).

12 April 1845

Bitton

I selected the Keynsham road for my route to Bitton, and, midway between Brislington and Bristol, met the Worshipful the Mayor thundering along in his close carriage, and 'all the accessories,' to say his prayers at St. Mark's. Seated on the outside of John Bunyan, with my face towards the free country, I did not envy him in the inside of a coach bound for Bristol. Not even for a seat in a civic coach would I now turn back with you to the crowded city from my rural ride.

It is very well for everyone to be satisfied with their own station; and so happy did I feel — so perfectly contented with myself on that Sunday morning, lulled by the drowsy, but not disagreeable, purr-like creaking of my saddle as I rode along — that I don't think I could have added a single item to my wishes. When, after a long winter, and continuation of cold easterly cutting winds, the spring seems suddenly, on some fine Sunday morning, to leap down upon the world with a somersault, and cry, as he scatters wild flowers and sunshine about, 'I'm come at last,' one's heart seems almost in a harlequin mood also. You welcome your shadow as it keeps you company along the road, as an old friend whom you hardly once got a glimpse of during the dull days; while the primroses, peeping in clusters from under the hedges, like little families of fair sisters, seem as if they had all come out during the night to wish you the joys of the season.

When I threw John's bridle to the boy at the White Hart, Bitton, though it was ten minutes past eleven by my watch, I thought I was still in time, as the good people of the hostelry had not left home.

"Hodge," said I, "have prayers commenced yet?"

"Yes, Sir, the bell be a done ringing."

"How is that, then, for your master and mistress, I see have not gone yet?"

Hodge shrugged his shoulders — a motion which said as plainly as possible, "Master and Missus are too anxious to serve their customers, to afford time to serve God."

I should hardly have known the vicarage as I passed it and the schoolhouse, on my way to the Church up that pretty little lane. In my old friend Mr. Curtis's time it was a plain building; on the present vicar entering it as curate it was tastefully improved, but on his becoming incumbent, it grew with his growth into quite a gothic edifice, with a great array of oriel windows: and on this same progressive principle, I expect to see it a palace by the time he has expanded into a Bishop.

On entering the Church, seeing *FREE SEATS* painted on the wall to my left, I turned that way, and had just placed my hand on a pew door when the rest of the inscription met my eye — *FOR WOMEN* at the same moment a grim old spinster — one of the village vestals of some three score years — in a rusty beaver bonnet, scowled at me, as much as to say, "You have no business here, you beant of our sex." A little disconcerted, I quickly withdrew my hand, and turning round I saw on the opposite side, *FREE SEATS FOR MEN*; and to one of these, as if to a city or refuge, I retreated, taking up my position by the side of one of the county constabulary. Mr. Vicar, is this your doing? — is it you that have been guilty of this almost eastern segregation of the sexes in the sacred edifice? I know it is sometimes done in conventicles; but this is the first time I have ever seen it followed in the Established Church, and I rise my voice against it, Mr. Vicar. Besides, to be just, the practice ought to be general. A little further up, amongst the seats that were not free, there was no such 'invidious distinctions,' and it is only with the humble that your arrangement, like the new Poor Law, interferes to separate man and wife. For my own part, I should have thought it far more edifying to be allowed to read out of the same book with some worthy old goody, and to hear her voice trembling through the Litany, than to be placed as I was, like a culprit, by the side, and under the surveillance of a county constable. It would not, perhaps, be so wonderful if I, an old bachelor, were capable of such exclusive notions; but in the head of a house, it is almost inexcusable.

Some of the malcontents throughout the kingdom have of late been getting up a great hubbub and opposition to chanting in the Church, on the grounds that the people cannot join in it. Had they been at Bitton with me on Sunday last, their objection would have been answered. Some portion of the services were chanted, and nothing could be more generally or agreeably done; and I am told it has been so for several years. Two or three rough young fellows in fustian jackets, who sat near me, got cleverly through it; even the old women were never at fault; and if there was any imperfection anywhere, it was with me and the county constable. The organist is the daughter of the village carpenter, self-taught, and, I believe unpaid. As the phrase goes, 'this is just as it ought to be;' it is a simple and suitable offering of lay service; and, to my mind, the organ of the village Church is never so appropriately played as when the village parishioner presides at it.

If I were the vicar, I'd preach a terrible sermon against irregularity (so far as time goes,) of attendance. The poorer portion seem to care little as to what hour they enter. Some two or three made their appearance as late as the Communion Service; and as if this were not sufficient disturbance, an old fellow, who, I suppose, calls himself a sexton, kept shuffling about inside the porch in a reversionary suit of the vicar's sables. I would advise this functionary to try and imitate the clerk, whose subdued, sober, quiet and correct manner, is quite in keeping with his place.

There were two, I might say three, interesting incidents in the service, on the day of my visit. One was the churching of women; a most solemn and beautiful service, and when introduced in its proper place imparts to, and I think derives from, the usual prayers an additional effect. The other incident was, the announcement by the vicar of his son's being a candidate for deacon's orders at the next ordination; and solemnly calling on the congregation, according to the custom enjoined in such cases, if they knew any cause why he should not take upon him the holy office, in the name of God to declare it. Had this practice been always acted upon in the true spirit in which it had been intended, the Church and the Priesthood would at times have been saved some pain and scandal. The third circumstance consisted in the sermon, on the day of my visit, being an occasional one preparatory to confirmation. It was preached from Ecclesiastes c.v.,v.4. — 'When thou vowest a vow unto God defer not to pay it, for He hath no pleasure in fools; pay that which thou hast vowed:' and was treated in a plain, sound, sensible manner. There was no eloquence; but he spoke to his congregation with a straightforward frankness, which showed that he was well aware of, and had no wish to conceal the fact, that this solemn rite was too lightly regarded, its obligations thought too little of, and its ceremony looked upon as furnishing more a day of show and amusement, than of solemn and grave import. How well, how distinctly, at the moment did I recall to mind my own confirmation. It was in Maryport Church, and I have now old Bishop Cornwall[1] in my eye, as laying his hand on my head, (it was not grey or bald then) he pronounced his benediction in these beautiful words, 'Defend, O Lord, this my child,' &c.

The Vicar of Bitton[2] who by the way, I must not forget to remark, read the lessons to my mind much too rapidly, is one of the most indefatigable men in the world. He is one of those men, who, if you placed him in the desert of Arabia, would I believe have half-a-dozen Churches up about him in little more than that number of years. I'm afraid to say how many he has built in the parish of Bitton, which was once almost as bad as Arabia; but I think I am correct in stating that he found it with one, and that he has managed to add four or five others, and by the time he is gathered to his fathers as many more will I expect stand as monuments of his untiring, his unconquerable zeal and services to a large district, once so destitute of the proper means of public worship. Where he gets, or got, the money for them all, heaven knows, I don't; but I should say he must have been a most intrepid beggar and indefatigable man, to do what he has done; he restored the mother Church; he rebuilt Oldland,[3] perched a pretty new chapel on Jeffery's Hill; and planted another amongst the coal pits of Kingswood,[4] and too good a Churchman to confine his labours to his own parish, he is setting one or two on foot at Siston, and in all he is as cool-headed as you can well imagine; he is too 'old a stager,' as somebody assured me, to be put out by a trifle; 'high and dry,' he rubs on enlarging the borders of the Church, while others are squabbling about her — erecting altars, while others are fighting about turning their faces towards to or from them. His energy would make him a capital Colonial Bishop, and if he could be tempted to take Hong Kong, the island, I'll be bound, would be full of Churches in less than no time. One only wishes he had a more grateful and better field for his exertions, for his parish is eaten up with Dissenters, whose ideas of religious duty are comprised in a few hours' cleanliness, on Sunday evenings, and 'sitting under' a *preacher* for some sixty minutes. It must be, and I doubt not is, very disheartening to the Vicar to see so scanty an attendance of poor at the parish Church; for though there are not many in Bitton itself, the poor being principally in Oldland, more ought to come, and would it they were not drawn off by the meeting houses, with which on a Sunday afternoon the region round about is literally *vocal*.

The restoration, repairs, &c., at Bitton Church, have been affected with great good taste and architectural knowledge. There is an inscription which records that the interior was altered, &c., in 1842, when the present equalization of sittings was effected, there being before that date double pews, and twelve inches higher that the present. I believe these alterations and improvements were done principally by private subscriptions. I know the front of the gallery is positively brilliant with emblazoned shields, which belong, as I have been informed, to those through whose donations the work was done; the 'pride of Heraldry' is put forth in all its pomp and power, of azure, argent and sable, so that one would fancy a whole company of Knights Templars had come to Bitton, and hung up their bucklers in a row, lions rampant, and falcons volant, and stags gazant, and bloody hands and sharp daggers, dreadful to look upon and numerous to describe. Whoever was the author of the idea it was a clever one: his family pride is a very good road to a man's pocket, and since the sale of indulgences was resorted to, to build St. Peter's, I have not heard of a more successful mode of raising funds to repair a Church. I do not know what amount, whether five or ten pounds, qualified a man to hang up his 'quarterings;' but I should be very glad to get a niche in the gallery at a moderate price, provided the painter or the parish will supply me with a coat of arms, as the family of the 'Church-goers,' however ancient, have not yet attained to that dignity.

While peeping about the building after prayers, I saw a piece of paper pinned to the green baize of one of them, on which was written, 'Mrs. Ellacombe's pew.' Whether this is done by the Vicar to vindicate his own good taste, and imply that this lady is alone answerable for this cumbrous piece of woodwork, I can't say, but I know this that the most suitable sitting for a clergyman's family, and the place and purpose, would be stalls. The other large pew is occupied by the tenants of the Rectory, for Bitton is an impropriate Rectory and a stall in the Cathedral of Sarum, the rich endowment being leased out to Laymen. The east window, which is a handsome one, was glazed only within the last

twenty years, being before that time blocked up, a gross act of barbarism, of which I could hardly have conceived any age capable. There is a north aisle or chantry, built about 1300, by Sir John Barr, and descending to the Newtons, has become their burying place. It is quite a gem in an architectural view, but being annexed to a private property, is kept locked up, and unless you have interest enough to get the key, you must be content with a peep through the key hole. The clerk, however, civilly opened it for me. It is principally early English: amongst the monumental memorials here found is one to Dame Newton, who had four sons and thirteen daughters: rather a large family of young ladies to bake for. Near this aisle, between it and the nave, is a little place, a kind of 'old curiosity shop' for the Vicar's antiquarian collection, comprising an ancient stone coffin, let in like a cupboard to the wall, and such as was much used in the thirteenth century; there are also two priests of about the same date, and a cross-legged monument, ascertained to represent Sir Walter de Button, who died in 1227, and which is all that remains to us, I believe, of a family of great importance in the thirteenth century, three of them being Bishops, one of Exon, and two of Wells.

In the stone coffin, suspended by a nail, is a card, on which is written an intimation, or an invitation, whichever you please to call it, to the following effect: 'If any Camdenian, Antiquarian, or member of an Architectural Society should visit this Church, the Vicar begs he will do him the favour to call at the vicarage.' Just the thing, thought I, for me; I'm an architectural amateur, and the Vicar must be at this moment sitting down with his family to his roast beef and horse radish; and there is something so suggestive of comfort in yonder vicarage, the smoke 'so gracefully curls' out of those Gothic chimneys, to say nothing of the subterraneous contingency of a cellar of old port, that I don't know when an invitation to a Sunday dinner, even though conveyed through the sombre medium of a stone coffin, ever came so welcome. I'll be with you in a moment, Mr. Vicar, said I, starting; but I had not got to the porch when a sudden thought struck me. No, no, it won't do, said I; even though the trap were baited with roast beef, I won't walk into it. The dearest lunch I ever ate I once had under nearly similar circumstances. I was down in Devonshire about fifteen years ago, and roving into a country church, which was being very tastefully restored, I saw a notice posted up to nearly the same effect, only that the invitation included 'all strangers:' the parsonage stood invitingly on a pleasant sunny slope close by, and I innocently enough walked up to it. The Rector received me very agreeably; we talked about the church, and I complimented him on the good taste with which the work was carried on. Of course it was not difficult to persuade me to have lunch, and I will say without disparagement to other people's, that I never tasted a finer Glos'ster, or a better tap, but I paid two guineas for it; for just as I was about to leave, my hospitable friend the Rector produced a book, in which was a long list of those who had lunched with him, and left two guineas behind them for the restoration of the church. I could not refuse, so I meekly signed my name, and put down two sovereigns and two shillings by way of embellishment. There may be a book, too, at Bitton, thought I — some ingenious, pretty, quiet, little web in the shape of a subscription list, to catch fly-about Camdenians and antiquarians, for the man must be no novice in the art of raising money who could contrive to build so many churches in so comparatively poor a parish. Besides, the chancel arch was restored only the other day, and all restorations are sure to leave a debt behind them; and on the present occasion I have barely enough about me to pay for John Bunyan's corn at the White Hart.

The present pulpit, which is a handsome one, was erected in 1838, and was the gift of a late parishioner.

The tower, which is a good specimen of very early Perpendicular work, merits the attention of the architectural amateur: there are heads of Edward III and Queen Philippa in the corbels of the drip: the spire on the turret of the tower was restored in the Summer of '43, having been demolished circa 1650. On entering the Church I was struck with a very simple but curious mode of chiming the whole set — the 'ingenious device' is, I believe, the Vicar's. Here, too, close by the West entrance is a free-stone mural tablet, which I think afforded me as much pleasure as anything I say on the occasion of my visit.

It is erected by the Vicar (and does his head and heart great credit,) to the memory of an old and faithful servant — a practice which I am sorry to not more followed, for it tends to excite an honest ambition in the humble, when they find those they serve gratefully appreciating and publicly acknowledging their merits. People complain that servants are not what they were, and it is in my opinion in a great measure because masters are not what they were: that old family footing on which the *domestic* once stood in the household, and that family affection with which he or she was regarded, has grown out of fashion, and belongs, except in a few instances, to the *temporis acti*. The words of the inscription, as well as I can recollect, were these:

This Tablet is erected to the memory of
JOHN MINGO,
by the
Rev. H.T. Ellacombe;
with whom he lived as servant 14 years, at the vicarage,
discharging his duty with
Exactness, honesty, and affection.

There is such a monument, and somewhat similar in purport, to an old servant, and erected by her mistress, in the little churchyard of Abbot's Leigh.

I should have said that the Church of Bitton is dedicated to St. Mary, and now consists of a nave or single aisle, and chancel.

1. P.M. Cornwall.
2. H.T. Ellacombe, curate of Bitton 1817-35, vicar 1835-50. At the age of 91 Ellacombe wrote *History of the Parish of Bitton* in 1881.
3. St. Anne, Oldland, 1829.
4. Holy Trinity, Kingswood, 1821.

Almondsbury

I have for many years, upon a certain morning in the week, been accustomed to visit the Bristol Library.[1] I do it for many reasons: I like to see the new books that come down — it is a habit I have, and I wish to enquire after the health of my excellent friend and old school-fellow John Pearce[2] and to tell him the news; for he is one of those men who believe time thrown away in perusing the paragraphs of a newsprint, while a single old book remains unread on the shelves round about him; and I think he has told me, he has not looked into a newspaper for twenty years — a source of some mortification to me, as I am too modest to call his attention to my lucumbrations, and I think he knows no more at this moment of the Church Goer, than if he were one of the Brahmins of India, or the bonzes of Japan. And, perhaps it is as well for my own comfort that he does not; for I am afraid my peripatetic impertinences would not meet with much favour in the eyes of such critical taste and hypercritical correctness; and I'd sooner have a bull fired at me from the Vatican, or a bill from Chancery, than the bad opinion of the elegant and orthodox defender of cathedral service.

But let it not be supposed that my esteemed school-fellow, as he sits deep recessed in his beehive chair, beneath the sculptured foliage of Gibbons is either indifferent or insensible to public affairs: on the contrary, though no broadsheet finds its way into or profanes that bookish seclusion and his old loves, the folios, would fall off their shelves in a fit of jealousy, if they saw any paper in their patron's hands more modern than the *English Mercurie*, he is glad to hear *traditionally* how things are going on outside in the world, to receive a synopsis of public intelligence. though it were only to deplore the decadence of those good old principles, which were in fashion when he and I were school-fellows, and 'George the Third was King.'

It may be weakness, but when I light on any of my old class-fellows, there are so few of us left in this transitory world — that it is quite a comfort to talk to, or about them. One consolation there is, that as he does not read the newspapers, he is not likely to know of the impudent liberty I have taken, and I hope no one will tell him.

I have wandered so far that I forget what led me in the first instance to refer to the Bristol Library; and from the Bristol Library it was a very natural digression to my old friend, as I could not for the life of me pass his beehive chair without a word of gossip. But now I recollect, I should have said, that having on the morning of my stated visit, some few weeks since, taken down Dugdale's Monasticon, I went into the inner room to make a reference. There were two gentlemen sitting by the fire, one had Bohn's Catalogue[3] in his hand, and the other, who appeared a Clergyman, was contemplating on a silver pencil-case, which he was twirling in his fingers. I had not turned over many pages when I thought I heard the word 'Church-Goer.' I cocked my ears, for vanity sharpens our senses amazingly. "I have no idea who it is," said the man with the pencil-case; "but as the number of Churches in the neighbourhood are limited, his impudence must soon exhaust itself." I had no ambition to hear more, so I shut Dugdale and walked off, solacing myself with the reflection that my censor was one upon whose corns I had inadvertently trodden. I am prepared, however, for these little tubs: I cannot ride round to old country Churches, and think 'to brush a web or two from off their walls,' without expecting to get a little dust in my throat: we cannot hope to sweep clean without raising a little cloud; for, to use the words of the Antiquary, 'the dust was very ancient, peaceful, quiet dust, and would have remained so a hundred years had it not been disturbed.'

There was more, however, in my censor's remarks than at the time I saw; for on Sunday morning I heard John Bunyan's tramp, tramp, and sudden halt at the street door, before I had thought whither my matin pilgrimage should be made. I looked about me, and on my first glimpse I seemed to have exhausted nearly all the notable Churches in the neighbourhood. On the Ashton side, to use what I believe is a sporting phrase, 'I had shot down all the manor:' Henbury and Westbury were already visited, and there was not an inn-stable in the direction of Stapleton, Stoke Gifford, and Winterbourne, in which John Bunyan had not eaten his peck of corn. At length, as I opened my mouth for the last bit of buttered toast, Filton came into my head, and in five minutes more I had turned John in that direction.

Having started early, I thought, as I did not hear the bell on passing the Anchor, that I was too soon. However, as I approached the Church, I found the silence was attributable to a far different cause. The little tower was standing, it is true, but the nave had disappeared before the industry of the Ecclesiastical Commissioners, and all that remained, at a disconsolate distance, were two-thirds of the chancel[4] and half of the Ten Commandments; rubbish and old rafters filled up the intervening space; the lion and the unicorn had gone to perpetuate the parish loyalty in a neighbouring barn, and not a vestige was left of my friend Poulden[5] or his pulpit.

"John," said I, "they have pulled down the Church to spite us: I had no great respect for the old edifice, but its abolition at this particular time is a pointed thing: it has been standing two hundred years, and they never thought of touching it until we thought of paying them a visit."

There was nothing for it, however, but to push on; I must get prayers somewhere. We had still an hour, and I determined to continue my course to Almondsbury, and hear my old friend Bishop Gray's son preach one of his father's sermons.

I hope none will draw an inference unfavourable to my sobriety, from the fact of my having put up at the Punch Bowl; but as John was the only party regaled within its precincts, no imputation can apply.

Man and boy I have been a hundred times at Almondsbury, yet I never stood on that hill without feeling its influence in every sense — the broad Severn and the rich intervening tract of marsh and meadow, and the old Church, with its pointed gables and its picturesque lead covered spire, beneath. I never heard

Church bells in any situation, I think, sound so well: there were joy and gladness in every tone, and the ringers passing in and out occasionally through the belfry door, which opened on the roof, gave an additional feature of animation to the scene. Having admonished two lads who were occupying themselves in a game of marbles, I strolled leisurely down the hill, and took my seat on a table tomb in the little churchyard, listening to the peals and looking at the people as they passed in. A pleasant thing is that to take a seat on some old tomb or headstone in a country churchyard, on a sunny Sabbath morning, and see the congregation arrive in all their Sunday finery; and Almondsbury, judging from what I saw, is not without its rural beaux or its village beauties. Some of them stared at the old fellow in the snuff brown coat, as he sat on a slab sacred to somebody's memory; and others giggled, and all wondered what brought me there, if it was not to look for testimony in the shape of an old tombstone, or on a pilgrimage to the grave of my great ancestor Prince Alcmond.

Almondsbury Church takes the visitor, who expects to see a plain country structure, quite by surprise on entering. Its handsome roof — its three aisles, separated by lofty pillars and pointed arches — its beautiful chancel and painted windows, seen through the columns that support the tower at the intersection — all give to the interior quite a cathedral-like effect. I can recollect when the Church was for the most part Norman; the arches low and heavy, and the chancel disfigured by a Grecian screen, which blocked up the fine east window. Within the last years, however, the whole Church and chancel have been extensively repaired, and altered to Early English;[6] the east window which is of three lights, with deep recessed mouldings, and disengaged columns, opened, and some good painted glass put in. The chancel, as seen from the nave, has a most pleasing effect: its seeming distance appeared to lend enchantment to the scene; and as the varied light poured in upon the snowy surplices of the officiating clergymen, the view was sufficiently solemn and picturesque to have frightened my poor aunt into the idea of Popery, especially as there is a picture of Christ blessing the bread — a copy from that celebrated one at Lord Methuen's. This last was the gift of a Mr. Hill, a *Dissenter*, and painted by himself. Who can despair of decorations when they have been known to come from such quarters? There is, near the altar, a very perfect piscina, lately discovered; also another smaller one in the south cross aisle. There are two fonts in the Church — a modern font, in the wrong place, the gift of the squire, which is used; and an old font somewhere else, which is *not* used.

Almondsbury Church was dedicated to the Virgin Mary, and consecrated by four Bishops, (what a muster of mitres!) in the year 1148. It is supposed to be the mother Church, having as Chapels of Ease those of Elberton and Filton. Somewhere about or inside this Church (if anybody could find them.) are the ashes of Alcmond, a Saxon Prince, father of King Egbert. And now the reader has got every bit and scrap of history or antiquarian information which I can either beg, borrow, or steal, about the parish or Church of Almondsbury.

It is a pleasant little village, free, I believe, from heresy and schism, and a populous neighbourhood, for the Church is well filled. On entering, I helped myself to a pew as noiselessly as I could, not to awaken three sons of the sod, who, early as it was, were asleep in the next seat. There were two young women in about the third pew from me; they will, perhaps, recollect an old man in a brown coat, who entered soon after; that gentleman presents his compliments to them, and begs that the next time a stranger visits their Church they will not turn round and stare him out of countenance, as if there had been a robbery of prayer-books, and they were endeavouring to identify the depredator. Nothing, however, could be more becoming than the bearing of the congregation generally.

The prayers were read by the Perpetual Curate, the Rev. Henry Gray.[7] I have a great respect for Mr. Gray, if it were only for his father's sake. I can recollect the old Bishop so well.[8] I have him in my mind's eye at this moment, riding about in his wig and apron; and I can never forget his bearing on the Sunday morning of the Bristol Riots,[9] when he steadily refused to omit through any fear of violence the service in the Cathedral. I was one of those who thought to dissuade him, owing to the critical state of things. "No," said his Lordship, and his answer was worthy of a Confessor, "though I can do nothing else in defence of the citizens, I will pray for them!" And pray he did, and preach too, though with partially closed doors, to a congregation that appeared anything but comfortable or at case; and I think the sermon, though by a Bishop, was lost upon them; as, from the frequent nervous peeps which they took out at the Green, I should say the people were not collected enough to be critical. When the Earl of Kildare was asked by Henry the Eighth why he burned the Cathedral of Cashel, he said, "because he thought the Bishop was in it:" and some, I have little doubt, were of opinion that instead of the presence of his Lordship being a protection against the populace, the fact might have been a further inducement to fire the pile.

Mr. Gray is an excellent and impressive reader, and nothing could be more correct, more decent, and more orderly than the manner in which the service was gone through. The singing, too was very fairly and respectably done by the children, and everything in and about the Church and parish evinced pains bestowed and interest taken by the resident clergyman.

1. The Bristol Library, King Street.
2. The Librarian was John Peace, not Pearce.
3. James Bohn, 1803-80. Bohn was a London bookseller. In 1845 he re-published Dugdale's Monasticon, and it may have been to this edition that Leech referred.
4. The church of St. Peter, c.1340. Enlarged and mostly rebuilt in 1845. A new nave and sanctuary were added in 1961.
5. James Bedford Poulden, rector 1831-76. Poulden was the leading force behind the enlargement of the church which Leech witnessed in the early stages.
6. The four bay nave was rebuilt in 1834 and the Norman arches removed.
7. Henry Gray, d. 5 June 1864.
8. Robert Gray, 1762-1834. Bishop of Bristol 1827-34.
9. The Bristol Riots, from Saturday 29 October to Monday 31 October 1831. Unrest was felt in Bristol as elsewhere in the country due to the rejection of the Reform Bill by the House of Lords. The opening of the Quarter Sessions and the arrival of the Recorder sparked off three remarkable days of violence in which Lawford's Gate, the Mansion House, and the Bishop's Palace amongst many other buildings were gutted by fire.

10 May 1845
Wrington

When I have rather a distant church to visit, I leave Bristol somewhat earlier than usual, at about the time when the milkmen are making their morning peregrinations from door to door, and this very coincidence, on Sunday week almost cost me a fall; for just on Redcliff Hill, some fellow who must have been a novice at his calling, gave such a sudden shrill shout of 'Meeulk!' and deposited his tin cans with such a clash on the flags, that John jumped in a panic at least three feet aside, and had it not been for the pummel and crupper I should have measured almost double that number on the ground. I like the cry of 'Meeulk,' whether it be made at the door or down the 'airy,' I have been so long accustomed to it. I like the calling, too, for those fellows in white smock frocks are so redolent of the country, they seem each morning, as they make their rounds through a crowded city, like refreshing envoys to us, from green fields and dairy farms; but I would not purchase even the picturesque at the expense of a fall and I hope all the milkmen who subscribe to my friend's paper, and read this notice, will be kind enough to deposit their cans at peoples doors, on Sundays, with as little noise as possible, if they don't wish to see me brought back to my lodgings some fine morning on a door.

I did not go direct to my destination; but wishing to have once more my old walk from Congresbury to Wrington by the river, I stabled John at the latter place, and proceeded along these pleasant green banks from which I have so often cast my May-fly.

I ought to be ashamed of myself for allowing such thoughts to enter my mind on a Sunday morning, but I could not help thinking 'twas exactly the day a taking day for trout; warm, and with cloud enough above to satisfy the most fastidious fisherman. 'Twas a beautiful day indeed; and though there was no extent of prospect, and the dim outline of the Mendips could barely be seen, yet the softness and poetry of the scene around me made amends for the loss of any more distant view. Every turn in the river threw a new picture out to the eye; here an old rustic unparapetted bridge, or a mill, with its dam and noise of falling water hardly breaking the Sabbath rest, formed a 'bit of foreground;' and there an old farmhouse, with its old trees, and its homestead and sheds, from which piled-up bundles of teazles¹ peeped out, made the prominent point of the landscape. The only persons I passed were here and there some rural labourer fishing water-cresses from the pool with a crooked stick for his Sunday dinner.

But here, while I have been gossiping, Wrington peals have been ringing in my ears, and Wrington tower, tall, beautiful, and symmetrical, like a fair vision, full in sight, to assert, as it were, the surpassing architectural taste and talent of other days. This is what makes English country scenery unlike any and all others in the world; when suddenly, as it were, in the midst of rural associations, which beguile the mind away from the recollection of man and society, some splendid church tower, some noble ecclesiastical pile, opens upon the view, to show the presence of civilization and the triumph of arts. To those who have ever passed this church, no description of its exterior appearance is necessary; to those who have not I would say, fancy one of the finest country Churches, and with certainly one of the most exquisite and imposing towers you have ever seen, and you have just as good an idea of the structure, and perhaps a better, than I can give you by a confused account of orders, and tracery, and niches, and drips, and buttresses, about which I sometimes talk until I am unintelligible to myself; what must it then be to the reader?

The first thing that attracted my attention on entering the churchyard, was a poor but new freestone Gothic monument, set in the gable end of a small thatched house, which abutted on the burying ground, and bearing the following inscription:

John Locke[2]
Was born in this house A.D. MDCXXXVI.
This stone was erected by the inhabitants of this Parish,
A.D. MDCCCXLI.

The tablet would have been complete had they attached the name of the writer of so elegant an inscription, where the pronoun *this* hisses so harmoniously three times in four lines. The parentage of such a composition should be placed beyond conjecture, for at present the honours of authorship oscillate between the schoolmaster and the parson. While I was copying the inscription on the blank leaf of my Prayer Book, a good-looking young woman, who I fancy is now an inhabitant of the mighty metaphysician's birth place, amused herself, in the absence of any more active employment for the 'understanding,' in laughing at me through the gate, while my ancient friend John Bennett, out of whose recollection I appear to have grown, was suspiciously dodging me at a distance. Somewhere here, too, in this yard are, I suppose, interred the remains of old parson Leeves,[3] the composer of the beautiful ballad of 'Auld Robin Gray,' which will live when all your Italian arias are in the Aegean. Old Leeves was Rector or Vicar of this parish, and of great musical genius, which was inherited by one of his sons, whom I recollect for many years scratching a double bass in the gallery, with great unction, against the combined voices of the parish school and parish schoolmaster.

At Wrington I loitered about the burial-ground for some time, as I had a good half hour to spare. There were a few lazy Sunday loungers lolling over the wall, with hardly sufficient energy of mind or body to turn round and look at me; so, for want of more interesting objects of view, I strolled on towards the *back-front*, I suppose I must call it, of the parsonage, and recalled to mind the catastrophe which occurred there when the late Parson Leeves' effects were 'submitted to public competition,' and buyers and bidders, auctioneer and all, suddenly disappeared through the floor; and really the tall tenement looks at this moment as if it were withheld by compunction alone from falling on the present proprietor. This is a pity; for it is in a pleasant situation, and I used to think it a pretty place long ago, when I strolled by in summer, on a Saturday evening, and saw the parson preparing his sermon by the open window, and occasionally turning his eyes for a thought towards the Mendips.

I don't know how old Wrington is, and I don't care; the inhabitants fancy it has great antiquity. My old friend Davies,[4] with whom I sometimes passed a Sunday, used to say, tapping the mahogany summits of his old tops with his cane, "In the time of Adam, sir, it was a market town of some importance, but ceased to be so about the time of Noah; and has not made much advancement since in that respect." Worthy Davies was the beau ideal of a Welsh parson; he was supposed to attend to the souls of the parishioners of Puxton; and I recollect going into church one Sunday as he was reading the service, lolling listlessly as he did so with his head on one hand; he was just in the middle of the Lord's Prayer as I entered; and he opened his mouth and yawned from ear to ear. The only excuse I can offer for him is, that it was a close summer's day, and he had been brewing all the week. However, my really estimable friend was not singular in this; there are a great many in the present day, who thank God 'they are not as other men are' and yet go through the beautiful prayers of the Church as if they were reading an Act of Parliament.

The peals had ceased, and the little sanctus bell had taken up the thread of their discourse, when I entered the church, which I did through the chancel door, and turned into the next pew that I found open, and which was one immediately behind the reading-desk — a situation from which I had an opportunity of seeing the miscellaneous collection of old printed parish papers, pack-thread, and spectacle cases, which the parson had stowed away on a shelf appropriated to such purposes. A lady, with a world of artificial flowers in her bonnet, was the only intern with myself. Had she been disposed to be communicative, I should have asked her something about the antiquities of the church, of which I don't know a ha'p'orth; but there was something about her that discouraged any advance towards familiar conversation. Perched on the seat of a pew opposite, close by the screen, was a little girl in a white bonnet and a red head, pulling away at the sanctus bell, the sound of which came down deadened and dreamily upon us.

I had abundant leisure to look about me and admire the proportions and details of one of the best parish churches in Somersetshire. Certainly, our Popish progenitors knew how to build places of worship; and though we can't admire their creed, we have good cause to be thankful for their industry; for it is well they built decent churches for us, as we are not disposed to do so for ourselves. At least we must confess, that to monkish taste in grouping pier and arch, parapet and pinnacle together, in one harmonious whole, we are indebted for such noble parish churches as Wrington, Yatton, Congresbury, Banwell and Backwell.

Nearly the whole of Wrington, and indeed almost all the churches in this part of Somersetshire, are Perpendicular. It is perfectly formed, consisting of a nave, north and south aisles, and chancel, with a good porch; the nave, which is divided from the side aisles by rows of arches springing from light and lofty piers, is lit by a clerestory, the windows of which are of good size and symmetry. There is an elaborate altar screen — I believe, more properly called Reredos — of perpendicular work; and which, if not new, has seemingly been recently repaired. There is also a fine rood screen — I mean the screen which divides the chancel from the main part of the church; and which, as the tourists say, is much admired for its beautiful flower and fret work.

The Church is, of course, full of the usual cumbrous traces of the village carpenter; at the west end of the north aisle there is a group of private apartments, enclosed with red curtains, something like the dinner boxes of a city chophouse; and there is a little gallery for the accommodation of a first and second flute, and the small boys who sing. This part of the service was very languid; the flutes were plaintive enough, and the schoolmaster sung as well as a weak voice and a stiff cravat would permit him, and even the lads were not loath to lend their aid; but the congregation were quite content to leave it all to them.

Mr. Thompson[5] is a neat preacher; indeed, I don't think I ever knew one to whom the term *neat* might be more truly and pointedly applied; he is neat in his appearance, he is neat in his reading, he wears a neat gown, and his compositions are neat. He does everything with a critical precision; and is one of those persons who, I should say, judging from what I saw of him, before writing his sermon, nibbed his pen with particular nicety, smoothed his quire of paper before him, placed his inkstand in a certain position, and never sat down to his work without equilateral editions of the Bible and Cruden's Concordance[6] at each elbow. His orthoepy (this is a fine word for pronunciation,) is faultless, nay, fastidious; and 'Pharoah' and 'Caiaphas' were 'mentioned' with an almost reverential respect for the dioeresis. Indeed, I should as soon expect to hear of a breach in the walls of Wrington church, as of a breach of orthography, etymology, syntax, or prosody, in the compositions of its Curate. His sermon, which was preached from Deuteronomy, chapter vi., verse 13, on the day of my visit, had all the characteristics of his style; it was distinct, clear, neat, and correct; you could not have picked a hole in it if, like a woodpecker, you went round and round it, trying it in every passage for a whole day: but it wanted muscle — it wanted originality — it wanted force; while it 'went on refining' rather too much for a rural congregation.

Now, if you say I expect too much, I admit it was a better sermon than one hears from nineteen out of twenty of the ordinary race of country Curates, who spend five days of the week making their cider, the sixth in making a sermon, and the seventh in preaching it; but you will bear in mind, that Mr. Thompson is a writer of sermons of some reputation, for the London market: he has written a book or two also, and is not to be measured by the same standard that you would apply to a mere working parish minister, who lives in a square parsonage all the days of his life, and eats beans and bacon without Greek, like Goldsmith's professor. In fact, we look for something out of the common in such a man.

The Rector is the Rev. John Vane.[7] I am not aware whether he is anything to Oliver Cromwell's friend, 'the Lord deliver us' Vane, or whether the obviousness of the quotation ever tempts the parishioners to apply it to their pastor; he has, however, been a very fortunate man, for he has two or three good country parishes, a London living; and is, or was, one of the chaplains of the House of Commons, having daily during the session to pray for the collective wisdom at something handsome ahead. He is a great favourite with all his farming friends, and seemingly believes the first object of study for a country clergyman should be composts; he appears to be as well acquainted with Liebeg[8] as with Jeremy Taylor;[9] is an authority on the succession of crops, and great on the subsoil plough. Mr. Vane makes a smart speech at an agricultural dinner, but I never heard him in the pulpit. He is, however, esteemed as a very liberal and kind-hearted friend in the country, and devotes much time and money to advance at least the mundane prosperity of his own and the neighbouring parishes. Though a courtier, too, he manages with much tact and intuitive cleverness the clods committed to his care; and if he is lucky in having so many parishes, the parishes tell you they are lucky in having him.

The congregation of Wrington is not large, but comprises a pretty fair sprinkling of the several classes in the neighbourhood.

1. Teazles would have been for sale to Gloucestershire, Wiltshire, and Somerset clothiers for raising the nap on woollen cloths.
2. John Locke, 1632-1704. English philosopher. There appear to be slight chronological differences to the nativity.
3. William Leeves, 1748-1828. Poet and composer.
4. Richard Davis, perpetual curate of Puxton, 1804-32.
5. Henry Thompson, 1797-1878. Curate at Wrington 1828-53 and Vicar of Chard from 1853 until his death. He wrote and translated several books including, in 1845, translations of Schiller's *Maid of Orleans* and *William Tell*.
6. Alexander Cruden, 1701-70. *The Concordance to the Bible* (1737).
7. John Vane (1828).
8. Justus, Baron von Liebig, 1803-73. German chemist.
9. Jeremy Taylor, 1613-67. Bishop of Down and Connor. *A discourse of the Liberty of Prophesying* (1646), *The Rule of Exercises of Holy Living* (1650), *The Rule and Exercises of Holy Dying* (1651).

24 May 1845
Weston-Super-Mare

"Weston! Who's for Weston?" said, or rather shouted, the man in green, throwing open the door of a second-class carriage at the same time.

"I, for one, am," I replied, about to step in.

"Please, first show your ticket, Sir," said he, interposing his great arm between my body and the carriage, and compelling me to unbutton my surtout, and undo all my comfortable preparations for the journey, in order to hunt in my waistcoat pocket for a slip of printed blue paper.

"That'll do," said he, as soon as he saw the corner of it peeping out, and I took my seat.

"Weston! Weston!, who's for Weston?" still shouted the conductor, continuing to hold the door in his hand.

"Here," said a decently dressed young mother, hurrying up with an infant in her arms, and followed by her husband, a respectable, manly-looking mechanic, with a fine little boy about three years old in his hand. Two young shopmen, as many young girls, an elderly man, and lady of mature age followed, and the conductor, with a bang of the door, left us, and proceeded to fill another carriage.

It is strange what a *microcosmical* tendency (if I may use the expression, and it has rather puzzled my fingers to write it) a man's mind naturally has. There is no one that reads this that has not experienced what I mean, that has not, when he has gone on board a steam-vessel, or entered a stage-coach or a railway-carriage, made for himself, for the time being, a little world out of the small circle into which he is by accident cast — that has not withdrawn himself from the multitude outside, to contemplate the little coterie which with himself are enclosed within the four partitions at that moment; it is, in fact, his microcosm, his little world: for however brief a space, he limits his speculations and conjectures to the business, the destinations, or the quality of his co-travellers and co-voyagers, and temporarily interests himself, or perhaps tries to make an impression, in and on each individual, as he never would have done but for this casual contiguity. He knows he, perhaps, may never see them again, that at most their lot is cast together only for an hour or two, still he will not permit even this time to be a blank, the activity or egotism of the mind will not be idle for a moment. And it is all for the best, this instinct is a main ingredient of sociability; man's wish to please might by some casuists be explained as an

effort at effect; and after all, no company is too small, or no time too brief, for display. Some naturalists have said that every leaf is a miniature of its parent tree; so every little social knot may be deemed an epitome of society at large; it is but the little wheel within the great wheel, and it is a small circle, indeed, that will not, even in a railroad carriage, give something like a synopsis of the main motives and dispositions that actuate society, and in the usual complement of six on either side you may see selfishness and sociability, ostentation and vanity, sense and nonsense: for instance, why did one of the shopmen pull off his glove, and use so many ingenious devices to show a bulky ring, if not to make an impression on the company, who in twenty minutes more would have forgotten both himself and his ring? What was he or his lump of jewellery to me? yet could I have placed my hand on my heart and

honestly said, that in pulling out the massive, old-fashioned gold watch which my father left me, I had not something like a secret pride or satisfaction in overpowering him with the superior weight of metal? Then, the young girl who sat nearly opposite me, was she insensible to even the momentary admiration of her chance companions, as she now and again smoothed her bonnet ribbon, or repaired the ravages of the breeze amongst 'the convolutions of her ringlets?' Then, there was the old hard visaged fellow, who crushed himself into, and the young mother out of, a seat, that he might have his back to the engine, was he no type of the selfishness of the world, which cares not who is exposed to the wind so that itself is not?

Now, I don't mean this for philosophy; for I don't wish, or don't want, or don't mean to be philosophical: I intend it for common sense, whether the reader will or not recognise it for such is another question. I am not one of those who affect to be reading or able to read profound moral lessons from Dan to Beersheba;[1] but I think a man may always find occupation, and perhaps innocent amusement for himself, if he only has the faculty (to use a common but comprehensive phrase) of 'making himself agreeable and at home' wherever he is. A wiser man than myself has observed that 'there is nothing too little for so little a creature as man; it is by studying little things that we attain the great art of having as little misery and as much happiness as possible.' There are some people have this talent to a marvellous degree, who are born with a pleasant and easy flexibility and freedom of manner which places them at once on a friendly footing with whatever company they may be thrown into for the moment; and the company themselves instinctively find it out; for poor human nature, notwithstanding all the hard things we say of it, is never slow to make the discovery, or to appreciate what is amiable or agreeable. I suppose people have found out by this time that I am given to talk occasionally of myself; perhaps they will still further bear with me when I say that my excellent father was in the habit of impressing it on my mind, that by doing or saying a civil thing I never could do wrong. I have tried to follow his advice, always endeavouring to temper each little sociable advance with suitable respect, so as not to offend any; and I find, looking at the matter even in an interested light, that I lose nothing by it, for my civilities are mostly returned fourfold. For instance, when my friend, the honest mechanic, came up to the carriage on Sunday morning, I tendered my services to assist his wife in with the band box and the baby, not, perhaps, that my assistance was any great advantage after all; for considering what little experience I have in babies, I cannot be expected to be very useful in that department at least, but they took the will for the deed — they saw I meant to be civil if I could; they were, therefore, obliged to me, and we were on the most friendly terms all the way, even to the eldest boy, who was a fine fellow, and took a most lively interest in the interior of my watch.

Seriously, however, there is no class amongst the multitudinous ones of which the mass of this great country is composed, the contemplation of which awakens so much interest, and creates so much pleasure, as the respectable, decent, and decently-dressed mechanic, who adorns the state of life to which it has pleased God to call him, and seeks, with a laudable pride, to make his own appearance and that of his family, as creditable as his little competence will permit: this man was well habited, and so was his wife, and even still more care and attention were bestowed to render the boy and the baby neat and becoming. And I have no doubt that their home was in keeping with their personal appearance, clean and comfortable; and, arguing from what I saw, I could mentally picture to myself the sanded floor and the bright fire irons, and the furnished dresser, and the clock, and the bird cage, and perhaps the little shelf of books, for I am confident that there are few, however humble their means, who, if they have conduct and the disposition, I'll say the ambition, to be so, may not secure domestic comfort, and even some few domestic luxuries for themselves. Only inspire a decent pride in their minds, and do what you can to aid and encourage it, and you do more, by raising the mechanical and labouring classes, to improve the nation, through meritorious and contented citizens and subjects, than if you were making long speeches through a long life; for if each were content to do a little instead of talking a great deal, it is marvellous how rapidly the sum of human happiness would accumulate.

I lost my friends at Clevedon Road station, having by that time established something like an acquaintance with all the family, especially the eldest boy, who was so fine a little fellow that, were I now to make my will, I should be almost disposed to remember him in my codicil. For want of better company, I read Izaak Walton until we reached Weston.

On entering my young friend Rogers', the successor of old friend Reeves, I found four single gentlemen engaged on double that number of mutton chops; and as I started without breakfast, I resolved so far to follow their example, as to substitute fresh eggs for fresh meat. One of them asked me if I came up by the train; and another, what I thought of Maynooth.[2] I said, I came up by the train, and I never thought of Maynooth. The politician said the grant was a dreadful thing; and I answered, that every one who spoke to me (for I spoke to no one on the subject,) said so; and as everybody knew more about it, I took their word for the matter; but to tell him the truth, it did not very seriously affect my appetite. Everybody scolded Sir Robert Peel, and perhaps he deserved it; but as I made it a point always to say to a man's face what I thought of him, I reserved my censures until such time as I should have the pleasure of dining with him. My neighbour stared at me for a few seconds; and I should not be surprised if he were at this moment labouring under the delusion that he had the honour of breakfasting with the sub-secretary of state a circumstance not so very unlikely, considering the fascinations of Weston and the speed of express trains.

I had time to take a few turns on the esplanade before service, and to recognise Bristol features in every second countenance I saw. I am not a guide-book, and therefore have nothing to say on scenery and all that; and even if I were, I could not give half as good a description as a second-class return ticket. Mrs. Piozzi[3] tells us that her Great Sage was wont to observe, in his own way, that 'the finest waters were those that afforded the most fish;' and, perhaps, upon this principle the sea which is within an easy distance of Weston, and which is said to abound in sole, though not the most picturesque, may still be admired. Some people abuse the mud, and some doctors praise it — the latter maintain it to be wholesome, etc.; and considering that I only meant to stay a few hours there, it was not worth my while entering into a critical examination of the arguments on either side.

After a brief promenade I sat down on one of the seats; and, whether it was the influence of animal magnetism or not, an elderly lady soon took up her position on the same bench. This seemed a move towards sociability: 'twas an opportunity, too, to know something about the Church, the parson, and the parish: and as I never let such an one slip, I inquired, after some observations on the weather, how she liked the clergymen; for this is the only mode by which I can obtain the little information I occasionally impart to the reader. The old lady was in raptures with them all — she loved the Archdeacon, she liked Mr. Forsyth, and she admired Mr. Rowley,[4] who was gone to get married — a very sufficient excuse, you'll say, for a temporary absence. "We have no Puseyism here, sir," she continued, with animation.

"Indeed! ma'am," said I, "and the lodges all let: you really are very fortunate."

"Indeed, sir, we are; and in these days when Tractarianism is so rife elsewhere. Do you know what, sir?"

"What, ma'am?"

"A friend, on whose word I can rely, told me yesterday, such is the sad lengths to which those people go, that Pusey is in the habit of waking his children at night and dropping hot scaling wax on their little noses, to teach them endurance, sufferance, and all that!"

I could only groan forth my horror.

"And you have, doubtless, heard, sir," she continued, "he is in the practise of sacrificing a lamb weekly."

"I have, ma'am, and observed, at the same time, that his butcher's bill must be enormous."

I was afraid someone had been imposing on my respectable neighbour, if, indeed, she was not one of Dr. Fox's friends at Knightstone,[5] come for the benefit of her health; so I changed the subject, lest possibly, it might be monomaniacal, and found she knew a good deal about the parish, and when not on the besetting topic was an agreeable gossip enough.

Wondering how one could get nobody to talk about *the* Church, though each had something to say about high Church or low Church, I followed in the wake of several Bath-chairs and many people to the sole place of Established Worship which the Westonians possess. Johnson, speaking one day of Dr. John Campbell,[6] the author of *Hermippus Redivivus*, said, "I am afraid he has not been in the inside of a Church for many years, but he never passes one without pulling off his hat. This shows that he has good principles!" I question if even Campbell, with all his reverential feelings could be induced to make his obedience in passing Weston Church, for it is one of the most raw, wretched, discreditable specimens of Christian architecture I ever beheld; a common hodman would have planned a better one. I have now before me a pretty little drawing, by a very clever person, of the old Church; which, judging from 'its counterfeit presentment,' was a pleasing and venerable structure. When people, however, began to fancy the plate, the Church was found to be too small, so instead of erecting a second they pulled down the old one, and raised the present one on its site, a farmer having heroically undertaken the construction of the new. Shade of Sir Christopher Wren and body of Pugin! just fancy a producer of swedes and a cultivator of potatoes building a Gothic Church;

but above all, fancy the kind of people that permitted him to do it. Were there no architects in the world, or was Weston out of it at the time? Alexander would have rebuilt the Ephesian Diana's Temple if they allowed him to place his name over the porch; the architectural farmer, the bucolical builder, ought to have inscribed his over the belfry-door, which is the only one he made for the admission of the congregation — he ought to have carved 'Parsley' in deep indented letters, on a dashing scroll, and posterity in gratitude would doubtless have added butter in abundance.

The Archdeacon has built a tolerably decent new north aisle, but I cannot applaud the judgment that tacks a new patch to such an execrable old garment; nothing but pulling down Mr. Parsley's[7] work will ever make it better than a great, ungainly, awkward, preaching house. There was lead, too, on the old Church, and there are slates on the present. Another thing, by the 82nd of Constitutions and Canons Ecclesiastical, the Commandments are required to be set up on the east end of every Church and Chapel, at the charge of the parish, and yet there was not a single letter of the Decalogue against the wall or elsewhere of Weston Church. There is, of course, a penalty for non-compliance, and if nobody else will I think I shall some day or other make them feel my virtuous indignation. I'll have a Proctor — I'll retain young Burges, or somebody else, and proceed against them to the uttermost extent of the law, until I make them feel that Canons and Constitutions are not cobwebs or soap bubbles. I see that my zealous and over powering friend, Edw. Parker,[8] writing a letter last week to the papers, reminds somebody that the Ninth Commandment is not repealed; one would fancy that the parishioners of Weston were of opinion that the whole ten were abrogated, or at least a dead letter, for they find no place for them.

Tremble then, churchwardens, for I suppose there are churchwardens, though I did not see any rods, lictors without fasces; there was, however, a large pew which savoured somewhat of the official, and which had been fitted up for them by the Rector,[9] the two small pin-cushions placed on the desk being of their own providing. The font is in keeping with everything else; instead of being placed, as the proper notions of ritualism require it, at the entrance of the Church, it stands, no very sightly object, nearly at the chancel.

There is a large pew in the north aisle, someone called a drawing room pew, which belongs to the Pigotts, and which is entered by a private door outside; it is quite an independent apartment, being protected from vulgar gaze by a world of woodwork, brass rails, and red curtains. I notice that for years people have been firing a great many letters at this freak, but seemingly all to no purpose; for though bombarded so long by paper pellets, the merino and the high panelling still stand, and Mr. Pigott still prays or sleeps on in his family pew unmoved, amidst soft cushions and Turkey carpets, which, however, are not in a particularly cleanly condition; though the sexton, who is fond of a good seat, and, like a sensible man, takes care of himself in this respect with as much solicitude as he does anyone else, ought to have a sufficient interest in the accommodation to look to it. As I have a regard for the personal comfort of this functionary, and it may not be always convenient for the occupiers to accommodate him, I would suggest that the churchwardens should build a pew for his private use, and in the best part of the Church, so that he might be always at hand when wanted. To intercept the breeze, there is a curtain placed over the west door of the new north aisle, which was hung there through the delicate attention of the Archdeacon: for which the ladies, however, are so ungrateful as to declare, whatever it was meant for, the only purpose it serves is to spoil their bonnets. The greater part of the chancel is, I believe, old; in it there are two mural monuments of ladies of the Pigott or Smith families — one a medallion, (I believe) by Chantry;[10] and the other a full length figure, I was told, by a pupil of his.[11]

One Church is not sufficient, nor anything like it, for Weston, a place where a new population makes its appearance, like a flight of swallows, every summer. The usual consequences are in such cases that the poor natives, like the aborigines of the back woods, are crowded out by civilization and the immigrants. The Church is always in the season densely filled, and in June or July you may think yourself particularly fortunate if you can obtain six square inches of deal board anywhere within the building, whether it be amongst high or low, rich or poor. The congregation upon most occasions is of a very composite character. For the sake of keeping up that fond feeling which temporary absence is said to freshen and improve, the citizens of Bristol are in the habit of separating themselves from their wives and families, or rather separating their families and wives from them, for a few months every summer, merely running down with a hamper every Saturday night and spending over Sunday. It has also begun to be the residence of retired *militaires* — some of those heroes, who after serving their country by consuming currie and East India Madeira under the tropics, retire with bloodless pensions to keep themselves cool in a marine residence for the rest of their lives. These are invariably the best attendants at Church, to which they impart rather a foreign air; so that if it were not for Mr. Parsley you might also fancy yourself at times in Calcutta Cathedral.

The services were most decorously gone through, and the singing, which was done from books containing, I think, eight hundred hymns, (what they want of half the number I cannot conceive,) heartily joined in. The Archdeacon, owing to ill health has not, I believe, officiated for three years; he is much liked, though indifferently aided by the parishioners in his attempts to improve the Church.

The prayers were read and the sermon preached by the Rev. — Forsyth,[12] in the absence of his brother curate, who, as my fair friend on the esplanade informed me, had gone to be married. The text was from Ephesians, chap. ii. v. 18; it was a capital sermon — earnest and persuasive, though moderate and modest. He touched upon forms and ceremonies, not factiously or fashionably, but with judgement, good sense, and temperance; which was most gratifying in these times of extreme notions on all sides. I have a dread of watering-place curates for the most part, as the idle population of old and young ladies generally do all they can to spoil them with praise and presents, and they get, as it were, unmanned; they contract a kind of fashionable religious effeminacy, which fritters itself away in classes, morning calls, and coteries of lady theologians. But there was none of this about the preacher on the present occasion; though young, he was no pulpit *enfant gate*; he was a commonsense, earnest, painstaking man; and I sincerely hope he buys all his slippers, for gratuitous slippers do more than weightier articles to weaken a man's understanding.

1. Two distant opposite points, Judges xx 1.
2. Sir Robert Peel had at this time just announced an increase of the grant to Maynooth, a college of training for the Irish priesthood to the Irish, but met with a Tory rebellion in Parliament.
3. Hester Lynch Piozzi, 1741-1821. *Anecdotes of the late Samuel Johnson* (1786).
4. The Archdeacon was the incumbent, Messrs. Forsyth and Rowley the curates.
5. The Baths of Knightstone were opened in 1822.
6. John Campbell, 1708-75. Campbell was an acquaintance of Johnson and Boswell. The slight misquote given above is from Boswell's *Life of Johnson*.
7. Richard Parsley, agent to the owners of Weston, the Pigott family and the real founder of Weston Church built 1824.
8. *See* Stoke Gifford.
9. H. Law (1840).
10. Sir Francis Chantry, 1781-1841. Sculptor.
11. Henry Weekes, 1807-77. Sculptor.
12. J.H. Forsyth.

31 May 1845
Horfield

I had not been at Horfield, until my present visit, since old Sayer's[1] time; I am afraid to say how many years ago. The reader is, doubtless, aware I allude to the writer of the History of Bristol. At the period to which I refer, I think he kept a school in the Old Park; at least he did at one time, and he had the perpetual curacy of Horfield, to which he used to go out on Sunday mornings, sometimes on foot, and sometimes in a pony-phaeton. For a couple of years, however, before death divorced him from his parochial charge, he had grown too feeble to get through the service without some refreshment; and I recollect full well, just before going up into the pulpit to preach, he used invariably to walk across to the pew in which an elderly lady, his sister-in-law, sat, (I think her name was Turner or Tucker,) and receive from her hands a little lump of sugar, saturated with some drops of brandy. Good old times those were; no one wondered, no one made a remark, and the little congregation, a dozen in number,) looked as regularly for parson Sayer's soaked lump of saccharine as they did for the bidding prayer; though, I confess, to me, for the first time, it had rather a curious effect, to see the old man walk across in his canonicals and hold his hand over the pew for his dole, while the worthy old soul within drew a little phial of Cognac from one pocket, and deliberately, drop by drop, let the due quantity fall on the fragment of white sugar which she took from the other. The Rev. historian having obtained his refresher, proceeded to mount the pulpit stairs, and as he did, 'munched, and munched, and munched,' like the sailor's wife in Macbeth, his vivifying morsel. Some old clergymen I have seen at times obliged to pause in the middle of the service, for two or three minutes together, to recover strength; and I recollect being one Sunday at Chew-Magna, when Old Doctor A., of Bristol, arrived to do duty; the worthy and learned Doctor was then nearly fourscore years, and he had not proceeded halfway through his sermon when he found nature begin to fail; so with the utmost self-possession and complacency he looked towards the singers, who sat in front of the gallery opposite, and thus addressed them:

"My dear children, neither my voice nor myself are as strong as they were, and I feel tired from the long exertion; so be pleased to give us a stave, and by the time you have finished I shall have recovered my breath." The rustic choir immediately arose, and gave him, not a stave, but the whole doxology;

which finished, the Doctor said, with emphatic gratitude, "Thank you, children," and proceeded with his discourse. Old Samuel Sayer preached a very sound sermon when you could hear him; he was learned and laborious, and a fair specimen of the old orthodox school, his love of the Church being only equalled by his hatred of heresy and schism.

Horfield in old accounts used to be reckoned two miles from Bristol; but if the building mania continue at its present rate, I suppose the city and the village will some day meet. On the occasion of my last walk, I met a number of untidy girls and unshorn men on the road, returning to Bristol after a morning's cowslipping, and actually 'oppressed with perfume,' loaded with poles full of that pretty flower, which was being transferred from its sunny home in the pleasant fields to smoky murky shelves and dingy tap rooms in a crowded city. Nothing could be a greater contrast than the difference between these brilliant and perfumed bundles, and the unkempt, unshorn, and unwashed creatures who carried them, and on whose soiled and smoky cheeks the fresh air and exercise of the country could not call up a glow. I can conceive nothing more conducive to health or consistent with innocent recreation than a Sabbath morning's walk in the country to the poorer classes, if they would first wash and clean themselves; but it seems to be a sort of luxury to the town mechanic to spend the brightest and best part of the day in an uncleanly and untidy condition, a practice which I believe deprives him of half the benefit he might otherwise derive from a morning's walk and the fresh air of the country. I think myself, when our humbler classes have acquired the habit of rising early on Sunday mornings, cleaning themselves, breakfasting, taking a walk in the country, and then returning to their parish Churches, it may be said that we have got on the sure road to moral and physical improvement.

I don't know any place that, in my recollection, has been so much improved, in fact, so completely metamorphosed as Horfield, or rather that portion of it on which stands what has been happily called 'the sacred close,' namely, the usual ecclesiastical group, comprising the Church, school house, and parsonage. It forms now as pretty and purely English a bit of landscape as you could see, standing some way in, on an eminence to the left of the main road, from which you get a glimpse of the little tower and parsonage, peeping out from, and bosomed by, beech and chestnut trees. The bells were ringing, and I sat for a while listening on the little wooden stile that led from the road into the fields, and almost loath to lose the influence of scene, and sound, and sunshine, by a nearer approach.

The view from the little churchyard, however, is far more beautiful; and for richness and extent, surpasses, I think, anything in the neighbourhood. The churchyard of Horfield is just what a country churchyard should be; no gloomy-walled burial-ground, nor formal trim, town-garden-like affair; of rustic irregularity, it retains all the character of a resting-place of the dead, where also the living might love to loiter away an hour in quiet and contemplation.

A simple hedge, overgrown with tangled woodbine and wild clematis, incloses it and the little church, the gothic school-house, and the old trees, which stretch their knotted arms over the green mounds where the 'rude forefathers of the hamlet sleep,'[2] while upon all the utmost care is bestowed, but so judiciously as to preserve its simple and country character. A little walk, winding amongst well-grown shrubs, leads from the school to the Church porch, and through this a troop of children in their rustic bonnets and grey shawls were passing as I entered the gate. Yet at one time this pretty and picturesque scene must have presented quite a different appearance. I have by me, on a smoky piece of paper, and written in a quaint and antique hand, some verses, the date of which I cannot tell, and the actual circumstances under which they were written I cannot explain; but they would seem to have been composed by some clergyman unattached, who received twelve shillings for a day's duty, and made a most uncomfortable journey from the Hotwells to Horfield to earn the money, under very adverse circumstances, of which he 'makes sad moan and most melancholy plaint.' As they are veritable verses and characteristic of the period, the reader will probably be glad to have an opportunity of perusing them:

A JOURNEY TO HORFIELD "

The clock struck eight, the morning clear'd,
The chocolate drunk, the coach appeared;
To Horfield bound — a dirty road,
A stomach sick with hippish load;
A rumbling coach, a grumbling wife,
With two friends more, annexed for life.
At length arrived to Horfield Green,
No Church bell heard, no mortal seen;
A puny Church, a surplice damp,
A churchyard soaked in watery swamp;
The reading-desk extremely cold;
A pulpit dusty, weak, and old;
A Prayer Book in dull print letter,
A Bible rather worse than better.
The congregation, great and small,
Made up but few — poor souls and all.
Three ancient dames, with wither'd faces,
Fell fast asleep in lower places;
Two grey-head dons, with gloves on pate,
Sate just above in nodding state;
One maiden fair, in yellow knott,
The only primrose on the spot;

The rest were chiefly farmers' men,
That gaped and listened now and then.
A doleful clerk, that sings or says,
Who's poorly versed in musick's lays;
In broken tunes, now in, now out,
'Twas all confused, like Babel's rout.
Then came the sermon, long and dull,
Adapted right to clodpate skull;
Some gaped, some slept; one sober lad
Beneath his arm a Bible had.
This book-learned youth had witt enough
To search the doctor's scripture proof;
He sat demure, with awkward face,
And doubled down the quoted place.
The sermon done, no dinner near,
A mile, at least, to cup and chear;
Churchwarden hog, not seen at Church,
Left hungry parson in the lurch.
The weather changed to snow and sleet,
Made chattering teeth and chilly feet.
The youth looked blue, the lady pale,
For want of somewhat to regale;
So further drive through mirey ground,
To reach the Ostrich, on the down,
The only place to stop and dine,
And whistles wet with beer and wine.
There, glorious sight! by great good luck,
Before the stomack hour had struck —
A loyne of veal in lordly dish,
And kale and bacon, all I wish,
Allayed the grumbling of the day,
And rous'd our spirits up to play.
We there sat down, content and snug,
With wine and beer and cider mugg;
Yea, cups of tea, the hostess' treat,
Appeared, to make the scene compleat.
Nature refreshed in cheerful way,
We drank and pledged and called to pay;
The coachman wheeled the cliff around,
And brought us home all safe and sound.
Horfield, farewell! thou starving soil,
Not worth the preacher's charge and toil;
Thy gift is shillings twelve — fifteen I spent;

Was ever priest on such an errand sent?
Through dirt and wet, and cold and hunger keen,
To teach sad boor, and ignoramus green?"

The writer certainly does not appear to have had a cheerful day of it — his lines were not cast in pleasant places; but, I think, the fervour with which he complains that

"Churchwarden hog, not seen at Church,
Left hungry parson in the lurch,"

is quite true to life, for nothing could possibly be more in keeping with the course of nature than that the chance clergyman should find a knife and fork laid for him on the churchwarden's mahogany.

Thinking over these lines, as I sat upon a headstone under the shelter of a fine old tree, and looked across to Stapleton and Stoke, with the rich and beautiful view that lies between, I could hardly believe I was on the scene so deplorably described by the forlorn author of the foregoing verses.

Near the door, and not far from the font, I found a modest seat amongst some quiet rustics, and joined in a simple and solemn service, in keeping with everything else I had witnessed in and about the place. It is true that a critical ear might have discovered a more perfect choir than the school children, but then they sang decently, with an appearance at least of devotional earnestness, though unaided by organ or instrument, and, what is still more rare than good singing, they conducted themselves properly. The Church is a neat but small structure, being, if I may use the expression, a miniature cruciform building, having nave, cross aisles, and chancel. There is a pretty east window with some painted glass, and the fine old trees which surround the edifice, when seen from inside, impart to the worshipper in that little temple a feeling of sylvan and solemn seclusion, enhanced by the reverential and subdued tone in which the services are read. Indeed, there was altogether about that little Church, and its simple congregation, an air of tranquility and retirement, which awakened in the heart, if no higher feelings, at least a sense of solemn repose.

In the cross aisles are small galleries, and the Church in other respects has rather a crowded appearance, the pulpit and reading-desk interrupting the view of the altar. In connection with the latter I have a word or two to say. From my boyhood upwards, and long before there was a word about the matter, I had been in the habit of following my excellent mother's example, and turning to the east on the Creed being read, and I still continue to do so, though I attach no particular moment to the observance or the omission of it; I, therefore, am far from objecting to a practice which I have always followed myself; still, were I the clergyman of Horfield, I should discontinue it, until such time as from the rearrangement of the interior I could more naturally and obviously comply with the custom, for at present the clergyman, in turning to the east, from the situation of the reading-desk, turns his face not to the altar, but close to and almost against the front panel of the pulpit, which to the congregation has an odd and almost absurd appearance. Of this, perhaps, the clergyman himself is not aware; but to my mind it certainly had a strange effect.

I found the Church neatly kept, the services decently and devoutly performed, the school children taught and clothed, and all through the exertions and liberality of a permanent Curate of some £80 a year; and I do as I should do, and have done, whenever I have found disinterestedness and zeal united, commend both, without regard to party distinctions, which I have no desire to recognise.

The sermon over, I confess I was not a little alarmed, and thought of my lady friends, when I saw the preacher descend from the pulpit, and immediately proceed with the offertory sentences, while the churchwardens moved out of their pews with two mysterious little wooden boxes. As the late agitation throughout the country has made me quite nervous on this point, I took up my hat and umbrella, and was preparing to escape, half in fear and half in displeasure, when shame caught hold of the skirts of my brown coat, and said, 'remain where you are ' and I did remain, glancing, however, furtively and timidly around to see if Pope Gregory was anywhere in the Church; in the meantime the collection quietly proceeded, the churchwardens moving modestly from pew to pew the clink of the poor man's penny and the farmer's sixpence, as they fell into the little wooden boxes, being the only sound that mingled with the solemn reading of the offertory sentences. I looked to see the people rise up and leave *en masse*; but nobody stirred, and I concluded that the 'special reporter' of the London *Times*, who might well say with the man in the play, 'poor people, they would never know half their misfortunes if it were not for me,' had, as he passed by on the high road, in his clemency, or ignorance, or contempt, abstained from blowing his horn against the little Church amongst the chestnut and beech trees. By this time the box had reached me; I instinctively put my fore finger and thumb in my waistcoat pocket, and before I could recover my presence of mind I had committed the sin of dropping a small coin amongst the pence and half-pence of the rustics. 'Well,' thought I, as my alms fell from between my fingers, 'if I have done wrong, I can't help it now; but can this be, after all, what they have been turning the world upside down about, what the city of Exeter has been all but burned for, and Henry[3] of the ilk has had his mitre nearly knocked from his head, (or his head from under his mitre,) and angry editors have written and mobs raved about?' 'Behold how great a fire so small a spark kindleth.' These simple people do not, thought I, seem to be aware of the precipice on which they stand; and the little girl by my side, who has just dropped her alms of one halfpenny so artlessly and so innocently into the box, is not, I'll be bound, conscious that she has just been doing that which has convulsed the Church to its centre, and rocked the thrones of bishops beneath them. Nobody appeared to be aware that they were doing harm in giving their pence and sixpences for the services of religion and the poor; and as ignorance was bliss in their case, I thought I'd restrain my ambition to turn agitator, and withhold from instigating the congregation to burn the parsonage. I was afterwards told that there is nearly £60 a year collected in this manner in this little Church, but then there are some mysterious old ladies who occasionally contribute through the parson.

The churchwardens having deposited the offerings in the alms dish, we were dismissed with the blessing.

I had passed through the little churchyard gate, and nearly reached the fields, when I heard someone running after me, and turning round saw a gentleman in black, whom I recognized as the churchwarden who had received my alms, panting and puffing, and trying to muster breath enough to hail me. It at once struck me that I had given him a sovereign by mistake, and that he had come or been sent to make restitution; but no such thing, he was the bearer of a double invitation, one from the parson to dine, and another from himself to lunch.

"Venerable Sir," said he, as soon as he could recover his breath, and lifting his hat with much politeness, "surely you will not pass the churchwarden's door without turning in to lunch. You must require some refreshment, as I perceive you do not employ John Bunyan this morning. Mr. Richards[4] also requests me to say that there will be boiled beef and plum-pudding at the parsonage at five, if you will do him the favour to remain until after second service, for dinner."

"Spirit of Fabricius and Aristides the Just," said I, indignantly, "here is a palpable attempt to corrupt the pure source of impartiality and justice. What, Sir! don't you think I have a soul above boiled beef, even with the accompanying allurement of plum-pudding? No, Sir, I'll even outrage my better judgement, and abuse your clergyman, to show my stern disinterestedness! and I struck my walking-cane with indignation full two inches into the greensward.

The churchwarden of Horfield grew pale, nay, I believe he trembled at an old man's warmth, as he observed deprecatingly, that they had no wish to bias my mind, but merely to refresh my body; I had doubtless by this formed my opinion of the parson and the parish?

"I have. Sir," said I, "and it was a good one, but the invitation has spoiled it."

"Well," said he, smiling, "I thought the hospitality of a parish would never be a crime in the eyes of the Church-Goer."

I smiled too, and with that smile I lost my resolution, reader; for I consented to return and lunch with the churchwarden; "but I repudiate the boiled

beef," said I, "I renounce the plum-pudding, besides I could not think of prey-
ing on a perpetual Curate, who gives more than he gets from the Church".

In a few minutes more I had tasted the churchwarden's 'home brewed and
double Glos'ter,' and at three o'clock I found myself again in the little Church
of Horfield; no longer, however, near the door, but seated in great dignity and
state in the churchwarden's pew.

1. Samuel Seyer, 1757-1831. *Memoirs Historical and Topographical of Bristol and its Neighbourhood*,
   1822-5. Seyer was Master of Royal Fort School, 1790, perpetual curate of Horfield 1813,
   and became rector of Filton, 1824.
2. Thomas Gray, 1716-71. *Elegy in a Country Churchyard* (1750).
3. Henry Phillpotts, 1778-1869. Bishop of Exeter 1830-69. Phillpotts was a high churchman and reactionary of the first degree. In the House of Lords he opposed every single
   reform including the Reform Act (which as in Bristol brought a mob to his Palace at
   Exeter), the Tithes Commutation Act and the Registration Act. The reference in this
   case is to the Reform Act.
4. H. Richards (1828).

14 June 1845
Bleadon

Bleadon is bounded on the East by the tail end of the Mendip hills, and on the West by a wide marsh; is four miles from Weston, and I can't say how many from Bridgwater. The parish is principally remarkable for its cattle and its Rector.

When I was passing by this Church to Lympsham some time ago, I was almost tempted to pay it a visit; however, I contented myself with approaching the stone cross, and pilgrim-like, registering a vow that the summer should not roll by, before I became better acquainted with the Rev. David Williams.[1]

Accordingly, on Sunday last I kept my vow, and having breakfasted at Weston, turned John's head towards Uphill, soon after nine o'clock. I at first intended to have gone to Morning Service at Bleadon; but having heard that the Rev. Gentleman indulged his congregation with a sermon only in the afternoon, I changed my route and resolution and rode to Hutton, an account of which, however, I shall defer for some future paper.

Having had prayers at Hutton, and dinner at an old friend's, at half-past two, I proceeded to afternoon service at Bleadon.

Bleadon, as a parish Church is a good building, but rendered cold and wretched to the eye by neglect and nakedness. On every side you behold traces of a Church, which seemingly has none to take care of it — a broken pathway, a bare, shrubless, treeless burial-ground, a broken roof, and decayed wall. You miss, in fact, all the 'circumstances' which make an English country Church so peculiar and pleasing a sight. The grass of the churchyard had been eaten bare by the yearlings of some poor parishioner, to whom 'God's acre' had been let or lent, and as I looked round, I thought I never saw before so desolate a scene, taking all things into consideration. I was told there was not one dozen in attendance in the morning, and in the afternoon there might have been two, a sorry proportion for so extensive a parish.

The interior of the Church, was quite as cheerless to my mind as the exterior — bare, and cold, and dreary; one pew was filled by a mourning party, and in the others were scattered a few showily-dressed young women, and still fewer men seemingly of the class of farmers; but there were little or no poor, and no children that I could see, the parish being without a single parochial school of any kind. The Rev. David Williams was in the reading-desk when I entered, going through the service, just as you would suppose the service to be gone through in such a church as I have described. He seemed to be suffering from flatulency, for at every other verse he was obliged to pause, afterwards wiping his mouth with an old brown handkerchief, and occasionally varying the act by using the sleeve of his surplice (which was far from clean) for the purpose. There was no singing or musical service whatever, the Rev. Gentleman objecting to it, as I have heard, on the grounds that it affects his head, but he has never complained of it affecting his heart. On some occasions, however, the Uphill singers have come over, and been permitted to 'perform;' but not very long since, being rather too energetic in their exertions, they were publicly, and from what little I know of country choirs, perhaps justly, rebuked by the Rector for their overpowering vocalism. — "If you can't sing better," said he, "don't sing at all — shut up that noise!" This familiar and almost household mode of censure is not very unfrequent, however, at Bleadon; he has occasionally paused in the midst of the Psalms, to correct the clerk for reading too fast or too loud, but by way of reprisals the clerk has sometimes had to correct the parson for reading the wrong psalm, an incident of this kind having occurred, I think, on Whitsunday last. At another time someone's dog followed the owner into church, and attracting Mr. Williams's notice, he called out, "John, turn out that dog — people should not make a kennel of the Church" — an observation which would have been not merely justifiable but meritorious, if there did not happen to be a yearling bellowing in the churchyard at the moment, where it was doing all it possibly could, by permission of the parson, to get fat on the 'green graves' of his departed parishioners.

I wish, however, it was only of mere oddities or personal peculiarities I had to complain; but I fear I shall be compelled to show by-and-by that other things are to be alluded to, and other matters mooted. But let me first go through the service, and refer to the Church, so far as I saw of both, on the occasion of my visit. As I said, there is no singing, the clergyman having ascended in his surplice from the reading-desk to the pulpit. I can fancy some of the advocates of the gown now bristling up with jealous alarm, and ready to exclaim against the Rev. David Williams as a Puseyite, and perhaps anxious to engage in a crusade against him. In this they can please themselves; and if they could stir up the namesake of the Royal Psalmist to do a great many things that ought to be done, and are left undone in the parish, perhaps I should not be disposed to dissuade them for their determination; but with regard to the surplice, I should think the Rev. David Williams cares as little about Puseyism as Evangelicalism; he has worn the surplice since his induction, and as many besides himself do for this reason, amongst others, that it saves the necessity of changing.

The text was, 'Her ways are ways of pleasantness, and all her paths are peace.' With the matter of the discourse, I have no complaint to make, and I am not the less disposed to be pleased with it because I think I heard it before. The language was good, and the sentences well turned, and whether made in

London or Bleadon, composed by the Rev. David Williams, or sold by Burns, it still taught a solemn, I will say an awful lesson, which I wish we were all willing to learn. It was preached in fourteen minutes, the entire service occupying, I should think, something more than three quarters of an hour.

The worshippers were few, and the worship cold. The priest delivered his part in a tone of apathy, and the replies of the people were faint and languid; the reading of the clergyman was not good, that of the poor clerk barbarous; the pews were dusty, and yellow damp-stains disfigured the walls of the chancel; there was no altar screen or reredos of any kind, and a rude railing enclosed a ruder communion table: some windows in the chancel had been roughly stopped up, and in fact nothing was wanting to make an originally good parish Church, a poor, wretched, desolate structure. It has a fair tower, and a very fair specimen of a stone pulpit; the former was struck, some twelve or fourteen years ago, by lightning, but I question if the stroke of neglect has not since proved more ruinous to the edifice at large.

On leaving the Church, I stood for a while in the churchyard, and allowed the little congregation (some of whom, from the late hour at which they arrived, could not have been more than sixteen or seventeen minutes altogether within the sacred edifice,) to pass by me, with the intention of having, if possible, a little serious conversation with the Incumbent, on the state of the building; for though there was no Uriah in the case, I determined David should not be without his Nathan. On second consideration, however, I changed my mind, and resolved to reserve for print all I had to say on the subject.

Those who have taken the trouble of reading these sketches, will probably by this time have discovered that whatever I am, I am not an ascetic, harsh-judging enthusiast; and that I think there is much more piety and virtue in the world than many are disposed to give it credit for. But still there are in my mind degrees of responsibility, the urgency of which no man ought to conceal from himself, and which, were he even so disposed, he ought not to be permitted to do. The Rev. David Williams has the parish of Bleadon, which, as I am informed, is worth £630 a year; he has also the parish of Kingston Seymour, which I dare say is worth between three and four hundred more; so that altogether he may be said to have about £1000 a year out of the Church, for this, he does at Bleadon two services and one sermon a week, such as I have described, and nothing more. I speak of Bleadon only, for I have not been at Kingston Seymour; but I may fairly presume things are not better managed there, than in the parish where the Rector is resident. There is no school of any kind at Bleadon; nor have I heard that the Rev. David Williams ever made a single effort to establish one there, and I wish for his own sake that anyone could convince me my information was not correct. It is true that some few years ago, two or three young ladies, daughters of respectable farmers in the parish, were impelled by the deplorable prospect before their eyes, to get up a school, to which the poor people seemed willing and even pleased to send their children; but the death of some, and the marriage of others, sadly diminishing the number of those who taught, the school fell to the ground, and the children of the poor were cast once more upon the roads, in idleness and mischief, for want of teachers; when it was the part of the Rev. David Williams not merely to have upheld the institution which they so amiably set on foot, but by anticipating the charitable act, to have prevented the appearance of being so far taught his duty by those whose spiritual guardian he is supposed to be. As I went into Church, I saw some boys idling about the gate; I spoke to them, and they seemed smart enough; and I could not help pitying the poor children, who with the capacities to learn, had none to teach them, and none, comparatively speaking, to care for them. A week or two ago I gave a shilling to teach the children of the poor Irish; I think I should be disposed to double the amount, if charity would begin nearer home, and some benevolent people out of the parish of Bleadon would undertake to establish a school in it. As I have no wish to suppress any circumstance I know, which may redound to the credit of the Rector, it is but fair to say, that he did not oppose the school, or discourage it, while he contributed one pound a year towards its maintenance; but then he neither originated nor maintained it, and I insist it was his business to have done one and the other, whereas all the active interest he took in it, did not amount to more than a twenty shilling subscription. The parochial order of things was inverted; the parishioners went to the parson, to beg his assistance to start a school, instead of the parson going to them: passive and at ease in his rectory, he saw it rise — passive and at ease in his rectory, he saw it fall; he saw the school shut up, and the children stray forth once more in ignorance and idleness into the roads and fields. But it is not merely that there is no school, — there is, I think, no parochial charitable association whatever in the place, and it is not to be wondered at, considering all these circumstances, that the ranters should have established a preaching room, and I believe some kind of a Sunday school in the place; their vehement groanings may be heard at a considerable distance, but whether they reach the parsonage or not I can't say; if they do they give the owner very little trouble, for the namesake of the royal psalmist is not very jealous of the spiritual allegiance of his people.

As I walked home from Church I fell into company with a poor man, and hoping that the Rector of Bleadon made up for his omissions in other respects by parochial visitations, I enquired if he often called to see the parishioners as a clergyman, if he visited the sick, etc. The reply I received removed no weight from my spirits; I shall not give our conversation, and sincerely hope much of what I heard was without foundation.

1. David Williams MA. FGS. 1792-1850, geologist. Rector of Bleadon and Kingston Seymour 1820-50, elected FGS 1828. Published papers on geological subjects.

5 July 1845
Pensford

There is a little inn or hostelry at Pensford, the name whereof I forget, if it be
not the Crown, but it faces the little Round House of the village,[1] here after
many unbarrings of a great gate I got admission for John, and having com-
mended him to the care of a rough looking rustic, I strolled out to see the
place. Pensford's only topographer describes it as being 'pleasantly situated in
a fine woody vale, almost surrounded with small hills, well cultivated, and having on their sides several hanging orchards, which form a pleasing rural scene
from every part of the town;' and he is correct enough, for as I sat on the bat-
tlement of the new bridge that spans the scanty river Chew, I found my view
bounded on every hand just as he has described. At most of the houses near
me the children were being dressed in their Sunday clothes, and for the fuller
benefit of light and air, their simple toilet was for the greater part being performed on the threshold; a primitive condition of things, which was still farther illustrated by now and again some little frolicksome curly-headed young
rogue starting off from his mother, and as he took a career through the highway in his buff, looking like a Pensford Cupid who had lost his wings. There
were some children who loitered by me, and upon whom the same trouble of
ablution did not appear to have been bestowed. I asked them if they went to
school, and they said they did 'to the chapel;' I enquired if they were taught to
wash their faces at chapel, and they said they were not, a fact obvious in itself.
There appears to be a good deal of dissent around; at one period I should think
the parish must have been greatly neglected, and schism allowed to spring up
and take root almost deep enough to defy future eradication.

As I still had some time to spare before service, and nothing more to see
from my seat on the bridge, I took it into my head to pay a visit to my old
friend Rogers, and see how his roses were getting on. Many years ago, when
I was a more energetic gardener than I can pretend to be now, I particularly
prided myself on my roses; and then I often walked over of an evening and
made a purchase at Pensford nursery, and walked back again with my plant.

Rogers had not forgotten me; he was dressed for church in his blue coat and
brass buttons, and buff waistcoat, and drab smalls and continuations, with a
tuft of Banxias in his buttonhole. I found him walking about his garden with
his budding knife, more really from the effect of habit than for use, in his
hand, though he very soon employed it to cut me a Prince Albert, which, as

well as every other kind, grows in extraordinary health and luxuriance there. I could not help thinking that a walk in that garden, where the wonders of God are so beautifully displayed, was no bad preparation for church.

On returning to the village, I walked into the churchyard, which, unless when the large iron gate is open, is inaccessible. On one side it is bounded by a little mill stream, and rather confined by small and poor looking houses; it is, however, cleanly kept; it was for the most part covered by rich grass, which was allowed to grow up rather too luxuriantly, but by the pathway near the porch were three or four seemingly infants' graves, which were 'turned into prettiness' by being planted with pinks and other flowers, that appeared to thrive as healthily on their 'mortal beds,' as if under the fostering care of my friend Rogers. There are people who would amuse themselves with a poetic train of conjectures on such an incident; to me it was enough to know that some young mothers, perhaps, or elder sisters had adopted this innocent and pleasing plan of depriving the infants' graves of all their terrors.

Seated at his ease on the bier beneath the tower, the old clerk, sexton, or grave digger, was pulling lazily at the bell rope when I entered the church, which was as yet quite empty. I got into conversation with him, though at first he was far from disposed to be communicative. I learnt, however, that the Rector was the Rev. Mr. Phillott,[2] who did not reside in the parish, and the Curate's name was Tilley,[3] who did. Before I have finished my interview, I heard the pat-pat-pat of innumerable little feet approaching through the churchyard, and in another moment the head of a column of little girls made its appearance through the porch, and filed by me to the gallery in two and two. They were, to the number of forty, neatly and uniformly dressed in frocks, bonnets, and pelerines, and looked clean and in good health. The mistress followed in the rear, and to her I addressed myself for information; she seemed a respectable and intelligent woman, and her observations were characterised by good sense. From her I learnt that the school was not a national school; it was founded by a General Owen, for forty children, to be taught and clothed. The Misses Ford, of Clifton, the nieces I think of the General, have the control and superintendence of it, and kindly supply any deficiency in the funds required for its support; for their gallant relative's intentions were rather disproportioned to his bequest.

There is not, I believe, any other school there, connected with the Church, a sore privation, considering there are boys as well as girls to be educated. I do not know, and I forgot to enquire, if the Rector ever tried to get up one; but if he did, I dare say he found the apathy of the great landed proprietors of the place immovable. General Popham, or General Popham's heir, has some ten or twelve thousand a year in the neighbourhood; out of this, perhaps, he may have given a guinea, at one time or another, in so called charity; but I believe twenty-one shillings are the utmost obligation the parish is under to his illustrious house. I often wonder where half the rich people expect to go when they die, they seem to be so perfectly insensible to everything like their duty. If it were not for the exertions made by the middle classes to relieve want, the possessions of the unfeeling great would have been long since perilled by the impatience of despair and poverty. Seven-eighths of the good is done, not by the lofty of the land, whose givings are too often miserably disproportioned to their means, but by the quiet and unpretending, upon whom the burden mainly falls. Here, for instance, are two or three parishes overrun by ignorance and dissent, and the clergymen, instead of receiving support from the legitimate quarter, to which they ought to look for it, do not, I am informed, even receive an answer to their applications.

The tower of Pensford is old, but the other parts of the edifice are poor and modern. It consists of a nave and south aisle, lit by plain, round-headed Roman windows; and the interior, though clean, is cold and naked; the altar is a miserable piece of woodwork, and the altar cloth is cotton velvet, once crimson, but now faded down to a dirty white.

On asking the clerk where I might sit, he intimated the whole church was open to me to select from, but pointed to a large pew near the altar, and over which the flue of the stove horizontally impended, being held up by hardly a stronger security than Damocles' sword. Independently of the schoolgirls, there could not have been much more than fifty persons present — a circumstance at which I was surprised, for the service was well and reverentially performed, the children singing with simple but most sweet and effective melody. The sermon was a sound and most useful discourse, calculated for, and suited to, the hearers. During the reading of the Liturgy, a singular incident, or rather coincidence, occurred, which had quite a solemn effect. The morning had been intensely sultry, but during the Litany the sky became overcast, and a long peal of thunder, accompanied by a heavy fall or rain, rolled over the little church, and congregation; its echoes had hardly died away, when the clergyman in the usual sequence of the service repeated the words, 'From lightning and tempest, good Lord deliver us;' an incident which showed the peculiar and beautiful adaptation of our incomparable liturgy, so sublime and comprehensive as it is, to every circumstance and situation of life.

On leaving the Church I thought it my duty to express to the schoolmistress the great satisfaction and pleasure with which I observed the conduct of the children during service, and the sweet and solemn manner in which they acquitted themselves in singing.

Having determined to attend afternoon service at Publow, I returned to mine inn, and had some refreshment. I asked an interesting looking little girl, the daughter of my hostess, and who attended me during my meal, the hour that prayers commenced at Publow.

"Three, Sir," said she, "I sing there."

"Oh, indeed," said I, "the Crown is then at the Publow side of the river Chew; but have you a choir there?"

"Oh yes. Sir, a bass viol, two flutes, and a clarionet, two basses, three tenors, myself, and two other young girls."

"Bless my soul," said I, "with such an orchestra you must be quite a lion in the country, have you a large congregation?"

"Yes, Sir, since we began to get up music, we are only six months at it, and we sing anthems."

"Then take away child," said I, "and make haste and dress yourself, for I shall have the pleasure of hearing you this evening."

1. The Blind House, — the village lock-up.
2. James Phillott (1815).
3. C.H. Tyler.

Publow

The walk from Pensford to Publow, over the hill and through the fields, is so beautiful — presents such rich and varied landscapes on every side, that it almost bewilders one's admiration. As soon as I reached the eminence, from which I had a view of the old church and its old trees, and the little river Chew winding slowly and smoothly around it, I took my seat on the dry and elevated roots of a beech, and looked down on the landscape, the grey tower, and the pointed porch half seen through the ancient yews.

If I did sleep I was awakened by a hollow musical sound, something like what Memnon's statue may be supposed to have sent forth, and on opening my eyes I saw a little man struggling under a big bass viol — doubtless the identical one appertaining to the choir of which the 'Maid of the Inn' at Pensford had apprized me. The violinist, dragging his viol with him. Having disappeared through some secret doorway or another, I proceeded, as the congregation had not yet arrived, to take a survey of the Church: and here let me say that when it may be securely done, without danger of desecration, it is desirable to leave God's house open during the Sabbath, for there is something soothing and solemn in a walk through its quiet and silent aisles at any period of the day.

Though it still wanted nearly half an hour of service time, the clerk was seated in the reading-desk, where, with his spectacles drawn up on his forehead, he was enjoying a siesta. He seemingly liked the refreshing coolness of the Church, and had, possibly, retired there for a quiet contemplative nap after dinner. While I meditated taking a sketch of him as he slept, he awoke; and rubbing his eyes and descending from his resting place, he civilly tendered me all the information I required, or rather all he possessed, about the Church.

There is nothing remarkable in the building, though the surrounding scene is perfectly beautiful, and the tower and the exterior have a venerable and pleasing appearance. It consists of a centre and two side aisles; and from the appearance of altar steps and piscina in the latter, I think All Saints, possessed two or three chauntries.

While I was taking my survey, the First and Second Flutes made their appearance, and were quickly followed by the Clarionet. I left the choir to their preliminary scratching and piping; and perching myself on an old altar tomb of some Publonian, departed this life a hundred years ago, I waited in the churchyard the approach of the clergyman and congregation. Here I was soon after joined by the First Flute, without his hat: he was a young rustic coxcomb, with his dark hair divided in front, and a remarkably good opinion of himself. Jumping up on the tomb and seating himself by my side, he entered at once into conversation with me; and on my enquiring as to the number of attendants, he gave me to understand, like my little friend at the inn, that the music was the main attraction.

"Our parson had not six to hear him until we came," said he.

"Then you, and not the parson, are the *populous* man," said I; but First Flute opened his eyes, and did not understand the allusion.

I am always glad to see young men and women in the parish take the trouble of getting up, and take a pleasure in, the musical services; for all this helps to give them an interest in, and attach them to their parish church; and I sometimes think that the Dissenters often lead off the humbler classes by their constant hymning. But I was a little annoyed with First Flute for his conceit, and the manner in which he spoke of 'our parson', as if inferior to the bass viol; so I left him and went into church.

The clergyman was already in the reading-desk, and with him a fine little boy in a brown Holland dress, who appeared to me, as he stood up behind papa, to be counting the congregation. There was a good attendance, which I was very glad to see, and the pews were pretty full; that in which I sat, however, was a most ricketty one; for every time I sat down or stood up, it creaked around and beneath me like a young earthquake. The service was reverentially performed; and I was curious enough to look up in the gallery to see if my little handmaiden of the Crown at Pensford, who so pointedly informed me of the share she contributed towards the parish music, was in her place; and there she was, singing away with all her voice, and, I hope, her heart too.

As my face was at the moment turned towards the singers, I did not see the clergyman go into the pulpit; on turning round, however, I was somewhat surprised to see that his little son had ascended with him, and perching on the seat behind papa, made a small family group more singular than appropriate.

The sermon (2 Peter i.4.) was a useful, plain, and pious discourse. The whole service was performed by the Curate, the Rev. Mr. Cornwall. The Rev. — Daubeny is Rector,[1] but he won't work; he lives at Cheltenham or Clifton — very convenient retreats for clergymen who were not born with a talent or taste for rural life. I believe the advowson is for sale, as one of the parishioners with whom I had some conversation evidently left me with an impression that I was come over to look at it preparatory to a purchase.

A field or two from the Church, I was overtaken by the Curate, who at once and very civilly accosted me. He drew my attention to the landscape, and seemed as ardent an admirer of the scene as I was. He complained that the brass company,[2] by raising the water of the river, had made both the burial ground and the Church quite damp, which I certainly perceived on my entrance to the latter, though I did not then know the cause. He spoke with much good sense of the difficulties of a clergyman, destitute of local and lay aid, in a large parish, full of dissenters, and where schools and clothing, and other charities are so much required. He also alluded to a subject of which I have myself often thought. He had not, I think, been more than a year in the parish; and in the place where he had previously been he had a town congregation of nearly a thousand persons; rather a contrast certainly with a small rural, simple attendance such as I saw that evening; transitions, however, to which moveable Curates are liable. I noticed that he preached in his surplice, as in fact they all do in the country parts of Somerset; and he said, with a smile, that it was not the colour of the garment, but of the doctrine preached in it that to him was of importance; and I need hardly say I fully concurred with him. Indeed, on the whole I found him a very intelligent, cheerful person; and I have little doubt he makes a useful and active clergyman. On reaching the top of the hill our roads diverged, so we parted — he to his home, and I to my hostelry.

1. James Daubeney (1834).
2. Brass Mill, one of the many on the River Chew.

26 July 1845
Blagdon

As I rode through Bedminster on the morning of my visit to Blagdon, a kind of Cobourg or market-cart, in which were a number of young men with black coats and white neckcloths, passed me; and soon pulled up, and deposited one of its semi-clerical-looking company in front of something like a conventicle. The conveyance then proceeded on its way; and as I was curious enough to wish to know what this meant, I pushed John to 'a prettier pace,' and was enabled to keep up with it, until another black coat and white neckcloth popped out near Bishport; the Cobourg still continuing its course, and, doubtless, dispensing more young ministers, like a shower of manna, by the way. This, I afterwards learned, was a conveyance belonging to the Baptist College in Stoke's Croft, from which it starts every Sunday morning for the country, with a cargo of young students, who are dropped in the manner referred to along a given line, and amongst congregations who are waiting their advent. The Cobourg having conveyed the 'last man' to the remotest chapel, waits until he has preached; and then, retracing its road, picks up the others in its progress, after they have got rid of their pent-up orations also. This is, doubtless, a good plan for young men to try their nascent theology and rhetoric on rural audiences; but, without wishing to say anything disrespectful of the College or the students, (who are also named on such occasions 'supplies') the return career of the Cobourg resembled, in my imagination, calling for empty cans, inasmuch as each young man had by that time discharged himself of his discourse.

Blagdon is a long ride from Bristol, but a beautiful one; and I should like to have had a fellow-traveller through Rickford Combe and the Vale of Burrington, for it is barren work riding amid the most picturesque scenery, and having nobody by your side to whom to say, "How beautiful!" My only companionship was the drowsy creaking of John's saddle and the singing of the birds. In the olden time, before the age of rails, I must have met, by Redhill and along the road, some Exeter coach; but as I passed the inn at the former place, which was once so famous for egg-flip, I could not help comforting myself with the reflection, that there was something more lone than a solitary horseman — and that was, a wayside inn after a railroad had run away with its customers.

On arriving at the toll-bar at Blagdon, I pulled out my penny to pay for John. "It is double 'pike today. Sir," said the man in charge.

"Indeed," said I, "are not people allowed to pass free to Church?"

"Yes, Sir, but they be the parishioners."

"And how do you feel, friend, that my residence is not within your boundaries?" I enquired.

The man looked at me archly, as he answered, "You could not be in the parish and people not know it. If you stayed at home, you'd have nothing to pay."

"There, my worthy neighbour," said I, giving him the two-pence; "it is well if a double 'pike be the only penalty I shall have to pay for my Sunday vagrancy."

Whether it was that they were looking out for 'a supply' or not, I can't say but most of the congregation of the sole Dissenting chapel at Blagdon were standing in front of the building, and seemingly on the watch for somebody. For a moment I was apprehensive that they might have taken me and John for what we were not, as they made rather a critical survey of both; so to prevent mistakes, I took refuge in the Seymour Arms, and having housed the quadruped, I proceeded along a very prettily kept pathway through the fields to the Church, from and about which there is one of the noblest and most extensive prospects I think I have ever seen, at least in Somersetshire. From the churchyard, as if from a platform, you look down on a vast vale, and right across to Redhill and Wrington, catching in your cursory glance the gabled roof of many an English residence, rising amidst its 'tall ancestral trees.' Hard by was a little clear spring, in which, as the day was sultry, I bathed my hands, and fancied that many a mendicant friar had done the same in the same spot before me.

Blagdon is not much of a country church; there is, I fancy, an affectation of city refinement about it: the tower is old and good, as in fact nearly all the towers in Somersetshire are; but the nave, which appears comparatively new, is gaunt and incongruous,[1] like something that attempted to be Early English, *and was nothing*. It has a great organ and a grand beadle, the latter with a capacity of red cape quite surprising for the country; he sat in a kind of prompter's box, which equally commanded the porch and the pulpit, and shewed me politely into a pew, the third from the reading desk, and the second in size.

I thought I knew the clergyman who was reading prayers as I entered, and on rubbing my glasses had no difficulty in identifying my young friend the Rev. Robert Taylor,[2] formerly curate of St. James's, in the City of Bristol, and now Clerical Secretary of the Society for the Conversion of the Jews. 'Ha,' thought I, 'I'm in for another twelve pence for Sir Moses Montefiore and the Baron Rothschild, those obdurate Hebrews, who have already cost me twenty shillings, and to no purpose.' But I was mistaken: the Clerical Secretary of the Jews had for the day given himself up to the Gentiles; he was, in fact, as I afterwards learned, preaching for the incumbent, the Rev. Mr. Wheeler,[3] who has been, I am sorry to hear, for some time in delicate health, and is consequently compelled to get foreign aid nearly every Sunday, so that the congregation have from this circumstance sufficient variety. To 'itching ears' this may seem a boon; but I question if in the long run it is an advantage to a simple and rural population to see new faces, and hear new styles every Sunday. In the present case, however, I cannot see how it is to be obviated, unless perhaps by the employment of a curate, which the incumbent, if he were not in the neighbourhood of a large city, must inevitably have recourse to.

It is surprising what a number of unattached clergymen there are available for such sudden and casual calls in Bristol: and I am assured that many of them make considerably more by this 'desultory work,' than they could by curacies. I was told by a gentleman who does not now reside in Bristol, that without seeking, or, as he expressed it, putting himself in the way of such work, he generally made between £80 and £100 a year by 'accidental Sunday services.' And I think it is quite fair that without making a market of it, clergymen should be paid by their brethren, who have been more fortunate than themselves, for their work, as we know there are many parish ministers, especially in the country, who are particularly fond of making use of their unattached friends, when they can have them for nothing. A clergyman who had no living or curacy, though a considerable independence of his own, assured me that he was obliged to change his residence on this account, and on going to a new quarter, he intimated he should be happy to do duty for any of his reverend brethren who might require his aid, at 'three guineas a day, and a pair of posters;' and the consequence was they did not trouble him. There is one incumbent of the diocese of Gloucester and Bristol, who is humorously likened amongst his reverend acquaintances to 'England,' in Lord Nelson's celebrated signal, inasmuch as he 'expects every man to do *his* duty,' and that for no weightier consideration than boiled beef and parsnips between services at the parsonage. However, there are faults on the other side of the question, to one or two of which I shall refer. The unattached Bristol clergyman to whom I at first referred, told me that he was one day waited on by three or four brother *sans*-cures, who informed him that they had determined to charge for one duty for the future one guinea, and for the whole Sunday two, and wished him to consent and concur in the agreement, which he declined to do, and in my opinion very properly, for it looked like striking for wages, and some graceless people might compare it to a clerical combination. It may be very fair for a young and unbeneficed clergyman to have two guineas out of a well-fledged Rector; but suppose a Curate, or a man with a large family and a small living, is obliged to be absent from sickness, or on unavoidable business, it would be very harsh to exact such terms from him; and to the credit of the clergyman in question, instead of charging in these cases, they have always, with the feelings of gentlemen and Christians, given their services gratuitously; but still I never liked trade combinations, and I must be permitted to have a prejudice against clerical ones, as somewhat unworthy of the cloth.

The interior of Blagdon Church seems spacious to the eye, but it has nothing whatever to boast of, being full of great pews, which it requires a person of considerable stature to peep over; and not content with this wooden defence from observation, the clergyman and some others have further enclosed themselves with thick curtains.

The only thing worth noticing in the building is a mural monument, on the north of the chancel, of comparatively modern date, with the following inscription, which I should premise was written by Dr. Langhorn, formerly Rector of the parish, to the memory of Mistress Ann, his wife:

> "With Sappho's taste, with Arria's tender heart,
> Lucretia's honour, and Cecilia's art.
> That such a woman died, surprise can't give;
> 'Tis only strange that such an one should live."

And 'tis equally strange that any man, who really *felt* for the loss of a loving wife, could sit down and write such a wretched and insipid conceit for her epitaph. Reduced to plain English, I suppose this means, that she read Spenser and Shakespeare; that she was attentive to her husband.

Blagdon is the first country Church in which I have been treated to a voluntary during service; and to my mind, I think we might have very well dispensed with it, or substituted a psalm instead. During prayers they unhitch the clapper from the bell, and the consequence is, that instead of hearing a tolerable sound, the abortive attempts of the clock to tell the hours to the parish, more resembled the inharmonious clatter of a pump handle than anything else I can compare it to.

The whole of the duty, with the exception of some part of the Communion Service, which was taken by the Reverend the Incumbent, was performed by the Clerical Secretary of the Jews, who preached an admirable extempore sermon, from the fourteenth chapter of St. John, sixteenth verse. When I entered the Church, immediately on seeing Mr. Taylor in the reading desk, I pushed a shilling into the corner of my pocket, towards purchasing the fee simple of Mount Zion for Bishop Alexander;[4] and three or four times during the sermon I had this same shilling between my finger and thumb, under the impression that the next sentence would be an appeal to our liberality. The discourse, however, passed over without any pecuniary reference whatever; but as I allocated the twelve pence in my mind's eye to the purpose, I think it is not fair to appropriate it to anything else, so that if the collector of the society will call on the editor of the *Bristol Times*, I have authorized that gentleman to pay over the same to any person properly and duly authorized to receive it. Otherwise I shall pay it into Miles's bank,[5] to the credit of the Bishop of Jerusalem.

The whole duty, with the exception of a part of the Communion Service, which was taken by the Rev. the Incumbent, was performed by Mr. Taylor. I can, therefore, only speak to Mr. Wheeler's reading, which was certainly more singular than correct. Indeed, I seldom have heard such a reader; some passages he delivered very low, and others swelled into great loudness, while the sense and signification of the text had no reference whatever to these sudden and abrupt changes of voice. If this arose from any natural defect I should abstain from referring to it; but it is evidently a bad style acquired and contracted.

As a parish minister, however, he is an active and painstaking man, and the cleanliness and care observable in everything connected with the Church, and celebration of divine service, is very creditable to him.

Near the Church is a neat school, which is retained in respectable efficiency by the combined liberality and attention of the Incumbent and the Misses Baker, the daughters of my esteemed old friend Samuel Baker, of Aldwick Court, and who I am happy to see inherit from their worthy father a love and devotion for the Church. As this comes from an old man, they will not I hope look upon it as a compliment.

1. Rebuilt 1907-9.
2. Robert A. Taylor, of 2 Gay Street, Bristol. Taylor did not hold any Bristol curacy at this time.
3. The incumbent was D.G. Wait (1819). D. Wheeler was curate.
4. Michael Solomon Alexander, 1799-1845. First Anglican Bishop of Jerusalem 1841-5. He died only four months after Leech published this article.
5. Miles, Harford, Battersby & Miles, 8 Corn Street, Bristol.

26 July 1845
Butcombe

This same afternoon I walked across to Butcombe, which is about a mile and a half from Blagdon. It is a little out-of-the way place on the side of a lonely valley. It is a small parish, and its few hundred of inhabitants are for the most part poor and uncultivated.

Though a portion of the road lay across some elevated meadows, commanding beautiful views, the greater part was lonely and desolate. Within about a quarter of a mile of Butcombe, I found a little fellow, some five years old, grovelling in the dust by the ditch-side and crying. I inquired what the matter was, and after I had repeated the question in a great many different shapes, he at length gave me to understand that he had 'a pain *there*' (placing his hand on his stomach). I felt I could not act the Levite, and pass by on the other side, while the child was ill; so learning from him that his mother lived in the village, I was preparing to carry him home on my back, when a farmer, who understood the habits of the natives better than I did, came up and relieved me of all responsibility by assuring me it was a fit of sulks — a discovery at which I was not sorry, as while I considered it my duty to carry the boy in case he was sick, I greatly doubted my ability to do so.

On a sign-board over the first house in the village (if a few straggling huts can be called by that title), is the name of 'Nimshi Clarke,' the 'son of Jehu,' and here I meant to have enquired the hour of service; but as the place was shut up, I was compelled to seek my information at the cottage opposite. This circumstance I relate, because it was attended with an awkward incident; for on pushing open the door, which was only partially closed, I disturbed a young woman in the act of robing for church. She seemed discomposed, but I was downright frightened: to have paused to apologise would have made the matter worse; so I had nothing for it but to retire precipitately, declaring to myself that I should never again be guilty of the indiscretion of pushing in a half-closed door, lest I might tumble on some rustic half-finished toilet.

The most favourable view you can take of Butcombe is from the churchyard, from which you look down on a wide prospect; though the situation must be somewhat cold in winter. It is an old but rather interesting little church,[1] with a small nave and chancel, and a south porch; the tower and a very tiny chapel is on the same side. There is also a portion of the shaft of an ancient cross there.

Service had not yet commenced, and the little congregation were scattered in groups of two or three around the porch, with the exception of a few old people who were resting themselves on the sedilia inside. On the whole, there was much rural, perhaps rude, simplicity and repose about the scene; with a slight shade, too, I thought, of loneliness. Some half dozen of the older people were gossiping in a subdued tone together, their attention being directed to an open grave. Never dreaming that I should know anything of, or have aught of interest in, the poor remains for the reception of which this hollow in the rich red earth was dug. I cursorily enquired for whom it was intended; and they told me it was for Stephen Keel, the brother of my late worthy old friend of Moreton farm. Poor Jenny had only been two months wearing the widow's cap for her honest husband, and here had Stephen now followed James, and fallen asleep with his fathers also. Last winter, as I sat in the capacious ingle by the bright fire with Jenny and James, the snow falling in broad flakes by the window, I believed that 'we three should meet again' in the same chimney-corner many a dark December; and since then, not only had one been drawn out of that little number, but a brother has followed him.

It is not often, I suspect, the little congregation of Butcombe find a stranger amongst them; and when they do, they treat him civilly. Farmer Morgan, who is one of the two great men of the parish, offered me a seat; and by way of making the compliment the greater, gave me one of his two pews entirely to myself, taking all his family into the other.

The Church is, I think, one of the smallest I have ever been in; but it is old and characteristic, and was originally far from meanly built; indeed, the few remnants of painted glass that in the east window still outlive some centuries of time, evidence better and more bountiful days. There is a rude gallery at the west end for the musicians — a very simple and rustic orchestra, comprising a great fiddle and a flute, and some singers, who did their best. As we worshipped in that remote place, I could not help thinking we resembled a 'Church in the wilderness;' so quiet and secluded did we seem in that little, retired, and ancient building. This feeling was, perhaps, enhanced by the chastened and reverential manner of the Curate who performed the service, and who, though quite a young man, seemed to be in very delicate health; his countenance was 'sicklied o'er with the pale cast of thought' and illness; and though his strength seemed barely equal to the duty, there was a resigned and, I thought, a cheerful tone of encouragement in his sermon, which he seemed, as it were, internally to apply to himself as well as to his hearers. To me there was a pleasing and, if I may use an apparent contradiction, a melancholy interest in his words; and I loitered about the porch after service, with one or two of the parishioners, in the hope that perhaps I might have an opportunity of exchanging a few words with one who, though quite a stranger, won so much upon me at first sight.

I was not mistaken; for he no sooner emerged from the porch, in his gown, with his surplice and bachelor's hood on his arm, than he spoke to my neighbours, and I took occasion to enter into conversation with him. I found him quiet, scholar-like, and gentlemanly; he alluded incidentally to his health, and said with a sigh, that while clergymen ought to have the strength of giants for their work, they were too often the least favoured in this respect.

The last straggler of the congregation had some time disappeared when I wished him "good evening," and as we left the churchyard, he in one direction and I in another, I could not help looking after him for some minutes together, as he walked slowly and thoughtfully towards his little cottage dwelling, doubtless to while away the long evening that yet remained, with his book and reflection.[2]

In my old and excellent friend Samuel Baker's time, the children of the parish had a most affectionate and attentive patron, who took the schools under his especial care and management — I have not been at Butcombe since his death, but I recollect of old accompanying him more than once across from Aldwick: he used to assist in teaching the boys and girls himself, and once a year he gave them all round a new suit of clothes, and never had man or tailor a more primitive way of measuring for the same. His plan was to call them out one after the other, and take their dimensions with his walking-stick, which was quite as tall as the majority of the candidates: the altitude of each having been thus ascertained, he dotted him or her down on a piece of paper, and left the matter of fit altogether to the discretion of the fashioner. There was one poor blind boy, to whom Mr. Baker was particularly kind. Curious as it may seem, the lad used to go to school, and Mr. B. always took him home on Sundays with him to Aldwick to dinner.

I am sorry to say I forgot to enquire after the lad when I was last at Butcombe; but I shall drop a note to my friend Farmer Morgan on the subject.

1. Restored 1868.
2. A few months subsequent to the writing of this sketch, Griffith Williams the Curate was laid in the quiet little churchyard. The non-resident incumbent was G.J.Sayce (1840).

Bibliography

The *Bristol Times and Bath Advocate*, 1843-1847.

The *Bristol Times and Mirror*, especially Monday August 14, 1893, (obituary).

A Catalogue of the Records of the Bishops and Archdeacons and the Dean and Chapter, Ed. Kirby, I.M., (1970).

CHILCOTT, J., *Descriptive History of Bristol*, (1844).

The Churchgoer: Being a Series of Visits to the Various Churches of Bristol, (Bristol,1845).

The Churchgoer. Rural Rides; or Calls at Country Churches 1st series, (Bristol 1847) 2nd series, (Bristol 1851).

The Churchbuilder, (1862 & 1868).

The Clergy List, (1844 & 1846).

COKAYNE, G.E., *The Complete Baronetage* 5 vols. (1900-6).

Dictionary of National Biography.

ELLACOMBE, H.T., *The History of the Parish of Bitton*, (1881).

FISHER, JOHN, *History of the Town of Berkeley*, (1856).

Gloucestershire Notes and Queries, Ed. B.H. Blacker, Vol. 4 (1890).

GREENWOOD C. & J., *Somersetshire Delineated*, (1822).

The History of the Ancient Society of St. Stephens Ringers, (Bristol 1928).

Hunt & Co.'s Directory, (1849).

JONES, IGNATIUS, *Bristol Congregationalism*, (1947).

LATIMER, JOHN, *The Annals of Bristol in the Nineteenth Century*, (1887).

LIVERSIDGE, M.J.H., *The Bristol High Cross*, (1978).

Matthews' Annual Bristol Directory and Almanack, (1846).

NICHOLLS, J.F. & TAYLOR, JOHN, *Bristol Past and Present*, (1881).

Notes, Historical and Architectural of the Church of St. John the Evangelist, Slymbridge, Gloucestershire, (Bristol 1845).

Parish Church Guides: *Bleadon*.

PEVSNER, N., *North Somerset and Bristol*, (1979).

ROLT, L.T.C., *Isambard Kingdom Brunel*, (1957).

RUTTER, J., *Delineations of the North Western Division of the County of Somerset*, (1829).

SOUTHEY, ROBERT., *Poems of Robert Southey*, Ed. Fitzgerald, Maurice H., (1909).

STORER, J. & H.S., *Delineations of Gloucestershire*, (1825).

VEREY, D.C.W., *Gloucestershire: The Vale and Forest of Dean*, (1970).

Index